The Bravest of the Brave

Civil War America
Gary W. Gallagher, editor

The Bravest of the Brave

THE CORRESPONDENCE OF

Stephen Dodson Ramseur

Edited by

George G. Kundahl

Foreword by Gary W. Gallagher

THE UNIVERSITY OF NORTH CAROLINA PRESS

Chapel Hill

© 2010 The University of North Carolina Press
All rights reserved.

Designed and set in Whitman by Rebecca Evans.
Manufactured in the United States of America.

The paper in this book meets the guidelines for permanence and
durability of the Committee on Production Guidelines for Book
Longevity of the Council on Library Resources.

The University of North Carolina Press has been a member of the
Green Press Initiative since 2003.

Library of Congress Cataloging-in-Publication Data
Ramseur, Stephen Dodson, 1837–1864.
The bravest of the brave: the correspondence of Stephen Dodson Ramseur /
edited by George G. Kundahl; foreword by Gary W. Gallagher.—1st ed.
p. cm.— (Civil War America)   Includes bibliographical references and index.
ISBN 978-0-8078-3373-5 (cloth: alk. paper)
1. Ramseur, Stephen Dodson, 1837–1864—Correspondence. 2. Generals—
Confederate States of America—Correspondence. 3. Confederate States of
America. Army—Officers—Biography. 4. United States—History—Civil War,
1861–1865—Personal narratives, Confederate. 5. United States—History—
Civil War, 1861–1865—Campaigns. 6. Generals—Confederate States of
America—Biography. 7. Generals—United States—Biography. I. Kundahl,
George G., 1940– II. Title.
E467.1.R2A4 2010   973.7'82—dc22   2009047819

Frontispiece: Etching of Stephen Dodson Ramseur as a major general
(Library of Congress)

14 13 12 11 10   5 4 3 2 1

For GEORGE K. COMBS

and the staff of the Alexandria

Library Special Collections:

LESLIE, RITA, BARBARA, JULIE,

MICHELLE, JOYCE, *and* ADA

Contents

Illustrations

Foreword

NEARLY THIRTY YEARS have elapsed since I first encountered the Stephen Dodson Ramseur Papers at the Southern Historical Collection in Chapel Hill. I had chosen Ramseur as the subject of my doctoral dissertation, planning to examine his Confederate career as a case study of how able young officers rose to prominence in Robert E. Lee's Army of Northern Virginia. I knew that Douglas Southall Freeman, whose books on Lee and his army stood as monuments in the field of Civil War military history, had characterized the letters as "a large, fine series." Freeman's description led me to believe the collection would yield important information about Ramseur's military development. I also hoped the correspondence would illuminate his personality, relationships with members of his family, and attitudes toward nonmilitary topics and issues. I soon realized the papers far exceeded my most optimistic expectations. Consisting of two groups of letters, one to Ellen Richmond (his cousin and later wife) and the other to David Schenck (his closest friend from childhood and later brother-in-law), the collection revealed Dodson Ramseur and his world in fascinating detail. All historians who work in unpublished materials dream of finding a rich, largely untapped lode of personal testimony—which is precisely what awaited me in the many folders of the Ramseur Papers. Every day I spent in Wilson Library, which houses the Southern Historical Collection, proved to be a joy. I found it hard to believe that no one had decided to exploit the letters for a book or at least an article. Ramseur wrote to Ellen Richmond in such touching, intimate terms that I often felt like an intruder reading his words. The letters to Schenck, more concerned with political, military, and other public subjects, rivaled the personal ones in interest.

The material relating to Ramseur's service as a regimental, brigade, and division commander in the Army of Northern Virginia shed much light on how he advanced to the rank of major general just past his twenty-seventh birthday. He fit perfectly into the culture of command created by Lee and personified by "Stonewall" Jackson. Lee sought aggressive, risk-taking subordinates who emphasized rigorous training and brought well-disciplined, hard-hitting units to the battlefield. Ramseur drilled his men endlessly, looked after their well-being in camp, and led by example in the heaviest combat—an approach that achieved gaudy success on fields such as Chancellorsville and Spotsylvania, brought multiple wounds (the last one fatal), and garnered praise from Lee, Jackson, and other famous superiors. The letters also sparked my long-standing interest in the question of Confederate national sentiment. Ramseur displayed an array of loyalties—to the United States while a cadet at West Point ruminating about Revolutionary figures, to his native North Carolina, to the slaveholding South, and, finally, to the short-lived Confederate republic. His generation of men from slaveholding families, who grew to maturity in the midst of escalating sectional controversies, seemed less attached to the Union and more willing to embrace secession than many older white southerners. Ramseur's letters reflect a strong sense of antebellum southern identity that quickly evolved into Confederate nationalism and a determination to sacrifice much to earn independence. Reading the letters helped explain why it took so long and so much blood and treasure for the United States to crush the southern rebellion.

More than once over the past twenty-five years, I thought about editing the Ramseur letters for publication. I knew such a book immediately would take its place alongside the most-quoted sets of published letters by officers in the Eastern Theater, including those of William Dorsey Pender and Robert McAllister. Other commitments always intervened, however, and I wondered whether anyone else would pursue the project. Word that George Kundahl had taken on the task came as a welcome answer to my question. Because of his editorial efforts, generations of readers and scholars will find, as I did in Chapel Hill many years ago, that Dodson Ramseur wrote letters of surpassing interest to students of the Civil War era.

GARY W. GALLAGHER

Editorial Method and Letter Sources

OVER 180 LETTERS written by Stephen Dodson Ramseur are known to exist today. Only a handful are official correspondence; the overwhelming majority are personal. They are addressed to family members, principally to his cousin Ellen "Nellie" Richmond, who became his wife, and to his best friend, David Schenck. The correspondence to his wife and family is archived in the Southern Historical Collection (SHC) in the Wilson Library at the University of North Carolina at Chapel Hill. Until late 2005, the Schenck letters resided there as well; they have subsequently passed into the hands of a private collector (PC). The primary source materials at Chapel Hill also include posthumous remembrances from Ramseur's friends concerning his life and death.

At the Office of Archives and History (NCOAH) of the North Carolina Department of Cultural Resources in Raleigh are a random collection of personal correspondence, official papers, and letters of appointment and certificates relating to Ramseur's military career. They are found in the Stephen Dodson Ramseur Papers. An exchange of letters with J. H. S. Funk concerning Ramseur's attack at Chancellorsville over and through the ranks of another Confederate command is also conserved there.

Finally, papers related to his application and admission to the U.S. Military Academy and miscellaneous official correspondence are found in the U.S. National Archives and Records Administration (NARA) in Washington, D.C. In Ramseur's Compiled Military Service Record (CMSR) is a haphazard compilation of Confederate military documents relating to attendance, pay, ordnance, and supply. Footnotes identify the location of each document in this volume using the abbreviations given above.

Earlier letters are devoted in large part to home life and local news to such an extent that they might discourage a reader from reaching the more important observations on matters, private as well as public, related to Ramseur's life preceding and during his military service. They refer to numerous individuals in the Lincolnton area and, later, in Caswell County, some of whom cannot be identified. Where possible, identification is provided; some individuals must remain simply "Kell," "Doc Julius," and "Miss Bonney."

The small number of surviving letters Ramseur received during his lifetime have largely been excluded, as they tend to focus on personal matters and "Home Loves," as he referred to his family. There are two exceptions: the first is the correspondence from his mother after Ramseur's departure for West Point, testifying to a mutual affection that was cut short by her passing away in midlife; the second is the sole remaining letter from Nellie, written after the clash at Stephenson's Depot on July 20, 1864, which is included to facilitate understanding of the controversy engendered by that episode and how Ramseur coped with it. After Ramseur's death, third-party documents detail circumstances surrounding his death, illuminate earlier chapters of his life, and help readers appreciate the high esteem in which he was held by contemporaries.

Reading these holographic letters is a challenge. Those in pencil are faded; those written in ink often have blots or bleeding from one side of the paper to the other. Cross-writing is common, as are perpendicular continuations in the margins. The penmanship is sometimes poor, as Ramseur wrote while in the saddle and, during two periods, used his left hand due to wounds in his right arm sustained at Malvern Hill and Spotsylvania. Gnawed corners and edges occasionally obliterate words. After trying to unscramble a particularly vexing combination of letters, I was amused at the sudden realization that it was a word from mid-nineteenth-century usage no longer common today. "Mote" and "tittle" are two examples. Only in a few places is the writer's fallibility evident, as when he mistakenly jots down the wrong month or day or forgets to enter the information altogether. A numbering system Ramseur used to supplement dating in September 1864 is of some assistance.

The spontaneous fluency and articulation of Americans who wrote by hand generations ago is a wonder to modern wordsmiths armed with software to edit and re-edit texts. Ramseur varied his vocabulary and sentence structure with only an occasional cross out or insertion. He used British spelling, notably "-our" at the end of words where "-or" is common in American English. The original spellings have been retained, as have misspellings. Ramseur tended to employ dashes where periods or commas would be expected. In most cases, these have been converted to the modern punctuation style for ease of reading. Again and again, the writer underlined words and phrases (shown here as italics) for emphasis. Only occasionally has it been necessary to add a comma or period. These additions could be rationalized by supposing that the original markings have faded. Abbreviations remain as written in most instances, as they are frequent and readily comprehensible. To facilitate a clear reading, long discourses covering more than a single topic have been divided into paragraphs. And to make for a more readable page in the printed book, levels of indent for paragraphs and various elements of the letters (salutations, closings, etc.) have been regularized, periods and commas have been uniformly placed inside close quotation marks, and words and phrases that originally appeared in full capital letters have been typeset in small caps. In truth, the challenge of the editorial method has been in deciphering the handwriting, not reformatting it to please the twenty-first-century reader.

The Bravest of the Brave

"WHENEVER YOU CAN SEND THEM, we shall be more than glad to get your father's letters. I know there will be much material in them that will be very helpful to students of Confederate History."[1] So wrote D. H. Hill, the general's son who served as secretary of the North Carolina Historical Commission, to the daughter of Stephen Dodson Ramseur. Hill had not personally known the writer but his father had, both from instructing Ramseur in mathematics at Davidson College in the mid-1850s and while serving with him during the Civil War. Maj. Gen. Daniel Harvey Hill would have observed Ramseur's endearing humanity in daily life and known of his bravery and leadership in times of strife.[2] If the younger Hill expected these qualities to be reflected in Ramseur's letters, he was not disappointed.

Stephen Dodson Ramseur was born into a mercantile family in a small North Carolina town and reared with the religious beliefs and values common to the South's slaveholding class during the antebellum period. His intelligence and drive led to a successful five-year course of study at West Point, after two years at a liberal arts college, followed by service as an artillery officer in the U.S. Army. In step with many of his southern peers, Ramseur resigned his commission in the spring of 1861 and joined his state's militia.

Ramseur's death on the battlefield at age twenty-seven brought closure to a meteoric rise from lieutenant to major general in a period of less than

1. D. H. Hill to Mary Dodson Ramseur, March 6, 1924, SHC.

2. Hill first met Ramseur at Davidson College, where he was a professor and served as his mentor and patron for the remainder of his life. Hill was appointed to the rank of lieutenant general in the Confederate army, although President Davis never submitted his name to the Confederate Senate for confirmation. Warner, *Generals in Gray*, 137.

four years. His advancement was the reward for excellent performance at each level of command. He participated in action peripheral to the naval duel between the *Monitor* and *Virginia* (née *Merrimac*) as an artillery officer and later led his infantry regiment into battle at Malvern Hill. As a brigade commander, he took part in Stonewall Jackson's flanking maneuver at Chancellorsville, saw action on the first day at Gettysburg, and fought valiantly in the Wilderness and at Spotsylvania Court House. He then served as a division commander during Jubal A. Early's Valley campaign, after accompanying Early on the raid from Maryland to Washington, D.C. In short, Ramseur was involved as a senior officer in many of the war's important conflicts east of the Appalachians. His incisive observations on these events are those of a competent, well-respected commander in the second tier of general-officer leadership in the Army of Northern Virginia.

In addition to providing a portrait of Ramseur's years in the Confederate army, and earlier at West Point, his letters describe his courtship and union with Ellen "Nellie" Richmond. In revealing his feelings about her and the events taking place in a nation at war with itself, Ramseur voices his attitudes on social matters, as well as on the military and political issues of his day. Ramseur's letters reflect the constant inner tensions generated by balancing national and state allegiances, family obligations and public service, and gender relations. The content is therefore of importance to a range of historians and other readers studying not just political and military campaigns, but the culture, religion, and social values of white southern society at the time of the war.

Ramseur's personal values radiate throughout the letters. Foremost is his unwavering faith in a loving God. Next is a sense of duty to his country, a profound feeling that repeatedly drew Ramseur away from family and loved ones to fulfill what he considered his foremost responsibilities. His letters also reflect courage, both in military service to his nation and in the personal risks he took on the battlefield, resulting in four wounds. Indeed, his friend since childhood characterized Ramseur as "the bravest of the brave" (see chapter 8). He was a man who lived as he thought right and died as a consequence. In sum, Ramseur's precepts and beliefs epitomize many of those held by southern gentlemen of his day.

In examining the experience of combat in the Civil War, historian Gerald E. Linderman identifies the set of values that constitute courage: manliness, godliness, honor, duty, and knightliness.[3] These ideals are reflected

---

3. Linderman, *Embattled Courage*, 8–16.

throughout Ramseur's correspondence, as illustrated by his thoughts during the pause before the critical events of 1863: "We certainly have a Stupendous task before us! A task which will test our manhood, and if successfully accomplished, will entitle those of us who unflinchingly perform the part allotted to us, to the full title of Heroes."[4] Like so many of his class in southern society, the most prominent of whom was Robert E. Lee, Ramseur was culturally, morally, and spiritually compelled by honor to defend his family, his community, and, just as important, his new nation.[5]

Ramseur fervently believed in full independence for the Confederate States. Repeatedly, he expressed hope that the North would tire of the fighting and suffering, and negotiate peace. He would accept no compromise to nationhood for the South, even though continuation of the war required him to remain far from home and family. While a self-acknowledged secessionist, he never mentioned slavery as his reason for pursuing the conflict. Yet his father owned slaves, and Ramseur employed and traded them.[6] He clearly expressed his feelings on the institution while a cadet at West Point, referring to slavery as "the very source of our existence, the *greatest blessing* both for master & slave, that could have been bestowed upon us."[7] By contrast, and with religious precepts foremost in his mind at Davidson College, he declared that he abhorred human trafficking, writing, "Is Mr Barrett still buying negroes. I sincerely hope he may soon see the wickedness of such a course."[8]

Knowledge of Ramseur's family is vital to understanding his letters. His paternal family was centered in Lincoln County in the North Carolina Piedmont. There were nine children in his immediate family in Lincolnton: Mary, Stephen Dodson, David, Sallie, Lucy (nicknamed "Luly"), Fannie, Charles, Addie, and Harvey. His mother's family (the Dodsons), as well as that of his wife-to-be (the Richmonds), lived in Caswell County on the Virginia border just below Danville. Caleb and Mary Richmond, who resided outside Milton, also had a son named Stephen Dodson and cousins Mary, Nellie, Caleb, George, Lou, and Nat. Young Caleb served on Ramseur's personal staff and is frequently mentioned in his correspondence. Ramseur's mother and elder sister, both named Mary, died in the 1850s; later refer-

4. Ramseur to his future wife, February 8, 1863, SHC.

5. Wyatt-Brown, *Honor and Violence*, 59–60.

6. The 1840 Census showed eight slaves owned by Jacob Ramseur. The 1850 Census indicated 20 slaves. U.S. Census Office, *Sixth Census, 1840* and *Seventh Census, 1850*.

7. Ramseur to Schenck, November 8, 1856, PC.

8. Ramseur to his sister Lucy, October 17, 1853, SHC.

ences to "Mama" and "Mary" in his letters to Nellie concern her mother and elder sibling respectively. Although Milton was a focal point for the extended family, relatives were found elsewhere throughout the surrounding area. His aunt and uncle, Dr. Charles and Priscilla "Prissie" Dodson, for example, appear repeatedly in Ramseur's writings.

Ramseur uses the name "David" when referring to his brother who served as a military surgeon. The more familiar "Dave" is reserved for Ramseur's lifelong confidant, David Schenck.[9] To confuse matters further, correspondence addressed to Schenck usually begins, "My Dear Brother." He is referred to in the third person as "Mr. Schenck" or "Mr. S." in correspondence with Nellie. And, when Schenck married Ramseur's sister, Sallie, their first-born was christened Dodson Ramseur, or "Doddie." Character identification is further complicated by Ramseur's using "Lue" as a nickname for both his sister, Lucy or "Luly," and for Nellie's sister, Lucy Ann. The context must be used to determine which sister is intended. A truncated family tree is provided as a reference to guide the reader through the tangle of Ramseur's relatives and their recurring names.

While not the majority of Ramseur's correspondence, the Schenck letters are rich in subject matter of interest to latter-day historians. A childhood friend, two years older than Ramseur and in later years his biographer, Schenck was an intimate. The closing of each message is often so syrupy as to suggest a sexual relationship to present-day readers, but such sentimentality was not unusual at that time. Historian Grady McWhiney cites these letters as an example of "latent homosexuality, if nothing more."[10] Ramseur communicated to Schenck his experiences at West Point, the details of battles, the reasons underlying his actions, and his hopes and fears for the future in a way he would not with a family member or sweetheart. Written less frequently during the war, these epistles tend to be long and insightful.

The most prominent aspect of Ramseur's letters is the overt religious tone. Not only is God invoked in almost every piece, but the writer sometimes employs biblical references, hymns and quotations from uplifting nineteenth-century tracts, many unfamiliar to modern readers. Every let-

9. After the war, David Schenck served as a state judge, was a leader in preserving the Guilford battlefield from the War of Independence, and authored volumes on North Carolina history. James R. Leutze, "David Schenck," in Powell, *North Carolina Biography*, 5:295–96.

10. McWhiney concludes his explication, "Ramseur's youthful difficulty in establishing his male sexual identity, perhaps exacerbated by the scarcity of females at Davidson College and at West Point, apparently eased as time passed." McWhiney, *Southerners and Other Americans*, 42.

ter pleads for more mail from the recipient, reflecting Ramseur's loneliness while in college, during five long years at West Point, and, finally, engaged in military campaigning.

The bulk of Ramseur's extant correspondence from his years at West Point and during his first two years in uniform is addressed to Schenck. In late 1862, Ramseur fell in love with his cousin, Nellie Richmond, to whom he began writing regularly. For the remainder of his life, Ramseur's thoughts were foremost of her, first as a sweetheart, then as a betrothed, and finally, as a wife. Nellie's father was a prosperous plow-maker and land-owner who, at one time, served as a state legislator. The 1860 Slave Census lists thirty-eight blacks and mulattos belonging to him, twenty-two above the age of fourteen years.

Correspondence with Nellie is openly affectionate. Ramseur unreserv-edly expresses his love, repeatedly regrets long separations, warmly recalls their brief times together, longs for the slightest bit of news about her, and always asks God's blessing on her and their marriage. Caring for others is a theme throughout his writing. While away from home, he regularly inquires about his family and friends and articulates his feelings for them. This concern is for relatives in both Milton and Lincolnton. Once war is under way, Ramseur writes of news and fears for chums from childhood, cadets he knew at West Point, and senior leaders and comrades with whom he is serving in the Confederate army. Indeed, his close companion while campaigning, chaplain Ephraim H. Harding from Caswell County, observed after the war, "It seems strange that one so affectionate, so almost womanly in his feelings, should have been so completely at home amid the dreadful scenes of the battle field."[11]

Ramseur's seven years of education at the college level is reflected in literary and historical references and in his use of words and phrases in Latin and French. What is remarkable is that Nellie, age nineteen during 1860 and with no schooling beyond that available in a small North Carolina town, would be thought to understand these allusions.

The nature of the correspondence changes as the war progresses. In gen-eral, reports of the unpleasant and unsuccessful become less common. With the exception of Ramseur's controversial decisions at Stephenson's Depot and his reactions thereafter, one must turn to other sources for accounts of his rare less-than-stellar performances and for explanations of his wounds. As the conflict lengthens and Confederate prospects grow gloomier, there

11. Harding, "Sketch," 40.

are fewer references to politics, as well as to friends and relatives. When troop levels plummet and Ramseur's command responsibilities increase through promotion, his attention focuses on the immediate situation. At the end of his days, the careful wording of letters to his new wife reveal a fear of alarming her during a pregnancy that Ramseur repeatedly declares is of the utmost importance to him. Tensions build on the battlefield and in his private life until, without warning, the writings stop.

1

The Formative Years, 1837–1855

BORN ON MAY 31, 1837, the eldest son of Lucy and Jacob Ramsour,[1] Stephen Dodson Ramseur was known throughout his life as "Dod" or "Dodson," his mother's maiden name. Dod took a special interest in nurturing his brother, David, who was two years younger. From the frequent, endearing correspondence between them, he also seems to have been very close to his sister Lucy, or "Luly," six years his junior. Sallie, born between David and Luly, assumed special importance by marrying Dod's best friend, David Schenck.

Dod's was the third generation of his paternal family to live in Lincolnton, a town in the rolling hills of the North Carolina Piedmont.[2] Located forty miles northwest of Charlotte, the settlement was named for Gen. Benjamin Lincoln, a Revolutionary War hero. Dod's father and grandfather were both successful entrepreneurs. Ramsour's Mill,[3] just north of town, was made famous by an armed confrontation between British loyalists and outnumbered patriots in 1780. His mother's family resided in Milton on the Dan River, just inside the state boundary ten miles southeast of Danville, Virginia.

In an era predating public schools, Dod attended the state-chartered Pleasant Retreat Academy, where he received a classical education in mathematics, chemistry, grammar, logic, Greek, and Latin. The primary influ-

1. For some unknown reason, Dod's father changed the spelling of the family name, which accounts for inconsistencies in subsequent documents. There were nine soldiers who served with North Carolina regiments during the Civil War with names spelled "Ramsour" and "Ramseaur," in addition to those with "Ramseur" as the surname.

2. The definitive work on Ramseur's life, from which much of the obscure information is drawn, is Gallagher, *Stephen Dodson Ramseur*.

3. The spelling of the Revolutionary War battle at the mill uses both "Ramsaur" and "Ramsour."

ence during this period was his mother, a staunch Presbyterian who helped shape his character using the Westminster catechism.[4] Their bond made her death in 1859 particularly painful to him. The slight youngster enjoyed roaming the woods and hunting in the fields surrounding the community. Perhaps Dod's skill with a musket was one reason he embarked upon a career as a soldier.

Dod's two steady chums were Schenck and Robert F. Hoke. The former was the son of a local physician and became Ramseur's Boswell. Schenck's extensive notations in a diary, letters saved from his friend during his schooling and military career, and the state history and reminiscences Schenck penned many years later, provide a thorough account of Dod's life. Only four days older than Dod, Hoke enrolled in the Kentucky Military Institute in 1852, but was required to return home before graduation to help his widowed mother run the family's diversified industries. This management experience undoubtedly helped prepare Hoke for the problems of military leadership that lay ahead as he rose to the rank of major general in the Confederate army.[5]

A year after Hoke departed for school, Ramseur left home at age sixteen to enroll in Davidson College, twenty miles to the east. Founded by Presbyterians in 1837, fewer than 100 students received instruction in a pair of small, two-story Greek Revival buildings facing each other. The young men were housed in one-story brick quarters nearby. Participation in religious activities was an integral part of Davidson's curriculum.

The idealism of youth prevented Ramseur from being satisfied with Davidson. He was understandably hurt when the severe regimen imposed by the faculty required students to stay on campus and study, thus preventing Ramseur from traveling the few miles home to spend a short time with family and friends. Even if his college experience disappointed him, it deepened his faith in God. His noble religious principles are reflected in a denunciation of slavery, a tenet he would later discard in the cauldron of intersectionalism boiling at West Point. The concept of personal duty was a value repeatedly expressed in his writing from Davidson, sometimes making Ramseur seem too serious for a teenager. His interest in politics and an abiding concern for family would never wane.

4. Cox, *Life and Character*, 13.
5. Barefoot, *General Robert F. Hoke*, 8–10, 13–16.

Davidson College, Oct 17th 1853

Dearest Sister[6]

I have learned my Latin lesson & have a short time to write to you, which will be more pleasant for me to do than to yawn over my Greek lesson. I can't describe my feelings on leaving Mr. Penick's, but I can assure you that the company of such a man as Mr. Penick is enough to keep anyone from feeling as I did.[7] I was very much surprised to hear of the objections Mr. Smith had to D. College. Altho' he may find many things to object to here, as regards the *course of study*, or rather the way it is taught, yet he can not object to this place on account of its being wicked. There are some wicked boys here that is true, but two thirds of the students are members of the Church. We have morning and evening prayer. Saturday night some of the students have a prayer meeting in one of the lecture rooms. Sabbath morning they have a Sabbath school which was gotten up by the students of their own accord, and at three o clock in the afternoon the Faculty hear all of the Students recite a Bible lesson. Does that not speak well for this place and does it not show that there is a true religious feeling with most of the students of this place, and besides this Davidson College has turned out more ministers than any other place in proportion to the number of Graduates. I don't think Mr. Smith can say this much for Newton.[8]

You asked me how I spend the Sabbath here. In the morning at Sunrise I go to prayers in the Chapel. From there we go to breakfast, and then it is about an hour until Sabbath school, which time I spend in reading my Bible. It is about 11 o clock when Sabbath School breaks up, and then we listen to a sermon from one of the members of the Faculty. After the morning sermon, I read some good book (I am reading [Philip] Doddridge's *Rise and Progress of Religion in the Soul*) which I hope may prove of lasting benefit to me. At 2 o clock all of the Students go up to the Chapel and recite a Bible lesson to Dr. Williamson,[9] which is very interesting and instructive, and we have another sermon Sabbath night. Yes Dearest Sister I try to spend the Sabbath in such a way as I think will please my Father in Heaven, and will be beneficial to my never-dying soul.

6. Very likely, Dodson's eldest sister, Mary, SHC.

7. A fellow student, Daniel A. Penick of Cabarrus County, Davidson College, *Semi-Centennial Catalogue*, 94.

8. A town in Catawba County, fifteen miles directly north of Lincolnton.

9. Rev. Samuel Williamson served as president of Davidson College at the same time he was teaching Mental and Moral Philosophy and Rhetoric. The faculty's curricula vitae are presented in the college's annual catalogues. See, for example, Davidson College, *Catalogue of the Trustees*.

I get along in all my studies more easily than I expected except Greek, and I can keep up with the class in that by studying pretty hard. I suppose the great wedding has taken place at Mr. Hendersons.[10] Tell me all the news when you write again. Have you seen Cousin Mary Ann & Mag lately?[11] Is Mr. Barrett[12] still buying negroes. I do sincerely hope that he may soon see the wickedness of such a course. When you [see] Mr. Abram:[13] tell him I will write to him as soon as I possibly can. Ask Pa if he is selling many goods now. Has he received the goods he ordered, and if so hope is pleased with them. How has the bottom corn turned out that was under water. Tell Pa please to see Mr. Craige,[14] and to ask him to assist me in procuring the appointment to West Point. Tell Pa please to do it as soon as he possibly can. Ask Mother if Pa had not better invite him to our house, so that he may become acquainted with all of the family, and tell her to talk all about it to him. For Dearest Sister, I tell you candidly I do not desire to stay here and graduate, for this place will not do to give anyone a first rate education. I know that it is owing in a great measure to the person, whether he is a schollar or not, but I do not believe it is possible for any one to receive as good an education here (the way things are now carried on). Let him try ever so hard. I already know two or three members of the Senior Class who talk much more incorrectly than Mr. *Font*, and I believe they stand as high in their class as any. I think Crockett is the only one in the Senior class who is a good English scholar, and he says he has forgotten nearly all he ever did know about it since he came here. Yes, I think there is something in the college as well as the individual, and I certainly think from all that I have seen of this place, and I am sorry to say it, that it will certainly go down unless Mr. [Daniel Harvey] Hill can do something to make it hold its head up.[15] My honest opinion is that Mr. Rockwell[16] is the only one of the Faculty that is fit to be a Professor and he is very worthy of a Professorship in any College. Besides this Dr. Williamson is so easy and partial that some of the students who are not as worthy

10. C. C. Henderson was a forty-nine-year-old merchant and father of nine in Lincolnton, U.S. Census Office, *Seventh Census, 1850*.

11. Mary Ann Hoyle Barrett was Ramseur's first cousin, and Maggie her newborn daughter.

12. Elisha S. Barrett, Mary Ann's husband, was a business partner of Ramseur's father.

13. An unidentified individual.

14. Elected as a Democrat, Burton C. Craige was the member of the U.S. House of Representatives from the Seventh District of North Carolina, which included Lincoln County, 1853–61. He later introduced the ordinance of secession passed by the state convention.

15. Ramseur is alluding to Williamson's easygoing approach that led to a student riot before Christmas 1854, quelled by Hill. Bridges, *Lee's Maverick General*, 24.

16. A graduate of Yale College and an ordained clergyman, Elijah F. Rockwell taught chemistry and geology during the 1853–54 term.

as some of the rest get along as well and better I believe with him than those who are really worthy. No Dearest sister it is impossible for me to form a very high opinion of Davidson, try as hard as I may. Don't let any one see this for it may produce a bad effect on their minds, and I want every-one to form an opinion for themselves concerning this place, but will be perfectly contented to stay here two years and then to go to West Point, (or if I can not succeed in procuring the appointment to the place) to stay here four years and graduate. . . .

S. D. Ramseur[17]

Davidson College N.C.

June 27th 1854

My dear Mother

I can give you no idea of my disappointment. I have been cheering myself up to perform my duties by the hope of making a visit home. How much pleasure did it afford me to think that I would be with my dear friends at home. Yes! after anticipating so much pleasure, I have been disappointed. My visit to my dear home must be deferred two more long months. Oh, it is a great disappointment. I am very sorry indeed that David[18] was troubled so much for nothing. I felt so sad to part with him. Was he not very much fatigued with his ride? I did not know. I did not even think that the Faculty would for one moment refuse to give me per-mission to go home when I was sent for, but there is a change at David-son since Maj Hill's arrival. When I asked for "*permission*," I told "The Faculty" that Pa had sent for me, and I wished to go home and I would promise to return on Monday evening. Prof. Gilland[19] first asked me if any of my friends were sick. I told him they were well, but that I wished to go home to see them. Also that I wished to attend Mr. Davis's communion[20] which would be at that time. Prof. Gilland then said that it was *absolutely* important that I should not neglect one single Greek lesson, for he said, that I had already been absent nearly six weeks and was not quite up with my class, so that he thought that it was my duty to stay. Maj. Hill said that unless this was an extraordinary case and it was very necessary for me to

17. SHC.

18. Ramseur uses "David" to refer to his younger brother and the more familiar "Dave" for his best friend, David Schenck.

19. Another clergyman, James Gilland was a professor of languages.

20. Robert N. Davis was a Presbyterian clergyman in Lincolnton, U.S. Census Office, *Seventh Census, 1850.*

be at home, that it was clearly my duty to remain here. Mr. Rockwell said the same thing and more. He said if I wished to stand high in scholarship and to receive a good report, it was necessary that I should attend carefully and punctually to every single recitation. Dr. Williamson said, that he knew and I knew that it was important for me to stay here and attend to my studies, but that as Pa had sent for me that he might blame him for preventing me from coming home. All the Members of the Faculty said many more things to me, telling what they thought I ought to do &c, &c and concluded to leave it to me, after letting me know that it was their wish and advice that I should remain and not fall back again. And I know that I ought to stay but I wished to go home. I want to see my dear Mother, Father, Brothers and Sisters. None but those who have experienced an expectation from friends and relatives can imagine what a great pleasure I sacrificed. I denied myself this pleasure, for I do not wish to be behind my class. . . .

It seems but as yesterday, when I loved to be with my darling Sister. Yes! the memory of that darling one, of her pure loving, pious heart, will ever be fresh and delightful. Oh! what a consolation it is for us to know that she is *now* freed from the anxious cares and burdensome sins of this wicked world. She is now an Angel worshipping in the presence of that Jesus she loved so fondly and served so faithfully while she was with us here in this world of sin and sorrow.[21]

[Dear Mother, July 24, 1854]

Sometimes I am so oppressed with my sinfulness that I can not but be sad. I fear sometimes that I do not perform my duty in every thing, but then I know that the blood of my Savior can atone for all of my infirmities. Oh! It is a precious thing to believe in God, to know that in all things whatever may happen, that it shall all work together for good for those who love God.[22] He is our protector, our preserver, and our merciful Savior. Oh how thankful ought we to be for all of his mercies to us. He gives us "every good and perfect gift."[23] Though we are sometimes called to go through "fiery trials," his sustaining Grace will support us; "he only designs our dross to consume and our gold to refine."[24]

21. Ramseur's eldest sibling, Mary, had died on April 28, 1854. Ramseur to his mother, July 24, 1854, SHC.
22. Romans 8:28.
23. James 1:17.
24. From the fifth stanza, "How firm a foundation, ye saints of the Lord," by William Cowper in John Rippon, *A Selection of Hymns from the Best Authors* (1787). SHC.

Dod Ramseur as a young man
(editor's collection)

The following letter of recommendation for Ramseur's admission to West Point from his mentor and idol, who would soon be a champion of the Confederacy, is curious for its brevity.

> D. College, N.C.
> Jan'y. 19th 1855
>
> This is to certify that Mr. S. D. Ramsour of Lincolnton, N.C. studied Algebra with me from Fractions through Quadratics, and also eight books of [Adrien Marie] Legendre's Geometry.
>
> He thoroughly mastered the principles in those branches and has now a mind trained to grapple with the difficulties of the more advanced Mathematics.
>
> D. H. Hill
> Prof. Math[25]

On February 6, 1855, Representative Burton Craige wrote to Brig. Gen. Joseph G. Totten, chief engineer of the army and inspector of the Military Academy, nominating Ramseur to represent his congressional district. Craige received confirmation three days later. Ramseur eagerly accepted the appointment on February 14.[26]

In his remaining time at Davidson, Ramseur focused on preparing himself for the academic rigors of West Point. Defending the career upon which he was about to embark, he wrote to his confidant, David Schenck:

> [March 17th 1855]
>
> I am devoting my time and attention to Mathematics alone. I am reviewing Algebra and Geometry, and studying Trigonometry. This *is rather preparatory to the West Point course.* And I will say here, that, as I am to serve my Country! I intend *to try* to live and act in such a manner that my Country will be proud of me. Yes! Dave, my days of idleness and pleasure are over. I feel now that Life is real! Life is earnest![27] and I feel too, that the time is approaching for me to work and to work diligently. God grant that I may be able to perform my *whole duty*, with a willing hand and a bold heart. Dave, you have always discouraged me in the course

25. Stephen Dodson Ramseur, U.S. Military Academy Application Papers, RG 94, NARA.
26. Ibid.
27. Henry Wadsworth Longfellow, "A Psalm of Life" (1838), first line, second stanza.

I am about to pursue. I know you always did this with the best motives, and altho' I always respect your opinion and have frequently followed your advice, yet in this matter, I beg leave to differ from you, for who knows but that "I may write my history with my sword" as the illustrious Scott once said.[28] . . .

Well Dave, I have nearly filled the last two pages with *fooling* and I think as I suppose you do that it is time to stop such. I saw in the Western Democrat today that Jim Caldwell is the Whig candidate for Congress.[29] I feel very much interested in this election. I want Mr. Craige to be elected again. I suppose the Know-Nothings will vote for *Jim*. If so I think he will be elected. I am very much afraid this will be the case. Burton Craige has performed his duty faithfully, he deserves the office again. I hope he may be elected, although in the present uncertain and distracted state of the Parties, the result is exceedingly doubtful.[30]

The young man who left North Carolina as an eighteen-year-old to attend West Point in May was described long after by a close friend and relation by marriage.

In person, General Ramseur was of medium height, his figure was slender but well proportioned, very erect and of fine martial bearing. His brow was large, prominent, well rounded—his eye[s] large and black and the whole expression open, winning, and striking. His face indicated in a most remarkable manner loftiness of character and purity of sentiment. He was a fine horseman, sitting his horse with grace, and managing him with skill.[31]

28. Winfield Scott's autobiography cites the *National Intelligencer* of February 25, 1855, as publishing this phrase contained in a letter penned in 1811. That date was a Sunday, however, and the newspaper was not printed that day. Scott, *Memoirs*, 42.

29. The census identified James A. Caldwell as a thirty-seven-year-old farmer, U.S. Census Office, *Eighth Census, 1860*. Later that spring he denounced the Whig Party and campaigned for Craige. Lucy Dodson Ramseur to S. D. Ramseur, June 1, 1855, Stephen Dodson Ramseur Papers, SHC.

30. PC.

31. Harding, "Sketch," 41.

2

Wearing the Military Uniform
of the United States

*The West Point Years and Service
as an Army Officer, 1855–1861*

IN THE YEARS BEFORE THE CIVIL WAR, the U.S. Military Academy was the nation's premier engineering school with a curriculum designed to prepare its graduates to build the river and harbor works, lighthouses, canals, and railroads needed by a burgeoning nation. It also served to prepare topographical and military engineers for times of war. The institution had been founded early in the nineteenth century, patterned after Sandhurst and St. Cyr, its counterparts in England and France.

In the wake of Napoleon's campaigns across Europe, the French influence was especially strong in military strategy and tactics. Two of the academy's stalwarts during Ramseur's years had studied in France. Dennis Hart Mahan,[1] professor of engineering and the art of war, spent four years at l'Ecole Polytechnique in Metz, and William J. Hardee, commandant of cadets, graduated from the cavalry school at Saumur. The Napoleon Club was the most prestigious intellectual society on campus, counting among its members Mahan, Superintendent Robert E. Lee, George B. McClellan, Gustavus W. Smith, and Dabney Maury.[2] Proficiency in the French language was required to read what were considered the most authoritative writings on the art of warfare. Hardee's revision of the U.S. Army's infantry manual drew heavily on French sources. Indeed, the academy library exchanged books with bibliothecas in France. It is not surprising, therefore, that Ramseur's letters are lightly sprinkled with Gallic expressions.

---

1. Dennis Hart Mahan was recognized as the nation's premier authority on defensive military works, as the author of the bible of the operational engineer, *Complete Treatise on Field Fortifications with the General Outlines of the Principles.*

2. Ambrose, *Duty, Honor, Country,* 138.

Ramseur's class was the second to be enrolled under an expanded five-year curriculum instituted at the direction of Secretary of War Jefferson Davis and implemented by Lee. The fifth year was added to strengthen offerings in the humanities—history, geography, and military law—and to introduce Spanish training to enable graduates to operate effectively in territory recently acquired from Mexico. Embarking upon an extended program of study could have seemed excessive for Ramseur, who already had two years of college under his belt. Surprisingly, eighteen of his classmates were older than he and, according to him, two dozen had already attended the best schools of higher learning in the country. Ramseur soon realized he would be challenged by subject matter and a level of competition in the classroom that he had not faced at Davidson.

Ramseur arrived at West Point located on a plain of about 160 acres overlooking a right-angle bend in the Hudson River, fifty-three miles above New York City. The first ordeal was to appear naked before three medical officers for a fitness examination, certainly a shock for a modest young man from rural North Carolina. He was then questioned by the Academic Board comprising the superintendent, commandant, and professors in the core disciplines, to determine his proficiency in basic arithmetic, history, and geography. Only afterward could he join the encampment of eight rows of tents (two per company) stretching out on the plateau in full view of the academy's permanent buildings. Continuing each year until the end of August, summer camp emphasized training in infantry tactics, employment of artillery, riding and cavalry skills, and swordsmanship.[3]

The routine was relieved by the attention paid by the fashionable young ladies. During the summer, the Hudson Valley was a favorite retreat for well-to-do families from northeastern cities who fled the heat at home and sojourned in local hotels. The attraction of a battalion of cadets in gray uniforms at thrice-weekly "hops" was irresistible for the daughters of vacationing captains of industry, finance, and commerce. New arrivals, or "plebes," had little chance with these maidens. In subsequent encampments, however, Ramseur could look forward to strolling with a debutante along "Flirtation Walk," an overgrown Revolutionary War sentry path on a bluff above the river with plenty of dark corners for innocent intimacies.[4]

Matriculation to West Point was a significant event for a small southern community. Only one cadet at a time could be appointed to the mili-

3. Wright, "West Point and Cadet Life," 193–96.
4. Aimone, "Much to Sadden," 14.

tary academy from each congressional district. The large number of visitors from home attests to the importance of Ramseur's achievement. His mother and father, a brother, other relatives, friends and their parents journeyed to New York State to visit Dod. Someone who did not come for a visit, Ramseur's childhood friend Bob Hoke, is repeatedly inquired about in Ramseur's letters.

Many of Ramseur's fellow cadets would confront one another on the battlefield shortly after graduation. Among the names familiar to Civil War enthusiasts are Lunsford Lindsay Lomax, Fitzhugh Lee, Edward Alexander Porter, George Crockett Strong, Joe Wheeler, Emory Upton, Judson Kilpatrick, Adelbert Ames, George Armstrong Custer, John Pelham, and Tom Rosser. Well known to Ramseur would have been Horace Porter, James Harrison Wilson, and Wesley Merritt, all northerners and members of his class who attained distinction soon after graduation.

How did they appraise Ramseur? Wilson considered him "as handsome and attractive a young man as could be found."[5] Another cadet wrote, "I remember him riding a fiery horse, and dashing at a dangerously high fence, to show a charming looking girl how the cadets were taught to ride."[6] To a New Yorker, Ramseur was "a Christian and a gentleman," no doubt due to regular attendance at Lt. Oliver Otis Howard's twice-weekly evening prayer meetings.[7] Gary W. Gallagher, Ramseur's biographer, opined that because he flouted academy prohibitions against smoking, chewing tobacco, and sneaking off to a local tavern, his classmates forgave his sometime puritanical bent.[8]

Tension between cadets from the North and South was beginning to arise as Ramseur was enrolled. As early as October 1855, Ramseur commented on sectionalism in the corps of cadets in a letter to David Schenck. Men from the Northeast tended to be assigned to certain units, those from the South to others, especially Company D, and all within the corps' ceremonial regulations to organize individuals by physical size. Taller cadets were placed in companies A and D. By the time he was assigned quarters for the 1858 semester, northerners were concentrated in one barracks, southerners in another.[9]

5. Wilson, *Under the Flag*, 1:19–20.
6. Wright, "West Point before the War," 15.
7. Schaff, *Spirit of Old West Point*, 56.
8. Gallagher, *Stephen Dodson Ramseur*, 27.
9. Aimone, "Much to Sadden," 13–14.

Drinking, staying out after hours, playing cards, smoking, and even fighting were common on antebellum campuses. In Ramseur's case, these relatively mild expressions of rebellion peaked a few months before graduation at Benny Haven's tavern beside the Hudson, an inn that catered to boatmen and cadets celebrating their independence by "skipping over the picket." Although a member of the class of 1861, Custer arranged a late-night party for his chums in what he considered the best class ever produced at West Point. He, Rosser, Pelham, and others saluted the stalwarts of 1860.[10] Ramseur's letters do not mention this caper, nor do they indicate that he finished fourteenth of the forty-one men who graduated from the class of 121 plebes who entered West Point in June 1855.

Two excerpts from Ramseur's first letter to his mother from West Point, dated August 15, 1855, illustrate his transition from upbringing to matriculation.

> Dear Mother, 'tis three months today I bade you "Goodbye." How sad to say "Good-bye" when we leave our childhoods home for a long time. It may be the last time, who knows? Good-bye, Mother, "It may be for years, or it may be forever" but still my thoughts shall continually wander back to home and the long years may glide down the stream of time. Difficulties will oppose, and wasting cares oppress us, but there is one string, which nothing but the hand of Death can still. It is the memory of a Mother's love which never dies. . . .
>
> You said that you were very anxious about my Roommate. This is indeed a matter of the *greatest* importance, and I am more anxious about this matter than anything else. Every thing almost depends upon ones room mate. Cadet Williams[11] from my state, told me that his roommate was the cause of his getting the great number of demerits which he received last year. If I can succeed in finding a pious, careful and studious Roommate I will be entirely satisfied. W. H. Gibbes[12] is a Son of the Editor of the South Carolinian. He is a very nice and complete *Gentleman*, but I do not like him sufficiently well in *all* respects, however I have made an agreement to room with him, provided he is in the same

---

10. Gallagher, *Stephen Dodson Ramseur*, 26–27.

11. Solomon Williams of Nash County, North Carolina, graduated with the class of 1858 after having been suspended for "deficiency in conduct." He served as a lieutenant with the U.S. Cavalry, 1858–61, and, then, as a colonel with the Twelfth North Carolina Infantry and Second North Carolina Cavalry, with whom he was killed at Brandy Station in 1862. Krick, *Lee's Colonels*, 371–72.

12. Wade Hampton Gibbes, from one of the first families of South Carolina, whose property in Columbia bears his name to this day, Gibbes Green.

Company with me. If he does not get in the same company with me,
I will room with my fellow statesman, John C. Gilmer,[13] a nephew of
Mr. Gilmer of Greensborough.[14]

"Camp Calhoun"[15]

West Point, Aug. 23d/55

My Dear Friend [David Schenck],

Your very kind letter was received a long, long time ago, and should
have been replyed to immediately, but I have been prevented from performing that most pleasant duty, by the *severity* of my *military duties*.
When the *Plebe* is not busily engaged, he is so much wearied from work
just performed, that it is an impossibility for him to take his seat on his
tent floor, with his writing desk on his knees, and in this *comfortable* position, to write a palatable letter. I do assure you, Dear Dave, if I had obeyed
the free impulse of my heart, I would have written *long before this*, for no
letter have I ever received from *anyone* that afforded me such *real* pleasure, as that of yours. As I eagerly traced those lines, everyone of which
breathed so much Friendship and Love, "Sweet Memory brought the
light of other days around me,"[16] and I experienced *true, calm happiness*,
to *which*, heretofore, I have been a Stranger at West Point. I do thank you,
from the bottom of my heart, for "writing to me as a Friend" for indeed
"I do appreciate that virtuoustie." And *now*, that *distance* separates us, (not
that "Distance that sends enchantment to the view")[17] and I am deprived
of the sweets of your Society, I still claim a place in your memory, and will
ever be proud and happy to receive letters from your fluent pen.

My Friend, you know, that I thought long, and considered well on the
probabilities of my success at West Point, before I applied for the station.
I imagined all the difficulties and hardships which I expected to encoun-

13. Gilmer did not graduate. His uncle was John Adams Gilmer, who served two terms in
Congress representing North Carolina, 1857–61, first as a member of the American, or "Know-
Nothing," Party and then as a legislator for the Opposition Party.

14. PC.

15. Each year's summer camp was named in honor of a different notable, many graduates of
the academy. In 1855, the corps was remembering John C. Calhoun who, as secretary of war under
President Andrew Jackson, approved West Point, New York, as the permanent home of the U.S.
Military Academy.

16. In "The Light of Other Days," Thomas Moore (1779–1852) wrote, "Sad Memory brings the
light of other days around me."

17. A common expression in nineteenth-century English, dating back at least as far as Thomas
Campbell, "Pleasures of Hope" (1799). Ramseur may well have become acquainted with the phrase
from D. H. Hill at Davidson College, as the former general used it when publishing *The Land We
Love* after the war. See, for example, the introductory page of Vol. 4, No. 3 (January 1868).

ter, but no one can *imagine* the severity of the West Point course. I have
often listened to what I supposed were exaggerated Stories of the sufferings of the *poor Plebes*, but I have found out by sad experience that these
Stories are too true. I have been here long enough to have some knowledge of military life (I mean the life of a Common Soldier, for while in
camp we are subjected to the same discipline, and have almost the same
labour to perform as the private Soldier of our Standing Army) and I do
not wonder that so few native Americans are to be found in our Army in
times of peace. They are too much attached to the glorious birthright, won
by their ancestors in the bloody Revolution, to live under the severe and
almost tyrannical laws, which are necessary for the preservation of order
and discipline in the standing army. You say, my Friend, that in accepting the appointment to W. P. I have staked much, and I assure you, no one
feels the responsibilities placed upon himself, more than I do. I know that
my talents must be exerted to the utmost, that all the energy I possess and
more too, will be called into requisition, that close persevering and constant application to my studies will be required, that a prompt and ready
obedience to all laws, no matter how severe or arbitrary, will be strictly
exacted. I know these things, and I am determined to perform every duty
faithfully and to the best of my ability and then if I fail—but no! "There's
no such word as *Fail* in the bright lexicon of Youth."[18] I will look upward
and onward. "Excelsior"[19] shall be my motto and "The spirit of laudable
Ambition."[20] I will try "ever to keep bright as I refuge in many a dark hour,
when purer motives fail."

I succeed very well in the military department. I think this is ac-
counted for by the natural fondness I have for the "ars militaire" [mili-
tary art]. I have received only *six* demerits, yet, while one half of my class
have over twenty, eight poor Fellows have fifty, and one has eighty. They
will certainly die of the "January Fever." If I do as well in the academic,
as in the military department, I will be satisfied, but I fear very much that
I cannot do this, because there are at least twenty-five men in my class,
who have graduated at the first Colleges in our land. Let me mention a
few cases. One graduated with first honor at Harvard. Another graduated
"first" at "Union College." Another graduated first at Princeton. Another

18. Edward George Earle Lytton Bulwer-Lytton (1803–73), *Richelieu*, 3.2.
19. "Ever upward," the motto of New York State.
20. Don Augusto Revilo Elppihw, *Nine Letters Particularly Addressed to the People of the Revolting
Spanish Provinces of the Caraccas, and to Other Spanish Provinces in North and South America: And to
the Whole Spanish Nation and the Civilized World* (Baltimore: Joseph Robinson, 1811), 5:16.

stood *very high* in four departments at the State University in Virginia, and still another graduated first in the scientific department at *Yale*, and many others have been over the whole mathematical course. These men have a decided advantage over that part of the class (to which I belong) who scarcely know the rudiments, but I will not be discouraged. I am *determined to do my duty*. I am aware dear Dave of the importance and honor of the position I now occupy, but more especially, of that which I will certainly occupy, if I remain true to God, to my Country, to my Parents, and to myself. "To thine own self be true &c"[21] [William] Shakespeare wrote, and the way for one's popularity and success in life is opened sure. In forming our characters for our own good, we are benefiting others likewise, and though difficulties and differences may arise, yet if one is true to himself the day will come when all will be righted.

Oh! how I wish I could have been a participator of the pleasures of your party at "*Old Ben's.*" I do wish that I could hear you whisper "something sweet," for my *ear* has been charmed with *no* "sweet words" since I left my dear old native Town. Dear Dave, do not let any thing *sweet pass* without letting me know it. Do not be afraid of "paper and ink giving too much dignity" to such things, for I do assure you with all earnestness that I enter with the deepest interest into all things pertaining to the Ladies. Bless their bright eyes, and ruby lips, I must insist on your telling me in your next, that "*something sweet.*" Oh! Dave, What must I say about the Ladies, my *heart is so full* that I do not know where to begin. This much I will say, I did not know that I loved so *many, so well,* until I had to leave them. I am glad to hear that *David* made an impressive *Debut.* I hope he will continue to improve. *And that walk!* Oh! Such a walk! 'twas Paradise regained. I can not say more. My paper is out and in five minutes I must attend Battalion drill. Say what you please, (for you know how I feel) to the dear Ladies of old Lincolnton.

Give my love to all of my Friends, to your Father, Brother and Sister, and to little Sue Jenkins.[22] My kindest regards. Tell old John to write to me, or if he will not write to be certain to come and see me Christmas. I would be very glad if he will conclude to bring Miss Sue Shipp along as Mrs. R. Tell Bob Hoke to write to me immediately, if not sooner. Kiss all of the Ladies, pull off their rings, squease their hands and anything else you think *prudent,* for me.

21. *Hamlet,* 1.3.

22. Two-year-old daughter of merchant James C. Jenkins, U.S. Census Office, *Eighth Census,* 1860.

I wish I had time to write another sheet. I want to *crow* over the miserable Know Nothings. Huzza a thousand times for gallant Craige and the Democracy of the 7th Congressional District of N.C.[23] Give me an account of the election at my old Home. Send me the vote of the State if it is convenient. I was so sorry to hear that Mr. [William] Williamson is again confined to his bed. Do you think he will recover? I want to say some thing about commencement, but I can not. Tell me all about it. Did you see Lily? What did she have to say for herself and Ed Sumner.[24] Did she ask about me? How did Jno. Rich vote? For Mr. Craige of course. I am anxious to hear the result in Clingmans[25] district. I believe it is impossible to beat him.

I will have to end my letter in the middle. Be certain to call on Mother frequently while I am at W. P. Give my best love to my dear Parents, Brothers & Sisters. Write very soon to your devoted Friend. S. D. Ramseur Excuse haste.

What does Capt Jno. F. Hoke[26] think of Know Nothingism since the election?[27]

West Point, N.Y. Aug 30th 1855

My Dear Father,

I have been very sad since you left me. I know that it is wrong to allow this feeling to take possession of me, but still I can not prevent it. To extend the *parting-hand* to an acquaintance or Friend for a short time, produces sadness in my bosom, but to say *"good-bye"* to my Dear Father, for a long time, perhaps forever, produces sadness deep, lasting, almost overwhelming. One thought, however, always cheers and upholds me. 'Tis this. If I perform *every duty* faithfully, and am zealous in the cause of Truth *now*,

23. Craige garnered 62 percent of the vote. *Congressional Quarterly's Guide to U.S. Elections*, 2:883.

24. Five years later, Edward E. Sumner was a civil engineer residing in nearby China Grove, Rowan County, North Carolina. U.S. Census Office, *Eighth Census, 1860*.

25. Thomas L. Clingman represented western North Carolina as a Whig in the U.S. House of Representatives, 1843–45, 1847–58, followed by tenure in the U.S. Senate, 1858–61, as a Democrat. He received 55 percent of the votes cast in 1855. Clingman later served as a brigadier general in the Confederate army. *National Cyclopedia of American Biography*, 7:200.

26. At various points in his life in Lincolnton, Hoke was a merchant, lawyer, and state legislator. He saw action as a captain in the Mexican War, leading to his appointment as adjutant general of North Carolina in 1861. Early in the Civil War, Hoke commanded the Twenty-third North Carolina Infantry and, later, served as colonel of the Fourth Regiment of North Carolina Reserves. Ramseur may well have first met Hoke as the uncle of his chum, Bob Hoke. Roberta Sue Alexander, "John Franklin Hoke," in Powell, *North Carolina Biography* 3:164–65.

27. PC.

I will receive a reward *hereafter*. If not in this world, in that happy, better world on high.

We marched out of Camp yesterday. All articles were removed to our rooms in the Barracks before 10 o clock. From ten to eleven the camp was thoroughly policed by the whole Corps. Not a *straw* was left upon the ground. From eleven to twelve the Cadets were employed pulling up tent-pegs, and taking off tent ropes, removing cloths, boxes, camp stools &c. At half past twelve, at the third tap of the drum, *all tents* dropped at the same instant and three *cheers* arose from the *Corps*, that sounded all along old "Crows Nest"[28] and that most delightful and highly celebrated "Washington Valley."[29]

Well, I have now a *fine room*, on the first floor. It is furnished thus. A bed, a table, a washstand, and one chair for each occupant. This looks like scanty furniture, but it is enough, more than this would be superfluous, and I do assure you, that after living more than two months in camp, performing the labours of a common Soldier, exposed to rain and cold, and being compelled to sleep on a blanket, I know well now to appreciate the comfort of my present habitation, especially my iron bedstead and my *mattress*. I am rooming as I expected with W. Hampton Gibbes. He is a fine Fellow, a real Southerner, frank, warm-hearted, and generous to a fault. I expect to have a pleasant time with him. 'Tis but few minutes until breakfast so I must close.

I received a letter from my Dear Mother yesterday. All were very well at home except Aunt Rebecca. She was in bed with a bad cold. I received your letter yesterday. I do not think there will be any danger in sending a package to me. I would rather you would wait until Mr. Jenkins[30] comes and send it by him, if he does not come direct to A. O. Ronaldson, care of Capt. Roe, West Point.[31] Do not have my name upon it at all. Ronaldson has received a good many packages for cadets. They are always directed to him. Excuse my great haste. I am on guard and had only a few minutes before Breakfast to write to you. Write to me when convenient. Your devoted Son, S. D. Ramseur[32]

---

28. A depression of 1,200 feet in the mountain closest to West Point.

29. The land route away from the academy toward Central Valley to the west, a lush depression where horses grazed under guard of Continental soldiers during the Revolutionary War.

30. James C. Jenkins, thirty years old in 1855, who had married Barbara Schenck, David's sister, and lived with his wife and four children, including little Sue, at the residence of Dr. Schenck, a widower. Sherrill, *Annals of Lincoln County*, 143; U.S. Census Office, *Eighth Census*, 1860.

31. Not a Federal officer; probably in the state militia.

32. SHC.

West Point, Sept 30th/55

My own dear Mother,

Want of time is my reason for not writing to you last week; but I am
not satisfied with this excuse for causing you the least anxiety or uneasiness. No. I have neglected to perform my first and most important duty.
I have done that which, when I left my dear home, I determined never
to do. I have broken a good resolution: I have failed to send my promised
weekly letter to my Mother. Yes, I have broken this good resolution, as
I have too many others. Oh! how unable am I to do any good thing or to
walk straight forward in the path of duty, unless the Lord sustains and di-
rects me. Dear Mother, I would have written, but I was so *unfortunate* as
to be reported for "light not extinguished at 'taps.'" (I was only a moment
too late in extinguishing my light, but according to West Point discipline,
a *half a moment* too late is as bad as *five* minutes, and we receive the same
punishment for being a "*Late*" whether we are one or five minutes behind
the time.) And this report gives not only three demerits, but also three
"*Wednesday extra's.*" For a description of a *Saturday extra*, I refer you to
Father, for I think he saw it practically illustrated. I will only say, that although it is by no means pleasant, yet I will submit to it, as to many other
things at W. P., with good humour, and while I march back and forth before the Barracks "*armed and equipped*," I will think of my home and imagine the many delightful ways that my dear Friends [illegible]

Lieut. J. B. Wheeler[33] was recently married to a Washington belle &
heiress.[illegible] are spending *these same Saturday afternoons.* Do you
ever imagine, while enjoying *delightful dinners*, that I am living on irish
potatoes and bread, and when you are enjoying rides and walks in the
country, do you ever think that I am confined to my room *twelve* hours.
Besides this, I have to drill from one to two hours each day! Do you ever
imagine, while you are enjoying the *luxury* of a *morning nap*, that I have to
rise at *five o clock*, go to reveille roll-call, make up my bed, sweep out my
room, and then pour over a difficult Algebra lesson? And then, if I happen
to have a little dust on my shelves, or a glove not smoothly folded, or my
chair not pushed under my table when I am at recitation, or wash-bowl
not clean and inverted or a thousand other little things whatch, a careless
boy, like myself, will neglect, *I am reported*, and receive the *dreaded* and
dangerous (for one hundred before January suspends or dismisses, as the

33. Junius B. Wheeler, a North Carolinian in the Class of 1855, spent a career in the U.S. Corps
of Engineers, rising to the rank of brevet colonel during the Civil War after resisting pressure to
join the Confederate army. Cullum, *Biographical Register*, 2:395–96.

Officers wish) demerits. I hope you will not feel uneasy, when I tell you that I have received at least twenty-four for the month. I received them all the first two weeks, and twas the result of *ignorance* more than carelessness. But I know better now, and I think I can do better. I am going to try to send home a report for next month, without one single demerit. But it is almost impossible to do this.

I received another one of your sweet letters on Wednesday last. Oh! you cannot imagine how it cheered me. Would that I could make known to you how much your letters encourage me, and console me. *Sometimes* when I have to perform *severe duty*, I feel *almost* disposed to give up the idea of *graduating* at West Point. Incessant toil continually subjected to all kinds of rough usage! *five years*! But, my dear Mother, it is only when *childishness*, and a desire to gratify my selfish wishes, predominates in my bosom that I feel thus. All that is noble and manly, the devoted love that I have for my Parents, the respect that I feel for my friends, the duty that I owe to my old native State, and my own interest and happiness, excite me to continued exertion, to overcome every opposing difficulty and to perform my whole duty. Thus, I will *graduate*, and *be a man*, a good and useful man. Then I hope to be qualified for my occupation or profession.

I think I could submit to all of the hardships of Cadet life, if I had *one pious* Friend; but I know that I have a Friend. One who is willing and able to encourage me and to sustain me in every trial and danger. But, I feel at times isolated, having none to whom I may make known my feelings, from whom I may receive words of comfort and encouragement, and with whom I may praise and worship God in the beauty of holiness. Oh! 'tis hard to cut off from the society of fellow Christians; to be surrounded by none but the devotees of pleasure and children of this world. O. that I could spend this holy Sabbath evening, around the fireside of my own dear home, where my Mother and Father, Brothers and Sisters all rejoice to praise our heavenly Father. Now, I know how to appreciate those prayers which are offered at the family altar. Now I know, what it is to be deprived of the society of pious Parents and companions. But, in all my loneliness and sadness, my dear Savior sustains and comforts me. He gives me strength to fight the good fight of Faith! He enables me, by the assistance of his grace, to act kindly to my companions and at the same time to perform my duty to my heavenly Father. Yes *Mother*, He makes me happy. Although sometimes placed in unpleasant situations, I am truly happy and look forward to the time when I shall be qualified and able to do good unto all men.

Dear Mother, I feel very anxious about my dear Brother David, who is just leaving Home where all is pure and holy, to be subjected to the trials and temptations of College life.[34] I do hope and pray that he may walk in that straight and narrow path, which leads to life everlasting.

I have not the certificate of schollarship with me. I think I remember giving it to you just before my trunk was packed.

Mother, I have been studying very hard for the last two weeks. We have very hard and long lessons, and they are required to be gotten perfectly. To give you some idea of the length of our lessons, I will tell you that I already have over and reviewed Algebra to the 6th chapter more than I have ever been over before. Just to think, in one month to be over one half of the Algebra. Davies Bourdon, at that.[35] We have been to Syntax and reviewed in "Bullions Analitical & Practical Grammar."[36] Twenty five pages is a lesson, both coarse and fine print. Here, my memory fails and I get along rather poorly. I do not think I can possibly stand higher than *Twenty-fifth*. This seems very low, but you must remember that my class is composed of the Chosen young men of the U.S.

Dear Mother, send me in your next some of my dear Sister's letters. Oh! I will love to peruse those sweet memorials of my darling Sister's affection for me. Write to me when you can conveniently. Tell the darling children to write to me. I have received letters from Crockett, Ed White, Ed Sumner, McFadden, Frontis Johnson,[37] Back Caldwell & several others, none of whom I have had time to answer. Tell Mr. Davis *I will* write to him just as *soon* as *I can find* time. Tell D. Schenck the same. Much love and many kisses to Father and my darling little Brothers & Sisters. Your devoted Son, Dodson

Mother are you willing to part with Harvey's daguerreotype, and to send it to me by the mail? And also Your's & Fathers and all of the children: It will be a great source of pleasure to me, to be permitted to look frequently at all of your daguerreotypes, and I think it will nerve me to still greater exertions to do my duty.

34. David Poindexter Ramseur entered Davidson College in September 1855, remaining enrolled there until 1857. Davidson College, *Semi-Centennial Catalogue*, 105.

35. *Elements of Algebra: Including Strums' Theorem*, by Charles Davies Bourdoun (Louis Pierre Marie), published in 1850.

36. Peter Bullion authored a text so popular that it was printed in five editions, 1849–77. Ramseur probably studied the 1853 version.

37. Frontis H. Johnston, a Presbyterian clergyman, later served for three months as a chaplain in the Forty-eighth North Carolina Regiment. Johnston was an 1855 graduate of Davidson College, where he and Ramseur may have become friends. Davidson College, *Semi-Centennial Catalogue*, 94; A. D. Betts, "The Chaplain Service," in Clark, *Histories*, 4:616.

Give my love to Aunt Betty and Aunt Fany. Tell George and Charlie[38] that they promised to write to me, and I would be delighted to hear from them. Remember me kindly to Benson & Capt Huss. How is Mr. Wm.son? My love to him. Also to Cousin Mary Ann, Mag and to Abram. Tell all of the Servants "howdye" for me &c. Ask Father how he had that bundle directed which he had sent to me from Phila. I have heard nothing of it except what Abram wrote to me. Love to all of my old Friends & Companions, to Schenck especially. Good bye.[39]

West Point Oct 27th 1855

My own dear Friend

Accept ten thousand, thousand thanks, yes more thousands will not express all I feel, for the two kind letters you have sent me in return for one. I can not give you the faintest idea of the great degree of pleasure your latest letter afforded me. When surrounded by those whom we love, and who love us, even then, 'tis pleasant to receive letters from old friends & acquaintances, but when distance, not that "distance which lends enchantment to the view," separates us from our "*old Nativity;*" when we are in the midst of strangers each striving alone for self; and when, subjected to the unrelenting discipline of military laws, then indeed 'tis cheering to receive letters from home, from *you*, Dear Dave, my dearest, warmest Friend, my bosom companion, from you whom I love, as devotedly as a Brother; yes, your letters all send a thrill of joyous emotion to my heart, for in them I so plainly see the reflex of that Original, with whom, some of the happiest (and saddest too) moments of my life have been. Your precious letters encourage me to *go on* with the work I have commenced; to bear patiently the hardships of the Present for Future good; to persevere against discouragement; "*to hope even against* hope";[40] indeed, to be a "*Hero in the Strife.*"[41]

Well, Dave, I have been pitching *Algebra*, pretty deeply for the past two months; I have also mastered Bullion's English Grammar, so that I can almost say it from beginning to end *by rote*; I have nearly finished Morse's Geography.[42] In this I can not do so well, for this semester we are required to draw all the maps on the black-board from memory. I have no particular

---

38. Ramseur's first cousins, George and Charles Motz, Aunt Fanny's sons. Otherwise, "Charlie" refers to Dodson's brother, Charles R. Ramseur.

39. SHC.

40. A derivation of St. Paul's writing about Abraham, "who against hope believed in hope," Romans 4:18.

41. Longfellow, "A Psalm of Life."

42. Jedidiah Morse, *The American Universal Geography; or, a view of the present state of all the Kingdoms, states and colonies in the known world*, published in multiple editions.

fancy for drawing, and cannot draw a respectable looking map, therefore I am not marked *high* on any Geography recitations. You see from this manner of teaching, that every thing must be thoroughly studied, and well understood. This is the case with every thing, whether we are engaged with schoolboy studies, or with the most difficult and obtuse sciences, all must be perfectly prepared, and recited. The *fashionable smattering*, which is all that is required at some of our Colleges, will not enable a man to graduate at West Point.

Sometimes, I think that if you could witness the wonders achieved by your Friend Dod, in one day, you would say that I really deserve *some credit*. And if *nothing happens*, and I *"go on" five years* hence, I will be a *Brevet Second Lieut*. in the U.S.A., stationed, *perhaps*, in a little *log Fort*, garrisoned by *dirty* Irishmen and stinking Germans; out on the frontiers, where I will have the most exquisite pleasure of shooting the poor Indians, or perhaps, of being knocked [illegible] by them and perish, "unmarked, untrophied &c." Rich compensations!!! For five years of hard labour; think you not.

I have frequently written about the severity and hardships of Cadet life, but I would not have you think that we are entirely without pleasures. Yes, there are many happy and glorious feelings that none but the Cadet can have. We have the most beautiful home in the World, there are pleasurable excitements and occasional amusements, such as a Concert every Saturday night in the Winter, by one of the best string bands in the U.S.; also a dance occasionally. No Ladies, however, are present to enliven the scene and to gladden the hearts of the "*Brass buttoned Angels*," as they call the Cadets, with their sweet smiles and kind words. We live in hope. We hope now that the time will soon pass by, and next encampment, we *hope* to meet our Father, Mother, and Friends. Then we will be no longer *Plebes*, but dignified Cadets. Then some of *us* have good reasons for believing that we will be made Corporals in the "Battalion of Cadets." Some of my friends say that I will be *first Corporal*. Then, after the encampment, we *hope* to visit our dear homes, my old native Town, on Furlough. After that, we hope to be First Class Officers, & then, to graduate &c.

I have made a good many friends, two very intimate and very dear to me. My roommate, Gibbes from S.C. He is a noble fellow, very handsome, smart, a great Lady's man, and he has a true southern heart. My other friend is a New Yorker, McFarland.[43] Do not be surprised and censure

43. Walter McFarland from Brooklyn, New York, graduated at the head of the class of 1860 and went on to spend the Civil War in the U.S. Corps of Engineers constructing Gulf Coast defenses at Fort Pickens, Florida, in Mobile, Alabama, and along the Mississippi, among other locations. Cullum, *Biographical Register*, 2:294.

me for trusting a Yankee, for there are some few noble spirits among the
Northerners. Among the Cadets, none are called Yankees except those
from Mass. N.H. Vt. & several of the New England *states*. With these the
southerners do not *associate* and indeed, they are generally kept at a respectable distance by all. I tell you Dear Dave, and I am proud to say it,
the Southerners are far superior to the Yankees in every respect except the
habit of close application to studies. They make much better officers than
the Yankees. To prove this, more than two thirds of the Cadet Officers are
always Southerners. The history of the academy proves that although a
great many more Southerners fail to complete the course, yet a majority
of those "found deficient in Studies" are Yankees. Southerners are generally dismissed on demerits, always having been accustomed to command
instead of to obey. As free and independent as the Sons of the South ever
will be, they cannot bear with patience and obey with promptness the
commands of the Officers of the higher classes. For this, they are reported,
get over one hundred demerits before January, and are, consequently,
dismissed.

Well, here I am on my last page. I declare I did not intend to write so
much about *the all important I*, but 'tis human nature to think about Self,
write about self, in short to be *selfish*. But I must stop this, and turn to
more pleasant themes. Your letter contained much to make me wish to
be with you. I would like very much to listen to *that tale* which you could
unfold, and which you think is too important to trust to paper & ink. You
know, dear Dave, that I am always anxious to know every thing that intimately concerns your own dear self, but with regard to such matters you
know what is best and most prudent to write. Your difficulty with Miss
Ellen Sumner will, from the tenor of your letter, perhaps prove quite serious. I know you are on the right side without knowing everything about
the matter. Ergo, I wish I could be with you and place myself entirely at
your service. I feel as if I would be thankful for an opportunity to be of
service to you. Write me all about the difficulty. Tell me this too. Whose
hand was that you squeezed, on the beautiful moonlight night. Oh! Dave
I wish [I] could visit Alexrs. field & swamp with you this evening. I feel
like I could "whortleberry over the *persimmons*" of a few old partridges. I
am nearly at the end of my last page. I have not said half that I intended.

As I will not have time to write to my old dear Mother for a few days,
I will commission you to tell her that I am, as usual, very well and send
more love than I can express to Father, Mother, Brothers, & Sisters. I will
write home in a few days. Yes indeed, my dear Friend, I do know how to
appreciate my dear Mother. I feel thankful to Heaven that I am blessed

with such a Mother, and my friend it is my earnest wish that you will visit my Mother, my home, *very, very frequently*.[44] Make my home a resting place from your labours. I know that you are and ever will be a most welcome visitor. Then, visit often my Mother, and when I return we will live as we have for the past few years as Brothers.

Write to me very soon. Give me another long precious letter. Tell me every thing that concerns yourself, for I assure you that it also concerns me. Say some thing sweet to all the Ladies for me. Especially to Miss Laura and Miss Sue &c. And now Dear Dave Goodbye. May heavenly riches & blessings be thine. Your Friend, S. D. R.

I must congratulate old Lincolnton! The President and Secretary of the Rail Road, both being chosen from the dear old Town.[45] What has become of old John. I have been expecting a letter from him from Ph'la. Has Mr. W. Wm.son recovered from his attack of sickness. Remember me [illegible] kindly to him. Also to Mr. R. Wm.son, to old Cpt. Slade[46] &c. Remember me to your Father, Brother & Sister. Tell Mr. Jenkins I have rec'd. two "*Saturday Extras*" since he was here as punishment for this wonderful [illegible] Sat. extinguished [illegible] at "Taps." Taps is at ten oclock. I was pulling off my coat & was just about ½ minute too late, but I was late, & must be punished. This is West Point on a small scale. I will expect a letter from you soon. Love to all at the [illegible]. I am and ever will be your *true* [illegible].

S. D. R.[47]

The three preceding letters reveal the depth of Ramseur's feelings for his mother and father, in addition to recounting his first impressions of cadet life. The following excerpt from a letter to David Schenck on January 19, 1856, reports the results of the dreaded January examination. The attrition rate was as dire as feared. The class would lose almost another third of its members before graduation.

Well, I will devote the short time which remains to who do you suppose? *My own dear self of course*. I have passed that fiery ordeal, the

44. Schenck's own mother died when he was a young child.
45. Haywood W. Guion was elected president and Benjamin S. Guion secretary of the Wilmington, Charlotte and Rutherford Railroad. Sherrill, *Annals of Lincoln County*, 158, 160.
46. Age fifty-four at the time of the 1850 Census, William Slade was proprietor of the Slade Hotel on East Main Street in Lincolnton. U.S. Census Office, *Seventh Census, 1850*.
47. Portions illegible due to water rot along the edge of the paper. PC.

January examination. I will give you the results: *thirty-four* young as-
pirants for military glory, were "found deficient" either in the military
or academic course. Poor Fellows! I pity them from the bottom of my
heart, A few months ago they entered the academy with high hopes
and bright anticipations for a life of future usefulness & honor, but alas!
Those fond hopes have been crushed, those bright anticipations are
darkened with a cloud black as midnight. Some have returned to their
home humbled, disappointed, miserable young men; others, too proud
and sensitive to return to their homes, are wandering over the country,
ready for any desperate enterprise. Among three "found deficient" I had
several friends, Bob Taylor,[48] nephew of the "Old Gen'l. Zac"[49] a noble
fellow, from Florida, and George Griffing,[50] son of one of the "Merchant
Princes" of New York City. He is a very talented youth, but unfortunately
his mind could not grasp the abstruse theories of Mathematics. I early
became attached to him, on account of his fine, open, manly counte-
nance, and I ever found him a true friend, and the very soul of honor. He
feels very badly, almost desperate. I think he will go to Russia and obtain
a commission in the Army of the Czar. Many others I could mention but
time forbids. This first examination has reduced our class to less than
two thirds of the original number. Oh! 'tis an awful responsibility which
rests upon us as Cadets. Oh that I may be able to perform the tasks, but
I look forward with a trembling heart, for I may fail; but no, I have now
a high stand, and *I'll keep it*: "Fail! Fail! In the bright lexicon of youth,
which fate reserved for a most glorious manhood, there is no such word
as fail!"[51]

48. Richard K. Taylor from Monticello, Florida, who apparently used the nickname "Bob," was
recommended for admission to the academy by his brother, who explained, "It is true we have
wealthy and honorable connections, but they have been of no service to us, and we have had to
scuffle as best we could (having lost our Father) since our infancy." Taylor enlisted in the Sixth
Florida Infantry in 1862 and, first, was assigned as an apothecary. In August 1863, on the request
of its lieutenant colonel, Taylor was transferred to the First Florida Cavalry Regiment, where he
was promoted to first lieutenant and was still serving in that rank one year later. James C. Taylor to
Secretary of War Jefferson Davis, June 20, 1855, U.S. Military Academy Application Papers, RG 94,
NARA; Taylor, Sixth Fla. Infantry and First Fla. Cavalry, CMSR, RG 109, NARA; Lt. Col. G. Troup
Maxwell to Gen. Samuel Cooper, July 30, 1863, Isham Blake, Fifth Fla. Infantry, CMSR, RG 109,
NARA; Department and Army of Tennessee, Special Order 72/1, March 14, 1864, RG 109, NARA.
    49. Major general and former president Zachary Taylor.
    50. There is no record of Griffing having served in uniform during the Civil War.
    51. PC.

U.S. Mil. Academy
February 2nd/56

My own dear Father,

Today I received my appointment as Cadet in the U.S.M.A. I took the "fiery test," January examination, and am now no longer a mere "conditional thing," but, henceforth a dignified, Brass-buttoned Cadet. You may imagine that I am in high spirits now since I have received my "warrant" and all is bright before me. Now, I am fairly started in my arduous path, and I feel confident, if I do my duty, I will graduate well. But there are many, almost insurmountable, difficulties before me, and sometimes I can't help for *fear*.

I hope, however, by continued and persevering application, to succeed. I was very sorry that I could not send you a better report. I wish I could have been First only for the sake of my Father and Mother. I did not do as well as I expected in English Studies, but I have a poor memory, and I did not succeed very well drawing maps. But I promise to send you a better report of my standing in Eng' Stu' in June. See how well I will keep my promise. But I think I did tolerable well; there are only three Southerners above me. McCreery[52] of Va. third; Sloan[53] of S.C. fifth, and Kerr[54] of N.C. fifteenth. The Yankees beat us, only because they have been trained from the cradle to apply their minds to their books. When they come to W. P. they *know how to think. We* have to learn after we arrive here. Why, I am vain enough to believe, if I could study as closely and constantly as most of the Yankees do, I could stand in "the Fives," but I am afraid I have comparatively very little application and less concentration; this is acquired by education, and if I can, I will have it.

52. William W. McCreery Jr. graduated eleventh in the class of 1860 and resigned his commission in the U.S. Army to become a lieutenant of artillery in the Confederate army. He served under Brig. Gen. John B. Floyd, Gen. R. E. Lee, Maj. Gen. John C. Pemberton, and Brig. Gen. James J. Pettigrew. Krick, *Staff Officers in Gray*, 207.

53. Benjamin Sloan graduated seventh in the class of 1860. He served in the U.S. Dragoons before resigning and accepting a lieutenancy of artillery in the Confederate army. His first major assignment was as aide-de-camp to Maj. Gen. Benjamin Huger, followed by command of a series of ordnance shops before becoming Maj. Gen. William H. C. Whiting's chief of artillery, 1863–65. After the war, among other positions, Sloan was president of South Carolina College, 1902–8. Krick, *Staff Officers in Gray*, 267.

54. John Marshall Kerr, the son of a member of Congress from North Carolina, John Kerr, graduated nineteenth in the class of 1860 and served in the U.S. Mounted Rifles. He was dropped from the rolls in July 1861 for failing to report for duty. In the same month, he was appointed second lieutenant in the Confederate Corps of Cavalry and died in North Carolina on March 10, 1862. J. M. Kerr, Confederate Generals, Staff Officers, and Non-regimental Enlisted Men, CMSR, RG 109, NARA; Cullum, *Biographical Register*, 2:508; Heitman, *Historical Register*, 1:594.

I wrote to Dave Schenck giving him a few of the particulars of the examination. Did he tell you of it? The examination was, as usual, very rigid and the Board rejected *all* who were deficient. Thirty-four poor fellows were "found deficient." Among them I had several friends, one, Taylor, from Fla. (Nephew of Old Gen'l. Zack) another Griffing from New York, and others. Vanderbuilt[55] studied very hard and passed. He stands forty-fifth. He is a noble fellow and one of my Friends. Gilmer came out fortieth. My roommate did very well in English Studies. He draws beautiful maps. He stood sixteenth. He did tolerable well in Mathematics—fifty-third, "Gen'l. St'dg." thirty seventh &c &c.

What cold weather we are having now. We suffer a good deal, not seriously though. I never heard of such cold weather in N.C. before. I see, in the last Standard that the Yadkin is frozen entirely across, and Luly wrote me that Mr. Randleman had frozen to death, a drunkards death![56] Oh! how awful! I do pity the poor people who have no blankets, no fires, no homes. May they be protected and provided for by the benevolent and wealthy. What a happy and noble employment, to clothe the naked, feed the hungry, sympathise with the unfortunate and comfort the distressed!!! How beautiful is our religion, considered merely as a theory! The brotherly love and self-sacrificing affection which it teaches us to entertain even for our enemies is a principle so beautiful and touching that it must melt every heart not made of stone. But how infinitely more beautiful is the pious life of a devoted Christian whose every action speaks loudly saying there is love to God and his fellow man burning brightly in his heart. Oh that I may I lead the life of the righteous, and "may my last end be like his."

Father do you intend to come North this Spring? Although I want to see you, Oh! so much! yet I will not be so selfish as to desire you to come North simply to see me. So Father if you do not wish to come North, do not let me influence you, but I will expect you and Mother, next encampment. Tell me what you think you will do?

What can the negroes work at on the farm this cold weather. How is the Factory doing now? What do you propose to do with your Danville property. I saw a piece in a Richmond paper about the growing impor-

---

55. George Washington Vanderbilt from New York graduated thirty-ninth in the class of 1860 and was commissioned in the infantry. When war broke out, he was posted to recruiting duty, September 1861 to April 1862. On leave of absence as a captain, he died in Nice, France, on January 1, 1864. Cullum, *Biographical Register*, 2:518; *Register of Graduates and Former Cadets*, 4–42.

56. The ground was described as covered with sleet and snow for over a week, a rarity in that part of North Carolina in those days. *North Carolina Standard*, Jan. 16, 1856.

tance of Danville. I think if you could hold that property a few years, it would bring a large price. It will pay for the trouble and anxiety that it will cost to keep it. Such is my opinion.

How is the Rail Road progressing? Do you think it will be in operation in June/57? What is your Company going to do. Where and what kind of a contract will you take. Who is your Surveyor? Give my love to all at my dear home. Tell Luly I'll write to her soon as I can. Have you heard from David recently. I have not heard from him since he returned to College. I don't know what to think of it. Love and kisses to Mother, Sallie, Luly, Fanny, Charlie, Ada and Harvey. With Love, your devoted Son S. DOD Ramseur[57]

West Point N.Y.
May 2nd 1856

My Dear Dave,

Let me congratulate you on your entrance upon the political stage. My *"Standard"* informs me that my dear Friend was a *prominent* Member of a Democratic meeting recently held in old Lincolnton, that *through him* the Committee reported *Resolutions* (which it did my heart good, to read, *as a Democrat* & also because I believed *Dave penned them*) and that *he* was appointed a Delegate to the District Convention.[58] Hurrah for my own dear Dave!!! You have embarked in the right cause, the noble old cause. You have talents, energy and ambition sufficient to make you an honor to the *"Old North State,"* one whom she will ever admire, trust and love. And my most sincere wish is that success may crown your every effort. May you win golden opinions and *richer rewards* from the democrats of old Lincoln for your devotion to the *good cause*. Be assured that your friend Dod is with you heart & soul, and if he may venture a word of advice, it is this, *Keep Cool*. Try and avoid *personalities*, and angry controversies, but, it is not necessary to add, "go a head" with a rush for *Bragg*.[59] "A little more grape"[60] will kill Gilmer *deader* than the "Great Pedee Wagoner." Do you not think so? Who do you think will be elected to the Senate[61] and who

57. SHC.

58. *North Carolina Standard*, Apr. 26, 1856.

59. Thomas Bragg was elected to two terms as governor of North Carolina, 1854–58, and later served as Confederate attorney general, November 1861 to March 1862.

60. A reference to the governor's brother, Confederate general Braxton Bragg, who achieved fame from Gen. Zachary Taylor's order during the battle of Buena Vista, February 23, 1847, "A little more grape, Captain Bragg."

61. James H. White, a Democrat from Gaston County who had helped in severing it from Lincoln County in 1846, was elected to the state senate.

[are] the candidates? I hope that fallen democrat and traitorous Know Nothing, who, on an occasion which I have not forgotten, treated *you* unkindly, impolitely & ungentlemanly, will not receive the nomination. What chance does Mr. Lander[62] stand for [illegible]? Oh! how I wish I could be with you and participate in the excitement of the approaching campaigns, for from the few indications that I have noticed, I think it will be a *hard fight*. May you be victorious, & may your honors be substantial & real.

May, bright merry May, gladdens our hearts with a smiling Sun and all the beauties of opening Spring. By the way, did the Fair Ones of our old Town crown one of their number "Queen of May," & did Dave enjoy himself exceedingly? Of course. You can not imagine how often & how forcibly the *events* of last May rush upon my memory, and awaken a little of the *old feeling*. Yes those moments when kind friends made my life so sweet, will be forgotten never! no, never! But the *drum* is summoning me to an unpleasant duty. My soul is willing to commune with you all evening. I wish it could be so. Please excuse the most imaginable haste, also *lead pencil*. I could not find a *pen*.

Accept my love and affectionate remembrance. Your's as ever, Dod

P.S. *Tell Father I am well & send love*. Give my love to John, & all your & my friends.[63]

[May 16, 1856]

My Dear Friend, you are going to "pitch into" the Political World. I am rejoiced that you are fighting in the good old Democratic ranks. You are assured that you are on the *right side* so you can "go it [illegible]." Do you think Thompson[64] will be elected. I hope so, altho' I must confess, I fear Cansler[65] *canoodling*; and, I presume, the immortal hero of the "National Bridge," will cast his *diminished* influence for *Dolph*. What do the good people of Lincoln think of Jno. F. Hoke, since his connection with the dark

---

62. William Lander had established a lucrative law practice in Lincolnton, which he continued while serving as district solicitor. Schenck was later his law partner for a time. An ardent secessionist, Lander served a term in the Confederate House of Representatives. Buck Yearns, "William Lander," in Powell, *North Carolina Biography*, 4:10–11.

63. PC.

64. Lew Thompson was a forty-nine-year-old lawyer in 1856, practicing in Lincolnton. Being born in Albany, New York, may well have contributed to his subsequent defeat. U.S. Census Office, *Eighth Census, 1860*.

65. John P. Cansler was a farmer living in Lincolnton, twenty-six years old in 1860, and, presumably, a friend of Ramseur and Schenck. U.S. Census Office, *Eighth Census, 1860*.

Lantern party?[66] Do you think his star has set, to shine no more with the *dazzling brilliance* of former days; Dave I don't know *why*, but ever since Jno. Hoke treated you so *rudely*, I have disliked him.

And you think Bragg will be elected by *12 000 majority*. Are you not too sanguine? Oh how sincerely I wish I could be with you, to enjoy the excitement, and participate in the struggle. But a cruel fate decrees otherwise and with a true military spirit I submit without a murmur.

How is the Rail Road progressing? Is old Lincolnton beginning to aspire to the dignity of a City? I understand the streets have been named, this sounds *kinder* [kind of] City like. You called on the Teacher, how were you pleased. I hope she does not possess the characteristics of her Brother, with whom I spent one year at D. College. Do you intend to go to the approaching Commencement? If so, give Lillie a call, et cetera. Hurrah for Old John!!!!! Tell him I wish him all the success in the world and if he is successful, tell him he must by all manner of means, postpone the consummation of his bliss until the Summer of /57. Tell him "*I speak*," to be a *waiter*. What do you think of his prospects?

Well my dear Dave I have written at such a rate that I am actually afraid you will be sorely puzzled to decipher this affair. But you must excuse all mistakes, *disconnection*, and haste. I had scarcely commenced writing when a crowd of my friends, *glorious fellows*, came in; I told them I had commenced a letter to you once before, & this time I did not intend to be interrupted. They told me to mind my business and they would take care of themselves. So! I have written this in the midst of talking, laughing and *dancing* &c. We are looking anxiously for the Plebes. Poor Fellows! Your Friend has been recommended by the Capn. of his Comp'y. for *1st* Corporal. And by the Adjutant of the Corps, for *2nd* Corporal of the Battalion. *2nd out of a class of 60!* I am indeed greatly surprised and gratified; for I now have reason to think that I possess some traits necessary to a good Soldier. Dave I hoped to finish this in time for the mail, but it is too late, & will not be mailed until Monday. Give my love to all of my old Friends, *the Ladies*, God bless 'em, more especially. Give my love to my dear Parents. I will write soon. May God bless you, Dear Dave. Goodbye.

The Same Dod

It strikes me that, if you can do so conveniently, you will greatly enjoy a visit to Chapel Hill. And if you can start so as to be there on the 6th Com-

---

66. A dark lantern ornamented a horn on the altar used for the secret rites of Know-Nothing societies. "The Cloven Foot," *Democratic Review*, 151–52.

mencement, your visit will be much pleasanter. I hope you will attend that Commencement and have a *good time*. What has become of E. E. Sumner? He wrote to me *a mighty friendly* [letter], with a *heap* of *advice* &c last Summer & I have not had, nor do I expect to have, time to answer it. Ask Bob Hoke if he has entirely forgotten me.

Write to me as soon as you feel like gladdening my sometimes *sad* heart. Oh! your letters are *so dear*!

Your's forever

S. D. Ramseur
U.S.C.C.[67]

West Point N.Y.
Sept. 13th 1856

My Dear Dave,

It has indeed been *too* long since I last wrote to you. This procrastination, be assured, is not the result of neglect or forgetfulness, but it is entirely unnecessary for me to say this, for you know me *too well* to have ever entertained such a thought even for a moment. One reason why I have delayed *so long* is this: Father told me that you intended to write one of your long precious letters as soon as you learned the result and particulars of the election, and I have waited for that anxiously looked for letter, although I confess I did not deserve to have you devote so much of your valuable time to myself and ought not to have expected it. Still, it was natural and I could not help it. Another reason why you have not been "troubled with a line" is that I have been very busily engaged, from the time my dear Parents arrived until the present time, either in the performance of duties or the pursuit of pleasures. But in the midst of them all, you were never forgotten. Often, when we were enjoying the merry "hops," when Beauty's eyes were winning us & Beauty's sweet words were charming us, when after our work was finished, friends, tried and true, would meet in social converse and beguile the tedious day, when sad and lonely (which was not often, I am happy to say, during the Encampment). Yes, at all times I wished that Dear Dave could be with me, to participate in our pleasures & sympathise with & encourage me to surmount difficulties yet to be encountered, the mere contemplation of which I shrink from with trepidation. If you had been with me, my cup of enjoyment would have overflowed!!!

67. United States Corps Cadets (U.S.C.C.). PC.

Well, mon ami [my friend], the Election is over: 13,000 majority!!![68]
Three cheers for Gov Bragg, and *nine* for the Gallant old State, which
knows so well how to appreciate and reward true merit: "First in the
hearts" of the people of North Carolina, for such a reward I would gladly
live, labor and die.

I was very sorry, if for no other consideration, for the honor and credit
of old Lincoln [County], that Mr. Thompson was defeated. I wanted our
glorious old county to be represented by a man who had *some* brains, but
in this I have been disappointed. What part did you take in the election?
I hope you added to the large number of your friends. In your next tell
me all about it, especially the part you acted. Dave, what do you think of
the present condition of our Country and of the approaching Presidential
election? Do you think the dissolution of the Union [is] a necessary consequence of the election of [John C.] Fremont? (for the contest will evidently be between Fremont & [James] Buchanan) What think you of the
"war in Kansas"?[69]

For myself, I believe an awful crisis is approaching, which will decide whether we shall still advance with rapid strides towards a *perfect
state* of civilization, as one great and united people; or, whether we shall
be troubled with divisions, distressed with enemies without and traitors
within, and destroyed by civil wars. Yes, a crisis has already arrived which
demands every Southerner to stand forth and battle for his rights, sacred
rights, bequeathed by Revolutionary Ancestors, dearer to him than life
itself. O God! strengthen the hearts and nerve the arms of every Son of
the South and enable them to march forth and maintain their rights with
the determination and dignity of Freemen! Does not your blood boil with
indignation as you read of abolition & outrages, cowardice & cruelty now
daily enacted in Kansas Territory? Would to God! I had the power, I would
punish them, one and all, as base black-hearted traitors to the Constitution and *our* Country. How I would like to command a regiment of Cavalry
and be ordered to disperse the villains & restore quiet! How I would delight to cut them down, like grass before the mower's scythe. But really I
am devoting more time and space to the "Black Republican hell-hounds"

68. Thomas Bragg, the Democrat, was reelected with 57,698 votes; John A. Gilmer, the American (Know-Nothing) candidate, received 44,970 votes. North Carolina Department of the Secretary of State, *North Carolina Government, 1585–1979*, 1401.

69. The Kansas-Nebraska Act in 1854 provided that the slavery question would be left to popular sovereignty. The territory of Kansas was thereby opened to organized migrations of pro- and
anti-slavery groups. For five years thereafter (and resuming during the Civil War), "Bleeding Kansas" suffered as a result of civilian warfare, most famously in the plundering of Lawrence and John
Brown's massacre on Pottawatamie Creek.

than I intended. I hope you will excuse me for I cant help feeling excited on the subject.

Oh! you can not imagine what real, genuine, quiet pleasure was mine when my Dear Parents & Brother were with me. I never have appreciated pleasure as I did that. Oh! did my very soul rejoice exceedingly. Have you seen Mother since she returned? I sent many messages to you & also my daguerreotype, which is not very good, but still looks something like Dod.[70]

You can not imagine how delighted I was to receive your ambrotype, dear old Dave! How natural! How like that original with whom so many happy hours have been spent. Oh! Dave! I love you too much, for to be separated from you makes me often unhappy. Do not smile at this as a *girlish feeling*, or a namby pamby profession. Oh No! it is the true and genuine devotion of an exalted friendship. After Father left, you may imagine I was sad, *lonely* & *dangerously* home-sick. But the Ladies, God bless 'em, would not long let me remain so. A few days before we "struck our tents" I became acquainted with one of the most charming Ladies I ever met. Her name Miss Hellen Stoddard,[71] her Home, Savannah, her disposition, sweet and affectionate, her mind, highly cultivated, and her *heart so warm & kind*. I assure you I was decidedly smitten and I would not be much surprised *if we meet again* &c.

I have enjoyed several flirtations amazingly well, kissed three beautiful Ladies, one of them the Daughter of the Count de Montholon,[72] French Consul at New York, who is mighty pretty, mighty *fast*, and mighty *affectionate*. But I'll tell you all about these things when I am on *Furlough, only nine months hence*! In the mean time I have to study like blazes (as Ed White would say). We have to perfect our selves in "Analytical Geometry," "Descriptive Geometry," "Shades Shadows & Perspective," "Calculus," & "Surveying" in these nine months, a course to which two years & a half is devoted in nearly every College in the land & then it is not half known. Besides we have French & any quantity of History, Composition & Declaration, and the Small Sword Exercise. Don't you think we will be kept busy. Won't you take pity on me & write to me long letters as often as you can & not expect any except my poor little scrawls (which are written just like I feel, without painstaking &c) in return. Really I have filled this letter without saying half I intended. . . .[73]

70. Quite possibly the daguerreotype taken with Ramseur's classmate Frank Huger. They appear in an informal pose in cadet uniform.

71. Born in England, the nineteen-year-old daughter of a planter from Massachusetts. U.S. Census Office, *Eighth Census, 1860*.

72. Charles Tristan, a French general who accompanied Napoleon I to St. Helena.

73. PC.

Dod Ramseur and Frank Huger at West Point
(courtesy of the North Carolina State Archives, Raleigh)

West Point N.Y.
Saturday, Nov 8th 1856

My Dear Dave,

How are you this wintry night? I am terribly *lonesome* (my noble room-mate, Gibbes, being confined to the Guard-room until Tattoo, for some unmilitary offence)[74] but, strange to say, in fine spirits. Join with me in huzzas for Buchanan & the indomitable Democracy. Our Country is safe for a *few* years more, & I believe those years to be *very few*. I never have, & do not now devote much time to politics, but any man of the small-est observation can plainly see, that the Union of the States cannot exist harmoniously; that there must, & *can & will be* a *dissolution*, wise, peaceful & equitable, I hope, but *at whatever cost*, it must come. The more I see of Northern people & manners & character, am I convinced that it must be so. Look at the vote of the North in the late contest. An *overwhelming* ma-jority for a renegade,[75] a cheat and a *liar*, only *because* he declared himself in favour of *abolishing slavery*, the very source of our existence, the *greatest blessing* both for master & slave, that could have been bestowed upon us. Say not that the *nationality* of the *noble* Democracy can prevent it.

The result in New Hampshire[76] alone is amply sufficient to satisfy any impartial mind that opposition to Southern institutions was the ruling principle. See what rapid strides the rankest Abolitionism is making over the entire North! From my heart I hope such a fate may be averted, but I confess the wonder is, how we have remained in peaceful connection so long. Our manners, feelings & education is as if we were different Nations. Indeed, everything indicates plainly a separation. Look out for a Stormy time in *1860*. In the mean time the South ought to prepare for the worst. Let her establish armories, collect stores & provide for the most desper-ate of all calamities—civil war. But, I did not intend to occupy so much space with my fears, which probably are very foolish & unfounded. I wish I could think so. Before leaving the Subject let me crow a *score* of times

74. It was not on this occasion, but in the wake of the John Brown raid in 1859 that Gibbes en-gaged in fisticuffs with Emory Upton, class of 1861, in what was described by another cadet as "the first determined stand by a Northerner against the long, aggressive, and unchallenged dictatorship of the South." Schaff, *The Spirit of Old West Point, 1858–1862*, 142–48.

75. John C. Frémont, the Republican abolitionist disliked by Ramseur, lost the 1856 presi-dential election to the Democrat James Buchanan. Millard Fillmore was the American (Know-Nothing) Party candidate. Frémont captured the electoral votes of the six New England states, plus New York, Ohio, Michigan, Wisconsin, and Iowa. Being from Pennsylvania undoubtedly enabled Buchanan to hold that state in the Democratic column.

76. Frémont garnered 54 percent of the popular vote in New Hampshire. *Congressional Quar-terly's Guide to U.S. Elections*, 1:652.

more over the defeated Scoundrels, Enemies of their country, their Sod, & themselves. Cheers! Long & loud for those noble & daring patriots who have achieved the glorious victory.

I am delighted to hear that you are so deeply in love with your profession. I feel confident that you will succeed, that your brightest anticipations will be realized. That such may be the case is the most sincere desire of your best friend, Dod. You must have a joyous time in the midst of all your studies at "*Log Town*."[77]

I wish I could be with you to talk over the good old times, & be strengthened in my determination to keep on the arduous path I have undertaken. Dave, I tell *you* what no mortal else suspects *even*, that I *am not satisfied at West Point*. You are surprised, but if you knew everything to which we are *compelled* to submit, & which can *only* be learned by experience (no mortal can describe it), you would think it perfectly natural. The government under which we are placed is the most *despotic in the world*. We have no rights & everything we possess is at the disposal of the authorities except our lives. It is ten times worse than ever before since Maj. Delafield, who has the reputation of being the best disciplinarian & most thorough Soldier in the Army, has been sent here as Superintendent.[78] Since his arrival, six weeks ago, eleven men have resigned. Heretofore a Cadet never was known to resign *voluntarily*. It is almost insufferable. Yes, I am dissatisfied, but I am *determined* to *graduate*. I came here to do it, & if I fail, it will be because I am *incapable*.

I will submit to their tyranny, provided it is necessary to make me a better Soldier. One thing is certain, we will have the satisfaction of knowing, *when* we *do graduate*, that we have endured an ordeal that none but *men* of the *true Stamp* could stand. I shudder to think of what we have yet to go through, but with a brave heart I will try to bear it all.

I do not want you to think that we are always gloomy & oppressed with our manifold duties & consequently enjoy very little social pleasure. Oh! No! I have some dear, noble, devoted friends at W. P. & with them

77. Schenck was studying at Richmond Hill law school, founded by Chief Justice Richmond M. Pearson. James R. Leutze, "David Schenck," in Powell, *North Carolina Biography*, 5:295. The grounds around Richmond Hill were known as Logtown because of the cabins in which the students lived.

78. This was Richard Delafield's second term as superintendent. It would continue until March 1, 1861, with the exception of five days in January 1861, when P. G. T. Beauregard held the post before keener minds in Washington realized that the incumbent might soon follow his native state of Louisiana out of the Union. Delafield first served from 1838 until 1845. When he took up his duties again on September 8, 1856, there was no honeymoon period for the cadet corps to enjoy while he learned the ropes.

have many joyous times, notwithstanding our hardships &c. But I'll stop grumbling.

Let me tell you about an Affaire de Coeur [love affair], that I have been carrying on for the amusement of both parties concerned for three weeks. A Lady, visiting one of our West Point Ladies, my friend, Miss Emma Thompson[79] by name, pretty, smart, & *fast*, of course, concluded she would have some fun by *flirting* with this individual, who never having been accustomed to "climb" on any occasion, counted himself *in*. I knew that there was nothing more in her sayings & doings than a real (& what she thought would prove) *telling* flirtation. But she hasn't *slewed* me. I saw what she was up to, & as it is Leap-year, I have *permitted* her to make all of the advances. The consequence is (I forgot to say she has gone & will be back again soon) I have been the happy recipient of a pair of beautiful *slippers* hooked by herself, her daguerreotype, *three* letters, *two* of them *four* pages & *crossed*,[80] & a basket of cakes, candies &c & I have the promise of *sweeter privileges yet*. This kinder [kind of] counterbalances the terror of *our* discipline. Would you not relish it?

I was delighted to hear that old Lincolnton was awaking & putting on a new appearance. Long may she prosper, & may the day soon come when she will be the Star of Western Carolina. Dave please excuse me for writing so badly. I've got a mean light (my lamp is on the "sick report,") a miserable pen, & was obliged to write fast in order to finish before Tattoo which is just being beaten. Good-night.

Dave, I hope you will excuse the careless haste in which this is written. I was very much hurried last night &c &c.

Remember me kindly to McDougall. I always thought him a clever fellow altho' I had very little, scarcely anything, to do with him. Ask him if he has heard from Kell or Neagle lately? Ed White[81] told me Kell was studying medicine. Well, mon ami [my friend], I must close. Good-bye. May a kind and merciful God bless, protect & save you is my constant prayer. As ever, Dod[82]

As a "yearling" in the second winter as a cadet, Ramseur continued to follow carefully the fate of his fellow North Carolinians. He anxiously

79. Daughter of an officer killed in the Seminole Wars. His family was permitted to live on post. They subsisted by providing board to a select number of senior cadets anxious to escape the mess hall. Morrison, "The Best School," 78.

80. Written horizontally and vertically on the sheet of paper.

81. By the time of the 1860 Census, W. E. White was a twenty-four-year-old physician practicing in Charlotte. U.S. Census Office, *Eighth Census, 1860*.

82. PC.

awaited his first furlough to return home but continued to study diligently. And, in an ironic exclamation, the enthusiastic youth expressed his pride at being an American. The first two snippets again come from letters to David Schenck, the last to Ramseur's mother.

[November 9, 1856]

You can not imagine how much we *"prison-birds"* as a Lady so appropriately called us, think & talk of our anticipated Furlough. Every evening we assemble, each separate *clique* in a particular room, after supper (our only leisure time, *half an hour*) light pipes, *smoke & talk* & laugh till we are interrupted by the Sentinel bawling, "Go to your Quarters: Is all right?" Where upon our pleasure is ended & with a groan, almost of despair, *we* take up our books, but not always are we able to break up the chain of happy thought & bind our minds down to the dullest & hardest of all subjects, Mathematics. Well, Dave, I am sorry to have to tell you that the representatives of North Carolina, in my Class, are not doing her much credit. In /56 there were *four* of us. One was *"found"* last year. Gilmer, Nephew of the great Know Nothing, a mighty *"good fellow,"* has now a great many demerits over the number which will dismiss him. Besides, he will be "found" on Studies at the next examination (in Jan/56). Ashe[83] too, a noble little fellow, Son of the Hon. J. B.[84] will, I fear, be found on Studies next Jan'y. Kerr, who came on the year before us & was suspended is in my class.[85] So I am the only one of the original four not in *present* danger. It grieves me much to have to write this, but is a sad reality. The truth is, far more Southern boys fail to master the West Point course than Yankees.

83. John Grange Ashe served as a company grade officer in the Confederate army from March 1861 until bad health forced him to resign his commission at the end of 1864. He was an infantry officer under Bragg at Harrington, Florida; with Brig. Gen. Robert Ransom as an AAG officer at Malvern Hill and Antietam; and a captain of artillery serving as an ordnance officer and AAG under Brig. Gen. James E. Slaughter in Texas. J. G. Ashe, Confederate Generals, Staff Officers, and Non-regimental Enlisted Men, CMSR, RG 109, NARA.

84. If Ramseur is correct concerning John G. Ashe's father, he was John Baptista Ashe (1810–57) who was elected to the Twenty-eighth Congress, 1843–45, from Tennessee. John G. was appointed from North Carolina by John Baptista's brother, William S. Ashe (1814–62), who represented North Carolina in Congress, 1849–55. John Grange Ashe, U.S. Military Academy Application Papers, RG 94, NARA. Ramseur may have confused his classmate's father with the most prominent Ashe in North Carolina history, as both men were nephews of John Baptista Ashe (1748–1802), a colonel in the Revolutionary War, member of the Continental Congress, and leader in the state convention which ratified the U.S. Constitution. He served in the First and Second Congresses, 1789–93.

85. John Marshall Kerr was disciplined for deficiency in conduct (too many demerits), March 27–July 1, 1855. Jefferson Davis, Secretary of War, to Superintendent, U.S. Military Academy, March 27, 1855, Military Academy Letters, Vol. 20 (June 28, 1854–March 5, 1856), RG 94, NARA.

Not for want of talent, so much as submission to the terrible discipline
& persevering application. They get tired & stop studying, & I defy the
brightest intellect to graduate here without hard study.[86]

[April 6, 1857]

Yes! I could to you "a tale unfold," of long and tedious hours spent in
the close study of Rhetoric, History, French and last, but by no means,
least, Mathematics; of *painful* hours passed in the practice of Light Infantry or Shanghai, and Artillery drills, Small Sword exercise, and, worse
than all, terrible Guard Duty. . . .

Good Gracious! How gloomy every thing looks out doors. From my
window, I look out upon Crows-Nest towering above the clouds, and upon
the white ruins of old Fort Clinton, surrounded by dark Cedars, an eloquent and lasting monument to the throes of that "Time which tried men's
souls."[87] I love the old Fort; and as I climb around its falling battlements,
or grope among its dusty dungeons, my heart swells with grateful, patriotic pride, and I thank God that I am an American.[88]

[May 16, 1857]

Since I last wrote, Fanny's & Luly's letters have been received. Thank
them many times for me. And Father has *also* sent me his written permission to come home this summer. Oh! I am beginning to appreciate that
I am soon to be with you all again. Precious Privilege! We have *only three*
more *weeks* to *study & drill*. Every body is rejoicing: (I ought to except
some poor fellows who *fear* the *result* of the approaching *examination*)
First Classmen, that they will soon be rewarded, for *four* years of toils,
hardships and patient perseverance, with that *invaluable* document, "A
Diploma of the U.S.M.A.," signed by the *learned* & Scientific "*Academic
Board*," and delivered by our venerable Superintendent. Is not this worth
labouring for? The Second Class rejoices at the idea of taking up the honors, dignities, responsibilities & *offices* which the departing 1st Class so
willingly resign. The Third Classman glories in anticipation of his Second-
Class Encampment, imagines himself a "dashing Sergeant," "the observed
of all observers" & last, but not least, a perfect Ladies-man. The Fourth
Class, of which honorable body, I am a member, have a glorious Furlough

86. PC.
87. Thomas Paine, *The American Crisis*, no. 1 (Dec. 23, 1776).
88. PC.

to think, dream & talk about. And the Plebes are beginning to hold up their heads & assume the importance of an *Old Cadet*. Poor fellows they have passed over a *hard road*.[89]

In the summer of 1857, Ramseur took his long-awaited break to visit friends and loved ones in North Carolina. The family life he enjoyed that summer would change radically in the ensuing two years.

Jacob Ramseur had thirty debts filed against him in late 1857 and 1858, totaling more than $24,000 in judgments and court expenses and costing him his mercantile business.[90] The social impact of his financial obligations, involving six co-defendants and twenty-five creditors, must have been devastating in a county of 6,000 white inhabitants, 496 living in Lincolnton, with many families interrelated.[91] The fact that he was placed into debt because of the dishonesty of his partner, a northerner married to Ramseur's first cousin, made the loss all the more difficult for a cadet who disliked most Yankees[92] while maintaining an abiding affection for kin. With his father transformed from a prosperous merchant to the clerk in the Laurel Hill cotton factory owned by his brother-in-law, Ramseur considered job alternatives to military service that would generate the income necessary to help support his siblings.

Then, in November 1859, Ramseur was devastated by his mother's death, and the family's closeness was tested once more. The impact of her husband's financial failure on the family's lifestyle was too much for her, at least this is the portrayal of David Schenck in his journal: "I have to record with painful heart the melancholy derangement of my dear mother-in-law Mrs. Ramseur. Oppressed with grief and care more than human mind could support, her reason became impaired on Monday last, the 14th, and has gradually increased until now."[93] Ten days later, she passed away. Her eldest son's keen sense of duty is seen in his concern for his siblings during these trials, just as it would be shown over and over again, later, on the campaign trail.

When his father lost his business, Ramseur began to consider ways to maximize his earnings after graduation in order to care for his family. The imposition of military duty on family responsibilities was difficult for

89. SHC.

90. Fieri Facias, Lincoln County Civil Action Papers, 1857–59, NCOAH.

91. U.S. Census Office, *Eighth Census, 1860*.

92. Gallagher, "A North Carolinian at West Point," 25.

93. David Schenck, Diary, November 19, 1859, SHC.

someone whose personal precept over the preceding two years had been duty to country and the profession of arms.

U.S. Military Academy West Point Nov. 8th/57

My dear, dear Dave,

Your precious letter was rec'd. more than a month ago. You know why it has not been answered before now. So I'll not lose time making excuses. Would to God, my dearest friend, I could make you know how dear you are to me! I love you as an elder Brother. May God bless you! May He ever keep genuine disinterested love bright and pure in our hearts! O Dave! Your letter did so cheer me! My heart whispered a thousand times whilst reading it. God bless my dearest, dearest, noblest friend. I thank God for such a friend. In this, the hour of terrible adversity, your kindness, sympathy and love comfort, console and strengthen me. Oh! Believe me Dave! Whenever or whatever I may be, I will ever be your *best* friend! I do not grieve for myself. Oh! no. But the thought that those who are ten thousand times dearer to me than Life itself may suffer in this selfish world continually oppresses me. The knowledge that they have been robbed of all earthly goods by the damning treatchery of a miserable Yankee, a villain, a liar, a fiend of Hell, a ——, too overcomes me. I try not to think of the author of all this. It will never do for me to meet him, for if I do I shall certainly crush him to atoms.[94]

My dear friend, I don't want you to think that I am discouraged, far from it. I feel a thousand times stronger than ever. I feel confident of success. My only regret is that I have so long to remain at W. P. that the time when I will be of essential service to those who are dear to me is *so far off.* Let me tell you my plan. I know you will take an interest in it. I will graduate. My salary will be $1300 pr yr. Of this, I'll need $800, the rest shall go towards educating my darling Sister. I'll remain in the Army three years, during which time I'll make myself a *No 1* Engineer. Then, I'll resign, and as Science & Worth are always in demand, I'll get suitable employment & wages.

I was talking with a (last June) Graduate, yesterday. He told me, that he could resign now, get a situation as Chief Engineer & $3000 the 1st year & $5000 pr. yr. as long afterwards as he chose. You know that at one time I

94. Elisha S. Barrett, listed as born in New York, thirty-two years of age, and living in Dallas, North Carolina in the 1860 Census. He was named as co-defendant with Jacob Ramseur in thirty-two lawsuits totaling over $30,000 in judgments and costs. Fieri Facias, Lincoln County Civil Action Papers, 1857–59, NCOAH; U.S. Census Office, *Eighth Census, 1860.*

said nothing would make me resign. I did not imagine then that troubles would come upon my home. But now I'll leave the Army without a regret. *I tell you Dave*, I believe I have a military genius (No; that ain't the word, *turn*, is better) for in all military exercises and studies I am among the first. Military heroes have been my study for many years. I feel that should I remain in the Army, I would make my mark. Dave I could write the above to no mortal except you. You know me too well to think it boasting or any thing of that sort. I think I will lead a far happier life by resigning. How can I be happier or better than by living for my home loves.

I told you once, that I would be perfectly miserable if I expected to live an Old Batchelor, but my views have changed. I look forward to the Future, and see myself beloved by my Brothers and Sisters, whose homes will be my home: and whose hearts will ever cling close to me. I want no dearer, no nobler object to life than I now have. I look upon these misfortunes as "blessings in disguise." They have made us all feel how dear we are to one another. We are not ashamed to be poor. We glory in our honour! Besides, is wealth necessary to happiness? No! Why Dave, I felt a deeper, purer pleasure since this calamity than ever before. Our family is peculiarly blessed in being an affectionate one. Love is the principle which governs us. Selfishness is not known to us. David, noble boy! has a plan in view too, by which he intends to live for our Parents & Sisters. And we, he & I, have our plan, which you may hear of some of these days. I have been amused, delighted, and often affected to tears by the letters of my darling little Sisters. Each wants to live for the others. Sally says she wants to go to school as long as she can, so that she may be useful; that she would rejoice in teaching in order to help Father. Here is an extract from a letter I rec'd. last Sat. from Luly. "I know I'll always be the least useful of the family. Sally can teach painting, embroidery and anything else; you (referring to me) can do anything & everything; Brother David, bless his sweet heart, is willing & anxious to do everything he can to help Father, and Fanny will be a famous music teacher. Oh! how I wish I had some great talent, by cultivating which, I *too* might be useful."

Noble Creatures! How can I be otherwise than happy being blessed with such affectionate Sisters! And my dear Mother! O Dave! It is not in the power of mortals to do her justice. Her reward will be in heaven. Struggling for such a Mother and such Sisters, what difficulty can oppose me? What danger turn me? What reverse discourage me? How can I stop short of full, complete, glorious success. Oh! my dear Dave, I will "bear myself like a man." As long as I have health & strength there will be no necessity of my dear, darling Sisters teaching school, or doing anything else to support themselves. O Dave! I feel as strong as Sampson. I look forward to the future with high, exulting hope. I try always to "do right" and I fear nothing. Oh! But *three years* is *so*, so long! How can I wait? There is a silent something that tells me "Be patient & fear not." "All will yet be well." And I believe it. "When God is for us, who can be against us. . . ."[95]

Two months later, Ramseur continued to muse about his future in these excerpts from a letter to David Schenck and, for the first time, expressed his view on the North-South controversy.

[January 24, 1858]

I am determined to graduate; then my armour will be bright and I will fight the "Battle of Life" in earnest! I have concluded that it will be best for me to resign as soon as I can after graduating. For in the Army, for the first four years I could not clear more than $600 pr. annum. As a Civil Engineer, I have the experience of every Graduate who has ever engaged in Eng. to insure me that I may confidently expect, at least $5000 pr. an. Tho' it will be like cutting off my right arm, for me to leave the Army, still I will gladly do it, to perform a Duty which I consider as the one object of my life! If I accomplish my object, then I will consider my Life as not vainly spent! May God give me strength and may I be enabled by Him to gain a sure victory. . . .

I wish I had time to write more, but it is nearly time for Tattoo so I must close. I would like to give you at length my notions of Politics. I am a *Secessionist* out and out. I am in favour of drawing the dividing line from the Atlantic to the Pacific. Let us establish a Southern Union, a glorious confederacy, whose foundation shall be Liberté et Égalité [Liberty and Equality].[96] The first infernal Yankee who shows his face across our line, to be tarred & feathered for the 1st offence & hung as high as Haman[97] for the second!

What do you think of my politics? I have the immortal Calhoun[98] with

---

95. Romans 8:31. PC.

96. "Liberty, Equality, Fraternity" became the national maxim of France following its revolution.

97. The chief minister of King Ahasuerus, Haman was hanged on the gallows he had prepared for the Jew Mordecai (Esther 7:10), i.e., to be hoisted on one's own petard.

98. John C. Calhoun of South Carolina—vice president, secretary of state, secretary of war, senator, and member of the House of Representatives during his long career in service to the United States—known as a champion of states' rights, slavery, and other southern causes.

me for now, the *"Balance of Power"*[99] is, or soon will be, lost to us if Kansas is refused admittance as a slave state. I think the South will be wrong to do anything but withdraw & establish an independent & glorious Nation! . . . [100]

Again, in correspondence with Schenck, Ramseur revealed a nervous condition undoubtedly aggravated by worrying about his family in Lincolnton. This affliction would resurface under the strain of warfare.

Two other subjects entered Ramseur's thoughts at this time. The first was the romance blooming between Ramseur's younger sister Sallie and his best friend. He could have imagined nothing finer than to welcome David Schenck into his family as a "brother." Complications involving religion were eventually resolved, and the wedding of Sallie and David took place in August 1859, though Ramseur was regretfully absent. Ramseur's second fixation was an opportunity to demonstrate prowess in a military campaign and garner recognition and advancement; war with the Mormons out west was a topic of fervent discussion in the barracks beside the Hudson.

U.S. Military Academy
February 4th/58

My Dear Dave,

I have just read a letter from Mother, which prompts me to write to you by the return mail. You know that I have written to you recently as I would have done to no other living Mortal. I will do so now. For I know you, Dave, and I love you.

Mother's letter was in answer to one I wrote, asking about Sallie's feelings. She says, "You know David's addressing Sallie took her so much by surprise that it was a long time before she could realize it. As I was very anxious that her affection should decide the matter, I did not say anything to influence her, & did not show her your letters until I knew that she did not love Dr. Rich[ardson]. I must say that Sallie has some of the sweetest traits of character I ever saw. It is very gratifying to me to see the innocence, simplicity and purity of her mind. There is no doubt now that her feelings are warmly enlisted for David. . . . I asked her tonight what she intended to David when he next came to see her, told her if she had any *objection* to tell him candidly. She said she had but one & she did not

99. The balance of power between slaveholding and non-slaveholding states was a pillar of Calhoun's concept of the federal architecture in America, and without opening the West to slavery, the equilibrium would be destroyed and disunion the natural consequence. Bartlett, *John C. Calhoun,* 371–72.
100. PC.

know how to tell him that, or whether it would be right to tell him. That she feared he was an High Ch. Episcopalian. Said she never could be an Episcopalian. . . . This is indeed a delicate matter. If David's religious views are settled, Sallie would not think it right to try to change them & it may prove an unpleasant barrier. For, I do think it is all important, my dear Son, for Man & Wife to have the same Religious sentiments. We can not expect Domestic happiness without it. . . . Sallie has been unhappy since she thought of this difficulty. Her feelings are deeply moved. I do hope and pray that the difficulty may not be the cause of unhappiness hereafter."

Although I knew that my dear Sister's mind was strengthened and her heart purified by religious principles, I was somewhat surprised at this objection. I do not think Sallie means it as an objection, but she regards it as a cloud that darkens the bright future.

I thought, it would be proper for me to mention this, especially as I have heretofore written so candidly to you.

My anxiety is now quieted, for I think that "All will certainly be well"! So mote it be!

Dave, I do hope you will excuse this hasty scratch. I have written as fast as I possibly could. Also excuse the last two I wrote you. Do write to me soon. May God bless you, My dearest friend.

S. Dodson Ramseur
Write very soon[101]

[February 28, 1858]

My Dear Friend,

Your precious letter of the 6th was received in due time. And I assure you that if I had followed the free impulse of my heart I would have answered it immediately, but Duty called me elsewhere. For the last week, I have been suffering, from a nervous attack (caused by excessive anxiety) to such a degree that for a time I was incapacitated for the performance of duty. . . .

At West Point, the same old monotony exists. The New York Herald tells us of the stirring times at Washington. You no doubt have read of the numerous duels on the tapis recently! One of the combatants, Lt Williams[102] of the 1st Dragoons, is on duty here as an Instructor in Riding. He is a

101. PC.

102. First Lt. Robert Williams of Virginia, class of 1851, served as a colonel in the First Massachusetts Cavalry, 1861–62, before being reassigned to the adjutant general's office for the remainder of the decade. In 1892–93, he was adjutant general of the U.S. Army in the rank of brigadier general. Cullum, *Biographical Register*, 2:290; Heitman, *Historical Register*, 1:38, 1:1042.

noble Soldier and his conduct throughout the whole affair was brave and chivalrous! He was fighting for a *friend*! The most interesting subject to us is the Utah Army & its movements, as we all have acquaintances and friends there. Military men think the Mormons will fight much harder than is generally supposed; that the little army now there is in decided danger &c. The whole "Frontier Army" has been ordered to be concentrated in Utah in the Spring & Summer.[103] The Secretary of War declares that Congress by rejecting the Army Bill, takes upon itself the responsibility of Indian depredations on our extended and unprotected frontiers!

We are all looking forward anxiously to next encampment. Some are transported with delight at the thought of Graduating. Some look to it, as a season of Rest and Gaiety. I look forward to it, as a time of rest & Reading, but principally as the *beginning* of the *fourth* year of my *bondage*. Yes, *two years more*, and I will be *uncaged*, and *then!*— But, I am obliged to close. My head is almost bursting. *Don't let any one at home know that I am sick*, for I am not in the *least danger*, and it would only *add* to their *many & grievous* cares.[104]

The following excerpt from Ramseur's letter of March 14, 1858, to his sister Luly is of interest for different reasons. The earliest indication of more than casual interest in his cousin, Ellen Richmond, is reflected in the first paragraph. She would become his wife in 1863. The second paragraph provides insight into cadets' informal interaction with their professors. The final comments may be viewed as not just Ramseur's but as those of his peers concerning the ongoing impasse with the Mormons.

I have not rec'd. a letter from Cousin Ellen in a long time. I believe I owe her one, tho' I wrote her a note (of 4 long pages) enclosed in my last letter to Cousin Mary.

I would like to give you a description of [illegible] dinner I spent last evening. Briefly thus [illegible] three other Cadets. I was invited to tea & [illegible] evening at Col. Hardee's, who has two mighty nice Daughters. One 17, the other 15.[105] This is the second *Tea* I have been

---

103. A conflict of jurisdiction between federal and court authorities led President Buchanan to appoint a non-Mormon as governor of Utah Territory in 1857. The expeditionary force commanded by Col. Albert Sidney Johnston, sent to accompany him, met with considerable resistance, almost reaching the point of open rebellion.

104. PC.

105. From the ages cited by Ramseur, the daughters who captivated him would appear to be Hannah, age seventeen, and Anna, age fifteen. U.S. Census Office, *Eighth Census, 1860*; Hughes, *General William J. Hardee*, 23.

invited to there. The moments flew rapidly & pleasantly by & Tattoo summoned us to Barracks. I hated to leave. Was quite captivated by Miss Annie who is a genuine Southerner in feeling, manners &c. These little Tea parties make our Saturday's very pleasant. I have attended several recently, nearly every Saturday have an invite either to Prof. French's,[106] Prof. Agnel's,[107] Col. Hardee's, Lt. Baird's[108] or Lt. Gibbon's.[109] The only place I dislike to attend is Prof. Agnel's. They are too stiff, rather French [illegible] I said I was quite smitten with Miss Ann [illegible], and if I had not determined to be *an Old Batchelor*, which determination I will be certain to *carry out*, I might have *surrendered*, before the dangerous darts of her sparkling black eyes and the killing sweetness of her smiles. But I am bound to be a *Batchelor*. May be *not* a *very old one*! Qu'en pensez vous? [What do you think about it?]

I have been troubled with a headache lately but it has now disappeared.

There is nothing new at W. P. Latest news from Utah, a skirmish between a "picket guard" of the Army & a comp'y. of Mormons. 4 Soldiers & two Mormons killed. It is thought that Col. [Albert Sidney] Johnston & his little Army are in eminent danger. If they are destroyed the blame must rest upon Congress for so murderously refusing to increase the Army while every principle of necessity, justice & humanity so urgently called for it.[110]

[March 27, 1858]

Dave, I fear I caused you too great anxiety on my account by my last letter. I did not intend to say that I was all the time suffering with nervous attacks, as you seem to think. 'Tis true, that *sometimes, not often*, I have had a head-ache severely enough to disqualify me for the performance of

---

106. John W. French was chaplain and chairman of the Department of Geography, History, and Ethics.

107. Hyacinth R. Agnel was professor of French.

108. First Lt. Absalom Baird of Pennsylvania, class of 1849, was assistant professor of mathematics. During the Civil War, he rose to the rank of brevet major general while serving as a division commander in the Western Theater. Cullum, *Biographical Register*, 2:233–34.

109. Born in Pennsylvania and raised in North Carolina, 1st Lt. John Gibbon, class of 1847, was serving as an artillery instructor and quartermaster at West Point. During the Civil War, he rose to the rank of major general commanding the XXIV Corps, Army of the James. Warner, *Generals in Blue*, 171–72.

110. SHC.

Duty.[111] *Sometimes*, too, it has been entirely *without* my power to collect and concentrate my thoughts for the deep & intense study required of a Third-Class Man. But those *dark days* are over. Two months more and we will pass the final ordeal of the terrible Third-Class Course. At present I am very well. I have been so for three weeks. Yes, I thank God for "a sound mind in a sound body." And I have been doing better than any time since my return from Furlough, as my report for March will show. The Storm is past! At first its terrible dangers breaking upon me so suddenly did cause gloom and sorrow and *almost* despondency. But after the first burst of grief and passion, Reason calmly resumed her wonted ascendancy. Now I am closely studying and patiently waiting coming events. My hopes are high and confident. Why not? There is no limit to the human mind. No object which can not be achieved by constant exertion! Oh! How I do long to enter upon the Great Battle of Life. I want to measure my strength with a "foe worthy of my steel"! And that time is surely coming tho' *slowly*. I know the responsibilities that rest upon me. I pray God will enable me to bear them all bravely, nobly. "My faith in Time is large, and that which shapes it to a perfect end."[112] Ah! Yes, all will yet be well. We may one day meet in high places & talk over our trials & struggles. . . .

What do the People think of the Mormon War? We may see some service against the Mormons yet. We certainly will if they turn it into an organized Guerrilla Warfare, which is likely. Qu'en pensez-vous? [What do you think about it?][113]

Entering his fourth year at the Academy, Ramseur was absorbed in the cadet command structure, as he had been appointed to an important position in the hierarchy. The corps was organized into a battalion consisting of four companies, each commanded by a cadet captain. The senior of the four, responsible for discipline throughout the corps, was designated "First Captain." Lieutenants filled positions such as corps adjutant and quartermaster and three slots in each company. All of the cadet officers came from the first class. The remaining first classmen were dubbed "High Privates" in cadet parlance. Second classmen filled positions as sergeants, the top two being the sergeant major or first orderly sergeant and quartermaster

111. A pathologist examined and analyzed Ramseur's thirty-seven appearances on the sick list at the academy. He found them to be mild and of short duration and concluded, "The number of admissions was above average, but from the diagnoses it appears that this record reflects concern with his health rather than poor health." Steiner, "Medical-Military Studies on the Civil War," 1016–17.

112. Alfred Lord Tennyson, "Love and Duty" (1842).

113. PC.

sergeant, followed by one first or orderly sergeant in each company. Lesser responsibilities were assigned to other sergeants. Third classmen served as corporals. The remainder of the cadets were privates. Ramseur naturally could not wait to share the honor of his appointment with Schenck.

[September 15, 1858]

Well, here is a *rapid* letter, *note* rather. I have any amount of *Good News* to tell you. Will you be surprised to hear that my anticipations have been realized, that I am now the 1st Orderly Sergeant of the U.S. Corps Cadets. Yes, I am promoted, and am enjoying my honours *hugely*! But this news is insignificant when compared with what I am going to tell you.

It is almost positively a fixed fact that the course will be changed. Instead of the present Five Year Course, the good Old Four Year Course (that has already made so many Scholars & Soldiers) will be substituted. In that case I will receive my diploma the 30th of June 1859 & my commission the 1st of July 1859. Oh! It is almost "too good to be true"; but I am not giving you an idle rumor now. The Sec'y. of War sent an Order to the "Academic Board" to convene, consider the propriety of shortening the courses, determine a programme of studies & forward it to the Department immediately. All of which has been done, the Board strongly recommending the adoption of a 4 yr. course. Every officer here believes the course changed. Gibbon told me yesterday. There was not a doubt of it &c.[114]

U.S. Military Academy
West Point N.Y. Nov. 20th 1858

Dear Dave,

I have long wished for an opportunity to write you a *long* letter. Today offers it to me, provided some unexpected *order* does not come, requiring prompt obedience. The northern wind is blowing chill and drear[y] without, and my lofty room appears the more comfortable from contrast. What would you give to behold the scene that is spread out before me? Would you be pleased with a description of my "Quarters."[115] We (Gibbes & I) are peculiarly favoured, having *two* rooms (only two Cadets, First Captain & First Orderly Sergeant, have this privilege) a bedroom and Study. Our Study is in one of the Towers, is octagonal shape, and has three windows, looking North, East & South. To the North the Noble Hudson, cov-

---

114. PC.
115. In the southern barracks.

ered with a thousand sails, spreads out like a *lake* of glass. Along its banks
dotted in the distance, piercing the "azure dome," are the famous *Catskills*.
To the East, *across* the River, I look at the Residences of Wealthy City Mer-
chants, who jump into the cars after Bkfst., go 50 miles to their counting rooms & return after Tea to the quiet Country Home. I often drop my
book & gaze with admiration at the beauty of some of them, almost *regal*
residences. After I picture a *family* gathered around the old hearthstone &
imagine their joys & comforts &c. But the South Window is my favorite.
Here, I sit in my straight-backed chair with my book open on the table
before me. Day & night I study, write and *dream* here.

O that I could penetrate the terrible distance that separates me from
those my heart holds dear! How sweet to look upon the faces of every precious one, to watch every shade of expression, and catch every beam of joy
and ray of Hope that exists there. Often, *too* often, my thoughts, refusing
to digest the abstruse facts which Science teaches, steal Home. Sometimes
full of gaiety, pleasure and Hope and sometimes (Ah! *Yes* 'tis *too true*) full
of sadness, sorrow and—*almost despair*. But *thank God* these dark moments are *few*. There are clouds, 'tis true, but they all have the "Silvery
lining." Hope, sweet & cheering (what is that silent something which says
"*delusive*"!) bears me up and urges me Onward! Yes, Dear Dave, when I am
suffering from thoughts that make my brain burn like fire, how cheeringly
sounds Longfellow's Psalm of Life. How precious, then, are the promises
of our dear Saviour! Oh! What would Life be worth were it valued only for
itself? Ah! Dave, I believe "Labour is worship"! Who would drone out life
in indolence and ease, which God has given to be spent in action. "God
like Action"!

Who would hesitate to encounter difficulties or turn pale at dangers,
when duty leads the way? I pray God to quicken my mind, to strengthen
my arm & prepare my heart for the Life that awaits me! My Dear friend,
I firmly, hopefully believe that a glorious victory awaits me! So may it be.

The course of Life I shall pursue often gives me cause for serious and
anxious thought. One thing is certain. I must make money. Possessing no
capital, my education must be my tool. Judging from the success of those
who have entered civil life before me, I am naturally led to anticipate a
like result.

Civil Engineering offers the best field. I do not doubt my ability to at-
tain the highest rank in this profession (I say this not in boast, as you well
know, nor in *ignorance*, for I have finished the Civil Eng. Course) but I
have *influence* to obtain *position*.

Another Sure but Slow source of profit is that which the Colleges of our Country willingly offer to us. A Professorship. This is not sufficiently lucrative to entice me. I rec'd. a letter from Ed White the other day in which more sundry inquiries made for Dr. Fox,[116] leading me to believe that he was desirous to obtain my services at Charlotte N.C. School. I answered candidly without betraying my suspicions. In fact, I have sorter [sort of] "*connoodled*" to bring myself into notice, so that if they should offer me a *paying situation* I will accept it. I believe in your plan of "strewing bread upon the waters"[117] when ever opportunity offers. What I want is *work that will pay*, the bolder & harder, the better. I am young and strong! I feel stronger and braver every day. I would be willing to *attempt most* any thing. If I failed I would do so struggling to the last, never giving up. Then conscience & humanity would acquit me. If I succeeded, the glory would be commensurate with the danger.

I would like Lt. Stone's fortune.[118] He was paid down $10 000 cash to resign & take charge of a N.Y. Mining Company's affairs in *Sonora*, besides to receive $5000 pr. yr. payable semiannually, and one hundredth of the *net profits*. This occurred last yr., & I hear from Huger[119] who knows him that he is making a tremendous fortune.

Three yrs ago Lt G. W. Smith[120] rec'd. a large sum to resign & take charge of some iron factories &c for three years. Now he is "Chief Street Commissioner" of N.Y. City with a salary $15 000 pr year.

Ah! If I could succeed thus! How happy I would be. How much good I could do with my money! &c.

116. A forty-one-year-old physician practicing in Charlotte, Charles J. Fox was the founder of the North Carolina Military Institute. He asked both Hill and Thomas J. Jackson to become involved with the new school, but only Hill accepted. Bridges, *Lee's Maverick General*, 27; U.S. Census Office, *Eighth Census, 1860*.

117. Ecclesiastes 11:1.

118. Upon graduation in 1859, Roderic Stone was made brevet second lieutenant of infantry and assigned to frontier duty first in Minnesota, and then in New Mexico. On leave of absence, he must have accepted the mining position. Stone had not resigned his commission and, when war broke out, he was mortally wounded as an infantry captain at the battle of Valverde, New Mexico, on February 21, 1862. Cullum, *Biographical Register*, 2:489.

119. A member of one of the first families of South Carolina, Frank Huger was among Ramseur's best friends at the Academy. Graduating thirty-first in the class of 1860, Huger resigned his commission in the U.S. Army in 1861 to join the Confederate army.

120. Gustavus W. Smith of Kentucky, class of 1842, fought in the Mexican War, where he was thrice brevetted. Later, Smith rose to the rank of major general in the Confederate army, commanding a wing during the Peninsula campaign and even serving a few days in Richmond as secretary of war ad interim due to the sponsorship of his ally, Adjutant and Inspector General Samuel Cooper. Warner, *Generals in Gray*, 280–81.

Well, it may be a wild dream but I do sometimes look forward to such success. Not that I expect Fortune to court me, but because I am determined to court Fortune! I would like above all things a chance to make a little money & a big reputation in my short furlough. If I could get a position on the R.R. requiring study, care, labour & a *theoretical* knowledge of Civil Eng'g. I believe I could do myself credit. Is there any chance for such a position, think you? But enough of No 1, for this time. At least until after I have dined on stale potatoes and *juiceless* beef. I would like to dine at Home. Do you believe it.[121]

U.S.M. Academy

West Point, March 1st/59

My Dearest Friend,

Good Luck affords me an opportunity to write to you. No doubt you appreciate the enormous quantity of work that is now exacted of us, and attribute my long silence to this cause. Never, I assure you, have I labored so hard, physically and mentally, as during the few months just passed. Altho' I have been continually on the go, my health of body and vigor of mind have suffered no injury. In fact, this discipline has proved beneficial to me. You will more clearly understand our position when you know that by the second shortening of the course, we have *all* the duties of *one year and a half*, to perform in about half that time. And you must know too that no *half-way* action is allowed at W. P. Perfection or *rejection* is the motto.

But a brighter day is dawning! Or rather, we are soon to be rewarded for the labor we have done. What a glorious reward! Your imagination must picture it. My pen will not even attempt it.

The First of March! Three months more! And a terrible and *final* ordeal will terminate our labors as Cadets. Then the wide world will be our field of action! Then instead of folding our hands in ease and idleness, the greatest incentive will wage us onward & upward. Glory, Honor, Wealth and all the rewards of the good & great awaits each and every one who proves himself a "Hero in the fight."

Nor is this all! Oh No! The Self-approval of our heart of hearts, the love and blessing of fond Parents; the tender, devoted affection of Sweet Sisters; the manly pride and confidence of dear Brothers; and the esteem and true friendship of associates—all, all will be the rightful property of him who proves himself to be a genuine Soldier, a true man, made in the image of God.

121. Extant letter ends without a closing and a signature. PC.

I tell you, my Dear Dave, I am entirely devoted to the profession of Arms. In all of its details are to be found such precise regularity interspersed with pleasing, exciting variety, as to make it most suitable to one of my temperament. If this is so in peace, how will it be in war? Then all the powers of mind, soul and body are called into powerful, manly, glorious activity! Oh! if I have a spark of the true Soldier about me, this is the life I would choose.

But my pen is running away tonight. You must attribute it to an exuberance of feeling, caused by the opening prospect. Besides, my dear friend, whenever I write to you my blood rapidly approaches the boiling point. Your love and sympathy encouraged me to labor and hope when clouds were dark and lowering. Now when the "Silvery Lining" has almost enveloped the so lately threatening clouds, I am glad and rejoice while communing with you.

I fancy you (judging you by myself) will not object to an *egotistical* letter so I'll continue in the same strain.

You know, on graduating, we are assigned to the different corps in the army according to choice. A limited number being assigned to each Corps, and we have choice according to Class rank. The first *five* are generally commissioned to the Staff (Engineers, Topog'y. Eng. and Ordnance Corps); the remainder to the Line Corps (Artillery, Dragoons, Cavalry, Mounted Rifles, and Infantry). I will graduate about 15th so that I can procure a commission in any one of the Line Corps that I may choose. The Mounted Service is considered the hardest and most dangerous, but in it, the promotion is a little faster and the pay a very little better.

This is my choice. I have but few objections to it, viz. Being only constantly stationed on the frontiers, a man sees little of civilization; has few chances of making money, unless it be by a lucky land speculation, or by saving up pay, expenses being small; can not well prepare for resignation; and can not *conveniently* marry. The Artillery is my second choice. In this, pay is less & promotion slower. Usually stationed on the Sea board, where expenses take all pay. Its advantages are good Society and the opportunity it affords to a man desirous of taking a "rib" unto himself.

After a careful consideration of the pros and cons, I have concluded, as I said above, to apply 1st for the Dragoons, 2nd for the Artillery. In the Dragoons, for the 1st year, I would be stationed at "Carlisle Barracks" Penn. In the Art. at "Old Point," Va. What do you think of my choice. Write freely and fully. . . .[122]

122. PC.

U.S. Military Academy
West Point, Ap'l. 8th/59

My Dearest Friend,

I am completely prostrated this evening. The *terrible* disappointment which I have recently suffered has almost unmanned me. Perhaps you don't know of it. Well then I'll tell you. The President has changed the four years' course back to *five*, ordering that my class shall not graduate till *June 1860*! Strange, unaccountable, unjust, outrageous as it may appear, 'tis *too* true. I need not tell you of the acute sorrow this has brought upon me *after having completed the course* and on the very eve of graduation. And why was it done? In order that the Pres. might appoint some of his friends as Officers of the army. For by graduating only the "first Division" of the 1st Class (twenty one members) instead of the whole Class (sixty three), the probability is that more vacancies, occasioned by deaths & resignations, will occur during the next year, than these *21* can fill, and consequently an opportunity will be offered to the Pres. to put in some of his friends. So on a *mere probability* of accomplishing his selfish ends, he is guilty of so great injustice to 42 men who have labored hard & faithfully for four long years.

We have completed the course, only requiring to pass the June Exam'n. to get our diplomas & be recommended to the Pres't. for commissions. The Acad'c. Board express themselves willing and anxious to bestow upon us the Diplomas to which they pronounce us so justly entitled. One of the most distinguished members of the Board (Prof. Mahan) said today "That he was delighted with our Class. We had acquitted ourselves like men. That we were equal to any and superior to many preceeding classes. Even in the lower Sections, where he always had some trouble, the conduct of the young gentlemen was unexceptionable." We had made all our arrangements for graduation. Our friends expect us. The unusual and extraordinary exertions (we have accomplished in one year what is usually allotted to 18 mos.) of the past year, have actually wearied us out. And *now*, in spite of all this, this unaccountable counter order comes to drown our hopes and condemn us to another year of imprisonment. Ties our hands when we are eager and ready to serve our country and to struggle for a name and fame.

Dear Dave, I am too sick to write. My head is almost bursting. I'll write again soon, more fully & more calmly.

We are not inactive. We have addressed a *statement of facts* to the Pres. & every one of us has written to all the prominent men of our States.

I wrote to Mr. Lander. That letter will give you the *facts of the case*. Write to Old Buck[123] for us. I confess I have no hope of graduating before /60. All our efforts will be vain for selfishness not justice is the controlling principle. I intended to write more but I can hardly see. Excuse this. Write soon. God bless you.

Your devoted friend

S. D. R.[124]

U.S. Military Academy
West Point N.Y. Ap'l. 29th/59

My Dearest Friend,

After *three weeks* as *Second Classman*, I who do lately stand with *first class dignity looking down* upon leper Animals, am becoming reconciled to my fate. So you say, 'twas indeed a sickening blow that scattered my bright hopes, but Such is the *fortune* of War.

Our Professors sympathize with us, and are exceedingly lenient to us. The fact is we have worked harder than any other class ever did. Cheered by the new prospect that was set before us, no amount of labor could be irksome. Our exertions *more than* realized the expectations of the Acad'c. Board. And when the *late* counter-order came out we were within ten days of the completion of our advanced course. Thus on the very eve of the consummation of the cherished result of four years of labor, after we were allowed to make all our arrangements &c, this miserable order has dashed all our hopes to the ground. It is needless to descant upon the surprise of the Acad'c. Board or ourselves at the unexpected event, remanding us to another year of probation at the Academy. Nor need I attempt to describe the deplorable practical effect upon the spirits of a set of young men, of a measure thus affecting their vast and dearest interests. A few weeks ago, and we looked backward over the past year of self sacrificing toils and the retrospect was gratifying. We looked forward to receiving our well earned diplomas and the commissions to which they were to be our title; to going home, meeting friends, all that. The prospect was delightful. We were all enthusiastic in interest for our prospective profession, and would have gone to the Army filled with the ardor that is the source of success.

123. President Buchanan.
124. PC.

Where now is the enthusiasm that strung our energies for usefulness? If we are not listless, dejected and disgusted, I must say, it is because we are *Soldiers*, and will try to be *men*. Of course, we can not tell what cause has produced this unwarrantable change. If it is for economy, will the relatively insignificant saving of expenditures compensate, in the Secretary's opinion, for *the rights* the measure violates and the widespread and lasting regret it causes? No, it is not *economy*. But it is the base Self-interest of that demagogue Floyd which has caused our trouble. He knows that twenty-two men (the number in the present First Class) will not be sufficient to supply the exigencies of the service for one year! He knows by keeping my class back at the Academy, he will be able to fill up the vacancies that are bound to occur in the Army by his Cit[izen] friends[125] who are about as well fitted for the commission as John B. Floyd is to be Sec'y. of War. We have kicked against the pricks and are still doing so. We have written to big men in all parts of the Country & they all agree to the justice of our case & sympathize with us. We have heard from several members of Congress, who say if the matter can not be reached other wise, they will at least have it investigated when Congress meets &c.

But enough of this, after telling you, if you have time, to write to Old Buck, *pathetically*, and to Floyd *complainingly*, and to both *forcibly*, stating our case & asking to graduate us. *The Acad'c. Board will graduate us any time on three weeks notice.* We ask for even-handed Justice. If the matter is referred to the Academic Board, we will be graduated immediately. Now if Floyd consults the good of the service, let him leave the matter to the most competent Judges! He consulted them on the change from *five* to *four years*, and it was on their unanimous recommendation that the first change was made. But this last swindling operation was done without even the knowledge of the Officers of the Academy.

Well, if we do remain another year we are determined to make the most of it, in every sense of the word. Our encampment will be a *gay one*. We will be the *Lions (First Class Men)*. Next year our Studies will not be so numerous or so difficult, for we will be principally occupied in the mere *review of subjects* on which, we *now stand ready to be graduated*. Did any one ever hear of such outrageous injustice. It is exactly the same thing as requiring a First Class, that had remained four years, mastered the course & made all arrangements, to wait & work another year.

---

125. With direct commissions as army officers.

I wish we could get hold of old floyd (his name don't deserve a Capital) & punish him as he deserves. But I'll stop writing on this subject. . . .[126]

All the complaints were in vain, as Ramseur must have known they would be. Ramseur's fifth year at the academy was not so disagreeable, as he conceded to his sister. More important, based upon Hardee's assessment of his military ability, Ramseur was appointed captain of Company B for the year 1859–60. The determined long shot from rural Lincoln County, North Carolina, attained the highest rank in the corps of cadets to which he could aspire, presaging his steady advancement in the looming war.

During his final year, Ramseur involved himself in an endeavor that showed not only his strong familial ties, but also how accessible Americans were to their president in the mid-nineteenth century. Aunt Fanny Motz had launched an impressive campaign to obtain an "at large" appointment to the U.S. Military Academy for her son George. It began with her letter to President Buchanan in November 1858. When that failed to achieve admission in June 1859, Fanny went to the White House in the fall to speak directly with the president. She then recruited three North Carolinians who had served with Buchanan in the U.S. Congress to lobby their old colleague—former senators Bradford Brown and William A. Graham and former representative Daniel M. Barringer. North Carolina governor John W. Ellis and Raleigh editor W. W. Holden were enlisted as well. These letters and Fanny's spoke of her penury as a helpless widow who had been cheated by a scoundrel and of George's patriotism and intellectual, moral, and physical suitability for West Point. D. H. Hill attested to the applicant's good character and strong academic preparation at Davidson College, where he was in the junior class.[127] Rev. Morrison, the first president of Davidson and now retired in Lincoln County, was properly restrained in his endorsement.[128] As he would do repeatedly throughout his military career, Ramseur came to the aid of his kin by writing, as well. But all their efforts were in vain. George would soon don a uniform, however, as he and his brothers served in the First North Carolina Regiment in the war to come.

126. PC.

127. George Motz was graduated from Davidson College in the class of 1861. Davidson College, *Semi-Centennial Catalogue*, 48.

128. Mrs. Mary Morrison was the sister of Governor Graham, and, therefore, most likely the link to his endorsement. Bridges, *Lee's Maverick General*, 23.

Ramseur announced his plan to his father on January 1, 1860, along with sharing his current intention to serve in the mounted service.

> Next week I intend to write a letter to Mr. Buchanan concerning Georgy. I will get his nephew (Cadet B.)[129] to send it to him so that it will not fail to reach him. I must confess my hopes for Georgy's success are not so bright as they have been. But still while there is a spark left I do not feel satisfied to leave any means untried. . . .
>
> On my return, I traveled with L't. Lane, of the Mounted Riflemen.[130] His account of the Mounted Corps has settled me in my decision. I will get commissioned in the Dragoons. This will enable me to save $400 or $500 the 1st year & $800 or $900 each succeeding year. As well or better than I could do if I would accept professorship at $1500 pr year, for my expenses in the latter case would be from $500 to $800. Besides I have a decided preference & talent for the Mounted Service. Of this more anon.[131]

U.S. Military Academy
West Point N.Y. Jan. 18th 1860

Honoured Sir.

I hope you will excuse this intrusion upon your valuable time. I address you in behalf of a noble woman, who is entitled to your sympathy and assistance. I refer to Mrs. F. A. Motz of Lincolnton N.C. The morning of her life was bright and joyous: She was happily married and the creations of this world contributed to render her happy. But Alas! Death took from her embrace the husband of her bosom, and left her with three little children mourning and desolate. Col. Motz was accidentally drowned in March 1851.[132] Since then his widow has been robbed of *all* of her property by the villainy of Col M's partner, who continued the business after his death. Her home with all of its endearing associations was publicly sold to pay the debts of this false-hearted man. Behold her a poor widow, with three

---

129. Edward Y. Buchanan, class of 1863, appointed at large, resigned in April 1861, due to the pending Civil War. There is no apparent record of his military service in that conflict. *Register of Graduates and Former Cadets*, 253.

130. First Lt. William B. Lane of Kentucky was a member of the U.S. Mounted Rifles. Heitman, *Historical Register*, 1:614.

131. SHC.

132. Andrew Motz perished when thrown by his horse into a creek near his factory. Sherrill, *Annals of Lincoln County*, 148.

little fatherless children, bravely battling for their support and education. She taught school until her constitution was completely shattered and she was obliged to seek medical treatment in Philadelphia to preserve life. On her return to N.C. she called on your Honour and made the application which I now beg you to grant, namely: an appointment ("at large") to West Point, for her Son George Motz.

Sir. She who has been so gently nurtured, and who when the Storm came, so heroically met it, cries to you, the Father of the whole nation, to aid her, by placing her son where he will be able to support his mother, while he serves his Country. Mark! She does not do this until her health is undermined and she is no longer able to educate her children or support herself.

I am aware that these appointments are reserved for the Sons of Officers, but Sir, there have been just exceptions to this rule in every administration; and I feel confident an exception can be made in no case more justly, than in that which is now asked. After more than four years service at the Military Academy, I declare, of my own knowledge, that George Motz is mentally, morally and physically competent to do honour to his Country, to his family and to you, Sir, should you give him the appointment. His father was an active and efficient Officer of the Militia. His Mother, Sir, has rendered valuable service to the Country by that most honourable and difficult task, the educating of the hearts and minds of Youth.

Sir. You will perceive that this is no ordinary case. I trust that you will see fit to grant the anxiously sought-for appointment to George Motz. This is the last beacon of the poor widow's hope!

In His Holy Word, God commands us "to comfort and aid the widow." Do this, Sir, and He "who is the Father of the fatherless and the Husband of the Widow" will abundantly bless you.

With sentiments of the highest esteem
I am, Sir, your obedient Servant

S. D. Ramseur
Cadet (Captain) U.S.M.A.

To
James Buchanan
President of the United States[133]

133. SHC.

As he closed out five years at the military academy, Ramseur was enjoying the study of military history, as contrasted with much of the standard curriculum to which he had been subjected. This fascination was expressed in letters to Luly, dated February 13 and 28, 1860, and in the first extant letter to his future wife on February 24.

[Feb. 13, 1860]

There is nothing new at W. P. & if there was I would not have time to write it. We are studying the Campaigns of Great Generals. You know how fond I have ever been of reading of the deeds of Heroes. Now, that the subject is studied critically and scientifically investigated, I am in ecstacies. My spare time is devoted entirely to this branch of Military Engineering.[134]

U.S. Military Academy
West Point Feb 24th 1860

My Darling Cousin [Nellie Richmond],

If I had obeyed the promptings of my heart, I would have written to you long ere this; but, you know, a Soldier must recognize Duty as superior to Inclination. Since my entrance at the Military Academy, I have never been so constantly at hard work, as during the two months just past. You know, I was congratulating my self that there would be but little for me to do this year; egregious mistake! But I am not sorry it is so, for if I am at hard work, it is also the most pleasant I ever did. Our course is now purely military. We have just completed a critical review of the celebrated battles of Great Generals, and are now entering upon the "Art of War," "Strategy" and "Grand Tactics." You can imagine what an absorbing interest such subjects must have for one who has been, from early boyhood, a great admirer of the World's renowned Heroes.

I mention this, Darling Cousin, that you may know I have been silent so long, not because I think of you less frequently or love you less devotedly, far from it! I do assure you the remembrance of your sweet friendship often, very often, greatly soothes the sadness that sometimes steals over me.

Does your memory still cherish fresh and pure the recollection of those joyous days we passed together at my sweet Home nearly three years ago? Pure, beautiful happy days! Oh! if happiness abides here on earth, then did

134. SHC.

I experience it. Not one thing, that Friendship could supply or Love suggest, was wanting to fill my cup of pure delightful pleasure to the brim.

My precious Mother governed and controlled it all. Her sweet affection prompted her to lay and execute plans for my comfort, my enjoyment, my well-being. Like heart-music her gentle, loving voice still speaks to me, exciting emotions purer and nobler than earth's aspirations. Oh! How my heart did bleed to see my poor Mother suffer so! But now her sufferings are no more, her "tribulation" is over. She is clothed in a "pure robe made white in the blood of the Lamb."

Dearest Cousin, is it not a precious thought, that she "is not lost; but 'gone before,'" to that heavenly home where her Spirit longed to be? How our jewels are gathering there? Almost every rolling year adds to the loved ones there, and brings our unending meeting still more near. Blessed hope! We too may join that precious band, for "*we* have an Advocate. Oh! Such an Advocate! With the Father, even Jesus Christ, the Righteous"!

Cousin Nellie, it has been so long since a letter passed between us, that I do not know what news to write. Shall I tell you that Grim Old Winter still tarries here? That our hopes are budding even in advance of the coming Spring, and that our pleasures are chiefly in anticipation of Graduation and Welcome Home?

I was joyfully surprised not long ago by a visit from David. He was with me from Sat. until Monday. He is very well and rejoices at the approach of the end of his course.

My Darling Little Luly writes to me very often. Is she not a jewel? Poor thing, I fear she suffers much away from home in such dark days.

Fanny too writes to me nearly every week. I think she is very like you, cousin. And, by that, I don't know who I compliment most for truly you both are very loveable.

Not long ago I rec'd. a pretty boquet with pleasant wishes for my happiness, from an *unknown* friend. The post mark was Newbern N.C. Can you enlighten me in any way, concerning the above? mentioned souvenir?

Instead of shivering in the midst of snow and ice, I suppose you are this evening enjoying the perfume of the crocus & iris, whilst the pretty birds are warbling in every tree. Truly I wish I were with you.

As the time for my graduation approaches, I become more anxious to have you visit West Point with Uncle Caleb and Aunt Mary.[135] If a visit north is still contemplated I do hope West Point will be in the programme, and that the time of that visit will be next June. Will I be disappointed?

---

135. Nellie's father and mother.

What is the news in Milton? Tell me about all the Dear ones there. Give a great deal of love to Grand ma for me. The Children at home are all wild almost at the idea of going to see Grand ma.[136]

With love to Uncle Charles & Aunt Prissie, to your dear Father and Mother and to my Dear Cousins I must close this letter. Please write soon. Pleasant dreams be yours tonight. With devoted love

Your Cousin Dod[137]

U.S. Military Academy
West Point, Feb. 28th/60

My Darling Little Luly,

If I had obeyed the promptings of my heart I would have written to you long 'ere now. But a good Soldier must recognize Duty as superior to inclination. You know, I used to console myself with the expectations of an *easy* time during the remainder of my term at the Academy. Egregious mistake! Since I became a Cadet I have never had so much hard work so constantly on my hands, but I am far from being sorry that it is so, for if I am constantly engaged, my work is also the most agreeable I ever had to do. Our course is now purely military. We have just completed a critical review of the celebrated battles of great Generals, and will take up next [Antoine-Henri] Jomini's "Art of War," "Strategy" and "Grand Tactics." You may imagine what an absorbing interest such subjects have for one who, from early boyhood, has been an enthusiastic admirer of the World's renowned Heroes. I mention this Darling to inform you of the cause of my long silence. Be assured I have not thought of you less frequently nor do I love you less devotedly. . . .[138]

War Department,
July 2d 1860

Sir:

You are hereby informed that the President of the United States has appointed you a Brevet Second Lieutenant in the Third Regiment of Artillery. In the service of the United States, to rank as such from the first day of July, one thousand eight hundred and sixty.

---

136. Grand ma was Mary Smith Dodson, both Nellie and Ramseur's mother's mother.
137. SHC.
138. SHC.

You will immediately on receipt hereof, please communicate to this Department, through the Adjutant General's Office, your acceptance or non-acceptance of said appointment.

John B. Floyd
Secretary of War

Bvt. 2d Lieut. Stephen D. Ramseur,
3d Regt. Artillery[139]

West Point N.Y.
July 14th 1860

Sir,

I have the honour to acknowledge the reception of my appointment of Brevet Second Lieutenant in the 3rd Regt of Artillery U.S. Army and to express my acceptance of the Same. My age at the time of Appointment was twenty-three years and one month. My Residence, when appointed, Lincolnton, Lincoln County, North Carolina.

I enclose my oath of allegiance duly sworn to & subscribed.

I am, Sir

Your obedient Servant

S. D. Ramseur
Bvt 2nd Lieut. U.S. Artillery

S. Cooper
Adj't. Gen'l.
Washington[140]

Ramseur's relationship with West Point did not end upon his graduation on July 1, 1860. A commission was appointed that year to examine the academy's organization, system of discipline, and course of instruction. Its chairman was the recently elected senator, Jefferson Davis of Mississippi. Its members included Maj. Robert Anderson and Capt. A. A. Humphreys, both poised to achieve fame in the coming conflict. Brevet Second Lieutenant S. D. Ramseur was called to testify. His responses to the inquiry aptly sum up his West Point years.

139. NCOAH.
140. NCOAH.

As regards the theoretical course of instruction, I think too little time has been given to artillery tactics. The ethical course is too long, particularly the study of moral science is unnecessarily extended. This whole subject is ridiculed, and should not be taught in the section room.

As regards the practical course, I think more time is devoted to infantry drills, proportionally, than is accorded at present to instruction in other arms.

The discipline has been much injured by cadets not being dismissed after getting the number of demerits to which the regulations restrict them. They are now careless about how many demerits they get. I think demerit should not be considered in making up class standing. For a certain number of demerits there should be punishments assigned, extra tours of guard duty, confinement to quarters, &c. There is a feeling in the corps rather to the prejudice of a cadet who raises himself about others by avoiding demerit.

Cadets go into the service ignorant of it in a great measure, and often not capable of judging what corps they are best fitted for. They ought to have some practical experience, before being permanently assigned to particular corps. I cannot, however, suggest a method by which this could be done.

The effect of restoring to the Academy cadets found deficient in studies, or dismissed by courts-martial for bad conduct, has been, particularly during the past year, very injurious to discipline.

A separation of the first class from the rest of the corps, and placing them in a higher position would, I should apprehend, be injurious to discipline.

The system of demerits I consider a good one, if it were properly carried out. I do not think the late regulation a proper one, which allows an appeal concerning demerit to be made to the Academic Board.[141]

I do not think there is sufficient practice in the field with astronomical and surveying instruments. There are theories taught in the philosophical course which cadets would not be able to put in practice, and I think all of the theoretical course would be better understood and remembered, if there were more practical instruction. This would require several months additional time.

---

141. At this point, the Commission took a recess, after which Ramseur continued his testimony.

I do not think instruments in the observatory could be used by the cadets without injury to their adjustment, with the present practical knowledge they have of those instruments.

I think that cadets who have no special talent for drawing learn little in that department. Practice in sketching from nature has been introduced since my class completed their course in drawing.

I do not think that the military exercises, riding, fencing, &c., at all interfere with the studies.[142]

There is no extant correspondence from almost nine full months Ramseur spent as an artillery officer in the U.S. Army. The newly commissioned officer first went home from West Point. He then reported to the artillery school at Fort Monroe, Virginia, where he would receive intensive instruction and practice in the employment of field guns. Before completing the course, however, Ramseur was ordered to Washington, D.C. for duty with a battery of light artillery.[143] On March 19, 1861, two weeks after being inaugurated as president, Abraham Lincoln signed a commission promoting Ramseur to the permanent rank of second lieutenant. He would not serve in that rank.

> Washington City D.C.
> April 5th 1861
>
> Col L. Thomas[144]
> Adjutant Gen'l. U.S.A.
>
> Sir,
> I have the honor to resign my commission as Second Lieutenant of the 4th Reg't. Artillery U.S.A. To take effect immediately.
> Very respectfully
> Your obdt. Servant
>
> S. D. Ramseur
> 2nd Lt 4th Arty.[145]

142. U.S. Senate, "*Report of the Commission.*"
143. Cullum, *Biographical Register*, 2:504.
144. Brig. Gen. Lorenzo Thomas succeeded Samuel Cooper as Adjutant General of the U.S. Army.
145. NCOAH.

Head Quarters New York
April 5th 1861
Orders
No. 5

2d Lieut. Ramseur having officially notified the Col. Commanding that he had left the resignation of his Commission in the hands of a friend in Washington, & that he had telegraphed to have it placed in the hands of the Adjutant General, He is hereby relieved from duty with the troops of this Command.

By Command of Col [Harvey] Brown

Geo. L. Haitsuff
Asst. Adjt. Genl.

To
Lieut. Ramseur[146]

Adjutant General's Office,
Washington, April 8th 1861

Sir:

Your resignation has been accepted by the President of the United States, to take effect the sixth instant.

I am, sir, very respectfully,
Your obedient servant,

L. Thomas
Adjutant General

2d Lieut. Stephen D. Ramseur,
4th Artillery[147]

146. NCOAH.
147. NCOAH.

3

Confederate Artillery Officer,
1861–1862

UPON SUBMITTING HIS RESIGNATION from the U.S. Army, Ramseur headed for the capital of the nascent confederacy in Montgomery, Alabama. Before departing Lincolnton, on April 16, 1861, Ramseur applied for a commission in the new Confederate army.[1] On the way south, Ramseur stopped to see his mentor, Daniel Harvey Hill, who was concluding his tenure as superintendent at the North Carolina Military Institute in Charlotte.[2] Ramseur quickly received an appointment as first lieutenant. On the way to his posting in the Department of Mississippi, however, he was offered a more attractive opportunity. Knowing of Ramseur's departure from "the old army,"[3] Hill had telegraphed Governor Ellis to report that his protégé's foremost wish was to serve his home state. Ellis endorsed the idea, and his eponymous light artillery battery (Company A, Tenth North Carolina State Troops) immediately elected Ramseur as its captain. The governor sent a dispatch offering him the command. Within a month's time, Ramseur was promoted to the rank of major in the state militia. On May 20, he had the honor of ordering a 100-gun salute outside the capitol to signal North Carolina's secession from the Union, followed by another round to mark the state's entry into the Confederate States of America.[4]

1. Register of Letters Received, Adjutant and Inspector General's Office, March–July 1861, Chapter 1, Vol. 45, entry 187, RG 109, NARA.

2. Gallagher, *Stephen Dodson Ramseur*, 30.

3. Civil War officers on both sides used this term when referring to the antebellum army vice the two military forces in opposition after 1860.

4. Clark, "Major General Stephen Dodson Ramseur," 70.

Sadly, seven weeks later, the Ellis Light Artillery provided military escort at the governor's funeral.

The unit was equipped with two twelve-pounder howitzers, three six-pounder, bronze smoothbore guns, and a three-inch rifle provided from the former U.S. arsenal at Fayetteville. Ramseur's forte was drilling his men in serving these weapons.[5] At a private estate converted into a military camp-ground outside Raleigh, Ramseur instilled discipline and soldierly bearing in his troops. In late July, he marched them into Virginia to Southside Hampton Roads, between the North Carolina state line and the mouth of the Chesapeake Bay, where they remained until the Peninsula campaign commenced the following spring.[6]

Adjt & Insp. Genl's Office,
Montgomery, April 22/61

Special Orders
No. 32
IV. Captain *Philip Stockton*,[7] Artillery, will proceed to Memphis, Tennessee, and such other points on the Mississippi River as have been verbally communicated to him, and carry out the instructions he has received from the Sec. of War. *First* Lieut., *Stephen D. Ramseur*, Artillery,[8] will report to Captain Stockton as an Assistant on the above duty.

By Order of the Sec. of War,

S. Cooper
Adjt & Insp. Genl.

Lt. Ramseur,
Montgomery,
Alabama[9]

---

5. Gallagher, *Stephen Dodson Ramseur*, 30–31.

6. Cox, *Life and Character*, 16.

7. Phillip Stockton rose to the rank of colonel and held the positions of chief of ordnance, Army of the West, and, later, commander of the arsenals in Jackson, Mississippi, and San Antonio, Texas. Confederate Generals, Staff Officers, and Non-regimental Enlisted Men, CMSR, RG 109, NARA.

8. War Department records indicate that in a letter dated April 22, 1861, at Montgomery, Alabama, Ramseur had declined a commission as a *second* lieutenant, artillery. Register of Letters Received, Adjutant and Inspector General's Office, March–July 1861, Chapter 1, Vol. 45, entry 11-R, RG 109, NARA.

9. NCOAH.

THE STATE OF NORTH CAROLINA

To Stephen D. Ramseur

We, reposing special trust and confidence in your patriotism, valor and military skill, have appointed, and do hereby commission you a Major in the Corps of Artillery and Engineers in our State Troops to take rank from the 16th day of May 1861, and we do hereby vest you with the authority appertaining to said office to the end that you may promptly and diligently perform its duties, as prescribed by law; in the discharge of which all officers and soldiers under your command are required to yield you obedience.

In Witness Whereof, HENRY T. CLARK
Speaker of the Senate, ex officio OUR GOVERNOR, CAPTAIN-GENERAL, AND COMMANDER-IN-CHIEF, hath signed these presents, and caused our Great Seal to be fixed thereto.

Done at our City of RALEIGH, on the 26th day of August in the year of our Lord one thousand eight hundred and sixty one and in the Eighty sixth year of our Independence.

Henry T. Clark
By THE GOVERNOR:
P Cowper
Private Secretary[10]

STATE OF NORTH-CAROLINA
DEPARTMENT OF WAR AND MARINE
RALEIGH, May 27th, 1861

SIR: You are hereby informed that the Governor has nominated, and by and with the advice and consent of the Military Board has appointed you a Major in the Corps of Artillery and Engineer in the *State Troops of North-Carolina* (authorized by "An Act to raise ten thousand troops," ratified May 8th, 1861). You will immediately on the receipt hereof, please communicate through the Adjutant General's office your acceptance or non-acceptance, and in case of accepting, you will fill up and subscribe the certificate and oath herewith, giving your name in full.

10. NCOAH.

You will report in person to Col. James A. J. Bradford,[11] Col. of Artillery
& Engineers.

Very Respectfully

Warren Winslow
Sec'y

Maj. S. D. Ramseur,
Artillery & Engineers,
Raleigh N.C.[12]

Camp Fisher, Near Smithfield Va
Sep'r. 7th 1861

My Dear Brother,

Your letter has just been rec'd and read. I confess it gives me the
"Blues" to have such a gloomy account from North Carolina. "A weak,
timid governor surrounded by broken down politicians."[13] With "few arms
and ammunition scarce" surely this is discouraging. That we must all suffer, and severely, I doubt not, but should we therefore hesitate or turn
back? A noble spirit spurns difficulties. A victory without dangers is too
cheap to be glorious! I feel assured that the patriotism and gallantry of
the Old North State will now shine forth with increased brilliancy. True,
Picayune[14] has struck us a hard blow, but let him dare to land and pillage![15]
The certainty of his punishment is fixed! In fact, I think the only incon-
veniences we will suffer will be the maintenance of a large force on our
coast and the interference with our privateers. My opinion is this move
is intended as a feint to draw troops from Va. This point is very important. Gen'l. [John C.] Pemberton has a force of 2700 infantry, 300 or 400

---

11. When war erupted, Bradford was an officer in the U.S. Army in charge of the Fayetteville
Arsenal. Resigning his commission, he was appointed colonel of the Tenth North Carolina Regiment and was captured upon the fall of Fort Hatteras. He was soon exchanged and returned to duty
in the Confederate army. Incapacitated for field service, Bradford was placed in command of the
post at Goldsboro, North Carolina, where he died of illness in 1863. John W. Sanders, "Additional
Sketch Tenth Regiment (First Artillery)," in Clark, *Histories*, 1:500–501; Matthew P. Taylor, "Sixth
Battalion (Armory Guards)," in Clark, *Histories*, 4:294; Clark, *Histories*, 5:680.

12. NCOAH.

13. Ramseur is referring here to Ellis's successor as governor, the former speaker of the state
senate, Henry T. Clark.

14. Presumably, a derogatory nickname for Maj. Gen. Benjamin Franklin Butler derived from
an antebellum black performer, John Picayune Butler.

15. On August 28–29, Butler had captured two small earthen forts on the Hatteras Inlet, Hatteras and Clark, in the war's first combined military-and-naval operation. Reed, *Combined Operations*, 12.

cavalry & my battery. With this force he is expected to defend the line of the James River from the upper port of Burrell's Bay to the mouth of the Nausemond [River], a distance of 30 odd miles. Suppose [Bvt. Maj. Gen. John E.] Wool attempts a landing in force at 3 separate points simultaneously. We can't prevent it. We can only fall back & give him battle against odds in the interior which is well adapted to defensible purposes. An attack on Norfolk should be made by first driving back this left wing, and gaining possession of the Petersburg R.R. But this will require 10 000 men & until Old Wool is strongly reinforced, we will rest inactive. Expect warm work here ere long and am trying to prepare for it.

I am very sorry to hear of Sallie's depressed spirits.[16] I would like for you to continue in your office for a few months, but it may be best considering Sallie's delicate health for you to be at home, unless it were practicable to have her with you occasionally, or in Raleigh, which I fear is not practicable. I have seen Dod[17] in Richmond since I wrote you. He says that he is pretty certain, tho' not confident, that Uncle Caleb has given Aunt Fanny the right of redeeming Meadow Woods in a paper separate from his will.[18] Dod says, does this oblige him to hold the property after 2 yrs provided Aunt F does not redeem it then. He thinks it anything but equitable to oblige him to hold the property until it can be redeemed by one *individual* who may never be able to redeem it. I *told* Dod that I was willing to give $500 for the right of redemption. He will mention in his letters home, Aunt F will hear it, & will make the proposition herself, if she entertains it favourably, which I don't expect. What do you think of the propriety of holding off from purchasing a home for a year or two?

Sunday morning. I rec'd. orders yesterday to be ready to move at a moment's warning & Gen'l. [John B.] Magruder sent a dispatch to Gen'l. Pemberton saying "that the enemy at Newport's News had rec'd. strong reinforcement in men with a large quantity of flat boats & that he was evidently meditating an attack on this side of the James &c." I am ready & expect warm work before long. Dr. [Peter E.] Hines, just returned from

16. Schenck had married Ramseur's younger sister in August 1859 at Aunt Fanny's farmhouse, Meadow Woods. Sallie was now pregnant with their first child.

17. Stephen Dodson Richmond.

18. Caleb Richmond had died on June 27, 1861, and as the eldest son, Stephen Dodson Richmond was now in charge of his father's holdings. Fanny Motz was still residing in the house at Meadow Woods built by her late husband. She had stated that borrowing by the unscrupulous Elisha Barrett, based on his co-partnership in her husband's factory (with Jacob Ramseur) and her own good name (not to mention the Ramseur bankruptcy), threatened to cost her not only her home, but servants and "all that I possess." Fanny Motz to President James Buchanan, November 16, 1858, George Motz, U.S. Military Academy Application Papers, RG 94, NARA.

Richmond, gives rather a gloomy account of the health of our troops at Manassas! He says they have poor tents, scarce provisions & little winter clothing. Let our people move in the matter of winter clothing. Soldiers must be fed & clothed, even if it takes every blanket from the beds at home. But with all, there is no grumbling. Every one is brave & hopeful. Our pickets are near the enemy's lines. In fact we have driven him from Hall's Hill, *one* mile from Arlington Heights, & we are 3 miles from his left at Alexandria.[19] I expect to hear of a big fight there before long. May the Good Lord be with us and bless our cause! Unto Him be all the gratitude for our success!

Let me hear from you at length whenever you have time to write. Take good care of your health. Don't overwork yourself. Don't eat too fast. Don't be too much troubled. The Lord is your High Tower. Trust Him!

'Tis strange we do not hear from David.[20] I suppose he is busy continually. Dr. Hines saw Maj [James H.] Lane of 1st N.C. Vols. in Richmond. He said David was at Yorktown. My men need money very much. We hope to be paid this, or next, week. I have been very economical. I have on hand $75. If they pay me soon, I will receive for July & Aug't. $324, which will pay for my horses & leave me $24. So that next time I can send home a little. If you will make me a visit of a few days I will pay your expenses. Small inducement, but I hope you will accept it. What is Capt Cameron doing?[21] Where is Morrison?[22] Give my love to all at home. Do you hear anything about "Ramseur's battery"? Tell the children to study, work, read & play so that they will not feel lonesome. Love to all.

19. Ramseur gave this report based on secondhand information from over 200 miles away in Southside Virginia. Hall's Hill is four miles west of Arlington Ridge and at that time was seven miles from the port city of Alexandria. The numerical inaccuracies do not diminish, however, the fact that the Confederates had pushed inside the Federal lines onto a defensive ridge with military value that would cause it to be occupied as a Union encampment site for the remainder of the war. At this point the Rebels were only two miles from the Potomac River.

20. Dr. David Ramseur had attended the Medical College of Philadelphia, 1857–59. He was appointed assistant surgeon in the Army of the Confederate States on July 19, 1861, although he did not accept the appointment until August 13. He had served in an identical capacity in the U.S. Army since October 19, 1860. He was not formally dismissed from the latter service until August 17, 1861. Davidson College, *Semi-Centennial Catalogue*, 105; Confederate Generals, Staff Officers, and Non-regimental Enlisted Men, CMSR, RG 109, NARA; Register of Letters Received, Adjutant and Inspector General's Office, Chap. 1, Vol. 46, entry 139-R-1861, RG 109, NARA; Heitman, *Historical Register*, 1:813.

21. By this time he was Maj. John W. Cameron in the Quartermaster-General's Department of the State of North Carolina. A. Gordon, "Organization of Troops," in Clark, *Histories*, 1:23.

22. Capt. William W. Morrison worked with David Schenck in the subsistence department of the state of North Carolina at the outset of the war. The department was reorganized in September 1861. A. Gordon, "Organization of Troops," in Clark, *Histories*, 1:37.

My Dear Brother, receive my love, pure & devoted as can be on this earth. God bless you. Dod

Don't forget to have me a pair of boots made in L-n. Also another pr of shoes. I can get them sometime *this* winter. I want a thick winter article. Goodbye. S. D. R.[23]

Ramseur's own correspondence is silent about his fall from a horse in July that resulted in a broken collarbone[24] and his serious illness when first reaching Virginia. A letter of September 25, 1861, from Stephen Dodson Richmond to his sister, Nellie, documented the latter infirmity.

I am glad to tell you that Cousin Dod is much better. When I first saw him, which was last Sunday week, he was very sick & I was quite uneasy about him. I found him very much improved. He has had a slight attack of typhoid fever. I do wish you knew Mr & Mrs Whitfield,[25] at whose house he is. The latter is the best nurse I ever saw, she keeps all his medicines in her room & sends it to him at the proper time. I had nothing to do there but keep him company. They have an old Negro woman who washed his face & made up his bed every morning. She called him the *Baby*, & she certainly was as tender with him as if he had been an infant.[26]

Camp Fisher, Near Smithfield, Va.
December 14th 1861

Maj. Gen'l. S. Cooper[27]
Adj't. and Insp'r. Gen'l. C.S.A.

Sir,
A number of volunteer Officers, whose term of service will expire next May, have informed me that they can raise ten (10) Comps. of Infantry for the War, as soon as their term of volunteer service expires. They have

23. PC.
24. Gallagher, *Stephen Dodson Ramseur*, 32.
25. Robert H. Whitfield was listed as a lawyer in Smithfield, Virginia. U.S. Census Office, *Eighth Census, 1860*.
26. Stephen Dodson Richmond to Nellie Richmond, September 25, 1861, Stephen Dodson Ramseur Papers, SHC.
27. Ramseur's newness to the Confederate army is shown by his addressing Cooper as major general instead of his proper rank as a full general. At this time, Ramseur held the rank of lieutenant in the Confederate States Army, although he had been appointed a major in the North Carolina regiment.

requested me to accept a Field appointment in the regiment they propose to raise, and have requested me to inquire of you, whether it would be best for them to be Commissioned by the State of N.C. for the War, or by the Confederate States. Also, whether they (or some of them) may be allowed to leave their present duties (say about next April) for the purpose of recruiting Companies for the War. Several of the Companies are already made up and can be transferred as soon as their term of volunteer service expires.

I am, General, Your Obd't. S'vt.

S. D. Ramseur
Maj: 1st N.C. Art'y.[28]

Camp Fisher, near Smithfield Va
Jan'y. 26th 1861 [1862]

To the
Hon Sec'y. of War,

Sir,

Mrs. Harwood's petition for the discharge of her Son has been received, and in my absence misplaced or lost.

I cheerfully recommend that her Son Charles Harwood, private of Comp "A" 1st Reg't. N.C. Artillery be discharged from the service. 1st because he is perfectly worthless as an artillerist and 2nd he will no doubt prove useful to his afflicted mother.[29]

I have the honour to be, Sir,
Your Most Obedient Svt

S. D. Ramseur
Maj. 1st N.C. Art'y.
Comd'g. L't. Bat'y.

P.S. I should have stated that said private Harwood is now in the Guard House under sentence of a Court Martial. His term of imprisonment expires on the 4th of March prox. S. D. R.[30]

---

28. Letters Received by the Confederate secretary of war, 1861–65, entry 8839 (December 1861), RG 109, NARA.

29. Harwood was discharged, January 29, 1862. He reenlisted at age eighteen in May 1863 and was killed at Funkstown, Maryland, July 10 of that year. Manarin, *North Carolina Troops*, 1:45.

30. Letters Received by Confederate Adjutant General and the Confederate Quarter Master General, 1861–65, entry 141 H 1862, RG 109, NARA.

Fort Pender[31] near Smithfield Va.

March 11th 1862

My Dear Brother,

I owe you an apology for not writing sooner, but I have been in a state of such glorious excitement since Friday last, that I could not compose myself to write to any one.

Well, you have heard of the great naval fight on the 8th and 9th Insts. I will give you a hurried account of an eye witness. Our Court adjourned sine die [without fixing a day for a future meeting] on the 8th about 10 a.m. I was preparing to leave Norfolk for my Camp when I heard a shout. The "*Merrimac* is going out."

Capt. Huger[32] lent me a horse & I hurried down to Sewell's Point Battery, thinking the Enemy might attack there. Col [John R.] Chambliss, comd'g. there, gave me charge of two rifle guns (32 pdrs.). The *Merrimac* steamed boldly & quietly up to the *Cumberland*, a first Class Frigate, and with her iron prow and 10 heavy guns sank her in 27 minutes. She then turned upon the *Congress*, also 1st Class steam frigate, and poured a heavy fire into her. In the mean time the *Minnesota* (1st Class steam frigate) set out from Old Point for the scene of action, & the Battery at the Rip Raps opened on us. Now was our time. I directed the guns at the Batt'y. to fire first at the *Minnesota*, then to diminish the elevation until we got their range, then to give it to them. The men were somewhat green in the handling of the guns & were necessarily [illegible] were by the enemy's fire from the Rip Raps. The first shots passed over the *Minnesota*. She made the distance from us greater (the very thing I wanted). We fired at her five times, when she got out of range & soon after went aground. This is what I desired. Before she could be got off (48 minutes) the *Congress* surrendered; & her colours were hardly hauled down when the *Minnesota* opened on the *Merrimac* at about 1 mile's range. Whilst looking on at the fight, I heard our lookout cry out that another ship is coming. I had the men at their quarters, guns loaded, run in Battery, & ready to fire. I pursued the same policy towards this vessel as towards the 1st. She proved to be the Frigate *Roanoke*. We fired six rounds at her and my fifth shot struck her *shaft* (the vital part of her propeller) which completely disabled her.

---

31. Named for Col. William Dorsey Pender, commander of the Third North Carolina.

32. Frank Huger was then serving as aide-de-camp to his father, who was commanding the Department of Norfolk. Confederate Generals, Staff Officers, and Non-regimental Enlisted Men, CMSR, RG 109, NARA.

She made signals of distress & two tugboats carried her ingloriously back to Ft. Monroe. All this time the fight was going on furiously between the *Minnesota* with those gunboats on the one side, & the *Merrimac* with the *Raleigh*, *Beaufort*, *Yorktown* & *Jamestown* on the other. The firing at times was perfectly terrific. I wish you could have seen the little *Raleigh* & her twin sister, the *Beaufort*. Skillfully and daringly they maintained the honour of our flag against immense odds. Joe Alexander and Capt Parker have now a glorious name.[33]

I was astonished and delighted at the *dash*, daring and cool bravery they displayed. Most sincerely do I wish that [illegible] share largely the honours and prize money with the glorious old *Merrimac*. Commodore Buchanan stood on the deck of his vessel all exposed throughout the entire day. Towards its close he was shot down by a Minie ball from shore, wounded in the leg, cutting a branch of the main artery of the leg. He is doing well. Night closed the 1st day's fight. The *Cumberland* had been sunk. The *Congress* burned & the *Minnesota* badly used up. The *Roanoke* having been disabled & hauled out of the fight. Sunday morning a very heavy fog prevented the fight from being renewed until about 10 o clock a.m. Then the famous *Ericsson* Iron battery[34] entered the lists against the M. & a formidable antagonist she proved to be. The fight between these two iron monsters lasted about two hours when the *Ericsson* drew off in a damaged condition. The *M.* had broken off her prow the day before in running into the *Cumberland*, & in her attempt to run over the *Ericsson*, she was so badly injured in this part as to leak badly. So that the *E.* just hauled off in time to leave the *M.* the winner of the fight. The Yankees must have lost *at least* 500 men, 2 1st class frigates totally & one almost totally destroyed. 'Twill take at least two weeks to repair *entirely* the damages of the M. In the mean time (I have been assured), she can go out at once if necessity requires it.

---

33. Joseph W. Alexander and W. H. Parker were two naval lieutenants captaining one-gun vessels in Commodore Franklin Buchanan's squadron. Alexander commanded the *Raleigh*; Parker the *Beaufort*. Parker received the surrender of the officers of the *Congress*, and the *Beaufort* then took the wounded and prisoners to Norfolk. The *Raleigh* assisted alongside the *Congress*, suffering a disabled gun carriage in the operation. U.S. War Department, *War of the Rebellion: A Compilation of the Official Records of the Union and Confederate Armies in the War of the Rebellion*, 9:8–13. Hereafter cited as *OR*, all references are to Series I unless otherwise indicated; where applicable, a part number will be added in parentheses after a volume number.

34. John Ericsson, a Swede, invented the screw propeller and designed and built the USS *Monitor* in 1861. Boatner, *Civil War Dictionary*, 266.

For fear Father's Day book might fail to reach you, I sent you one. Also one to Miss [illegible] Alexander with a note of congratulation. With reference to Roanoke Island,[35] I am delighted to learn that the *people* (I hate the phrase!) are getting right & fastening disgrace & condemnation on the cowardly *or* ignorant officers who had the command of *brave* men. I believe in Napoleon's plan. *Hang* every officer who surrenders! We are fighting for *existence* as well as honour & right, but what were the first without the last! As to F't. Donelson, tho' "the Peop's." applaud Floyd to the skies I consider him *now* a scoundrel beyond hope of redemption! Here is an exact parallel. Suppose my batt'y. were overpowered. I must surrender or cut my way through. I say to Capt Manly[36] I won't surrender, nor will I cut my way through, but I'll shift the responsibility on you. You may do as you like. I leave the room. Say to all who will follow me, I'm going to sneak off under cover of this night. Capt M. says ditto to Lt [William J.] Saunders. Capt M. & I take off a large force, demoralize the balance & leave Lt S. alone with such a diminished force he can't escape. He can't fight his way out with his diminished force. So he surrenders. Buckner was wrong, but was not Floyd and Pillow far, far more so. I tell you had F. & P. possessed *moral* courage there would have been a different result at Donelson.[37]

My Battery is now separated, 2 guns being at Chickatuck & 4 at Fort Pender, which is near Col P's old reg't.[38] Our entire Brigade is being gradually moved towards Suffolk. Gen'l. Huger's plan is to mobilize his forces (of which he has now not more than 15 000 at the outside) near the Rail Roads, to await the developement of Gen'l. [Ambrose] Burnside's plans & then to pitch into him & press him hard & to the death. If he (Gen'l. B) gives us two weeks longer to prepare, we will whip him *certain*, notwithstanding the immense odds in his favour.

35. Roanoke Island, North Carolina, fell to Burnside's Federals on February 8, 1862, providing control of Pamlico Sound and a base for future naval operations. Ramseur's anger must have been directed at Brig. Gen. Henry A. Wise, the nominal commander who was incapacitated and did not participate in the engagement, and Col. H. M. Shaw, the acting commander of the vastly outnumbered Confederates. *OR*, 9:170–73.

36. Basil C. Manly succeeded Ramseur as battery commander, and the battery retained his name until the end of the war. John A. Ramsay, "Additional Sketch Tenth Regiment: Light Batteries A, D, F and I," in Clark, *Histories*, 1:551–53.

37. After failing miserably to follow up on their early success against the Federals at Fort Donelson, Tennessee, Generals John B. Floyd and Gideon Pillow fled in the night, leaving their subordinate, Brig. Gen. Simon Bolivar Buckner, to surrender the sizeable Confederate army.

38. Thirteenth North Carolina Infantry (originally the Third) was formed in May 1861 with Colonel Pender as its first commander. By this time, Col. Alfred M. Scales had succeeded Pender. R. S. Williams, "Thirteenth Regiment," in Clark, *Histories*, 1:653–54.

My Batt'y. is in fine condition, & if I am not deceived will do every thing that is expected of it. I have talked with the men & they are ready for the fray. I repeat what I have written before that I intend to make my motto "victory or death."[39] In fact until we come to this determination we will do *nothing*. Old Abe's policy is to "bust nobody" absurd, cowardly and contemptible. Let us show them we are terribly desperately in earnest. Let us lay waste our beautiful country & leave him a wilderness to possess. Let us hang traitors as did our forefathers & let us swing cowards [illegible] than Haman. I am rejoiced to hear you favour a *Dictator*.

The Yankees have a one man power at the helm & hence heave all together. Let us stop our miserable political squabbles & as one man put our shoulders to the wheel, pulling & pushing, working & suffering all things, until our independence is achieved, & whoever baulks or hesitates or disobeys, let him be put out of the way, speedily, surely, eternally.

With reference to my dear self, there is no chance of my getting a reg't. here. If you can have me chosen for a reg't. for the war—if the Bethel comps.[40] have not selected a Col., suggest my name & let it run. Or if you see any good chance for an Inf'y. reg't., you may put forward, in fact I desire you to put forward my name.

Nothing more of interest here. Our Brigade will bivouac for three days near here this week. Give love to all. I'll send you $100 by my 1st chance. I want you to buy plenty of flour & meat to do Father for two years. Have you heard from David, has not he some money on hand? I am anxious to finish up the last note. *Then* I'll be content. I can't come home 'till the fight is over here. Kiss Sallie & Doddie[41] for me. Love to all. [illegible] mercy keep, & bless you & all my home loves

Yr Brother, S. D. Ramseur[42]

39. Gen. George Washington's watchword for the attack on Trenton, New Jersey, Christmas Day, 1776.

40. Companies that fought on June 10, 1861, at Big Bethel Church, Virginia, the first land battle of the war. The Confederate force consisted largely of the First North Carolina Regiment commanded by Col. D. H. Hill. Edward J. Hale, "The 'Bethel' Regiment: The First North Carolina Volunteers," in Clark, *Histories*, 1:89.

41. Dodson Ramseur Schenck.

42. PC.

Camp Pender Va. Ap'l. 5th/62

My Dear Bro.

I have just rec'd. orders to report the batt'y. in full marching order, for service in the Peninsula. The news is that McClellan with over 100 000 men is advancing towards Yorktown. This is reliable, taken from dispatches captured yesterday. I am glad that I will be one of the 15 000 (*only*) who will have the honor of resisting him successfully, or of dying in the attempt.

If I should fall, tell my dear loved ones not to mourn for me, for I give them the assurance that I die willingly in the defence of our glorious South. May the Lord prepare me for a better world! I am determined never to surrender. If taken, it will be by being overpowered & disarmed. I have sold my horse & have given Mr. Whitfield $400 to send to you by the first opportunity. Hope you'll get it safely. My horses are in Raleigh. When you go there have Mark (ostler at Claytons) to give them gentle exercise every day. It will do you good to ride half hour daily. Let them remain there until you hear from me. Of course you will sell them at once if I fall. When you get to Raleigh, if I have not yet been elected Col. of Inf'y., see Barringer[43] & tell him I am entitled to Lt Col of Art'y. He & Gen'l. Martin[44] can fix it.

I read that portion of your letter concerning the probable action of the convention towards the Confed. Gov't. to Col [Alfred M.] Scales. He said tell Mr. S. for God's sake not to be the instrument of bringing more trouble, more difficulties in the way of our Confederacy. God knows there are breakers enough ahead already, without our own people bringing *more* in the way. Tell Schenck as his friend I have said this, & he will believe me. Give love to all of my dear friends. Magruder told me the other day when I was there, that he wanted to give me the post of honour, which means the post of danger. I leave to you to give my name to history, tho' it is humble.

May God bless you & all, Father, Luly, Fanny, Charles, Ada & Harvey. Bring up my dear little nephew to be a Soldier & tell him about his Uncle who loves you & Sallie & Doddie so well. God bless you. Write to me care of David at Wms.burg. God bless our cause & give us the victory. Never despair.

Your Brother in love. S. D. Ramseur[45]

---

43. Daniel M. Barringer was a former congressman (1843–49) and advisor to Governor Clark.
44. James G. Martin was Adjutant General of North Carolina State Troops.
45. PC.

To Stephen D. Ramseur

Greeting:

We, reposing special trust and confidence in your patriotism, valor and military skill, have appointed, and do hereby commission you a Colonel of the Forty-Ninth Regiment North Carolina Troops to take rank from the 12th day of April 1862, and we do hereby vest you with the authority appertaining to said office, to the end that you may promptly and diligently perform its duties, as prescribed by law; in the discharge of which all officers and soldiers under your command are required to yield you obedience.

In Witness Whereof, HENRY T. CLARK Speaker of the Senate, ex officio OUR GOVERNOR, CAPTAIN-GENERAL, AND COMMANDER-IN-CHIEF, hath signed these presents, and caused our Great Seal to be fixed thereto.

Done at our City of RALEIGH, on the 28th day of April in the year of our Lord one thousand eight hundred and sixty-two and in the Eighty-sixth year of our Independence.

Henry T. Clark
By THE GOVERNOR:
P Cowper
Private Secretary[46]

46. NCOAH.

4

Regimental Commander,
April–October 1862

IN THE SPRING OF 1862, the counties around Lincolnton raised a unit that was mustered into service as the Forty-ninth North Carolina Infantry. Its members elected Dodson Ramseur as their colonel. Over the next six months, they would fight only once under his command, at Malvern Hill. Ramseur's correspondence is silent concerning that engagement. Instead, his letters provide insight into Ramseur's thoughts about himself and his views on the war. As a new regimental commander untested in combat, Ramseur was naturally apprehensive about his first pitched battle lying ahead.

Camp 49th Reg't. N.C. Troops
Near Goldsboro N.C. May 14th 1862[1]

S. Cooper
Adj't. Gen'l. C.S.A.

Sir,

    I have appointed Mr. James W. Wilson,[2] Quarter Master of my Reg't.

---

1. On May 1, 1862, Ramseur had written to the Quartermaster General from Raleigh asking why Capt. Charles D. Hill, quartermaster of the Thirteenth North Carolina Infantry, had not reported to the Forty-ninth regiment. Only a notation of the correspondence still exists. Register of Letters Received, Quarter Master Department, March–August 1862, Chap. 5, Vol. 4, entry 62-R, RG 109, NARA.

2. Wilson hailed from Alamance County, just south of Caswell County.

Stephen Dodson Ramseur during the Civil War
(courtesy of the North Carolina State Archives, Raleigh)

(49th N.C. Troops), Mr. Ed. P. George,[3] Commissary, and Lieut. C.A. Durham,[4] Adjutant.

Please send to my address at this place commissions and bonds for the Q.M. and Commissary. Lieut. Durham was commissioned by the state of N.C. as 1st Lieut. on the 22nd day of April 1861. He was in the 12th Reg't. N.C. Vols. Lieut. Durham derives his Commission to date from the date of his first entry into service, that is, from the 22nd day of Ap'l. 1862.

I have the honour to be Gen'l.

Very Resp'y.

Your Obd't. Svt.

S. D. Ramseur
Col. 49th Reg't. N.C. Troops[5]

Near Goldsboro, May 21st 1862

My Dear Brother,

I am too weak, the Dr. says, to drill, so I'll chat awhile with you. Well, I have had a pretty severe attack of dysentery. Am nearly well now, and expect to return to duty tomorrow. I did not write home at first, because I thought I was only afflicted as Frank Huger says with the "beller ache." Under this impression I continued to perform my work until I was obliged to go to bed. I'll be more careful here after.

On the reception of your letter I wrote you & sent by hand to Charlotte. As those sort of letters are frequently lost, I will say here, as I did there, that I am perfectly willing to convey that part of our land beyond the R.R. to you. I'll enclose a note to that effect to Mr. Thompson. Col [Junius]

3. Edward P. George of Mecklenburg County had served previously as commissary with the Thirtieth North Carolina Infantry. He left uniformed service in July 1863 when appointed purchasing commissary for three counties in southeastern Virginia. Forty-ninth North Carolina Infantry, CMSR, RG 109, NARA; Adjutant and Inspector General's Office, Special Orders, July–October 1863, Chap. I, Vol. 14, Spec. Order. 173/11, July 22, 1863, RG 109, NARA; Manarin, *North Carolina Troops*, 8:416.

4. Before the war, Cicero A. Durham had been a cadet at the military institute in Charlotte headed by D. H. Hill. After serving as adjutant of the Forty-ninth North Carolina Infantry, he became its quartermaster, earning the sobriquet, "The fighting quartermaster." Durham was mortally wounded at Drewry's Bluff, Virginia, on May 13, 1864, and died the following month. Manarin, *North Carolina Troops*, 12:26; Thomas R. Roulhac, "Forty-Ninth Regiment," in Clark, *Histories*, 3:128.

5. Letters Received by Confederate Adjutant General and the Confederate Quarter Master General, 1861–65, entry 552 R 1862, RG 109, NARA.

Daniel informs me that the Pay Master here has gone to Richmond for money. When he returns, your humble Servant will call on time for $380, of which, I think I will send $300 home and wait for another month to pay my Raleigh debts, which are individual. The other you know is a family affair. The fact is I am very anxious to wind up those notes of Mr Thompson.

Your description of "New Home"[6] did much toward cheering & comforting me. In fact it brought tears of gladness & gratitude to my eyes. May a Kind Providence enable me still more opportunity to aid [illegible] dear little Darlings at home. I do assure you, the sweetest pleasure I ever enjoy is that which flows from the knowledge that my home loves are comfortable and happy and that I have been the instrument, in God's hands, to help make this so.

Tell Father my earnest wish is for him to devote all of his energy to the cultivation and improvement of "New Home." I prefer that this should monopolize all his efforts. I intend to write him a letter this eve'g., which I will enclose and want you to read, requesting him to stay away from that factory and devote all his energies to our new home. If you don't think it expedient, or if you think me too hasty in these perilous times (for I might be killed, you know, and then he would need the money he makes at the factory) don't deliver the letter which I will enclose to Father. I am anxious to have all the available produceable land put under cultivation. I tell you, food is going to be *gold*. I tell you again, that every spare dollar of Confederate money or any other paper money in your hands, you had better invest at once in hams that will keep, in wheat, flour &c. Impress this fact on Father.

And now for a chat on the war. Our prospects at Corinth are *bright*. [Maj. Gen. Henry] Halleck's Army is in a critical condition. He is afraid to advance. He dare not fall back. When [Maj. Gen. Mansfield] Lovell joins [Gen. Pierre Gustave Toutant] Beauregard, Old Borey will attack and drive the Yankees through Tennessee & Kentucky. The defeat & retreat through these countries will annihilate Halleck's Army. It will be more disastrous than was the retreat of the British from Lexington.

In Virginia, I fear the prospect is not so bright. In fact, I verily believe

6. As a result of his financial collapse, Jacob Ramseur had been forced to move his family out of their three-story brick home on Northwest Square. At first, the Ramseurs lived at Meadow Woods, home of Fanny Motz, but by this time they apparently had moved again to a place later referred to by Dodson as Oak Spring. Brown, *Our Enduring Past*, 138; David Schenck, Diary, April 12, 1859, SHC.

that unless this Gen'l. [Joseph E.] Johnston attacks McClellan in the next seven days, we will be forced to evacuate Virginia. And why? McClellan is now waiting only long enough to organize his grand attack on Richmond. Give him seven days and he will have [Maj. Gen. Irvin] McDowell to join him with 25 000 men. He (McClellan) will send 25 000 men to the South side of the James, there joined by 30 000 from Wool (at Norfolk) and 15 000 from Burnside's Army will form a column of 70 000. This column will threaten our Right flank, cut off communication South, and operate in conjunction with McClellan's main army of 140 000 (at least) or 170 000 (at most). At the same time, we will be pressed by [Maj. Gen. John C.] Fremont with 35 000 men & [Maj. Gen. Nathaniel] Banks with 40 000 men in N.W. Virginia. Suppose they unite to overwhelm [Maj. Gen. Thomas J.] Jackson with his 30 000, drive him back upon Richmond or, which I believe is *the* plan, if they hold him in check until Richmond falls, what will become of him? Now, I believe the only way to avert all these evils is for Johnston with his 80 000 to attack McClellan with his 150 000 & drive him back to Fort Monroe. This alone can save the evacuation of Virginia![7]

[illegible] my Regiment I am little encouraged. The fault lies in the Company Officers and the power to fill the lowest vacancy by election. I have a good many offrs. who ought to be dismissed for incompetency. I have *seven* that I would force to resign tomorrow did I not know that the chances are that their places will be filled by men even as incompetent.

I am astonished at the miserable foolish weakness of those military (?) men who recommended such a course to the convention of N.C.[8] However, if I could get these offrs. & men to show a little *pluck*, a slight desire to meet the foe, instead of fearful & anxious inquiries, do you think we'll go today? Where will we go? We aint ready for a fight yet. Do you think so? &c &c! I'm somewhat afraid my reputation as a Soldier will suffer if it depends on these men. However, I hope for the best, & will leave nothing undone that I can do to make them effective troops.

Write to me frequently and fully. Don't expect a letter from me often. If any thing turns up, I'll let *you* know. Col Daniel's Reg't. went to Weldon

7. In general terms, this is the military operation that unfolded in the Seven Days Battles, June 25 to July 1, 1862.

8. The North Carolina State Convention had enacted an ordinance providing "that all volunteers . . . shall be thrown into companies and proceed to elect their company commissioned officers." *Weekly Standard*, February 26, 1862.

this morn'g., a preliminary step towards Richmond, I think. I expect to follow soon. Give my love to all. Kiss Sallie and Doddie for me. May God bless you and all of my darlings at Home.

Your affte. Brother, S. D. Ramseur[9]

Petersburg Va
June 1st 1862

Dear Brother,

I have just arrived here with four of my Comp's. The remaining six will be here tonight. I am the Senior Officer present here. About 1700 troops. Gen'l. [Robert] Ransom arrives to night. I have already sent off 3 Comps. of Inf'y. & one Batt'y. to the banks of the Appomattox. A Gen'l. Engagement is going on near Richmond. A dispatch just rec'd. says the carnage dreadful on both sides, the Yankees twice ours. The Yankees were driven back some distance & at last accounts were slowly falling back fighting desperately. No more now. I'll write when I have time. I am very tired. My *Militia* give me a *heap* of work to do.

Love to all. Expect to be off to Richmond tomorrow. God bless you.

Yr Bro. S. D. R.[10]

Camp 49th Reg't. N.C. Troops
Near Petersburg Va June 5th 1862

My Dear Brother,

I arrived here with all my effective men last Sunday. The Reg't. numbered then 32 Offrs and 609 enlisted men. Since that time, five days, one hundred and nine have taken sick, or *pretend* to be sick, sufficiently well to fool the Surgeon. So that I have now but 500 Effective Strength, out of a paper strength of 900; and a real strength (last Sunday) of 609. When men get sick without exposure (for though we have been in the rain for two days) what can I expect when they are required to make forced marches, sleep on the wet ground & fight battles after all of this.

I tell you (and it is only for you, because in case of disaster I hope you will vindicate me) I do not put much confidence in my men. Now understand me, and don't think this is spoken lightly or from *timidity*. I have studied them closely and well. I have laboured hard to teach them. When

9. PC.
10. PC.

I speak of coming strife, of how I would do under certain circumstances, of what I expect them to do &c &c they look scared & anxious. When in Goldsboro I detailed 14 men for a Scouting party, and when they appeared asked each man if he was willing to go. One backed out. I sent him off with disgust & only this I believe kept the others from following like. I believe the large majority of the Reg't. instead of being anxious to hasten on to Richmond, are actually dreading any orders that will move them towards the enemy.

Not a Soul knows my fears. I am laboring hard to cultivate a proper feeling. Should my Reg't. run, God only knows what will become of me. If I should survive such a misfortune, I will publicly denounce the whole crowd as Cowards & leave the Reg't. instanter. But tho' the evidences of gallant & eager troops are not to be seen & as you have said, "our old, un-demonstrative men from the West are true as steel when aroused," I still hope for much good yet to be accomplished. I assure you I am to the ex-tent of my humble ability do[ing] my duty.

I send you my pay accounts for April and May. Do not collect them un-less something should prevent my doing so. Should I collect them I will in-form you, so that you can tear them up. I cant say how long we'll be here. Gen'l. Ransom commands; my opinion is we should have at least 100 000 troops here to resist an advance up this side of the James. The Yankees can land five times as many troops as we have here in four hours.

The bloody fights of Sat. & Sunday last[11] no doubt were greatly exagger-ated when they reached you.

The opinion of military men is that it was a gallant fight on both sides. We drove the enemy back, and after taking some plunder fell back to our original position. What then is gained. We lose brave men and our best Officers as many, if not more, than the enemy. Our country is in mourn-ing, whilst very few Northern homes mourn, because the enemy's slain are mainly foreigners. Our N.C. Troops behaved with great gallantry and are much praised.

If we are successful at Richmond the Yankees are *goners*. There is much apprehension for the safety [of] Stonewall Jackson. Rumour says he is about to be overwhelmed with troops from McDowell; Banks; Fremont; [Maj. Gen. John A.] Dix; and [Brig. Gen. Robert H.] Milroy's Commands. I do not believe the above rumour. I do believe we will hear that Washing-ton City is in our hands before one week rolls by. Beauregard has *with-*

11. The battle of Seven Pines or Fair Oaks.

drawn from *Corinth*!! Where has he gone? What do you think of Butler at New Orleans?[12] Isn't his course enough to make the blood of the meekest & most timid boil over with indignation? And Wool too, the Old Villain, *Starving* the people of Norfolk into subjection to the hateful Yankees.[13]

I have not heard a word from David. If he knew I was here I think he would write. Tell him to write to me. Give my love to all the children. May God bless you all. And may we all be ready when he calls. Remember my dear Brother, that should I fall, I do it willingly, gladly and with the hope that I may be rec'd. into the Company of the Saints On High. Therefore, my wish is that my friends should not mourn for me, but rather think of the time when we shall all meet to part no more.

Don't let this letter make you sad. I am not so. I am anxious about the behaviour of my Reg't., but not sad. I would willingly give my life to have my Reg't. behave with the same glorious gallantry as did Col. [George B.] Anderson's 4th N.C. State Troops.[14]

Every thing quiet today. Gen'l. Lee is in Command.[15] I expect the grand fight will come off soon. Gen'l. Lee says there'll be no more retreating, that the watchword of the Army must be and is "Victory or Death." May God give us the victory is my earnest prayer.

Give my love to all the Loved Ones at New Home, to Aunt Betty & all. Kiss Sallie & Doddie for me. Write soon. May God bless you all.

Your Brother S. D. Ramseur

Captain [James T.] Davis is the best Offr I've got. If I had ten Comps. like his I could whip *1500 Yanks*. He sends regards. Also *your* Adj't.

---

12. On May 15, 1862, Maj. Gen. Benjamin F. Butler, commander of U.S. forces occupying New Orleans, issued Order No. 28, declaring that any woman showing contempt to a member of the Federal army should "be treated as a woman of the town plying her avocation," due to repeated insults suffered by Union soldiers up until then. Butler's "Woman Order" was the object of criticism in the North and abroad, not just in the South, and was one of the causes of his removal from New Orleans later that year. Boatner, *Civil War Dictionary*, 945–46.

13. The Richmond press had just published Gen. James E. Wool's ultimatum to the residents of Norfolk, "Take the oath of allegiance or starve." *Richmond Enquirer*, June 4, 1862.

14. At Seven Pines, the Fourth North Carolina had fought and maneuvered through thickets and over a heavy abatis and waded through waist-deep water and across plowed fields mired in mud to capture an enemy redoubt and scatter the defenders. The regiment was on the field from early afternoon until dark, when it was described as "completely exhausted and very badly cut to pieces." Only fifty-four men answered the roll call. Col. George B. Anderson, the original commander, had been elevated to brigade command, leaving Maj. Bryan Grimes to lead the regiment. *OR*, 11(1):951, 955–56.

15. The wounding of Joseph E. Johnston at Seven Pines on May 31, 1862, led to Robert E. Lee's appointment to command the Army of Northern Virginia.

I could not find a blank pay account. So I'll just inform you that the C.G. [Confederate Government] owes me from 1st of Ap'l.[16]

Head Quarters 49th Reg't. N.C. Troops
Petersburg Va. June 6th 1862

Gen'l. S. Cooper
Adjt. Gen'l. C.S.A.

Sir,

I have the honour to request that commissions and blank bonds be sent to Mr. E. P. George, whom I have appointed Commissary. And Mr. James W. Wilson appointed, Quarter Master. These gentlemen are ready to file their bonds *now*. It may put them to considerable inconvenience to do it after awhile.

The date of Mr. E. P. George's appointment was May 1st 1862. The date of Captain Wilson's appointment was 18th of May. Both of these gentlemen have been on duty from date of appointment & their commissions. I respectfully request, may be dated from time of appointment. Mr. C. A. Durham, was appointed & has been performing the duties of Adjutant since the 15th of May. I desire that he may be commissioned as such from date of appt.

I addressed a communication concerning the commissions early in last month, having never heard from it, I presume press of business crowded it out. I most respectfully beg that these commissions be forwarded at an early day.

And I have the honour to be, Sir
Your Obd't. S'vt.

S. D. Ramseur
Col: 49th Reg't. N.C. Troops[17]

Head Quarter 49th Reg't. N.C. Troops
Petersburg Va. June 11th 1862

My Dear Brother,

I have an opportunity to send you a *letter* and some money by Mr. Ware of Cleveland. We have been over a week in a state of expectancy.

16. PC.

17. The request was approved by order of the secretary of war. Letters Received by Confederate Adjutant General and the Confederate Quarter Master General, 1861–65, entry 618 R 1862, RG 109, NARA.

Once I was ordered out at Sundown to meet the Yankees, said to be landing at City Point, 12 miles off. I formed "my Militia" in fifteen minutes. Made them a little speech, told them some of them were my neighbours & I knew what stuff they were made of. Others I did not know but they were North Carolinians & that was enough to know. I told them of Butler's order disgracing humanity & told them such were the men they were to drive back. Asked them if they would follow where I lead, if they would remain & fight while I staid with them &c, finally wound up by asking them to make as proud a record for the 49th as the Glorious Fourth (Anderson's) had now for itself.

It would have done you good to hear their cheers. They cheered for me, said they would stick to me &c, & to tell the truth I feel that *we will* make a name for ourselves that the State may yet be proud of, if one of those unaccountable panics should not strike at the dangerous moment.

Very little news here. Jackson is playing the mischief with the Yankees. It is reported that Hill's[18] & my Reg'ts. are to start to him tomorrow. I hope most sincerely this is true. I want to get under a *moving* man. I'll write you if we go.

I drew $375 pay today from Maj. [J. F.] Simmons. This brings me up to 1st of June. I send you $300 which I hope will cancel the note. I am very grateful to Him who is the Giver of All Good, that I have been enabled to send this aid to our dear Home Loves. Surely the happiest thoughts I enjoy are connected with "New Home."

I made rather a bad trade with Mr. Sanders.[19] The large horse is going blind, the small one is sick. I offered $200 & the large horse for a little gray today, but it was refused. I am very well. Got your beller ache medicine. My men are improved. Acknowledge receipt of the $300 enclosed. Love to all, kisses to Sallie, Home loves & Doddie. Hope I'll be with Old Stonewall soon. God bless & keep you.

    With love,
    Yr devoted Brother

Have you heard from David?[20]

18. Most likely, Maj. Gen. A. P. Hill.

19. Robert Sanders worked for a blacksmith in Lincolnton. U.S. Census Office, *Eighth Census, 1860.*

20. PC.

Head Quarters 49th Reg't. N.C.Troops
Petersburg Va. June 23rd/62

My Dear Brother,

I wrote you by Mr. McDonald. Mr. McAfee[21] starts to Shelby tomorrow. I therefore send you a few lines by him. I suppose you have rec'd. my *picture* & find me as good looking as ever. My Reg't. has been held in readiness for the march all day long. Our destination is not known tho' I think we will proceed to Drewry's Bluff & cross the James there & find ourselves in front of the Enemy's Left wing. I am induced to think this from the *fact* (*if it* be a fact) that Stonewall is at New Hanover Courthouse with his army. We will then deliver the grand battle in front of Richmond, Stonewall pressing with 40 000 men upon the Yankee's Right flank, whilst the balance of our forces attack along his entire front & Left.[22]

If we should be successful in this attempt, McClellan would be forced in confusion back upon the James. His means of retreat cut off, and his entire army annihilated. It will prove a desperate fight, and the victory will only be won by the most determined bravery and daring.

Should we whip McClellan, our Armies can march northward & put to confusion the fresh Yankee levies. Halleck too would be in a bad box, if, as is stated, he is en route to the East, for he would arrive just in time to be beaten *in detail*.

All of these bright prospects turn upon the defeat of McClellan *during the present week*. God grant that we may overthrow entirely our base & merciless invaders!

I understand that our Army about Richmond is in rather bad health but in most excellent spirits and feel confident of Victory.

I take with me five hundred and seventeen (517) men, *only*, fit for a fight. I had to detail forty men permanently for a battalion of Sharp Shooters for the Brigade. This Battalion is composed of four comps, of 75 enlisted men each, Cap'n. & 3 Lieuts. I have recommended and expect to secure for George Phifer[23] a Lieutenancy in this corps, which is by far the

---

21. Lee M. McAfee was a lawyer in Shelby, Cleveland County, southwest of Lincolnton, and the Forty-ninth Infantry's first major. Upon Lieutenant Colonel Eliason's resignation in June 1862, McAfee became the regiment's deputy commander. He rose to the rank of colonel, commanding Ransom's Brigade in his absence at the Crater at Petersburg in July 1864. U.S. Census Office, *Eighth Census, 1860*; Thomas R. Roulhac, "Forty-Ninth Regiment," in Clark, *Histories*, 3:127, 142, 153.

22. Ramseur's concept is generally congruous with how the Seven Days Battles evolved.

23. Ramseur's first cousin and his bugler in the Ellis Light Artillery in 1861, George Phifer was the first sergeant-major of the Forty-ninth Regiment and went on to command its Company K as a captain in July 1863. He died one year later at Petersburg. John A. Ramsay, "Additional Sketch Tenth Regiment: Light Batteries A, D, F and I," in Clark, *Histories*, 1:551; Thomas R. Roulhac, "Forty-Ninth Regiment," in Clark, *Histories*, 3:125, 128.

most desirable service. Lieut. Col. Eliason[24] has resigned, & his resignation has been forwarded to him. I regret this exceedingly, as he was my main support. However we must do our best under the circumstances.

Why don't you write me something of Aunt Fanny & how she behaves. I would much rather know the state of affairs as they really exist than to indulge in imaginary evils for which tho' I have little time, yet sometimes they *will* creep in to mar my quiet moments. How are all the Loved ones at Home? Have you read Ben Wood's speech?[25] Such sentiments will not fail to work a good result. Has Father drawn any pay from the factory lately? Tell him I request that he will draw his *wages* up to the 1st July, & lay in a good supply of bacon & flour & salt if it is to be had. Write me about the improvements &c at our New Home, "Oak Spring," as you call it. I hope fruits & flowers may abound. Tell Father to cultivate *Fruit. Good fruit.* Has Charlie improved at school. I desire him to return next session. I'll pay his tuition if I am spared. Give my love to all.

Kiss Sallie & Doddie for me. I hope my Nephew will not suffer from teething. May God keep you & yours & may he have us all finally in His Holy Kingdom. As ever most Truly & Affectionately, Your Brother,

Dod[26]

The Southern Express Company

The following Dispatch was received by Telegraph at 11 o'clock June 28 1862. Dated Richmond June 27.

Addressed to Lincolnton mailed David *Schenck*

Rumor says Col Ramseur of the Forty Ninth N.C. is killed. It is not so. He is well & all the members of his staff.

D. F. Chambers[27]

---

24. William A. Eliason was second in command of the Forty-ninth North Carolina Infantry. Thomas R. Roulhac, "Forty-Ninth Regiment," in Clark, *Histories*, 3:125, 128.

25. Wood was a "Copperhead" member of the U.S. House of Representatives and proprietor of the *New York Daily News*, charged by a federal grand jury for the "frequent practice of encouraging the rebels." Mushkat, "Ben Wood's Fort Lafayette," 162.

26. PC.

27. David F. Chambers, Company B, Third North Carolina Infantry, Stephen Dodson Ramseur Papers, SHC.

The Southern Telegraph Companies
Lincolnton
Received at Raleigh July 1862

By telegraph from Richmond; To J. A. Ramseur

Slightly wounded yesterday. Borne from field. Reg't. suffered severely. Can give no particulars. Kindly taken care of in Richmond corner 9th & Capitol Street

S. D. Ramseur[28]

Adjutant and Inspector General's Office,
Richmond, July 10, 1862.

[Extract]

SPECIAL ORDERS,

No. 159

xxx Leave of absence for sixty days for the benefit of his health is granted Col. *S. D. Ramseur* 49th Regt. North Carolina Volunteers.

By Command of the Secy of War

Jno. Withers[29]
Ast Adjt. Genl.

Col S. D. Ramseur[30]

Richmond Va
Oct 27th 62

My Dear Brother,

I arrived here safely last Friday night, after spending Sunday & Monday in Raleigh and W[ednesday] & T[hursday] in M[ilton]. All well in M. Uncle Charles[31] thinks my arm is a bad fix. He fears I will be disabled for a long time. I have been assigned to the care of Dr. [Charles B.] Gibson, the most celebrated surgeon here. He gives me *no* encouragement. He says

---

28. SHC.
29. Capt. John Withers, assistant adjutant general to Adjutant General Samuel Cooper. Krick, *Staff Officers in Gray*, 308.
30. NCOAH.
31. Charles Dodson, Ramseur's kin and a physician in Milton.

my idea of joining my reg't. is insane. He treats me pretty much as John[32] did but from the questions he asked me this morning he intends to cut my arm open. He thinks the ball carried some of my clothing into the wound & that it (the clothing) is not yet extracted & hence the nerves are slow in uniting. Enough of No. One.

I have been to several negro sale establishments. I have not yet seen a negro of the description you gave me, but I think I will purchase you a No 1 boy (to all appearances) 27 yrs old for $1250. I think this better than to give $1000 or $1100 for such as are offered here.

I am advised by competent judges to wait a few days, 1st because negro property is falling & 2nd because the Petersburg & Weldon R.R. is in danger.

Rest assured I'll do my best for you, with all the light before me.

Please inform Col Wm. Johnston[33] that I'll send a negro to him. Same for you. I did not see him when I came on.

I fear David's chances for promotion here are slim. I'm doing what I can for him. Give my love to all. Write soon.

Direct to Box 805.

Love & kisses to my Nephew. God bless you all.

Truly Yours

(Box 805) S. D. Ramseur[34]

Ramseur had been seriously wounded in the right arm at the battle of Malvern Hill on July 1. He was struck above the elbow, the ball mangling the muscles and tissues of the upper arm, rendering it useless. Ramseur was carried to the home of M. S. Valentine in Richmond where the severe pain persisted, raising concern that his arm would remain paralyzed.[35] It was a month before the invalid could travel back to North Carolina.[36]

32. In all likelihood, Ramseur's friend, Dr. John Richardson, who practiced in Lincolnton.

33. The first commissary-general of the state of North Carolina. A. Gordon, "Organization of Troops," in Clark, *Histories*, 1:37; K. P. Battle, "The University of North Carolina in the War, 1861–'65," in Clark, *Histories*, 5:649.

34. PC.

35. Harding, "Sketch," 34.

36. Writing from Richmond, Ramseur requested a furlough on July 7, 1862. Register of Letters Received, Adjutant and Inspector General's Office, Chap. I, Vol. 50, July–November 1862, entry 447, RG 109, NARA. Ramseur asked for an extension of his leave on August 24, and then applied from Lincolnton for further delay on August 31, 1862. The last request was referred to Gen. R. E. Lee. Register of Letters Received, Adjutant and Inspector General's Office, Chap. 1, Vol. 52, July 1862–July 1863, entries 915-R, 955-R, RG 109, NARA.

Assigned to Ransom's brigade in Huger's division, the Forty-ninth had not been ordered into combat until twilight. They advanced in the face of withering fire from muskets and artillery, coming within twenty yards of the enemy's guns before falling back.[37] Leading the charge, the regimental commander was hit almost immediately, but refused to leave the field of honor until his troops were forced to withdraw.[38] Ramseur's men admirably displayed the courage and discipline he had instilled in them. Their commander's success in rapidly molding an effective fighting force from a band of civilians did not pass unnoticed in the upper echelons of the Army of Northern Virginia.

37. *OR*, 11(2):795.
38. Cox, *Life and Character*, 18.

5

Brigade Commander (I),
November 1862–October 1863

·

THE WOUND SUFFERED BY Ramseur at the conclusion of the Peninsula campaign was so severe he had to be evacuated to North Carolina, where he remained for much of the remainder of 1862. Meanwhile, the Army of Northern Virginia engaged in two of its famed battles, at Second Manassas and Sharpsburg on Antietam Creek. In the latter engagement, Brig. Gen. George B. Anderson, another North Carolinian, was mortally wounded. Lee selected Ramseur as the new commander of Anderson's brigade, consisting of four North Carolina regiments: the Second, Fourth, Fourteenth, and Thirtieth infantries.[1] On November 5, orders were published promoting Ramseur to the rank of brigadier general.[2] Even though his arm had not completely healed, he joined his new command in January 1863.[3]

From that appointment until his wedding at the end of October 1863, the extant letters of the new brigade commander concentrate on love and war. Ramseur had spent part of his convalescence visiting with his cousin, Ellen Richmond, at Woodside, her father's frame house on high ground two miles outside Milton. Familial fondness in earlier years had developed into true ardor, and they agreed to marry. Consequently, his love for Nellie

1. The correspondence log reflects that D. H. Hill wrote two letters, one on August 5 and another on October 6, 1862, recommending Ramseur be promoted to brigadier general. Register of Letters Received, Adjutant and Inspector General's Office, July–November 1862, Chap. 1, Vol. 50, entry 1270-H; Chap. 1, Vol. 52, entry 1105-R, RG 109, NARA.

2. An entry on November 15, 1862, in the correspondence log indicates that Ramseur had written the War Department to request that his promotion take effect. Register of Letters Received, Adjutant and Inspector General's Office, July 1862–July 1863, Chap. 1, Vol. 52, entry 1312, RG 109, NARA.

3. One southern lady alleged that Ramseur's arm was still paralyzed the following June, causing a dinner companion to have to cut up his meal for him. Avary, *A Virginia Girl*, 237.

Ellen Richmond Ramseur ("Nellie") (photograph courtesy of the North Carolina Collection, Wilson Library, University of North Carolina at Chapel Hill)

and eager anticipation of their union in autumn were dominant in his correspondence at the outset of 1863, reflecting an unusually strong affection for his betrothed.

Conversely, as Ramseur's attention was drawn away from Lincolnton and to his fiancée and military responsibilities, David Schenck's marriage to Sallie and his relocation to Lincolnton led him to assume the duties of family caretaker. This change in Schenck's role is reflected in much of the subject matter of Ramseur's letters during 1863–64 to the confidant he addresses as "Brother."

As winter turned to spring, Ramseur's thoughts became centered on the forthcoming military campaign. Camped on the banks of the Rappahannock River outside Fredericksburg, he foresaw fighting that could well bring a successful end to the war. His stellar performance in the battle of Chancellorsville, in which he was wounded in the shin, nevertheless engaged him in a controversy that became the subject of his writing at one point. While extremely painful, the wound was not so serious as to prevent him from participating in the Gettysburg campaign, a focus of subsequent letters.

When summer drew to a close, Ramseur's mind and pen were busy with plans for the nuptials to take place as soon as fighting slowed for the winter, a time when he could put aside military duties and head for Milton and his beloved.

Confederate States of America,
WAR DEPARTMENT
Richmond, November 1st 1862.

You are hereby informed that the Department has appointed you Brigadier General

In the Provisional Army in the service of the Confederate States: to rank as such from the first day of November one thousand eight hundred and sixty two. Should the Senate, at their next session, advise and consent thereto, you will be commissioned accordingly.

Immediately on receipt hereof, please to communicate to this Department through the Adjutant and Inspector General's Office, your acceptance or non-acceptance of said appointment; and with your letter of acceptance, return to the Adjutant and Inspector General the OATH, herewith enclosed, properly filled up, SUBSCRIBED and ATTESTED, reporting at the same time your AGE, RESIDENCE when appointed and the STATE in which you were BORN.

Should you accept, you will report for duty to General R. E. Lee.

Geo. W. Randolph
SECRETARY OF WAR.

Brig. Gen'l. S. D. Ramseur
&c &c[4]

Richmond Va.
November 22d, 1862

I certify that I have carefully examined Brig. General S. D. Ramseur and find him unable to perform military duty in consequence of gun shot wound of right arm and recommend that he be granted a furlough for 60 days.

C. B. Gibson
Surgeon P.A.C.S.[5]

Lincolnton, N C
Dec 25th/62

My Own Precious Nellie,

How can I tell you what pleasure your letters have given me? Next to a visit from your own sweet self they are most welcome. And now will my Darling accept an excuse for my selfishness? I have been looking and waiting so anxiously for your sweet letters. I have been living so happily in thoughts and dreams and love of you that a whole week has rolled by leaving me still rejoicing in my happiness without having expressed to you, the source of all my joys, how infinitely much I owe to you, how inexpressibly much I love you for all this newfound happiness. I would like to tell you, my Dearest Nellie, what sweet thoughts, what pleasurable emotions, what complete happiness your love gives me! To know that you rejoice to think of me when absent, that you count the days and weeks till my return, that you love me so fondly, that you live for me, that you are mine to cheer, cherish and comfort, mine to rejoice in prosperity, to sympathise in adversity, to urge to high deeds; my own Sweetest Darling Precious Nellie:

---

4. NCOAH.

5. Provisional Army of the Confederate States (P.A.C.S.). Letters Received by Confederate Adjutant General and the Confederate Quarter Master General, 1861–65, entry 1362 R 1862, RG 109, NARA.

I say to know all this and more, renders me enthusiastically, inexpressibly happy; it makes me purer and better as well as happier.

Sometimes I think it strange that you, my Darling, my long cherished ideal of womanly perfection in the sweetness, purity and beauty of her nature, that you should love me as you do! I rejoice that it is so. You are just what I would have you be, my own beautiful Nellie, and I will try to be worthy of you. What higher incentive to deeds of daring than a sense of duty, can I have unless it be your sweet love?

I can not write news, but oh! I have so much to tell you when I see you (2nd week in Jan). I judge you by myself & *know* you want to see me.

Darling Nellie! Please write often, do not wait for my left hand to reply. Your written words go right to my heart. Lue & Fan[6] want very much to see your letters, but in vain. All send love to all, & a happy Christmas. I hope this will reach you on yr birthday[7] & whisper that I love my beautiful Nellie better than all the world beside. May our Heavenly Father bless & keep you.

with love unalterable from your Dod[8]

Written with left hand, *wounded* in right hand[9]

Lincolnton Jan 1st/63

My Darling Nellie

This bright morning I am making you a Spirit visit. I wish for you a New Year full of joy and happiness and can I not hopefully expect the accomplishment of my wish.

My Darling if my love can make you happy, let me assure you that it is a growing passion. Every day I love you more fondly and more devotedly. The sentiment fills every corner of my heart until it has become as essential to my happiness as the heart is to existence. But it is impossible for me to write as I think. My pen cant keep pace with my thoughts. So I will have to learn patience (hard lesson) until next week when I will see you and tell you *all*. You don't know how much I want to see you! How long the days are! How wearily the hours drag along when I am away from my beautiful Darling!

This is Father's Fifty fifth birth day! We will all enjoy a family dinner out here! How I will wish for you! In your last you scolded me *a little* for

---

6. Ramseur's unmarried younger sisters, Luly and Fannie.
7. Ellen Elizabeth Richmond was born on December 18, 1840.
8. SHC.
9. Inscribed in another hand on the back of this and subsequent letters.

not writing oftener! If my precious Darling knew how much I desire to write, if she could read my hourly thoughts, she would no longer complain, but she would write me long and frequently thus stimulating my thoughts, and adding to my joy. Will not my Darling Precious one keep her promise in this respect? If you knew how anxiously I look for the mail and what a welcome, deep and heartfelt, your letters receive, you would write very often.

I was again unfortunate last week in addition to my little wound. I rec'd. a severe cut on my left hand from a knife in the hand of Miss Fanny. This accounts for this more than common badly written scrawl I am almost ashamed to send you this, but I know you will excuse every thing in my letters as you kindly overlook all my other faults, knowing that I love you so truly, so tenderly, so devotedly, and that this love is making me purer and better every day. Love & a happy New Year to all. All send the same.

May our Heavenly Father bless, protect and keep us and all we love. As ever

Your own Dod[10]

Direct to Ramseur's Brigade
D. H. Hill's Division
Jackson's Corps
near Fredericksburg Va
Jan 29th 1863

My own Darling Nellie

Had I followed the promptings of my heart I would have written you a *long* letter every day since I left you; but my heart has been too full to allow expression from a left hand. Have you, my Heart's Darling, thought of me as often and as tenderly? & have you a good excuse for writing but *one* short sweet note? I am sure if you knew the delight your little note gave me you would send such more often.

My Brigade is now on picket duty on the river bank, Yankee pickets in full view on the other side. The snow is 11 or 12 inches deep, the atmosphere is quite cold. Our troops necessarily suffer a good deal from the inclement weather. My arm is doing very well. Tonight the moon is shining brightly on the white snow & nature in her purity suggests thoughts of my little Darling. Oh! my Precious Dearest Nellie! How sincerely I wish

10. SHC.

this war would come to an end so that we may enjoy the sweets of Love together! Will that not be a happy day which brings the fruition of our hopes?

I told Misses Mary Garnett & Bettie Saunders of our Engagement & asked them to wait on us both. Both said such an arrangement would be delightful. But enough of news. I am surprised that I have written so much.

And now my pulse of my heart! Dearest Darling of my soul! Believe that my thoughts are constantly on a visit to you whenever they can steal away from my Brigade, which is very often, especially in the still hours of night. Love to all. Caleb is well.[11] May Heaven bless & protect my little Darling is the constant & earnest prayer,

Of your own devoted

Dod[12]

Head Qrs Ramseur's Brigade
D. H. Hills Division
Jackson's Corps
Army near Fredericksburg
Feb. 6th 1863

How long, my heart's Darling, must I wait and hope for a messenger from you? Surely, Surely not many more weary days. Do you know how, after a long day's work, sitting dreamily by my Camp fire, my heart yearns for you? How Sweet memories of recent days spent with you are fondly cherished and oft-revived! What happy dreams and gentle anticipations, of "a good time coming" when we "twain shall be one," are repeatedly indulged! Yes My Darling, if you knew all this and a thousand times more, would you let me wait so long again for a letter. I do not write this My Own Precious One in a spirit of complaint but in order that you may have the more pleasure in writing to him, whom to make happy, you have said is your greatest pleasure.

I am necessarily very busy now and will be for some time to come. My Brigade has been so long without a Brigadier as to be partially disorganized; however, by hard work I hope to have my Command in fine fight-

---

11. Caleb Richmond had contracted typhoid fever in the summer of 1862. Ramseur's letters thereafter contain assurances to Nellie of her brother's health or, when he is sent home on invalid status, inquire about his condition.
12. SHC.

ing trim when "fighting Joe"[13] has the temerity to advance upon us. The
Yankee Army is massed in great numbers on the other side of the river.
Their pickets, silent and gloomy, walk their posts not more than 300 yds.
from our own. There has been no firing between the pickets since the
battle of Fd'sburg. where this arrangement was made. This beautiful and
fertile country is almost ruined by the two hostile armies. Broad forests
and magnificent groves are fast disappearing before the solder's axe: fields,
uncultivated, are torn and disfigured with earth works and rifle pits, while
on every eminence generally crowned with a princely mansion so recently
the home of hospitality, elegance and domestic bliss, huge batteries frown
upon the well trained lawn and artillery horses trample upon flowers &
shrubbery. But this scene must be witnessed to be appreciated.

Are you not surprised that I could have written all this & have said so
little about your Sweet Little Self? My sweet little charmer does not know
how effectally Cupid has me bound. Ah! The long weary months that
must pass away before I can meet you again! How can I endure such a
long separation! I will be cheerful my own Precious, for I am very hopeful.
May you be so too. Let us very frequently commune with each other. Your
letters will supply abundant and most welcome food for my thoughts. And
your love and sympathy will move my heart to the performance of every
duty.

May God bless my Darling. Good night with love & a kiss from yr own
Dod[14]

Army Northern Va

Feb 8th/63

My own Darling Nellie

Since I last wrote you I have again moved my Brigade after two weeks
of very severe duty. Now I am just beginning to be comfortable. Your letters, one by Capt Hunt,[15] the other of the 25th ultimo, came to cheer my
loneliness and were received and entertained with *all* the welcome of
a welcoming-well heart. I am certain some of your letters have not yet
reached their destination, for a period of *fifteen* days elapsed without a

---

13. Sobriquet for Maj. Gen. Joseph Hooker, commander of the Army of the Potomac, derived
from the tag line of Associated Press dispatches from the Seven Days Battles. Boatner, *Civil War
Dictionary*, 409.

14. SHC.

15. Leonard H. Hunt was a druggist in Caswell County before enlisting in April 1861. He had
advanced to brigade inspector on Brig. Gen. Dorsey Pender's staff. Krick, *Staff Officers in Gray*,
167.

letter from my heart's Darling. And you read part of my letters to Mom! She says write more about the war. I do not like to write about the war, for is it not this horrible war which renders this separation from my little Darling so cruel a necessity? However I never shrink from the dark realities which loom up in the hidden Future.

I do not think the War near a close, hence I did not agree to a proposition "to wait until the war is over." The Yankees wish to have forgotten the cause of our first Revolution. They have *recklessly, yea madly, invested a weak miserable creature, Abram Lincoln with dictatorial power.* His word is henceforth *Law to Yankeedom.* Every thing turns upon the chances of war. I have this consolation, three hundred thousand men go out of Abe's service next May. His new troops can not possibly be raised, organized, and efficiently instructed before July. Hence we will, in this Spring Campaign, be required to meet the old armies which we have always beaten. Some persons think the Yankees will not submit to a draft. This too I believe will be affected by the result of the coming campaign. We certainly have a Stupendous task before us! A task which will test our manhood, and if successfully accomplished, will entitle those of us who unflinchingly perform the part allotted to us, to the full title of Heroes. I have no fear as to the result! One glance at the noble men around me, who have given up home and all that is dear to them, teaches that such men prefer death to slavery. Such men, my Darling, are invincible.

Oh! May the Lord vouchsafe to us the victory! May He, who turns pride to shame, and vain glory to emptiness, who is powerful to raise up and to destroy, may Our Father's God be our Strength and Shield! Our mighty Protector and Our Deliverer.

And now My Precious Darling you must promise me not to let my views give you "the Blues." You must not allow yourself to become melancholy or despondent, for such a state of mind invariably invites sickness. Be cheerful & happy and light hearted. Rejoice, as I do, in the hope of a "good time coming."[16]

Tuesday morning
[February 10, 1863?]

My Darling Nellie,

How can I, with a left hand, tell you the thoughts and feelings and emotions which Love for you calls forth? Should I write pages long and numerous. The burden of my story would be My Precious Darling!

16. SHC.

My heart's Treasure. I love you above all. More than all. Oh! so tenderly, so truly, so dearly, so devotedly, so earnestly, so enthusiastically.

Your love makes the world appear bright & beautiful to me. I care not for its difficulties, I fear not its dangers. I will brave them all and triumph over them all with your love around me as a panoply & shield.

I think of you constantly, such sweet tender thoughts. This is my chiefest delight.

All of my friends are rejoicing with me. Write me fully, freely & often. My Precious Beloved One let your heart commune with mine, even as I would commune with you in terms which my poor unskilled left hand fails to express. I look so anxiously for a sweet messenger from you. This will be my only solace whilst absent from my heart's Darling.

And now my Darling I must close without expressing even a small fraction of the tender, all absorbing love I feel for you: but you must not judge from the expression, but from the love that is in your own heart *how* we love. Accept my love, *my* heart full as *you* know it is. May the Lord bless, protect and keep you and me until we shall be happy in loving Him together as one.

Good bye yrs. always Dod[17]

D. H. Hill's Div.
2nd Corps
Near Fredericksburg
Feb 12th/63

My Own Darling Nellie

You are so good & kind and so precious. A few days ago I rec'd. yr letter (in Caleb's). Yesterday, the one written soon after we left sweet Woodside. And today yr precious letter of the 2nd inst. came to cheer my heart.

I can not tell you with what joyous emotions I tore open the envelope & communed with you!

Oh! the inexpressible, rapturous joy of mutual love! Sweet thoughts of my little Darling are always gladly welcomed and joyously entertained whenever the care and duties of my station make room for them.

This morning is cold and rainy and I have been sitting long and silently by our bright, cheerful fire. I have been so taciturn Caleb asks "why I am blue?" with a cunning twinkle of his eye which tells that he knows I am not blue. Tho', I may be unsociable. My little Darling can guess that my thoughts have been visiting her. I have been thinking of the walk we took

17. SHC.

back across the branch. When my own beautiful Nellie so sweetly said, "Yes, my Dearest, I will love you always, your fortune shall be my fortune and your home, my home. I care not how humble, so that your great, honest heart is there to warm it." I remember how beautiful you looked then. Every feature, every changing expression of your sweet face is faithfully daguerreotyped in my heart! That hour was worth days and weeks of passionless existence. Oh! for the day when I shall again clasp my own beautiful Darling to my heart!

"When Woman's pure kiss, sweet & long,
Welcomes her Warrior home!"[18]

That day will come, my Precious! Some of would-be Prophets declare we will have an honorable and lasting peace before next winter.

So mote it be! Will you let me scold you just a little my Darling. You must not think of me as "shivering with cold & suffering all kinds of hardships." Caleb & I are comfortable (comparatively) & we want all who love us to know it. My arm is doing better than I had any right to expect. I have had very few of those severe spasmodic pains, tho' I have ridden several miles nearly every day & frequently in the snow & rain. I write home very seldom, so you must make mends for my neglect.

I expected you would scold me for telling Miss Mary Garnett our sweet secret but I am so proud—so happy whenever any body mentions you. I cant prevent showing it. Miss M. said she would love above all things to spend the spring at Woodside (so would I) & that if she could, she would.

Give my love to Mama, Sis Mary & all. May God bless you & make you happy my Darling. Yrs ever, Dod

Every [illegible] blot it's by [illegible] of my left hand. Write soon & very frequently. You can not write too much. Good night. Sweet dreams be thine Dearest.[19]

Picketing on the Banks of the Rappahanock
St. Valentines Day [1863]

Queen of my heart! Sweet Partner of my Soul!
Though vallies wide, and rivers 'twixt us roll;
No mountain high, no river's widening tide,
Can my true Spirit, from thine own, divide.
Veritas [Truth][20]

18. The American poet, Fitz-Greene Halleck, "Almwick Castle," (1827).
19. SHC.
20. SHC.

Head Qrs 4th Brigade
D. H. Hill's Div'n.
2nd Corps d'armée
Near Fredericksburg
Feb 17th 1863

My Precious Darling

Did I send you a wordy messenger, expressive of my feelings as often as my thoughts fly away to find you in your sweet home, you would be called on to read a lengthy epistle morning and evening daily. But in addition to other obstacles, the great difficulty to be overcome is this troublesome and unsatisfactory left-handed way of expressing thoughts and feelings which require rapid, enthusiastic and free expression.

Last night I gazed upon the bright stars in a clear sky, and thought how sweet it would be to have you by my side, to hold your hand in mine, and listen to you call me "Darling." This morning I look out upon hill and plain beautifully draped in Nature's pure white, and I long oh! *so* ardently, to be with my own beautiful little Nellie! Sitting by a bright fire looking out upon the fast falling snow, while the soldiers are felling mighty monarchs of the forest resounds on every side, making strange contrast with the hail pattering on my tent. I am disposed to muse, to dream and to dream Loved one of you. Thus I have been sitting, musing for an hour. I have remembered pleasures past and anticipated joys to come.

In every thought, every fond recollection, every joyous anticipation my little black-eyed Beauty is the principal figure. The chief character around which all others revolve, the precious Darling of *my* heart, without whose sweet Presence *all* would prove a bewildering blank, a dreadful desolation.

The pleasures of memory, Darling Nellie, are very sweet to me; but delight even more to dwell upon the sweet joys anticipation offers me. Sometimes I picture our future home a sweet modest little cottage where you and I as mistress and master dwell with love and happiness. Sometimes our home is a grand residence where every comfort and luxury wealth can bestow is showered upon us and where great and small delight to do us homage. Sometimes I imagine you have followed your Soldier *husband* far away from your childhood's home and on the banks of the majestic "Father of Waters" live loving and beloved. Sometimes too I imagine a gay and beautiful home in one of our eastern forts where my beautiful Nellie will be the bright star of a high-toned society and the firm advocate of all that is good and pure and beautiful. But, whatever or wherever my home, whether it be the lordly mansion rich in the profusion of worldly goods or the humble cottage where honour and truth love to dwell, whether it be a moving out among the great wilds of the Wilderness West or gay "quarters" in an eastern garrison where the "pride, pomp and circumstance of glorious war" convey a false idea of its stern reality I say, *whatever* or *whereever* my home, *there must my Darling Nellie be the Joy of my Life! reigning Queen of my heart!! My own gentle precious loving, beloved little Wife!!!*

I have just been interrupted by an order from Gen'l. "Stonewall" to move this Brigade without delay up the River. So I must bid you good bye my own precious Darling & march ahead. Love to all. I had much more to say, but orders must be obeyed. May God bless & keep you.

Devotedly Dod

Caleb is well & sends love. S. D. R.[21]

Hd Qrs of Brigade
Feb. 22nd/63

When I last wrote you my own Darling Nellie, I was seated in my little tent by a warm fire. My pleasant thoughts were suddenly interrupted by an order from Gen'l. Jackson directing me to march up the river. After a march of 7 miles thro' deep & blinding snow wading thro' deep creeks I reached Camp 9 p.m. Since then my Brigade has been constantly on picket immediately in front of the Yanks. Last night snow fell again & is still falling being now fully 15 inches deep. A large fire & heavy blankets keep us comfortable. I am writing you a "few lines" Dearest in accordance with yr request. I wish I could write you a long letter for my heart is *so* full, but I must stop. What would I not give to spend this evening with my own Dearest Nellie!

The Yanks have been dishonoring Washington's birthday by firing salutes right across the river from us. Write to me my Darling very often. Your love is my greatest joy, my chiefest delight.

Oh! for the sweet privilege of being with you once more. Give my love to all. Caleb is well.

Accept my own Beloved, my heart—full of love. (Do you know how much that is?) Write soon. Pray for me. May our Father in Heaven bless us & unite us to love & serve him. Bless your heart Darling. Good bye

Yours ever Dod[22]

21. SHC.
22. SHC.

Head Qrs 4th Brigade
D. H. Hill's Division
Near Fredericksburg
[Received Feb. 27, 1863]

Hon James Seddon
Sec'y. of War

Sir:

I have the honour to nominate Capt James Wilson (Q.M. of the 49th
N.C. Troops) as Major and Quarter Master of this Brigade, now vacant.
Should this nomination be confirmed you will please have Capt Wilson
ordered to report to me immediately.[23]

I am, Sir,
Very Respectfully
Yr Obd't. Sv't.

S. D. Ramseur
Brig. Gen'l. Comd'g. 4th Brig[24]

Hd. Qrs 4th Brigade
Near Hamilton's Crossing
Feb 28th/63

Will my little Darling be surprised to learn that I am afflicted with a
severe attack of the "Blues"? And why? I have not rec'd. a messenger from
you for *thirteen* days! I wont quarrel with you because I know you have
written and all the fault is chargeable to the mails.

But my Precious Nellie let me suggest a partial remedy for this state of
things: in order that I may receive you letters more frequently, you must
write more fully and more often.

Number your next letter 1, and every letter after that one in the natural
order. This will inform me of any that may have been lost.

We have had some terrible weather since I last wrote you. The snow
has been over twelve inches deep. Last night and today a warm spring
like rain has washed much of the snow away. And this evening the atmosphere warm and balmy. O for one hour with your sweet little self! What
happiness we would crowd in that hour! I sometimes feel little murmur-

23. Wilson was assigned to Ramseur's brigade staff on February 28, 1863.
24. James Wilson, Confederate Generals, Staff Officers, and Non-regimental Enlisted Men,
CMSR, RG 109, NARA.

ing when I think *how long* it must be before I can see my heart's Darling. I wonder if my beautiful little Nellie knows *how* truly, tenderly, warmly, all-absorbingly her Soldier Sweet heart loves her! Ah! my bright-eyed Nellie, you *do* not know how my heart clings to you! Do you?

I wish I could take a stroll about Woodside this lovely night. The stars would twinkle more brightly and Luna would shine more benignantly. All nature would add to our heart happiness!

But my Darling I must overcome these longings. Duty, stern and high, must weigh supreme. We are however encouraged to hope. Many see bright omens in the North Western sky. You know my opinions on the duration of the war. I see nothing to produce a change as yet. When Old Abe is impeached and driven out of office, or when he abdicates in favor of some other, we may have some reason to hope for a cessation of hostilities.

I rec'd. a long letter from Capt Huger today.[25] Answered immediately informing him that his services would be required on Tuesday the 1st day of Sep't. proximo as groomsman at our wedding! What does Mama say?

My Darling, you must excuse short letters &c. I write as often as I have time or opportunity. Do write often. Oh! how I long to be with you tonight!

Caleb is well & wondering why *we* dont hear from home? He is very attentive to his duties & is learning fast. He will do his part well. Love to Mama, Cousin M, Lue[26] & All. My heart is full of love for you. May God help & keep my Darling & unite us soon to love & serve Him. Ever your own devoted lover.

Dod[27]

Army Northern Va
March 2nd/63

I have been very much occupied for the past ten days; have rec'd. two precious letters from you since my last was written. How good you were my Darling! How worthy my heart's best love! Oh! my sweet one, you have my love, pure, tender and devoted. Would that I could behold "the light that is in your eye, and be with you to hear you tell the happiness that is in your heart"! How rejoiced I am to be assured "that your health is perfect"

---

25. Huger was now commanding a battery of light artillery in the Army of Northern Virginia. Confederate Generals, Staff Officers, and Non-regimental Enlisted Men, CMSR, RG 109, NARA.
26. Nellie's two sisters, Mary and Lucy Ann.
27. SHC.

that "every one speaks of *how* well you look." How much more delighted I would be to confirm their decision by secular demonstration.

You write from a sweet home, my beloved Nellie of the happy spring time, of the music of birds and the tender language of flowers! Can you estimate *what* an incentive your picture gives to an imagination already prone to anticipate the good time that is coming. A modest little cottage with you, my heart's Queen, to preside over it, will be a reward for present trials and privations which we will appreciate with hearts full of gladness and Thanksgiving.

In such a glorious cause as that for which we now struggle, and for such a home as that we hope for and desire, is it not worth our while to bear uncomplainingly willingly the cruel separation and severe hardships of the present? Yes, a thousand times, yes. Then let us be cheerful, joyous and happy, avoiding even the appearance of sadness and melancholy. Let us bear bravely the trials and danger of the present and thus prove ourselves worthy to become recipients of all the future good we hope for.

Since I wrote you last, Capt. Huger has made me a visit. We talked much of you. He told me to say to you that I once promised to say a good word in his behalf to you. That I had cheated him. And he could only forgive me on the promise from you of a large share of your friendship. I enjoyed Frank's visit mightly. Miss Cellie is to be married at Columbia on the 11th or 13th of April next.[28]

I was surprized yesterday to receive a letter from Father from Richmond. I wrote him to return by Milton and see my sweetheart. Hope he will, & that he and Mama will talk the *matter* over to suit themselves. Doct is still in R.[29] I fear hopelessly in love. I hope you will succeed in persuading Sallie to make you a visit. I fear she will give it out.

And now any beautiful Nellie I must close. I have written very little, but my heart is full. My thoughts visit you often. Not a day passes but that a visit in spirit is made to my heart's Darling. Oh! May the time soon come when I can visit you in person and call you my own Darling Nellie, my beautiful little wife. May God bless you my Sweetest Love, and may the time soon come when He will unite us, hand and heart, to love and serve Him! Ah! Nellie Dearest I do love you as few women were ever loved before. Write often! Darling of my Heart! Good bye. Ever your own Dod

28. Celestine Pinckney Huger, daughter of General and Mrs. Huger, married John Preston Jr., at Trinity Episcopal Church, Columbia, on April 29, 1863. Originally from Abingdon, Virginia, the Prestons were exceedingly wealthy. Meynard, *The Venturers*, 491–93.

29. Meaning that his brother David, the physician, was still in Richmond. David P. Ramseur, Confederate Generals, Staff Officers, and Non-regimental Enlisted Men, CMSR, RG 109, NARA.

When the campaign opens it will doubtless be an active one. The preliminaries are already on foot.

I will have but little time to write on an active campaign, so I write now to warn you & to ask you to be hopeful & cheerful as a Soldier's black-eyed love should always be. With love & a kiss my Darling goodbye.[30]

Army Northern Va.[31]
Near Fredericksburg
March 26th/63

How can I tell you my heart's Darling how much, how fondly, how devotedly I love you! Just now, I feel that I would give everything I possess to be with you my Sweetest Nellie. And can it be that I must wait until the Summer passes slowly away and our rugged work is done, before I can receive a welcome (Oh! how welcome!) embrace from my own Beloved! Away with such sad thoughts! Duty calls me away and though sometimes my heart *aches* to be with you, yet I remain here willingly in the service of our Country's glorious cause. That we will soon achieve our independence I am certain. The vandal hordes of the Northern Tyrant are struck down with terror arising from their past experience. They have learned to their sorrow that this army is made up of veterans equal to those of the "Old Guard" of Napoleon: that though clothed in rags and barefooted every man of this glorious army is a true Hero. I honestly believe Hooker is *afraid* to advance & for several days last week, the roads were in (comparably) good condition. I was ready to hear the ominous "to the front" at any moment, but lo! "Fighting Joe" allows the chance to slip, preferring to postpone the day of his defeat and humiliation. I assure you, I do not believe this Army of brave men, whose efforts have so often been blessed by our Heavenly Father, relying upon His favour, our righteous cause, brave hearts and strong right arms can ever be conquered by a vandal foe. From the west and from Charleston too, we have cheering accounts. You remember I wrote you some time ago that the duration of the war would be short or long according as we are successful or unsuccessful the com-

---

30. SHC.

31. On March 18, Ramseur had written from Fredericksburg to ask permission for Major Wilson, his quartermaster, to go to Richmond and procure clothing for his brigade. The request was approved. Register of Letters Received, Quarter Master Department, March–July 1863, Chap. 5. Vol. 7, entry 8-R, RG 109, NARA. Earlier in the winter, on January 31 and February 7, Ramseur had asked that Miller be relieved from duty with his brigade. Apparently, that request had been denied. Register of Letters Received, Adjutant and Inspector General's Office, January–March 1863, Chap. 1, Vol. 54, entries 113-R, 189-R, RG 109, NARA.

ing campaign. I fully believe this. The Yankee papers, even the most rabid, declare that we must be whipped, crushed, "pulverized" during the next three months. *If not*, "the country will hold Pres't. Lincoln & his advisers *responsible*." What does this mean? Verily "all they that take the sword shall perish with the sword."[32]

The announcement of dinner yesterday stopped my writing. I have just returned from the 14th Reg't. where I listened to a very earnest and touching sermon by Rev. Mr. Powers, Chaplin of 14th.[33] The congregation was large and attentive. As I looked upon bold faces and manly forms crowding around the preacher, I thought the scene might resemble that presented by Moses teaching the children of Israel in the Wilderness.[34]

And when these brave men, who have never quailed before the enemy, bowed down in humility before the Lord of Hosts, and brought His mercy and deliverance from a cruel foe: I felt that the Lord would hear, and that our God would set at nought the evil designs of our relentless oppressors and graciously grant us all the blessings of peace and security. Oh! May we live faithful subjects and loving obedient children of our Heavenly Father! May he repel the invader from our land and soon permit us all to return and worship Him in peace under our own vine and fig-tree! Let us pray My Darling Nellie, for this result: tho' far apart, let us invite night & morn'g. in our petitions at a throne of Grace, that the Lord will bless us, protect us and soon unite us to love and serve Him.

This is the first real Spring like day we have had up here. Yesterday we had snow & hail & then a rain to wash it away. Last night the moon emerged from the clouds and this morning we listened with comfort to a sermon in the open air. May there not be something auspicious in the beautiful weather of this day set apart by our good President?[35] Let us accept it as a good omen!

Now, my Darling Nellie, I am going to quarrel with you a *little* before I close. It is more than a week since I rec'd. your last letter. Can you not write to me oftener my Dearest Sweetest Love? Could you know the effect yr letters produce on me, my thoughts feelings and actions, I would never have to quarrel with my good, little Nellie, for neglecting to write often to me. Would I Dearest! Caleb's well & sends love to all at home. Give my

---

32. Matthew 26:52.

33. William C. Power was Methodist chaplain in the Fourteenth North Carolina Infantry, CMSR, RG 109, NARA; A. D. Betts, "The Chaplain Service," in Clark, *Histories*, 4:607.

34. On many occasions during forty years in the desert, Moses gathered the Israelites and instructed them. Exodus 16:1, and following.

35. March 27 was designated by President Davis as a day of fasting and prayer across the Confederacy. *Richmond Dispatch*, March 27, 1863.

love to Mama, Sis' Mary & all. Write to me soon & tell me what Father said to you. And now, my beautiful Nellie, goodbye, with a heart full of love I am yr/devoted Lover Dod[36]

Army Northern Va
April 5th 1863

I am very lonely this eve'g. Dearest Nellie, and must write to you, even tho' it be a short and hurried scrawl. You don't know how much I have been disappointed yesterday and today in not receiving a letter from you. Do you remember saying "that you expected to write two letters to my one. Maybe more." Has my Darling kept her promise? or do I write too frequently for you to double on my letters?

Ah! my Sweetest Darling, my beautiful Nellie. *Do* you know *how* I love you? *How* I long for you? How live for you? If I complain of y'r. not writing oftener it is because I love you *so* much! and you must excuse my selfishness on this ground.

I have just written a letter to Luly. I told her that I expected to return to N.C. early next Fall & that then *we* would desire the pleasure of her company at Woodside. Lue says every body is talking about our "rumoured engagement." I suppose the rumour has reached *one* who will not fail to use all the power of her acute intellect to throw obstacles in the way of the accomplishment of our wishes & vows. I fear that strange woman I once loved so well, will endeavour to arouse our good Grandmother's opposition, but I hope my fears are unfounded. By the way, has Grand ma yet said anything indicatory of her feelings in the matter which so much concerns us?[37]

'Tis two years ago today since I resigned my commission in the U. S A[rmy]. Two years full of great events and wonderful changes. But I will not speculate. What would I not give to be with My Heart's Darling tonight? Snow fell, to the depth of 11 inches yesterday, tonight the moon is shining brightly on nature's pure vestment. How we would enjoy the scene to witness it *together*, yet as one!

I am of the opinion that active operations will commence here in the course of the next two or three weeks if Hooker does not soon attack. I believe Gen'l. Lee will Hunt him up & call him to an account. We all feel

36. SHC.

37. As Ramseur and Nellie were first cousins, "Grand ma" was their mutual grandmother, Mary Smith Dodson.

confident of victory! And tho' I would rather the Yankees make the attack, yet I am willing to leave *all* to Gen'l. Lee.

I have purchased another horse, have named her Belle. She is a beautiful dappled grey, gay and graceful. My other horse, Duke, is greatly admired. Would that you could accompany me in some of my rides along the piket lines. Think you we would talk much of the hateful Yankees?

I must close now my Dearest Nellie. Tho' I have written little, it is more than I intended, but it is almost impossible for me to leave you. Sweetest, Dearest, beautiful Darling write *often* and fully to one who loves you more fondly, more devotedly, more enthusiastically than this poor pen can express. May Holy Angels minister unto you. Accept a heart full of love & a good night Kiss. May God bless you!

Devotedly your own Dod[38]

> Near Fredericksburg Va
> April 11th/63

My Precious Nellie

"You deprived yourself of the pleasure of writing to me for *ten* days to pay me back for my long silence." I am fully paid: the debt is cancelled.

If I have not before this written you that I would write as often as opportunity offered, I now make that statement and know that I will be fully credited. I am sure you must be aware that I can not write as often here as my heart would desire. I am suffering.

I have just returned from a very pleasant ride to Division Hd Qrs. And tho' the cause of my visit was business of great importance, I was induced to forget the war & war business and make a flying visit to the Darling of my heart. Oh! my Sweetest Nellie I do so long to see you! Do I love you too well? I think not. I love you dearly very dearly, with all the devotion of a large warm heart. You are my heart's Darling. Without you and your love this world would indeed seem a barren wilderness. All this you know and more. Your heart teaches it to you. Does it not my Darling?

Last evening I took tea at Mr. Dickensons, who has quite a pretty daughter. 'Twas a pleasing episode in this wearisome Soldier life of ours.

No news here. Have we not glad tidings from Charleston.[39] May the finale be as brilliant as the opening of the fight. Some how I have some misgivings as to the result, but I hope I am to be most agreeably surprised at our success at C'ton.

38. SHC.

39. On April 7, nine Federal ironclads under Flag Officer Samuel F. Du Pont steamed into Charleston Harbor but were repulsed by heavy fire from Confederate batteries and withdrew.

Caleb is well. Says George wrote him a very blue letter, which it is right hard for him to get over.[40]

I was surprised a few days ago by a visit from Dr. David.[41] He is looking remarkably well. Says he intends to court Bettie Lepar this time next week. If she says yes all right. If, no, he has made up his mind to take it "airy" as possible.

Excuse a short letter my love. Do write often. Give my love to Mama, Sis' Mary & all. Oh! how I want to see you. With earnest prayers for your health and happiness & with more love than I can tell, I am your own Dod[42]

Army Northern Va
April 14th 1863

My Heart's Darling,

I awoke this morning to the music of birds. The air is balmy and spring-like. The Sun is shining brightly and all nature seems rejoicing in the delightful change. My heart *yearns* for you this beautiful morning, so suitable to tender and heart-thrilling emotions. I have just returned from walk. How much I missed my *own* sweet Nellie, your heart must tell you. Sufficient to say, I rec'd. your precious letter of the 9th Inst. immediately on my return & could not resist the desire to write to you, tho' by so doing I fear I will not give you an opportunity to write two letters to one, unless you write more frequently than in times past. When you think of the hardships of Camp life, remember Dearest that my tent is *only* desolate & gloomy when a sweet messenger full of love and hope fails to come from the Darling of my heart. How differently I feel & act when my beautiful betrothed sends me frequently sent letters full of her devoted love! Say you, I am selfish. I plead guilty, but attach no criminality thereto. Deprived of all or nearly all other pleasures, is it strange that I should be selfish of the heart's best, purest, dearest pleasure? But I shall leave this to your own *heart*, trusting that you will write as often, and only as often, as your heart dictates.

Your last beautiful letter, so full of hope, has cheered me greatly. My heart reechoes the wish of yours "and we, I trust, will *soon* be permitted to live together a Christian life, loving and obedient children of our merciful

40. Caleb and Nellie's younger brother, still at home in Milton.

41. At this time, David was assigned to the Wayside Hospital in Petersburg, Virginia. David Ramseur, Confederate Generals, Staff Officers, and Non-regimental Enlisted Men, CMSR, RG 109, NARA.

42. SHC.

God." It is a sweet and precious assurance, my beloved Nellie, that night and morning you pour out your heart's pure prayers for me! Oh! May He who hears & answers prayer grant all your petitions!

So the Miltonians are "gone gossiping." I am sure they can not say aught but that is highly complimentary, and you know true compliments are pleasing. David says Bettie pays him so many comp'l. that he is continually deferring the time when she will be obliged to come square up to the mark, and say "Yes" or "No." Dr. has been to see me, and he says he is determined to be held in suspence no longer. He goes to Petersburg today for the purpose of asking Bettie to change her name. Hope he may succeed.

I take another sheet without knowing when I'll stop, or how long before I can write again. Exciting reports are coming in. This much is true. The Yanks have withdrawn their pickets in our front & heavy firing is heard on our extreme left where their largest masses are concentrated. Their balloon is up on that part of their lines. I am expecting marching orders.

You say my own beloved that I must not unnecessarily expose myself. That I wish not. My life is dearer to me *now* than ever before. For your sweet sake, My Darling Nellie, I will endeavour to perform my whole duty, fearlessly but *carefully* and *prudently*.

If I should fall, my sweetest one, remember that the Lord doeth all things well. Do not murmur but trust in Him.

Should a battle occur soon, which I think not impossible, do not believe the first reports. Should anything befall Caleb or myself, I will request Maj. Wilson (my Quarter Master) to write you all the facts. But how gloomily I am writing. I believe with you, My Loved One, that all will yet be well, that a good time is surely coming when those who have been so long absent battling for dearest rights will return to claim the respect and love of their Countrymen, when hearts and hands will be joined in holy wedlock, and when the joy and happiness of delightful Peace will abound throughout our beautiful Sunny South! Until that joyous time let us be hopeful, faithful and prayerful.

Caleb is very well. He looks better than I ever saw him before. I will take all possible care of him, tell Mama. I teaze him much about Gussie's engagement. I think he regrets it very greatly. I do not remember what I said about G's engagement, but presume I expressed astonishment & regret. Tell her for me that I wish many good things for her & him she has accepted, that I hope they may yet realize even more of happiness than they now anticipate.

Give my love to Mama, Sis Mary, George, Lou & Nat. To Grandma

Uncle C[harles] Aunt P[rissie] & the little ones. And after sending so much, the supply left for your precious little self is inexhaustible, unbounded, inexpressible.

And now My Dearest Nellie Darling of My Heart, Good bye. May God bless & protect us and soon unite us in Love to serve Him. I send you a kiss Dearest. Devotedly Dod[43]

Army N Va
Ap'l. 24th 1863

My Heart's Darling,

Two sweet letters I have rec'd. since I last wrote to you. I have been very busy recently having been appointed President of a Board for the examination of offrs. for promotion. In addition to the above, I have to perform all the duties of my office. Your letters my Darling are truly sad. My heart sympathises deeply with you. Would that I could be near you now, for I feel too deeply to trust to mere words to give expression to heart feelings. My Beloved, you must not allow such poignant grief to oppress your heart.[44]

All is well with your Dear Brother! What a crown of Glory he inherits! What a life of blessedness he leads! What unspeakable, never-ending happiness he enjoys! How sadly different had he tarried in the "vale of tears"?[45] How great would have been *his* share of the sorrow and suffering we all must bear! His fair form would have been a target for Yankee bullets. His fine constitution would have been subjected to the diseases and hardships of the camp. And his great soul would have been continually at war with Sin and Satan!

Do not longer grieve my precious Nellie: for your Brother and all your long absent loves have "gone before" to realms of bliss prepared for them and all God's people, by our own risen and ever blessed Redeemer! Let us rejoice rather and be exceeding glad that our Redeemer lives and reigns continually making intercession for us at the throne of Heaven. May the Holy Spirit descend into our hearts and may the Grace of God rest and abide with us, enabling us to look forward with a confident hope to a happy home in heaven where *all* of our loved ones will be gathered forever more!

43. SHC.
44. Refers to the death of Stephen Dodson Richmond, Nellie's older brother, of typhoid fever one year earlier in May 1862, shortly after transferring to the Forty-ninth North Carolina Regiment as its adjutant. Manarin, *North Carolina Troops*, 12:26.
45. William Shakespeare, *Othello*, 3.3.

I rec'd. a sweet letter from Fanny t'other day. She says she is growing jealous of you, that I write home less frequently than ever before. You hear the charges against us. Will you not defend me in a long letter to my little pet? In the way of news here, there is absolutely nothing. We are living in our usual monotonous way. Gen'l. Jackson's wife came up last Monday from which we infer that the Army will not move immediately.[46] The weather too is bad. Rain! Rain!! Rain!!!

I have a bunch of violets given me by a very pretty lady near my camp. How I wish you could make her a visit! Wouldn't *we* enjoy it? How are all at Woodside. I earnestly hope that Mama is quite well again. My sweetest Darling, do write me often and fully. Your letters are my most precious treasures! Oh! my beautiful Nellie! How *much* I want to see you! How devotedly I love you! How *poor* in the heart's best feelings would I be without you! Can I, must I wait five long months before I can see you & call you my own sweetest Nellie! Love to all at Woodside and in Milton. I am sorry indeed to hear of Aunt Prissie's declining health. How is "Sis Mary" & little Richmond?[47] My love to both.

When may I expect another letter. Improve the present Dearest, for when the campaign opens it will be impossible to get a regular mail. May Holy Angels watch over my Heart's Darling with tender care. Dearest: Good bye. Devotedly & forever your own Dod[48]

Army No. Va.
Ap'l. 25th/63

My Dear Bro.

I am at Division Hd Qrs today as Pres't. of a Board for the Examination of Offrs for promotion. Whilst waiting for an Offr. to appear for Ex'n. I'll write you a few lines.

I am glad to hear of the success of your cotton investment. If you take my advice, you will accept the offer of 35 cts for your stock on hand. This will almost be 100 pr ct on cost. That is enough & you would do well to close at that rate. A bird in the hand is worth two in the bush, think you not so?

46. Anna Jackson, "Stonewall's wife," had arrived by train with their newborn daughter on April 20. The timing of that birth and Jackson's death soon thereafter bore an eerie similarity to Ramseur's last days.
47. The wife and child of Rev. E. H. Harding, Nellie's sister and nephew.
48. SHC.

I was glad to have such a cheering account from home. I have thought of selling Ned. If the rascal does not come square up to the exact line of duty I think he ought to be shipped at once. At present prices he ought to bring $1500. If that sum can be had for him, I say unhesitatingly let him slide. Will you see to this, or am I troubling you too much.

There is no news here. I believe the enemy will either hold on in quiet on the other side or will change his base to the South side of the James.

I hope we will not be forced to fight him behind his breast works. At all events I do not believe we will keep still here much longer. We will either attack the enemy in his strong position, or we will drive him out by a move on Washington. I can see no end to the war. Am disappointed at the result of Gen'l. Hill's Expedition & in the same of [Maj. Gen. James] Longstreet's at Suffolk.[49]

Have not heard a word from David since he was with me. What do you hear? Love to all. Let me hear from you. Affte. Yrs S. D. R.

I want you to buy me two fine saddle horses. Get Wallace Rembrandt[50] to assist you & hire some man to bring them on to me at once. I have sold, or rather expect to sell my big bay for $900. I'll send you the money by the man who'll bring the horses. Give to David $800 in the purchase & replace it by what I send you. I want two good saddle horses, 6 or 7 yrs old, about the size of old Brimmer in his best days: to cost about $400 or 450 each delivered here.

I have bought me another horse cost in N.C. delivered $300. Delivered here $350. Am offered $500 for her. Have on hand $300. Do not know *how* to send it to you.

I want you to buy me when my money reaches you $100 or $200 of salt. This precautionary 300 000 000 lbs salt will be needed for the Con-

---

49. These engagements were part of a strategy of gathering food supplies from along the coast, while at the same time reducing the Federal presence there. D. H. Hill's expedition consisted of two distinct military operations. In mid-March, Hill attempted to capture the Federal headquarters at New Bern and failed. He tried again at the beginning of April to invest Washington, North Carolina, with strength inferior to the garrison's. When, two weeks later, Union supply ships swept past the Confederate batteries, it became obvious that Hill's blockade would fail. Longstreet's siege of Suffolk, Virginia, began on April 11 and was no more successful. On April 22, for example, he reported that his force had met with "a serious disaster" four days earlier when a Union gunboat surprised a Confederate fort on the Nansemond River, resulting in the capture of the battery and 125 men. Ramseur would have been exposed to optimistic rumors published in the Richmond press, along with hard news that Hill had withdrawn from Washington and that Union forces were receiving heavy reinforcements at Suffolk, despite Longstreet's investiture. *OR*, 18:188–89, 1014; Bridges, *Lee's Maverick General*, 173–77; *Daily Richmond Examiner*, April 17–18, 20–22, 1863.

50. Wallace M. Reinhardt, not Rembrandt, was a farmer residing on the property adjacent to that occupied by the Ramseur family. U.S. Census Office, *Eighth Census, 1860.*

federacy next winter.[51] Where will it come from. Say nothing about this. Yrs Dod[52]

A. N. Va

Ap'l 29th/63

My Dear Bro.

The enemy seem at last to be on the move. Heavy firing (Art'y. & musketry) has been heard about a mile on the left of my front for several hours. I am now "in readiness to move," & awaiting orders.

I send you letters from my Sweetheart which you must put away carefully. You shall hear further from me if nothing happens to prevent.

Please buy me two fine horses & send them on to the Army as soon as possible. I do not wish them to be larger than Old Brimmer was. Get Wallace Rinehart to help you in the purchase. Fanny wrote me somebody had a pair of boots for $25. Buy them for me. The boots Father sent me were too small. Caleb has them. Write soon. Love to all. May our Heavenly Father bless & protect us all.[53]

As Ever Yr Affte. Bro.

S. D. Ramseur

To counter the Federals crossing the Rappahannock River en masse in late April, Lee ordered Jackson to reposition his corps to the west. Jackson selected Ramseur's brigade to be in the van. Ramseur pushed his troops ahead under cover of carefully managed artillery until the gray coats were no more than a mile from Hooker's headquarters at Chancellor's House. Continuing to advance the following day, Jackson's command surprised and easily routed the Federals commanded by Ramseur's religious mentor at West Point, Maj. Gen. Oliver O. Howard. That night, Jackson was mortally wounded by fire from his own soldiers. The next morning, May 3, after the Rebel attack stalled, Ramseur offered to lead his men forward to regain the momentum. When the soldiers of another command refused to leave the protection of their breastworks, Ramseur's troops charged forward, step-

---

51. Salt was required not only for human digestion, but to keep horses and cows healthy, preserve meat and fish, and conserve animal hides until they could be tanned into leather for harnesses. Before the war, the United States annually imported 12 million bushels of salt. The adjutant general of Alabama estimated that, even on a reduced basis, the Confederacy would require 6 million bushels or 300 million pounds a year, the figure cited by Ramseur. Lonn, *Salt*, 13–18.

52. PC.

53. PC.

ping on and over the cowering Confederates, and despite absorbing a withering fire from their adversaries wrested earthworks away from the Federals. Calling for support so that he would not have to abandon his forward position, Ramseur was reinforced by several units, including the renowned Stonewall Brigade now commanded by Col. J. H. S. Funk. Although Ramseur's regiments suffered casualties at Chancellorsville amounting to more that 50 percent of their combatants, this last encounter earned Ramseur well-deserved praise from his superiors. It also touched off a controversy.

He. Qrs. Paxton's Brigade
9th May 1863

Genl. Stephen Ramseur

Dear Sir,

The report has reached me that you had remarked that Paxton's Brigade had disgraced its-self upon the field on the morning of the 3rd, refused to go forward when ordered and permitted other troops to run over them. I had hoped the brigade had sustained its reputation on that occasion. Gen'l. Rhodes [Robert E. Rodes] I understood was under the same impression but when informed of the facts has admited he was mistaken in the brigade. I also hope you are mistaken. I will briefly state the facts.

At the commencement of the engagement we were the 2nd line on the left and our right resting on the plank road. After sunrise we were ordered across the road and placed upon the extreme right, advancing over some earthen works behind which lay a brigade. We continued our advance over another line of battle, where we were warmly engaged some twenty minutes our right being infiladed, and forced to fall back some hundred yards when Genl. Paxton fell.[54] Here we reformed when Genl. Steuart [Maj. Gen. J. E. B. Stuart] ordered me to take command, and put the brigade in motion to relieve (as I understood) your brigade who were out of ammunition. I immediately advanced to the relief of the line in front, who were gallantly holding their ground with thinned ranks and empty boxes. We continued the charge up the hill driving the enemy from his fortifications in rear of the log house some half a mile west of Chanclersville.

I do not remember any troops passing over us, or they refusing to move forward when requested or commanded. Our casualties speak for us, losing more than one third of what we took in the engagement.

54. Brig. Gen. E. Frank Paxton was killed by a Minié ball while his command, more famously known as "the Stonewall Brigade," was advancing early on the morning of May 3. Robertson, *The Stonewall Brigade*, 187.

I hope from the above statement of facts, you will find you are mistaken in the brigade. Please favor me with an immediate answer.

In haste, I am sir very respectfully,

Your obt. Servt.

J. H. S. Funk Col[55]

Cmdg Paxton's Brig

P.S.

Captain [Meriwhether Lewis] Randolph of Genl. Rhodes' staff informed me that the Genl. admitted he was mistaken in the brigade as several Virginia brigades were on our left.

J. H. S. Funk

Col[56]

A wound suffered at Chancellorsville provided Ramseur a credible reason for a brief visit to Nellie just across the North Carolina border at Milton, from which this next letter was written.

Woodside Ap'l. [May] 10th/63

Dear Brother,

. No doubt you are surprised at the date of this letter. I find on arriving here that none of the dispatches I sent here have been received & conclude therefore that you have not heard one word *directly* from me since the great fight commenced.[57] I was wounded by a piece of shell, in the foot, Sunday eve'y.[58] The skin was not broken, but the contusion was severe. I have been quite lame but am walking pretty well now. I expect to start back to the Army next Thursday or Friday.

My Brigade has covered itself with glory. My loss has been *very* heavy. I was complimented on the field for the skill of my maneuvering & the gallant conduct of my troops.

On Sunday I charged over two, or large parts of two, brigades from Va. who refused to march onward & meet the leaden storm of Yankee bullets. I [ran] over these *timid* friends, over the first line of breast works, driven the Yanks out of their second & third lines, & in conjunction with some troops from [Brig. Gen. George P.] Doles' & Rodes' brigades drove the

---

55. Col. John Henry Stover Funk, commanding the Fifth Virginia Infantry.
56. NCOAH.
57. Battle of Chancellorsville.
58. May 3.

enemy from his battery of forty guns & thus secured the position of Chancellorsville to our troops.

Such is a very brief sketch. If the newspapers do not mention me (I have not paid correspondent with my brig. as many others have) the official reports will, and that with high praise. Hence, I am content to wait. Gen'ls. Stuart & Rodes made my brig a speech of thanks &c, as they came out of the fight. Truth is mighty & will prevail in spite of the papers. If you see anything about my brig in the papers, please save the extracts for me.

I am sorry I will not have time to come home. I think my foot will be well in a few days & I will then hurry back to the army. Have you bought my horses? If possible send them on at once. Love to all at home. I'll write soon again. Write as soon as you get this & direct to the Spotswood Hotel, Richmond.

With love to all, ever yr affte. Bro: S. D. R.[59]

Spotswood Hotel
May 17th 1863

My Darling Nellie,

I have just returned from church and am very lonely. Yesterday all day, and frequently today my thoughts wandered back where my heart is, with you. It has been a hard struggle for me to leave you. I sincerely hope that I may soon return again and claim you as my own beautiful Bride. Indeed I regret, deeply regret, that we were not married during this last visit. Tell Mama so, and that my earnest desire is that, as soon as I can possibly come to N.C., our union may be consummated. I may come back again unexpectedly, so My Precious Darling be prepared!

There is no news here. Send your letters to S.D.R. Maj Gen'l. Rodes Division, Army Northern Va.

I went to church this morning with Miss Bettie Saunders & tonight with Miss Mary Garnett. They are as sweet as two ripe peaches. Of course I talked a great deal about you, especially to Miss M. & invited them both to *accompany* me to *my* wedding as soon as I can get away from the Army. Both say they will certainly do so. Travelled on here with the Hon John Kerr,[60] who asked me if *we* were engaged. Told him "Yes & would be married as soon as circumstances would allow." Oh! My Sweet Little Darling how I do long for your presence!! It is *so* hard for me to part from you, you

---

59. PC.

60. Kerr would have been well known to Ramseur, not only as the father of his West Point classmate, a member of Congress, and unsuccessful Whig candidate for governor in 1852, but also because the Kerrs lived in Yanceyville, the seat of Caswell County, which includes Milton.

who are the better part of my life, my own beautiful Darling Nellie! But let us hope that the terrible war will soon be brought to a close and that we may be allowed to complete our wishes very speedily.

Caleb went over to Petersburg this morning with Miss Ella Taylor. He has not yet returned as I expected him to day so I suppose I will have to remain in this disagreeable place until Tuesday. *Gen'l. Lee* is here, so I suppose there will be nothing doing in our army for some time yet. Continue to pray for me, my Heart's Darling. I have been preserved, miraculously preserved, thus far, and I really believe it is in answer to *special* prayer. Write to me very often, fully freely and without reserve. Your letters are most precious, and are my chief delight now. Write to my little Sisters frequently. Give my love to Mama, Sis' Mary & all in Milton. May our Heavenly Father bless you and keep you & protect you and me until in His own good time, He will permit us to be united to love & serve Him. Take special care of your health for your own Devoted Dod[61]

> Hd. Qrs. Ramseur's Brigade
> Maj Gen'l. Rodes' Division
> May 22nd 1863

My Dear General

I take great pleasure in writing you of the splendid conduct of my brigade of yr old Division in the recent fight. We were advanced at a critical moment at Chancelorsville when the fortune of the day seemed to be hanging in the balance.

Yr old Division swept forward like a tornado, carrying everything before it. My Brigade had the task assigned it of carrying the enemy's formidable breastworks situated immediately in front of our embrasure battery on Chancelors hill, of forty two guns. This was done in most gallant style. Of course three lines of Yankee Inf'y. with such a support could not be run over without heavy loss. My list of casualties is a sad but eloquent tribute to the heroic devotion and unconquerable bravery of my glorious brigade. I carried into action fourteen hundred men. My loss was seven hundred and eight. Brig. Gen'l. Junius Daniel's Brigade is arriving here, one regiment pr day. Brig Gen'l. [Alfred H.] Colquitt has been sent to you in his stead. I learn that Gen'l. C. did not have more than 125 men killed & wounded and nine entire companies captured during these fights.

I have heard that your desire was to send up to this Army a full N.C. Brigade, and receive in its stead a N.C. brigade whose depleted units might

61. SHC.

be filled up from the conscripts & dodgers now in N.C. Am I correctly informed in this matter?

Is it possible for you, General, to do anything towards apprehending deserters and arresting this baneful crime in *this* Army? I have rec'd. some sixty conscripts, over thirty of whom have deserted.

We all mourn with you the loss of our great and good and invincible Jackson.

I hope, General, you are now enjoying good health, and that this blessing is extended to Mrs. Hill and yr little ones. Have you any news in yr Department? Please excuse haste &c. With sentiments of high esteem and sincere friendship

I am, General,

Truly Yours

S. D. Ramseur

Maj Gen'l. D. H. Hill
Comd'g. Dept N.C.[62]

Camp near Harrison's Xing
May 22nd/63

My Dear Brother

I rec'd your short letter at Richmond and was glad to hear from home.

After a short and glorious campaign with 53 000 men Gen'l. Lee has beaten and driven back in disgrace & with terrible losses Hooker's "finest army on this planet,"[63] which at the lowest possible estimate numbered one hundred & twenty five thousand men. These recent fights are justly regarded in properly informed circles as the most brilliant & successful of the war. Professedly knowing ones ask, "Why did we not bag the whole concern" & such like questions. Is it not enough that we drove largely more than twice our numbers from the strongest field works I have yet seen? The victory of our arms was decisive in this, that had our army been repulsed & defeated it would have been irretrievably ruined & Richmond would have fallen. Had we had [Maj. Gen. John Bell] Hood & [Maj. Gen.

---

62. D. H. Hill Papers, Accession 32032, Box 2, Library of Virginia, Richmond.

63. This characterization of the Army of the Potomac was by now well known. It had first appeared in the *New York Herald*, been published in southern newspapers, and used by Hooker soon after taking command in a meeting with a prominent Republican politician and newspaper editor from Pennsylvania. Ramseur may well have seen the moniker in *The Standard* [Raleigh], May 8, 13, 1863; *Daily Richmond Examiner*, April 22, 28, May 8, 1863. See also McClure, *Recollections of Half a Century*, 347.

George E.] Pickets Divisions of Longstreet's Corps with us (some 18 000 men) I believe we would have visited a far heavier loss on the enemy. Have you seen any mention of my brigade in the papers or have you heard anything about our conduct in the fights? I have this consolation that we are & will be most highly recommended in all the reports of my Superior Officers.

Brig. Gen'l. [Alfred] Iverson comd'g. a N.C. Brig I learned behaved badly himself, his brigade doing well. I learn that charges will be preferred against him.[64]

My friend [Brig. Gen. Dorsey] Pender acted as he always does with conspicuous & daring gallantry. Gen'l. Lee told him on the field that "he was sorry that he did not have a Division for him to command."

I was truly sorry to learn in Richmond that Bob Hoke was seriously wounded.[65] I had previously heard that he was but slightly wounded and would resume his command in a few days. Go to see him for me and congratulate him on the splendid charge I hear his brigade made.

I will send you a copy of my report, which you may read to some of my particular friends & then file it away for me. Be careful not to allow any one [to] publish it, such publications being highly unmilitary.

I was sorry I could not get home. I had 30 days, but Hood & Picket & troops from N.C. were hurrying up to Gen'l. Lee & induced me to think he meditated an advance & if so I wanted to be with my gallant brigade. Hence I am here where all is quiet.

I am glad to hear of Jack Phifers liberality to Father.[66] By the way, Charley[67] wrote to me for some money. I wish you would send him $5 for me & charge it to my account. I see that some Confederate Bonds are worth more in Richmond than others.[68] What denomination are mine? What are they worth? I can not send for my horse for some time yet. If you can buy

64. No record has survived of any such charges being brought. Ramseur's observation seems to reflect the common antipathy toward Iverson held by many officers and men in the Second Corps of the Army of Northern Virginia. See, for example, Robert K. Krick, "Three Confederate Disasters on Oak Ridge: Failures of Brigade Leadership on the First Day at Gettysburg," in Gallagher, *Three Days at Gettysburg*, 100.

65. Hoke was struck by a bullet that shattered his shoulder bone while leading a charge at Marye's Heights outside Fredericksburg during the battle of Chancellorsville. Barefoot, *General Robert F. Hoke*, 84.

66. The husband of Jacob Ramseur's sister Elizabeth, John F. Phifer, had given S. D. Ramseur's father a job when he became bankrupt and, apparently, was still helping him financially.

67. Ramseur's younger brother.

68. Ramseur may well have been reacting to the effect on Confederate bonds of the act of March 23, 1863. It was one in a succession of measures pushing back the maturity dates on the series of interest-bearing and non-interest-bearing notes issued by the Confederate treasury, thereby changing their market values. Ball, *Financial Failure and Confederate Defeat*, 140–43.

me another horse for $300 or $400 you may do it, and I will get it some time soon.

My sweet heart was prettier & prettier than ever. If I could have done so, I would have gotten married on my last trip to Milton. Give my love to all at home. Kiss Lucy & Doddie and Sallie for me. Love to all at Oak Sprg. Write soon. With much love as ever Yr Devoted Brother S. D. R.[69]

Hd Qrs Ramseur's Brigade
May 22nd 1863

Col. J. H. S. Funk

Sir.

Your letter of the 9th May was rec'd. last night. I hasten to reply.

First let me express the great satisfaction your "Statement of facts" affords me. I was slow in believing that the veterans, once commanded by our beloved and departed Hero, the Immortal Jackson, could or would ever falter in the discharge of their duty.

I will briefly state the occurrences of Sunday, May 3rd, in order that you may understand *why* I reported to Maj Gen'l. R. E. Rodes that I had passed over [Brig. Gen. John R.] Jones' Brig. and a *part* of Gen'l. Paxton's. Having been in the advance Friday and Sat'y., our Division was placed in the 3rd line on Sunday. Soon I was ordered to advance to the Support of our 2nd line. Arriving at the Enemy's first line of breast works at a dangerous crisis, I found behind this line a large body of troops, 3, 4 and sometimes 6 deep. I immediately halted my Brig. & told these troops the order was to advance, directed them to move forward, that I would support them. Not a man moved. I then enquired what troops were there. Several men answered, "I belong to the Stonewall Brig." I asked for Gen'l. Paxton whom I knew as a brave man and true. They could not tell me where he was, but stated he had moved to the Right. I then moved on to the right, asked again about 75 or 100 yds. from the men I had just questioned as above, what troops they were lying in my front. I was answered "we belong to the Stonewall Brig." I hastened on to the right, about fifty yds. farther to the right, where I found an officer in a Major's uniform. In answer to my questions he told me that he belonged to Jones' Brig, that Gen'l. Jones was not there & that Col [Thomas S.] Garnett comd'g. the Brig had been killed.[70] The troops on his right were those of Jones' Brig. These troops I

69. PC.

70. Jones had left the battlefield with an ulcerated leg, and as his replacement on the morning of May 3, Garnett was shot in the throat. Furgurson, *Chancellorsville 1863*, 227, 229.

urged to go forward. They did not move. The crisis was on us. A general advance of the whole line I knew had been ordered. Therefore I ordered my Brig forward over those of Gen'l. Jones' and over those who told me that they were of the Stonewall Brig. My officers & men have been under the impression that they ran over Paxton's or Jones' Brigades. I am happy to correct our impression which does injustice to the Brigade called after the Immortal "Stonewall," which I will do most cheerfully by having your letter published to my troops at Dress Parade.

The number of men who said they belonged to the Stonewall Brig. I do not know. I take it they were either lost from their regts., were skulkers, or were other then they represented themselves to be.

I have but to add that I have always depreciated all miserable jealousies between troops from Sister States contending for a common and glorious cause, and this matter has been spoken of by me with caution & regret. In order to explain my terrible loss (more than ½ of the force carried into action), I conceived it to be my duty to report to Maj Gen'l. Rodes that though frequently sent for after my Brig. advanced to come to my assistance and twice by myself ordered forward, the troops I had passed over refused to move the enemy from a gap on my right flank, from which position he was pouring a destructive enfilading fire into my line, and by which I lost most of my men.

I am Col. very Respectfully

S. D. Ramseur
Brig Gen'l.

P.S. I would have rec'd. your letter earlier had I not been absent on account of my wounds. I returned on the 20th Inst. S. D. R.[71]

CAMP NEAR HAMILTON'S CROSSING
May 23, 1863

SIR: In obedience to General Orders, No. —, dated May 7, 1863, I have the honor to submit the following report of the operations of my brigade in the series of skirmishes and battles opening at Massaponax Creek and ending in the splendid victory at Chancellorsville:

Wednesday a.m., April 29, the brigade was placed below Massaponax Creek, to dispute the enemy's crossing, and remained in that position occasionally annoyed by their artillery (by which I lost a few men) and kept

71. NCOAH.

on the alert by picket firing, until Thursday evening, when we were with-drawn to a point near Hamilton's Crossing.

Friday, May 1, at 3 a.m., we were aroused for the march, and led the advance of Major-General Rodes' division in the direction of Chancellors-ville. At a distance of 7 miles from Fredericksburg we were detached from our own division and ordered to report to Major-General [Richard H.] Anderson, when we advanced upon the enemy, who fell back in confusion before our sharpshooters for several miles, strewing the way with their arms and baggage, this brigade with General [Carnot] Posey on our right and General [A. Ransom] Wright on our left, for upward, perhaps, of 2 miles, being in advance.

About 6 p.m. we found the foe in force upon our front, and supported by batteries that poured grape unsparingly in the woods through which we were still advancing. Night approaching, a halt was ordered, and we slept on our arms, with a strong picket line on the outposts.

Saturday, May 2, we were relieved about sunrise, and shortly thereafter marched by a series of circuitous routes, and with surpassing strategy, to a position in the rear of the enemy, whom, at about 5 p.m. we were ordered to attack.

This brigade was directed to support Brigadier-General Colquitt, with orders to overlap his right by one regiment, and was placed accordingly. At the command, we advanced with the division, preserving a distance of about 100 yards in rear of General Colquitt. Brisk firing was soon heard upon our front and left, indicating that General Doles had encountered the foe. At this point General Colquitt moved by the right flank, sending me word by an officer of his staff that the enemy was attempting to turn his right. I immediately moved by the right flank, but heard no firing in that quarter. Again he sent his staff officer to inform me that the enemy was passing by his right flank, when I directed him to say to General Colquitt (in effect) that the firing indicated a sharp fight with General Doles, and that my impression was that his support was needed there, and that I would take care of his right flank. General Colquitt moved to the front, with the exception of one regiment, which continued to the right. I then pressed on by the right flank to meet the enemy that General Colquitt's staff officer twice reported to me to be in that direction, and prosecuted the search for half a mile, perhaps, but not a solitary Yankee was to be seen. I then came up to the division line, and moved by the left flank to the support of General Colquitt, whose men were resting in line of battle on the field General Doles had won.

Saturday night our division occupied the last line of battle within the intrenchments from which the routed corps of [Maj. Gen. Franz] Sigel had fled in terror. My brigade was placed perpendicular to the Plank road, the left resting on the road, General Doles on my right and Colonel [Edward A.] O'Neal, commanding Rodes' brigade, on my left. I placed Colonel [Francis M.] Parker, Thirtieth North Carolina, on the right of my brigade; Colonel [Risden T.] Bennett, Fourteenth North Carolina, on right center; Colonel [William R.] Cox, Second North Carolina, left center, and Colonel [Bryan] Grimes, Fourth North Carolina, on left.

Sunday, May 3, the division being, as stated, in the third line of battle, advanced about 9 o'clock to the support of the second line. After proceeding about one-fourth of a mile, I was applied to by Major [William J.] Pegram for a support to his battery, when I detached Colonel Parker, Thirtieth North Carolina, for this purpose, with orders to advance obliquely to his front and left, and rejoin me after his support should be no longer needed, or to fight his regiment as circumstances might require. I continued to advance to the first line of breastworks, from which the enemy had been driven, and behind which I found a small portion of Paxton's brigade and Jones' brigade, of [Maj. Gen. Issac R.] Trimble's division. Knowing that a general advance had been ordered, I told these troops to move forward. Not a man moved. I then reported this state of things to Major-General Stuart, who directed me to assume command of these troops and compel them to advance. This I essayed to do; and, after fruitless efforts, ascertaining that General Jones was not on the field, and that Garnett had been killed, I reported again to General Stuart, who was near, and requested permission to run over the troops in my front, which was cheerfully granted. At the command "Forward," my brigade, with a shout, cleared the breastworks, and charged the enemy. The Fourth North Carolina (Colonel Grimes) and seven companies of the Second North Carolina (Colonel Cox) drove the enemy before them until they had taken the last line of his works, which they held under a severe, direct, and enfilading fire, repulsing several assaults on this portion of our front. The Fourteenth North Carolina (Colonel Bennett) and three companies of the Second were compelled to halt some 150 or 200 yards in rear of the troops just mentioned, for the reason that the troops on my right had failed to come up, and the enemy was in heavy force on my right flank. Had Colonel Bennett advanced, the enemy could easily have turned my right. As it was, my line was subjected to a horrible enfilade fire, by which I lost severely. I saw the danger threatening my right, and sent several times to Jones' brigade to come to my assistance; and I also went back twice myself and exhorted and ordered it (officers and men) to fill up the gap (some 500 or 600 yards) on my right, but all in vain. I then reported to General Rodes that unless support was sent to drive the enemy from my right, I would have to fall back.

In the meantime Colonel Parker, of the Thirtieth, approaching my position from the battery on the right, suddenly fell upon the flank and handsomely repulsed a heavy column of the enemy who were moving to get to my rear by my right flank, some 300 or 400 of them surrendering to him as prisoners of war. The enemy still held his strong position in the ravine on my right, so that the Fourteenth and the three companies of the Second could not advance. The enemy discovered this situation of affairs, and pushed a brigade to the right and rear of Colonel Grimes, and seven companies of Colonel Cox's Second, with the intention of capturing their commands. This advance was made under a terrible direct fire of musketry and artillery. The move necessitated a retrograde movement on the part of Colonels Grimes and Cox, which was executed to order, but with the loss of some prisoners, who did not hear the command to retire. Colonel Bennett held his position until ordered to fall back, and, in common with all the others, to replenish his cartridge boxes. The enemy did not halt at this position, but retired to his battery, from which he was quickly driven, Colonel Parker, of the Thirtieth, sweeping over it with the troops on my right.

After replenishing cartridge-boxes, I received an order from Major General Rodes to throw my brigade on the left of the road, to meet an apprehended attack of the enemy in that quarter. This was done, and afterward I was moved to a position on the Plank road, which was intrenched, and which we occupied until the division was ordered back to camp near Hamilton's Crossing.

The charge of the brigade, made at a critical moment, when the enemy had broken and was hotly pressing the center of the line in our front with apparently overwhelming numbers, not only checked his advance, but threw him back in disorder, and pushed him with heavy loss from his last line of works.

Too high praise cannot be accredited to officers and men for their gallantry, fortitude, and manly courage during this brief but arduous campaign. Exposed as they had been for five days, immediately proceeding the fights on the picket line, they were, of course, somewhat wearied, but the order to move forward and confront the enemy brightened every eye and quickened every step. Under fire all through Wednesday, Wednesday night, and Thursday, without being able effectually to return this fire, they bore all bravely, and led the march toward Chancellorsville on Friday morning in splendid order. The advance of the brigade on Friday afternoon was made under the very eyes of our departed hero (Jackson), and of Maj. Gen. A. P. Hill, whose words of praise and commendation bestowed upon the field we fondly cherish. And on Sunday the magnificent charge of the brigade upon the enemy's last and most terrible stronghold was made in view of Major General Stuart and our division commander, Maj. Gen. R. E. Rodes, whose testimony that it was the most glorious charge of that most glorious day we are proud to remember and to report to our kindred and friends.

To enumerate all the officers and men who deserve special mention for their gallantry would be to return a list of all who were on the field. All met the enemy with unflinching courage; and for the privations, hardships, and splendid marches, all of which were cheerfully borne, they richly deserve the thanks of our beautiful and glorious Confederacy.

I cannot close without mentioning the conspicuous gallantry and great efficiency of my regimental commanders. Colonel Parker, of the Thirtieth, who was detached during the fight of Sunday to support a battery, and having accomplished that object moved forward on his own responsibility, and greatly contributed to wrest the enemy's stronghold at Chancellorsville from their grasp, as well as prevent their threatened demonstrations upon the right of my brigade; the gallant Grimes, of the Fourth, whose conduct on other fields gave promise of what was fully realized on this; Colonel Bennett, of the Fourteenth, conspicuous for his coolness under the hottest fire, and last, though not least, the manly and chivalrous Cox, of the Second, the accomplished gentleman, splendid soldier, and warm friend, who, though wounded five times, remained with his regiment until exhausted. In common with the entire command, I regret his temporary absence from the field, where he loved to be.

Major [Daniel W.] Hurtt, Second North Carolina State troops, commanded the skirmishers faithfully and well.

To the field and company officers, one and all, my thanks are due for the zeal and bravery displayed under the most trying circumstances.

To the gentlemen of my staff, I owe especial thanks for services rendered on the march and upon the field. Capt. Seaton Gales, assistant adjutant general, and Lieutenant Richmond, aide-de-camp, were with me all the time, promptly carrying orders under the very hottest fire. I take pleasure, too, in speaking of the bearing of Private James Stinson, courier, a youth of twenty, who displayed qualities a veteran might boast of, and of the conduct of Private J. F. Beggarly, also a courier to headquarters.

To Dr. [George W.] Briggs, senior surgeon of the brigade, my thanks are due for his skill, zeal, and care of the wounded.

I am, sir, very respectfully, your obedient servant,

STEPHEN D. RAMSEUR
Brigadier-General, Commanding

Maj. G. Peyton,[72]
Assistant Adjutant-General[73]

Ramseur's actions on May 3 and shortly thereafter illustrate both bravery and his strong sense of duty. The conduct that generated controversy was not a spontaneous act. Ramseur recognized the need to attack when ordered to do so. He repeatedly implored troops occupying the trenches immediately in front of him to advance. Receiving no response, he sought guidance from higher authority more than once. When approval came, his decision to climb on and over these gray coats to lead his men in a charge, demonstrated a commitment to risk his own life to win the battle. Twice Ramseur returned from an advanced position to ask for support. Throughout this engagement, he was constitutionally unable to stand by idly while other Confederate soldiers shirked their duty.

Ramseur included this episode in his official report, citing the dodgers as members of units in the vaunted Stonewall Brigade. To his knowledge, that was who they were, and despite his adoration for the venerated Jackson, he believed it his duty to identify the shirkers to his superior. Word of Ramseur's criticism provoked a complaint from Col. Funk, the 5th Virginia commander, on May 20. Ramseur politely answered it on May 22 and, the following day, submitted his report. Two decades later, William Terry, who commanded the 4th Virginia that day as a major, wrote that he had spoken with the North Carolinian about the misidentification on the eve of the Wilderness campaign and again the evening before Ramseur perished at Cedar Creek. On both occasions, Ramseur was said to have admitted the mistake which he agreed to correct, but never did.[74] His belief was unshakeable, regardless of who might be hurt or what pressures were brought to bear on him.

72. Moses Green Peyton, assistant adjutant general to Rodes.
73. *OR*, 25(1):994–98.
74. Terry, "The 'Stonewall Brigade' at Chancellorsville," 364–70.

Head Qrs 4th Brigade
R. E. Rodes' Div'n.
May 25th/63

My Precious Nellie

Your sweet letter accompanying letters sent me by Maj. Wilson was rec'd. a few days ago. How glad I was to get it my little Darling! You must imagine 'twas the first messenger to visit me since I left you sadly. Does my Heart's Darling know what a struggle was going on in my bosom between inclination and duty? Ah! 'twas a hard, hard necessity compelled me to give you up, even though it should be for a very short time.

I have been hard at work with my gallant little brigade ever since my return. The brigade has been very much united recently on the score of a return to N.C. Rumours of that kind being abundant in camp.[75] My own opinion is that we will not be sent to N.C. In fact, I think I can safely say there is no chance for such a move. Should we move however, I shall take the earliest opportunity to ask the fulfilment of promises my Darling has made me. Then the question rests just so, to remain in Virginia and do my duty with this glorious army, or to go to N.C. get married and fight the Yankees to boot. Will you be ready?

Brig. Gen'l. Daniel's Brigade has arrived here. I went over to Col Moorhead's[76] camp this evening. Saw Capt Smith[77] who was well, and found that Mr. Harding[78] had gotten provision from Col M. to come on by the train. He stopped I learned at Hanover Junction to see Dr. Wilson[79] and is expected here tomorrow and will be camped within one mile of my Hd Qrs. Daniel's Brig. having been assigned to our Division. This will be very pleasant for us.

And now my Precious Darling, after writing so much news I must try to express (I know it will be *faintly*) how much, how devotedly I love you.

---

75. Ramseur's old mentor, Maj. Gen. D. H. Hill, now commander of the Department of North Carolina, had requested the transfer of Ramseur's brigade in exchange for a comparable command at greater strength. Recognizing the exceptional asset represented by Ramseur's leadership of seasoned veterans, Gen. R. E. Lee declined the proposition. OR, 25(2):835, 852–53; 51(2):720.

76. Col. John H. Morehead of Guilford County, commanding the Forty-fifth North Carolina.

77. Thomas M. Smith of Caswell County was commander of Company I, Forty-fifth North Carolina Infantry. Cyrus B. Watson, "Forty-Fifth Regiment," in Clark, *Histories*, 3:36.

78. A Presbyterian clergyman, Ephraim H. Harding of Caswell County had been assigned as chaplain of the Forty-fifth North Carolina Regiment in Daniels's brigade. Harding would become one of Ramseur's closest confidants, as well as a courier for mail between Ramseur and Nellie; and, after Ramseur's death, Harding would become his biographer and the author of warm remembrances of their friendship. Harding, "Sketch."

79. May well have been Dr. William R. Wilson of Granville County, the Twenty-fourth North Carolina Infantry. W. N. Rose, "24th North Carolina Regiment," in Clark, *Histories*, 2:269; P. E. Hines, "The Medical Corps," in Clark, *Histories*, 4:635.

My thoughts make you flying visits whenever I can escape from my Army work. I have left my *whole heart* with you. You are dearer to me than all the world beside. For you, I love to overcome difficulties and count dangers but trifles. For you I would acquire fame and wealth. For your sake I would become good and great; and to be with you, to call you my own beloved Nellie is the greatest happiness I desire. Oh! that this war would soon be stopped by our Heavenly Father so that loving hearts might be united. My Sweetest Darling, I cant tell you my love. You must *feel* it.

Dr. Wm. Hoge[80] is preaching for our Div'n. I have heard two excellent sermons from him. Continue to pray for me my sweetest Nellie. Your prayers for my safety have been answered. Pray also that I may have full abundant convincing assurance that I am in deed and in truth a child of God. Write to me very often. Love to all. May our Heavenly Father bless & keep us to love & serve Him through a long life of usefulness. Devotedly your own Dod[81]

Hd Qrs. Rodes' Division
May 27, 1863

Respectfully forwarded. I approve the application warmly. Am extremely anxious to have Gen. Ramseur's Brigade made as strong as possible, and to have his regiments increased as much as possible. The Regimental and Brigade Commanders are each among the most efficient officers of their grades and hence the more men they have the better for the service within certain limits. Gen. Ramseur's application refers especially to full Regiments now in N.C. . . . If no other arrangement can be made I would be willing, nay, under a sense of duty, would recommend, that Ramseur's and Johnston's Brigade, should be consolidated and placed under the command of Gen. Ramseur as the more efficient commander of the two.[82]

---

80. Brother of the more famous Moses Hoge, William J. Hoge moved from a temporary position in Charlottesville to a permanent calling in Petersburg in 1863. He died from typhoid fever the following year, contracted in Petersburg's hospitals and camps, where he ministered. *National Cyclopedia of American Biography*, 10:465.

81. SHC.

82. Col. Robert D. Johnston took charge of the Twelfth North Carolina Infantry when its commander was killed on May 2. The Twenty-third North Carolina to which Johnston was assigned was shattered at Chancellorsville, losing 50 percent of its strength. Rodes may have intended to refer to Johnston's regiment, not a brigade. Or perhaps he was thinking of Iverson's brigade, poorly led by an officer disliked by many, including Johnston's regiment. This reorganization subsequently occurred after Gettysburg. *OR*, 25(1):947; V. E. Turner and H. C. Wall, "Twenty-third Regiment," in Clark, *Histories*, 2:230–31.

Gen. Ramseur's command, and that of each of his Colonels, all of whom are superior offrs. ought to be increased at all risks short of damaging the efficency of the Army.

Respectfully,

R. E. Rodes,
Maj. Gen'l.[83]

Head Quarter's Ramseur's Brigade
May 29th 1863

My Dear Brother,

I send you a copy of my official report of the battles at and near, Chancelorsville, also, a copy of an application for more troops with the official endorsement of Gen'l. Rodes. Therefore you will perceive from this latter paper that Gen'l. R. has such confidence in me as even to recommend the increase of my Brig. by taking that of another Brigadier from him. I wish you to preserve these papers for me.

Gen'l. Rodes came to see me a few days ago. He told me that L't. Gen'l. A. P. Hill, *that* morning told him that he was present Saturday Evening and heard a Staff Officer of Gen'l. Jackson say to Gen'l. Lee, "Gen'l. Jackson sends his compliments and wishes that Gen'l. Rodes and Gen'l. Ramseur may be promoted on the field."

It is very gratifying to me to know that my conduct in my first field fight as Brigadier has received the approval & commendation of all our noble and illustrious leaders.

Our victory at Chancelorsville is rightly considered by all military men as the greatest and most wonderful of the war. Hookers plans were admirably and skillfully conceived, but the attempt at execution was a miserable failure.

The news from Vicksburg is very, very discouraging.[84] The Yankee Pickets have been calling out to ours, "Vicksburg has fallen. We've taken Vicksburg with 57 pieces of art'y. and 40 000 prisoners" &c &c. I don't believe these stories. Yet I cant help but feel anxious about our affairs in the West. Should Vicksburg fall the Northern peace party will be crushed out

---

83. From the copy of an endorsement to a request by Ramseur to increase the strength of his brigade. David P. Ramseur to R. E. Lee, February 22, 1866, Lee Headquarters Papers, MSS3 L 515, 592–94, Virginia Historical Society, Richmond.

84. Ramseur may well have been referring to Brig. Gen. Ulysses S. Grant's second assault on Vicksburg one week earlier (May 22), which was characterized by the Richmond papers as a Union victory when, in fact, the Federals had been repulsed. Ballard, *Vicksburg*, 350.

and the war greatly prolonged. We must trust more implicitly in Almighty God. We are weak and powerless without the aid of his Strong Arm. Oh! May the Lord bless our arms and enable us to drive back forever our cruel and powerful enemies.

I was, and am, sorry, I did not go home. Every thing indicated a move of this Army and I desired to be with my gallant little band; hence I hurried back, but found every thing quiet up here.

If you can get any reliable person to bring my horse on to me, send him at once. I would like for you to send me two horses. I need two, & it will be cheaper & better to send him at once. Dont buy the 2nd horse younger than 6 years. He need not be a fine horse, so he is tough and serviceable. Write to me soon. Give me a long letter on crops, family affairs, money matters &c. Have you sold your yarn?

Gen'l. Lee reviews our Division today. So I must be up & doing in preparation.

Love to all. I hope you can find an opportunity to spend a week or two in Milton. Write very soon. Love to the children at Oak Spring and to Father. Write soon. May our Heavenly Father bless and keep us and all those we love, and may He hasten the time when we may all be united to love and serve Him in peace and quiet.

Yr devoted Brother

S. D. Ramseur[85]

Head Qr's Ramseur's Brig.
May 29th 1863

How can I tell my Heart's Darling the rich, bounding, overflowing love which filled my heart as it always does whilst I read your last beautiful, tender precious letter! 'Tis indeed sweet to be loved by such a pure, lovely, beautiful, devoted little Darling as my own precious Nellie. 'Tis my delight to think of your love and the precious moments we have so recently enjoyed together. 'Tis pleasure, deep and heartfelt, to look forward to the speedy coming of that "good time," when we will join "hands and hearts," and Oh! My Beloved! 'tis my greatest consolation, my best comfort, my strongest encouragement, my joy and my hope to know that "morning and evening your heart is poured out at a Throne of Grace in my behalf!" Sweetest Nellie! Your love and your prayers are of infinite value to me.

85. Simon Gratz Collection, Case 5, Box 16, Historical Society of Pennsylvania, Philadelphia.

May the time soon come when we may be united in love and together may we unite in prayer and thanksgiving to the God of Love and Mercy.

And you want to hear what the Army of N. Va. is doing. Today Gen'l. Lee reviewed our Div'n. We made a splendid appearance, but 'twas very bad to see the thinned ranks of our veterans. So many now are in the cold grave. So many are languishing upon beds of pain. We are awaiting "Fighting Joe's" movement and are engaged in watching him closely. Yesterday heavy clouds of dust indicated that the Yankees were moving towards Acquia [Aquia] Creek. It may be in the ultimate intention of moving the mass of his forces to the Peninsula or the South bank of the James river. We have had no intimation as yet of any movement on his part. No doubt Gen'l. Lee will be ready to meet him at any point and with his veteran army so often blessed by our Father in Heaven, and drive him back with loss and disgrace. We feel very anxious about Vicksburg, tho' the news today wears a more cheering prospect.[86] Should Vicksburg fall, which God forbid, I believe the war will be prolonged almost indefinitely. If we are victorious at V'g. our army there will be released. [Gen. Braxton] Bragg's army at Tullahoma can be greatly strengthened and Rosecrans may be driven through Kentucky.[87] Oh! that this may be done and that our avid foe may be brought to see that the Lord is on our side, and give up the contest as useless and vain. I confess as matters now stand I can see but little reason to hope for a speedy conclusion of the war.

I have been sitting gazing at the moon shining beautiful and bright into my tent. I have wondered whether my Nellie was looking at it at the same moment. I imagined so, and that Luna was a medium of communicating our thoughts to each other. Am I right? Yes, my Darling Nellie. I *do* wish I could walk and enjoy the beautiful roses with you at Woodside & would that we could enjoy Nature together! But I must close tho' very reluctantly. I saw Mr. Harding today. He is very well & I think a *little* blue at the slim chance of his being home to Presbytery. He & Caleb send love to all. I suppose Sally is well by this time. Give her & my hopeful nephew my best love.[88]

---

86. The ray of optimism may have been due to the sinking of the gunboat *Cincinnati* by Confederate batteries on May 27, when Maj. Gen. William T. Sherman attempted to neutralize Fort Hill, a strongpoint on the Mississippi.

87. Bragg's Army of Tennessee would withdraw from Tullahoma at the end of June. It had failed to drive the Federals from Kentucky during its invasion of that contested state the previous autumn.

88. Ramseur's sister, Sallie, and David Schenck had become parents for the second time on November 20, 1862. Ramseur was apparently unaware that the baby was a girl named Lucy.

Love to all at Woodside. Continue to write me very often. You can not write too often. Accept my heart full of love. May God bless you my own sweetest Nellie.

With a good night kiss. Yr own devoted Dod

I wrote you from Richmond. Did you receive that note? Miss Mary Garnett was well & sent you love in abundance. She's coming to our wedding. Write very soon my Darling and believe me ever your own devoted Lover S. D. R.[89]

Army N. Va
June 3rd/63

My Heart's Precious Darling

We have just rec'd. orders to prepare for the march, and I expect will be off tonight. Where or why we go, none but Gen'l. Lee & his Lieuts. know. I think the Yankee Army has moved toward Washington, & we are now about to move in that direction. Let me beg you not to feel uneasy on my account. At least My Darling One, endeavour to believe that all is well till you hear the contrary. Do not believe any disastrous news until fully confirmed. Continue my Heart's Beloved, to pray for me at a throne of Grace. Your prayers, my Darling One, have availed much heretofore, and I know you will feel encouraged when I tell you how much I rely on your prayers.

Your sweet precious note in Caleb's letter reached me last Sabbath, my 26th birthday! What a charming, beautiful birthday present! After reading & rereading, I could express my feelings by explaining Oh! precious Darling Nellie to be with you and tell you how I love you is almost the only desire of my heart.

I would have written you a long letter before this, but I have been quite unwell. Am better today. You must excuse this brief note, & don't feel anxious if you fail to hear from us for a long time. When on the march mail facilities are poor. Saw Mr. H.[arding] today; he dined with us & is well.

Give my love to all in Milton. I'll write soon as possible, and now my Heart's Darling, I bid you, very reluctantly, goodbye. I cant bear the idea of being deprived of your sweet letters even for a short time.

May our Heavenly Father bless, protect, and keep us in safety under the shadow of His Almighty wings. And may He hasten the time when we may be united to love and serve Him. With a Heart full of love and with a long sweet pure kiss. Believe me fondly & devotedly your own Dod[90]

89. SHC.
90. SHC.

Along with other elements of the Army of Northern Virginia, Ramseur's brigade broke camp on June 4 and began a circuitous journey northward. When Lt. Gen. Richard S. Ewell's corps crossed the Potomac River on June 15, Ramseur's brigade was in the van. Rodes's division drove across the Mason-Dixon Line into Pennsylvania, stopping just across the border in Greencastle. Ramseur seemed pleasantly surprised at the ease of the invasion of Yankeedom, so far with minimal cost in Confederate lives.

> Green Castle, Penn.!!!!
> June 23rd 1863
>
> My Heart's Darling,
>
> I take advantage of the first opportunity since leaving Culpeper to write to you. Our advance has been wonderfully rapid and gloriously successful. Our troops are in the finest spirits and when we meet the enemy's vast horde we will give a good account of ourselves. Up to this time we have had no serious engagement. Our loss (in Ewells Corps) all told is less than 200 killed & wounded while we have captured between 4500 & 500[0] [prisoners], vast stores, large amounts of artillery ammunition &c &c.
>
> My Brigade was the first to get into the enemy's territory. I can not write you our numbers or designs for fear that this may fall into the hands of a "bushwhacker." Suffice it to say that we expect to make a bold and successful campaign.
>
> And now my Precious Darling, let me tell you that whilst I have been cheered and delighted with the action of my Brigade, I have sometimes allowed myself to become very sad and heart sick at not hearing from you. As the distance between us increases I feel more deeply my love for you. Oh my sweetest Nellie I hope the time may soon come when our wishes will be realized.
>
> Ah! Here is the order for the march and I must stop. All is well. So am I. I cant tell when I can write again. Do not I beg you distress yourself on our account. Do not take trouble or interest. In great haste. May the Lord watch over, bless and protect you & may He soon give us a peaceful & quiet home where we may love & serve him together. With a heart full of love.
>
> Devotedly & fondly
> Your Own
>
> Dod[91]

91. SHC.

Carlisle Barracks, Penna.
June 28th 1863

My Precious Darling

We rec'd. a mail last night and I was fortunate enough to get three letters from you. It is impossible my Sweetest one to tell you how rejoiced I
was to receive these expressions of your love and devotion. It makes me
inexpressibly happy to be assured that you love me and live for me. And
you have such a sweet way of telling me all your love. Today I burned three
of your letters. How sorry I was to do so, but I knew of no *safe means* of
sending them home.

Are you surprized to find that we are so far advanced into the Enemy's
territory? We are, or rather we are surprized that we have met with so
feeble resistance thus far. We feel sure however that we will have some
stern and bloody work to do before this campaign is ended. God grant that
success may attend our arms and that this bold campaign may result in a
glorious and honourable peace. Then might we may expect to realize our
happy dreams! our sweet anticipations & earthly bliss.

In Hagerstown, Md. we met some fair and beautiful sympathizers of
the South. I said some sweet things to some of them and kissed a few rosy,
ruby lips. I take some credit to myself for converting a Wisconsin Girl,
very pretty, pert and *plump*, from the error of her northern notions to be a
good and zealous sympathizer in our cause. At this place, we are occupying the old U.S. Barracks which in the days of yore were inhabited by the
gay and happy young Officers of Dragoons & Cavalry. We arrived here yesterday. So hurried was the flight of the Yanks that many household orna-
ments & luxuries were left behind. This morning I breakfasted on Salmon
left in ice &c &c.[92]

I know not whether this will reach you, so it is not prudent for me to
detail our plans. Let this suffice: they are bold and well conceived and thus
for me have reason to hope for success. I write in great haste, having accidentally learned that a courier was going to Richmond. Caleb is pretty
well. Tell Mama not [to] feel uneasy about him. I will take all possible care
of him. Write to me often. I will get your letters soon or late. I will write
you by every opportunity. And now, sweetest Nellie, precious Darling of

92. Built in the eighteenth century to defend against Indians, by the time of the Civil War the
Carlisle Barracks was a cavalry recruiting and training station housing less than 300 officers and
enlistees. It had been hastily evacuated two days before the invaders arrived. The Confederates
may have been dining on provisions demanded of the townsfolk by their cavalry upon first arriving.
Nye, *Here Come the Rebels!*, 303–5.

my heart, good bye. Oh! you are assured, you must be, that my love for you is growing, is great as the universe. Love to all. With a heart full for your sweet self, I am your own devoted Dod[93]

Gettysburg Penn
July 3rd 1863

We were overwhelmed yesterday by numbers. Today we will have a hard fight—I pen these few lines from my saddle, hope you will receive them. My love is for you. You are my Heart's Darling. If we meet no more on earth let us hope to meet in Heaven. My Darling I hope your prayers have been & are answered. And that my heart is Christs. Love to my Darling at home. Caleb sends love. May the Lord bless you & me, and may He soon bring this cruel war to an end, and may we soon be united to love, to serve our Father in Heaven. God bless you my precious Darling. Receive my heart's best and fullest and purest love. Good bye.

Forever your own

Devoted Dod[94]

Hagerstown Md
July 8th/63

My Hearts Darling

Once more, by the mercy of God, I was allowed to write you a few lines. We have just fought one of the bloodiest and most terrible battles of the war. The Enemy occupied a Gibraltar of a position.[95] Nevertheless our gallant troops stormed & restormed them sometimes successfully but finally we were compelled to withdraw from the unequal contest. My Brigade behaved splendidly as it always does. I captured a Brigadier & 2700 men, and killed a great many. My horse was shot & killed under me.[96] I made many hair breadth escapes, thanks to an all Kind Father. I am still spared to you.

Caleb is well. Mr. Harding also. My Darling the intensity of my love is

---

93. SHC.
94. SHC.
95. Referring, most likely, to Cemetery Hill opposite his lines.
96. Ramseur received compensation for his gray mare. Receipt for $400 paid, August 4, 1864, Ramseur, Confederate Generals, Staff Officers, and Non-regimental Enlisted Men, CMSR, RG 109, NARA.

felt more keenly more deeply in these times of danger. I verily believe that God has spared my life in answer to your prayers. Oh! may we both live to love & serve Him together.

I cant tell you what will be the next move of our glorious army. Whilst we have suffered terribly (N.C. particularly) our men are in fine spirits and we expect to defeat & drive back the enemy whenever he has the tenacity to advance.

Capt Hunt is well. Also Lt Hines.[97] This is in great haste & with my right hand.

Oh! My Darling *how* I want to see you. May the time soon come when our land will be blessed with peace & we may be united in holy & happy wedlock. God bless you & keep you for your lover's sake. With love inexpressible

Your own devoted Dod

Write often. Direct to S. D. R. care Maj Gen'l. Rodes through Gen'l. Lee, Army N. Va.[98]

Ramseur's contribution to the Confederate effort at Gettysburg took place on the first day of the battle, July 1. Rodes's division arrived after fighting had already begun. Hurrying his force against the right side of the Federal line, Rodes watched as O'Neal's brigade was decimated, failing to protect its flank. Calling on Ramseur's command, held in reserve until then, produced a far different result. The Yankees were driven back, giving up almost 1,000 prisoners. After Ramseur's troops broke the Federal line, Rodes's brigades pushed into Gettysburg, where they paused. Ewell's decision not to contest Cemetery Hill prevented them from advancing farther. The following evening, Ramseur was halted on the brink of attacking the northwest face of the hill, now a strongly fortified Union position. On the third day, his troops watched in horror from afar as the attacking Confederates were mowed down while trying to take Cemetery Ridge.

97. At this time, Samuel H. Hines was a first lieutenant in Company I, Forty-fifth Carolina Infantry. He hailed from Milton, where he was a clerk before the war. His health was a concern as during the winter he had been hospitalized for five weeks suffering from Remittent Fever, and then given sick leave for several months. Manarin, *North Carolina Troops*, 11:107; Joslyn, *The Biographical Roster of the Immortal 600*, 139; Forty-fifth North Carolina Infantry, CMSR, RG 109, NARA.

98. SHC.

Camp Near Martinsburg
July 17th 1863

My Heart's Darling,

Caleb is leaving for the rear. I hope he may be able to get home. I have time to write but a few words.

You have no doubt seen that our glorious army was repulsed at Gettysburg. We have now reached the famous valley of Va. Here I think we will remain holding the Enemy in Check, unless he moves by Leesburg toward Richmond, in that event we will have to cross the mountains to confront them.

My glorious little Brigade *has again covered itself with glory* and we are still ready and anxious to meet the Yankees on fair ground. But I will leave Caleb to give you the details of our fight. C. is not much sick, simply chilled. My Sweetest Darling tho' all things look dark and gloomy at this time, I do not feel doubtful of the final result. I firmly believe our Cause to be right & just and surely a God of justice and mercy will bring us through all our tribulations to a final and glorious Peace.

Oh! my Sweetest Nellie how my heart yearns to see you. After dangers and toils of the day are past in the silent house of the night my thoughts are of you. My heart beats for you. I feel *near* you.

May God soon, very soon, cause the cruel war to end. And may He in the Kind Providence, speed to unite us in love to serve Him. Accept Darling of my heart, *all of my* heart's love.

I cant tell when I can come to see you. I can not venture to hope to be with you next Sept. But do not be despondent, but hope with me, & remember Love that I will come to you as soon as Duty (you know how sacredly I endeavour to discharge duty) will soon allow me to leave my post.

Let us hope My Darling that our Heavenly Father will bring all our desires to our hearts. May we both live to see the fulfillment of all our hopes, and may we be surprised at the joys we yet have in store. Write to me *very very* often. Direct to Maj Gen'l. Rodes' division Ewell's Corps, Army Northern Va.

Love to Mama, Sis' Mary & all and Darling Nellie to your sweet self. I send more love than my poor pen can write. May the Lord keep you and cheer you and bless you is my constant prayer. Pray for me Darling. Your prayers are precious to me, Sweetest Darling.

Good bye with a kiss from one who loves you better than all the world besides. Your own Dod[99]

99. SHC.

Madison Court House
July 29th 1863

Again, my Hearts Darling, after ten days of the hardest marching I ever experienced, I enjoy the precious privilege of writing you a few lines. Mr. Harding is [illegible]. He has written home every opportunity during our march. He is very well & the life of our party. Caleb, I hope, reached home safely. I heard of his leaving Staunton. Tell him to be sure to have his vacancy *registered* at the Danville Hospital & to write to me often. Will George[100] have to join the army. Tell Caleb I do not want him to return until he is entirely recovered. You must see that he does not come back too soon.

What must I say my sweetest one about our bleeding country? This is certainly her "dark hour." Let us not be discouraged. Our cause is right and just. Our enemies are wicked & cruel. Our God loves justice & mercy. He will avenge us. He will protect and deliver us.

When I last left you I fondly hoped that I might return next Sept and claim you as gay Hearts own. Not now. I can not see any prospect of a furlough. As soon My Sweetest Nellie as Duty will allow I will apply for a furlough. Till then, be cheerful, happy hopeful & contented.

Oh! My Sweetest Nellie how my heart yearns to be with you! Morning and evening, all day and all night, I think of you & long to be with you.

Yesterday I had the head ache. I told Mr. Harding if I could only feel your hand on my head for a moment, I would be cured. So with my heart, could I be with you, *feel your presence*, I would be happy indeed. Oh Nellie my life, my love, my Hearts Darling, I love you more devotedly, more intensely, more all absorbingly every day. The chief desire of my heart now is to live in a quiet happy little home & care not how humble it be, blessed with your love. Let us hope that happy day is not far off.

You remember I have always declared that we might expect Recognition when & only when European Powers discovered that one party or both were terribly exhausted. It is the policy of selfish Europe & more selfish England to keep our country separated. It is likewise their policy to see us as much exhausted & crippled as possible. When all this is accomplished, I look for them to intervene. Not before. What does Uncle Charles think of my opinion in this matter.

I am kept more busy now than ever before. Brig Gen'l. Iverson has been

---

100. Nellie's youngest brother, age eighteen in 1863.

relieved from the command of his brigade for misconduct at Gettysburg.[101] His brigade has been added to my command. So you may imagine my hands are full, especially as Capt Gales is sick & Caleb absent. But I am very well. My strength seems to increase with the necessity.

Darling Nellie, do write to me often. I have not received a line from you since we went to Penn. Direct care of Maj Gen'l. Rodes, 2nd Army Corps, Army No. Va. Nor have I heard from home. What of my loved ones there? I have not written home since the fight knowing that you would keep them posted. I have not been mistaken have I? Excuse this hasty letter and write by next mail. Dream of me tonight. I look at the beautiful moon & stars & imagine you are looking at them with me, and that you are exchanging thoughts with me.

May the time soon come when we can look at them together. Tell Mama to keep Caleb until he gets right well. Give her my best. Love also to Sis' Mary. Tell her I have laid hands on her other half[102] & don't intend to let him go till he cries Enough!

Love to Aunt Prissie, Grandma & all. Nellie Sweetest Darling, it is so hard to leave you. Think of me & pray for me. God bless, comfort, protect & keep you for your own Devoted Dod[103]

In Camp near Orange C.H.

Aug. 3rd 1863

I can not allow Mr. Harding's letter to go to Woodside[104] without a note to you my loved one. My last letter was brought to a sudden close by marching orders. Then I expected to have had a brush with the Yanks before now, but the Cowards are afraid to attack us. If they move us from here it will be by sending troops to the James River or elsewhere. They will not dare to attack us in front on a fair field. But enough. And you think Darling that I write as if I was sad and depressed. I am sad, my sweet one.

---

101. Positioned in the middle of Rodes's division when it moved forward toward Oak Ridge on July 1, Iverson's brigade suffered heavy losses (65 percent of 1,384 men); with a wide-open clearing behind them, the unprotected Confederate brigade was surprised by Federals hidden in Sheads's Woods. Iverson was severely criticized for not personally coming onto the field, leading his brigade in its advance, and discovering the nature, strength, and deployment of his adversary. He was later sent back to Rome, Georgia, to organize his state's troops. Robert K. Krick, "Three Confederate Disasters on Oak Ridge, Failures of Brigade Leadership on the First Day at Gettysburg," in Gallagher, *Three Days at Gettysburg*, 100–105.

102. Chaplain E. H. Harding.

103. SHC.

104. Harding would be writing to his wife, Mary, Nellie's sister, at the Richmond family home.

I lost some of my dearest friends in the last battle. Poor Pender, so full of every noble and manly spirit, so rich in the heart kindness, so brave and glorious in battle!! I can but shed tears over his fall.[105] And his poor wife! May the God of the Fatherless and the widow sanctify this affliction to her and give her strength to bear it. Poor McCreery[106] too, fell, while gallantly charging with Col. Burguin's Reg't.[107] He and Col. B. are buried in the same grave in the land of the stranger, yea worse than stranger land, in the land of our inhuman base, cruel cowardly Enemy! There among the humble Soldiers, heroes all. I have lost some warm friends and supporters. But this loss is not all. Our great campaign, admirably planned & more admirably executed up to the fatal days at Gettysburg, has failed, which I was not prepared to anticipate. But my Hearts Darling, though sad and grievously disappointed, do not dream for a moment that my confidence in the final success of our cause, the complete and glorious triumph of our arms, has abated one jot or one tittle. I look the thing square in the face and am prepared to undergo dangers and hardships and trials to the end. We have yet much to suffer. We will suffer it all bravely and heroically. A glorious and honorable Peace will be our rich and lasting reward.

My Sweetest Nellie, how I want to be with you! My thoughts are constantly flying away to you. Yesterday I went to church in town & then with Maj Wilson to Mrs. Crockfords[108] to dinner. Imagine how we enjoyed old ham & chicken, but 'specially corn & tomatoes & potatoes! Mrs. C asked me if I was married? Said "No Madam, but as soon as the exigencies of the service will allow I intend to go to N.C. and get a wife." "That's good, said the gentle Madam & if the Army remains here, you must bring your wife to stay with [erased]." "That I will Madam, and I predict you will find her as lovely as I have told you."

105. A fellow North Carolinian, Maj. Gen. W. Dorsey Pender was a division commander in Lt. Gen. A. P. Hills's Third Corps. He died on July 18, as the result of a leg wound suffered the second day at Gettysburg.

106. Captain McCreery, a Virginian, was one of only two southerners to finish ahead of Ramseur in the West Point class of 1860. Serving as assistant adjutant and inspector general on Brigadier General Pettigrew's staff, McCreery was shot in the heart while waving the Twenty-sixth North Carolina Infantry Regiment's flag during the brigade's assault on McPherson's Woods on July 1. Krick, *Staff Officers in Gray*, 207; Gragg, *Covered with Glory*, 129.

107. Col. Henry K. Burgwyn Jr., age twenty-one and commander of the Twenty-sixth North Carolina Infantry Regiment, had taken the flag from the lieutenant who succeeded McCreery and was, in turn, shot twice; when turning to hand the colors to a private, Col. Burgwyn was himself mortally wounded in the side. Burgwyn was judged by some accounts to be one of fourteen regimental standard bearers shot that day. George C. Underwood, "Twenty-Sixth Regiment," in Clark, *Histories*, 2:407; Gragg, *Covered with Glory*, 129–30, 135.

108. Wife of John Crockford.

Sometimes Darling I hope to be with you next month and think I have reason to hope. We must wait patiently. One thing is certain: just as soon as I can be spared if even for seven days, I am coming to claim you as my Darling Wife.

Oh here goes the mail carrier & I must close. Love to all. Tell Caleb to write to me, and not to return until he is entirely well. Has the recent call for troops taken George?

Sweetest Nellie, write often. You can not write too much. Your letters are the sweetest dearest pleasures I can enjoy.

Dearest Nellie Goodbye. May our Heavenly Father bless you more abundantly than I can ask or even think. With love inexpressible

As ever and more than ever

Your Devoted lover

S D Ramseur[109]

Camp near Orange C.H.
Aug'st. 10th/63

My Dearest Darling

After patiently waiting a long time I today rec'd. your last letter (no date). *You* know *how* rejoiced I was to get it!

To be with you Darling at beautiful Woodside is the constant wish of my heart which frequently finds expression from my lips. I have thought of you more frequently, and if possible, with more tenderness for the past week than ever before. My heart yearns to be with you, to be constantly with you. I feel that a sweet little home of our own, up in our beautiful mountains, with none to interfere with us, with no outsiders to bother us, left alone in our love in the midst of God's beautiful and magnificent creations would be all that my heart could desire. Oh! my Sweetest Nellie. To be with you and enjoy your love is my first and dearest wish! Can I tell you how happy your words of love and sympathy render me?

My Darling, if you live to love me and make me happy, surely I will be happy. May I be worthy of the confidence you repose in me and may the time soon come when we may be permitted to enjoy life's pleasures and share life's sorrows together!

I had written thus far yesterday when a carriage drove up to my tent, then another and another filled with *Ladies: two* pretty ones. Imagine my surprise and *pleasure*! I do love your sex! I sent for the band, which discoursed sweet music. The ladies expressed themselves highly pleased &c and departed after leaving pressing invitations to call, to take dinner, tea &c. I was almost bewildered & said some sweet & some imprudent things, squeezed *one* hand & rec'd. a gentle pressure & sweet look in return &c. &c. After these bright creatures departed, I could not but think on the better part of creation. How readily my thoughts sped on to the *best* of the "better part." Darling Nellie my thoughts of you were so sweet last evening. I knew you were at that very hour paying me a "Spirit Visit."

My Sweetest One. Is it not hard to be *patient?* When I think of the bare possibility of not seeing you this fall, my feelings almost overcome me & a murmur is in my heart if it does not find expression from my lips.

But Darling, I think there is a strong reason to expect a *short* leave this fall tho' not so soon as Sept. How will twenty days do? Can we not have all our plans carried out in that time. And then Darling, will you not come back with me to the neighbourhood of the Army? To have you with me & know that you are well and happy to enjoy your precious society and feel your love is happiness I long for Oh! so eagerly, so earnestly.

May our Father in Heaven cause a stop to be put to this terrible war and may He bless us speedily in the union of our hearts & hands!

Oh! My Beloved! Could the warm enthusiastic emotions overflowing my heart be expressed on paper, I would send you a large volume! But I must leave your imagination free. Let your own heart be your guide. To every feeling, every wish, every strong hope, you cherish, remember in my heart of hearts its counterpart is found. Write to me oftener my precious Darling. Working here day after day in some monotonous way, what have I to cheer me? What is there to vary the ceaseless round of military duty? What, to call me back to, a brighter world full of hope & love? What, but your sweet messengers of love! Please write oftener. Send me a note in Mrs. Hardings letters. Write whenever you can steal awhile away from other duties. Do not wait for replys. Truly my own Beloved, I write as often as possible. Tell Caleb not to come on 'till he is perfectly well.

Give my love to all. I am very well, better than at any time since I left Fredericksburg. Do write me long & frequent letters. Ten days interval between the last. I fear the mail has something to do with it. My own Sweetest Dearest Darling Nellie, accept my heart full of love. May our God be with us & bless us!

With a Kiss Darling Nellie

Your own Dod[110]

110. SHC.

Camp Near Orange C.H.

Aug 15/63

My Own Precious Nellie

When my work is done and I have a leisure hour at my disposal, it is always eagerly seized and appropriated to your sweet self. I have no Brigade drill on Saturday, hence, you have this letter today.

Mr. Harding brought me a precious little note from you yesterday evening. Imagine how glad I was to receive it, after having just been informed by my mail carrier, "No letter for the Gen'l." Mr. H. has gone back to his Reg't. for which I am sorry. I miss his bright, cheerful Christian sympathy. He comes to see me often. A sense of Duty took him back. He said he was afraid opportunities to do good, might be left, whilst he remained away from the Reg't., which he might improve if there. I think he is right!

I have worked very constantly this week, making only one visit to the Ladies. Tell Caleb there are more pretty girls in this neighbourhood than in any Section of Virginia that I know of. Also, that I am now having Division Drills on a Small Scale. I have consolidated Iverson's (old) Brig. into two Regts. under Col [Thomas M.] Garrett.[111] Have placed the 2nd & 14th under Col Cox, and the 4th & 30th under Col Grimes. Pretty Girls on fine horses ride out to our drills and the drill hour is looked forward to with pleasure by officers and men. Our Army is being increased quite rapidly. My Brigade is 150 stronger than when I went to Penna. The gain is caused by the return of my (Chancellors[ville]) wounded heroes. I am sorry to say there are a good many deserters from Our Army. W. W. Holden[112] is responsible in great measure for the desertions among N.C. Troops.

I am sorry to learn that Caleb is again afflicted with those horrid chills. Tell him not to come on until he is perfectly well. To consider this *an order*. I have learned him to obey orders. Tell him I detailed a man to take care of his horse soon after he left, but all his efforts prove unavailing. The horse is still disabled, and Capt. [William C.] Coughenour's horse (in charge of the same man) is hopelessly lame. Horses are selling here at from $800 to $1500.

Don't you think I have been liberal to devote so much of yr. letter to Caleb. Would you be surprised My Heart's darling, to see me next month? I reason in this way about it. Gen'l. Lee will be as well prepared, at the expiration of four weeks, to attack the Yanks, as he can be during the Winter.

---

111. The remnants of Iverson's brigade, which were transferred to Ramseur's charge, remained until September, when Brig. Gen. Robert D. Johnston was selected to take command of them. Wert, "Robert Daniel Johnston," 3:199.

112. William W. Holden was editor of the *Raleigh Standard* and an influential opinion-maker in the state.

The Yanks are weaker now & will be for four or five weeks than they will be after that time, for they are daily sending off men to bring on their newly drafted men. Hence I conclude that if Gen'l. Lee attacks (as I think & hope he will) it will be done before 15th Sept. If Gen'l. Lee does not attack, I don't believe the Yanks will. And therefore, I expect to gain a Furlough in either event.

You can not imagine *how* happy I am even in the anticipation of meeting you so soon! It is dream day and night! Not long ago I dreamt it was our wedding night and I saw you in your Bridal costume. Never did eyes behold a lovelier Bride! The dream I hope will soon be a reality! I know that my eyes will never behold a sweeter Bride!

Will it not be *nice* to make a bridal tour to my home. If *people* bother us there, to go on to our glorious mountains and look out for a location for *our home*! Oh My Sweetest Dearest Nellie! Our home! I will leave you to think about it. My heart overflows at the thought.

I wrote Luly & Fanny eight pages yesterday. I have neglected them shamefully of late. I shall look to you to defend me. I fear the Girls will think I have transferred all my affection to you, but I will try to be a better Brother and at the same time a better Lover. Does my Darling know how broad and how deep and how great is my love? Would that I could be with you to tell you all I feel! Last night after a tremendous storm in the evening, the stars shone out so beautifully bright. They spoke so eloquently to my heart of my Loved Absent Darling! Oh! that the time will soon come, when we can walk hand in hand and enjoy God's beautiful Creation together yet as One!

How can I express all I feel my Darling Nellie! My letter would be filled with exclamations of joy and Love! And somebody said it will not do to write too much love, for fear of becoming wearisome. Speaking for myself, *I* never weary of reading your words of love & I know I never tire writing my love. I believe my Darling feels as I do on the same subject.

I was interrupted at the end of my third page, and resumed writing on a new sheet. So you must pass on to the next sheet & read this page last. I hope you'll excuse this letter. My thoughts can not be *connected* when I am interrupted every few minutes. If I were not a good natured man, I would get mad at somebody. Write to me very often my Darling Nellie. Your letters are my comforters. Give love to all. Tell Caleb he is not keeping his promise to write to me. I am looking for a long letter from you today. May I not be disappointed. Good bye, My Loved One. May Our Heavenly Father love & bless you.

As Ever, Darling, Your own Devoted Dod[113]

113. SHC.

[late August 1863]

My Dear Brother

Your long letter rec'd. the other day. I am indeed sorry to know you have reasons for yr apprehensions. The Army, I think, I know, is *sound*, and will do honor to the State. If the people at home do not condemn us in dying in this cause. Can it be possible that Holden's influence is as potent for *evil* as you think? I can not think so. Are there not true men enough to put him down? The *party* meetings, Holden speaks of in the Army were not *party* meetings. I speak for my Brigade & say that it was an *almost unanimous* (no open dissenters, probably as many as 30 who took no part) condemnation of Holden & his Tory party.[114] Desertion is the only evil I have to contend against & I submitted a plan to Gen'l. Lee the other day to stop deserters, for which he complimented me highly. But I must hurry on.

I expect a furlough between the 19th of Sep't. & the middle Oct. Cant say exactly when. So prepare *everybody* for my wedding at any day between the above named dates. I'll telegraph you when I'll get to Milton, & I want you all to come on post haste. I never would cease to regret your absence on such an occasion & may, must insist on yr being there, in spite of business & every thing else.

You made me a liberal offer of a present in yr last letter. I'll let you off with a present to my wife next month.

Love to all. In haste, S. D. R.[115]

Camp Near Orange C.H.

Sept. 2nd 1863

My Darling Nellie,

I was greatly disappointed yesterday and today in not getting a letter from you. Mr. Harding rec'd. a letter from Cousin M. yesterday in which she says she fears it is impossible for you to be ready to be married before the last of this month, probably not then. This alarms me, my Dearest. If I do not come home *now*, I do not know *when* I can have another opportunity to do so.

My Darling do not allow the absence of great or small things interfere with the consummation of our hearts best desires! I do not believe, I know, you will not disappoint me in this dearest anticipation. I expect to

114. Holden's willingness to make peace with the U.S. government is compared to Tory loyalists among the colonists wanting to remain under the British crown during the time of the American Revolution.

115. PC.

be through with my work on the Court Martial the latter part of this week. Other business will detain me until the latter part of next week. And then, if Gen'l. Lee thinks I can be spared from the army for a short time I expect to leave then for yr. home on Monday the 15th inst. On the evening of the 17th I will arrive at Woodside and be married that evening. Then the balance of the time is at your disposal. I shall apply for 30 days. May get 25, but think it highly probable only 20 will be granted me. However I will notify you more fully, when I will leave here. Let me know your wishes. If possible they shall be conformed to in every particular. Remember that we must be married as soon as possible after I leave the Army. I can get to M[ilton] the 2nd day after leaving the Army, but I promised you three days notice & that is the longest possible time I can wait. Please write me fully on this subject. Write to me oftener Darling. You don't know how *desolate* I am without yr letters. I have written in the greatest possible haste which you must please excuse. Oh! My Sweetest Nellie to be with you in your own beautiful home this eve'g. is all my heart desires. Accept my Heartfull of Love. As ever & forever Your Own

Dod[116]

Camp Near Orange C.H.
Sept. 7th 1863

My Own Precious Nellie,

I can not tell you how greatly disappointed I have been every day for the past week, as I have been daily informed "No letters for the Gen'l." When I last heard from you, you were suffering with a severe headache. I am fearful that you have not yet recovered. Are you unwell, my Darling? Write me the worst, for I assure you realities are much more easily borne than this dreadful state of suspense.

Do you know it will be fourteen days tomorrow since I rec'd. yr last letter, which was that brought by Caleb. I feel sure that you have written to me in the mean time, and that the miserable mails have failed to bring me your letter. This causes me the more anxiety, for fear some of my letters have not reached you.

I hope My Sweetest Nellie, you do not think me unreasonable in urging the immediate consummation of our engagement! I can not tell how long the Season of quiet we are now enjoying will last. Should an active Campaign be carried on in Oct. I am sure I could not get a furlough until Jan'y. at soonest, probably not then. I do feel it is due us both that we should

116. SHC.

be united hand and heart as we both so earnestly desire. I could give you reasons for such a consummation that would cover pages, but it is unnecessary for I know your heart cordially reechoes the chiefest desires of my own. I am some what embarassed by the uncertainty of the day on which I shall reach Milton. I can not say *positively* I can be in Milton on the 16th but *think* I can. If R Roads or Yankee movements do not now or soon prevent such an undertaking on my part. At all events, I will not arrive in M. sooner than the 16th Inst. and unless something unlooked for happens, I will be with you on that day, or very soon thereafter.

If possible, I will go to Danville on Tuesday the 15th Inst. & thence to M. on the evening of the 16th, or if I have not time for this, I will have to come directly from Richmond to Milton on Wednesday. The only objection to this is the *possible* detention of the cars by accident and the lateness of the hour of our arrival. My Furlough I am almost sure to get, unless the Yankees move before this time next week. I will telegraph you as soon as I get it & tell you positively when you may expect me. I have written to my home Loves to tell them that I certainly expected to be married on the 16th Inst and begging them to be sure to be present at that time. I sincerely hope My Sweetest Darling, all that I have done meets with your approval. I know my Heart's Darling, you fully appreciate my haste. It is one of the necessities of war. I would prefer on your account waiting until Oct. but that delay involves the chance, yea the probability of a still further delay 'till Spring &c.

By the non arrival of a letter from you during the past two weeks, I am unable to act on any suggestion you might make. You can thus imagine my greater disappointment during this time. If However, it is *impossible* for you to conform to the plans I have proposed, I will submit as gracefully as I can, asking you to make known the change to my home Loves.

I would have written this letter sooner My Precious Darling, but have been waiting daily for a sweet messenger from you, making known all your plans and wishes. That letter not having come, & the time to write to my home having come, I was obliged to adopt the course within. I hope to receive your letter this even'g. Yes, I will write you by tomorrow's mail. Send to the telegraph office next Saturday and Monday.

Please excuse this hastily written letter. I must close for the mail. Mr. H. & Caleb are well. Love to all. Accept my heart full of Love my Heart's Darling! May God bless you.

Ever your own Dod[117]

117. SHC.

Camp Near Orange C.H.
Sept. 8th 1863

My Darling Nellie,

Your letter of the 28th Ult. was received yesterday. You see that it has been ten days on the way.

I am sure my Precious Darling, I cannot wait until the 30th of Sept. & for the following reason's. First, my furlough will be half out before that time, and we would not have time after our marriage to visit Lincolnton, which we both desire very much to do, and which I think we ought to do. Second, My Furlough can not be put off to a later day, for reasons given you in a former letter. Finally, I promise in my application to return to my post and duty, whenever I may be summoned. You can see then the necessity for our marriage as soon as possible *after I start* on Furlough. For I might be recalled even before the marriage, provided it were put off too long. Consider these reasons, my Darling, and let us agree to a compromise. Though I'm afraid to wait a day.

Then let us agree on the 23rd of Sept, as our Wedding day. I would willingly yield to your wishes in this matter, but My Darling, I am more fully impressed with the uncertainties of military life than you are. And therefore when I get a furlough *this* month, I think I ought to gladly take it, and not unwisely wait till next month when I *may not* get it. Then I shall take it for granted, My Sweetest Nellie, that you will consent to the 23rd and I will today write to Father & Mr. Schenck to honour us with their presence on that day.

I was only joking about bringing Ladies with me. You don't suppose I would allow myself at such a time to be "bothered" in such a way. I have seen Maj Huger who will try to get a furlough to go with me, but he does not expect to succeed. If he does succeed, He & Mr. H. & Caleb will be my companions from the Army. I hope Dr. David and George Phifer can & will also accompany me. I will call on Caleb & Doctor, & Maj Huger & G. Phifer, for Groomsmen. I have also written to David Phifer[118] to attend. I will state the day in all these letters as the 23rd. So My Darling, you must consent to that day. It is too late to change it now. Oh! Sweet Precious Nellie how my heart overflows with love for you. As the time *slowly* approaches for the fulfillment of our Engagement my Love increases and grows until it has taken possession of my whole being. I perform my duties

---

118. Ramseur's first cousin, the eldest child of his father's sister, Mary Adeline, resided in Concord, North Carolina, and was listed as twenty-one years of age in the 1860 Census. U.S. Census Office, *Eighth Census, 1860.*

with dispatch in order that I may have *more time* to devote to *My* Nellie. During the busy, noisy day my thoughts fly away to seek you in your bright beautiful home. And when the moon and stars look upon our sleeping host, and quiet reigns on all sides, Oh! how my heart yearns to be with you My Best Beloved! May our bright hopes all, very soon, be fully realized. May we enjoy the beauties and pleasures of this world for many long years in happy union. May we grow in love and tenderness towards each other. And Oh! may we indeed go hand in hand helping and encouraging each other in the narrow path that leads to our Heavenly Home!

I must close this hurried letter. It has been written in the midst of business with soldiers all around me, waiting to have their cases acted on. So please excuse it. I know my kind little Darling will agree to all I have written in this letter and will be ready to welcome me with a welcoming well heart on the 23rd Inst. Will you not, Darling?

Mr. Stanfield[119] came yesterday. He is with Mr. Harding. I have not yet seen him. Caleb looks better than I ever saw him. He has not had a chill since he returned, but I think he attends at least three parties a week & does not return until the small hours of the morning. I suppose the children will be with you when this reaches you. As I wrote them we would be married on the 16th you mustn't allow them to encourage you in postponing the event!

Please write to me. Don't you think you have treated me *very badly* in not writing to me at this anxious time! Love to all! Accept my heart full of love. May God bless you & keep you for yr own Devoted Lover, S. D. R.

Be sure to have Grandma & Aunt Prissie with us on the *23rd*[120]

Camp on the Rapidan River
Sept 17th 1863

My Beloved Nellie,

I am heartsick. My disappointment has almost unmanned me. But no, I will perform my duty here & there. I'll come & claim your love. The Enemy has advanced in forces to the Rapidan.[121] His attitude is threatening. We are in position to meet & hurl him back, should he have the temerity to cross. For myself, I don't believe there will be a great battle here for some time, but until further developments it is clearly my Duty to remain here.

119. L. A. Stanfield was a clergyman in Milton. U.S. Census Office, *Eighth Census, 1860.*
120. SHC.

121. Union forces were moving from the Rappahannock toward the Rapidan, pressing against Lee's army weakened by the transfer of Longstreet's corps to the western theater.

You can imagine my Heart's Darling, *what a trial* this is to me! I know you will love me all the more for performing my whole duty. I cant tell you when I will be able to come and claim you as my Beloved Wife! But as soon as I can possibly leave the Army I will come to you my Darling One! Oh! How my heart yearns to be with you now! May the cruel separation be very short! I think & hope it will be.

I'll write you a long letter tomorrow. The messenger is waiting for this so excuse great haste. Do not be uneasy. I don't think there will be a fight. Accept my heart overflowingly full of love. Be ready for a surprize visit. May God bless you & me & May He speedily unite us in Love to serve & glorify Him.

> As Ever & Forever
> Your Own
>
> D

Affairs may change in a few days. If so I will be with you in a few days.[122]

> Camp on the Rapidan
> Sept 25th 1863

My Dear Precious Nellie,

I sent you a pencil note on Wednesday last, which I was ashamed to send altho' it was the least I could do under the circumstances, and which I fear you were unable to read. Everything still remains quiet in our front, altho' the Yankees are plainly visible, their pickets being still in hailing distance of our own. Last week I would not have been surprised had the Yankees attacked us. *Now*, I fear they entertain no such intention. Should they have the boldness to cross the Rapidan on our front, I feel very confident they would be defeated, routed, overthrown. With this confident feeling of our ability to repel & defeat the Yanks in our present position, you can imagine my anxiety for them to advance is great and eager. Again I declare my belief that there will be no advance of the Enemy on this line, and I make this repetition for the purpose of allaying all of your fears and quieting all your apprehension. Can you imagine, My Darling Nellie, how, almost, desolate I feel these beautiful bright days and calm, lovely nights, away from your love and your Precious Self? This very disappointment is what I feared, when I so suddenly and seemingly unreasonably, appointed the 16th as our Wedding Day. But I must bear this disappointment like a

122. SHC.

good soldier, who still keeps the Hope of an early consummation of his heartfelt wishes bright before him.

I must confess that I am perplexed at the thought that I am detained here unnecessarily. My Duty however is very plain. I *must* remain *here* until the emergency, that now threatens, is passed. It requires a great degree of self denial on my part to make such a resolution but I know that My Heart's Darling, would not have me desert the post of danger and duty under *any* circumstances. I know that My Nellie would rather deny herself and disappoint the expectations of her friends than to have me absent from My Gallant Brigade in time of need. I know My Darling will love me all the more because I have thus followed the course of Stern Duty.

In consequence of the suddenness of our move, I did not have an opportunity to notify a few friends of the impossibility of my presence at Woodside on the 23rd and the consequent necessity of a postponement of our marriage. I must not be surprised, therefore, to hear that you have been placed in the embarrassing situation of entertaining one or two Gentlemen, who came to see you married? Am I right in my conjecture? Have my little Sisters yet made themselves visible at Woodside? I hope so. I think 'twill be better for them & for you to be together nowadays. I must insist upon it, that you put away all anxiety, all foreboding of Evil. In short do not anticipate sorrow! Never take trouble upon interest. Be cheerful, happy & gay anticipating with genuine pleasure that the "Good time is coming." Oh! My Darling Nellie! I can not tell you how genuinely enthusiastically happy I am in the thought that your heart is mine, that you love me above all others, and soon that this love is to be pledged and sealed in Holy Matrimony. My Sweet Nellie knows *how* I love her, and how the pride and delight of my life will be to love her and makes her happy & contented in this life.

We are now so far from the Rail Road that our mails are not regular. If therefore you fail to receive letters from us do not be uneasy. I hope, My Precious Darling, you will write me often and fully. Should your letters come in my absence, they will be immediately sent to me. As to the continuance of the present state of affairs, of course, I can not speak with certainty, but I think and hope I may be able to leave, in quiet, during the next week or next month. Possibly our wedding day will yet be the Anniversary of Mama's. Certes [Assuredly] is it. I am coming as soon as possible and I want My Nellie to be ready for me on very short Notice. Say three days!

Caleb & Mr. Harding are well and both send love. Give my love to all. Write to me as soon as you read this. Accept my best love, Beloved Nellie.

Pray for me. May God bless you & me, and very soon May He unite us to love each other in His Fear. Devotedly Your Own Dod[123]

Camp on the Rapidan
Sabbath Eve'g. Sept 27th [1863]

My Heart's Darling,

Your letter by my Cousin D[avid] Phifer was rec'd. today. You must imagine my surprise and delight to hear from you. 'Tis indeed very great comfort to me to be assured that you are happy and cheerful notwithstanding *our* great disappointment. I have endeavoured to perform my whole duty cheerfully and well. Sometimes, not often, I have felt like crying out against my bad fortune. Your letter today reassured me in the path of duty. Your love, my Precious Darling, is to me a reward richer and more highly prized than any thing on Earth.

I can not tell you how great my disappointment has been and is now. My thoughts have been constantly stealing away to you. You were right, My Precious, to imagine that *I* was making you a spirit visit last Wednesday. Long into the night and until the small hours of the morning, I walked alone before my little tent, looking at the beautiful Moon, which was looking at My Heart's Beloved! Yes, My own Precious Nellie, I have been with you in spirit day and night since my great disappointment. Oh! *How* I *do wish* I could have made one of the party at Woodside last Wednesday! *How Happy* would *We* have been! Ah! Me! This cruel, cruel war!

I know My Darling, that you deserved every compliment that was paid you for your graceful and beautiful conduct under such embarrassing circumstances! I thought of you and the circumstances, and Mr. Harding & I spoke of it several times. I wish I could have taken a *peep* at you, so that I might witness your triumph and share the delight of your friends.

Oh! My Sweetest Nellie! How *can* I stay away longer? If these miserable Yankees do not attack us soon, I will either insist on my furlough or I will strongly urge an immediate attack on the Yanks. I verily believe that we can go over the River & whip them with our small force.

I have just been interrupted so I will have to close suddenly My Darling. You must excuse this scribbling. It has been written by twilight. I am Gen'l. Offr. of the Day, and have now to visit our advanced posts. The full moon is rising. As she lights me on my way I'll fly in thought to you My Love!

Oh! to be with you even but one short hour!

123. SHC.

All well. Love to all. Hope I may get off the latter part of this week or first of next. It is however impossible to say *when I can* get *Home*!

Dearest Darling of my Heart! Good bye. Accept a kiss full of love and tenderness from your devoted, Dod[124]

Ramseur was confronted at this time with a situation common to military command. The governor of North Carolina wrote to the Secretary of War that Maj. Wilson had been elected Chief Engineer and Superintendent of the Western North Carolina Rail Road and urged that his resignation from the army be accepted. The request was granted on October 3. Four days later, Ramseur requested that Capt. Buckner D. Williams of the Thirtieth North Carolina Regiment be selected as Wilson's replacement. It was not until November 14, after the Adjutant and Inspector General's Office reported it could identify no other qualified officer candidate, that Williams was finally appointed quartermaster of Ramseur's brigade.[125]

Hd. Qrs. Ramseur's Comd.
Oct. 8th 1863

Lt. Col. Pendleton
Adt. Gen'l.

Sir,

Please inform me specifically whether the Lieut. Gen'l. Comd'g.[126] wishes me to move at once with my whole Brigade to join the Div'n. Col. Garrett has not yet arrived tho' three Regiments of Johnston's[127] Brigade are already here. By moving tonight, I will leave the whole line now guarded by my Brigade, from two miles above Morton's Ford to three miles below, exposed. Col. Garrett will hardly reach here before daybreak.

I have the honor to be,

Very respectfully,

Yr. Obt. Servt.[128]

124. SHC.

125. Zebulon B. Vance to James A. Seddon, September 21, 1863, James W. Wilson, Confederate Generals, Staff Officers, and Non-regimental Enlisted Men, CMSR, RG 109, NARA; Ruckner D. Williams, Confederate Generals, Staff Officers, and Non-regimental Enlisted Men, CMSR, RG 109, NARA; and Register of Letters Received, Quarter Master Department, November 1863–January 1864, Chap. 5, Vol. 9, entry 10-W, RG 109, NARA.

126. Richard S. Ewell.

127. Brig. Gen. Robert D. Johnston was also a native of Lincoln County and just ten weeks older than Ramseur.

128. Ramseur's signature has been cut out of the letter.

P.S. Capt. [Charles W.] Fry's Battery[129] is here, under my command. Do you wish it to move also with me? S.D.R.[130]

> Hd. Qrs. 2d Corps
> 10 ½ P.M. 8th Oct. 63

General

The Lt. Gen. Comd'g. wishes you to move your own brigade at dawn to Orange C.H. to join your Div'n. Leave Johnston's here. Direct Col. [illegible], who is here to relieve your pickets & those of [John B.] Gordon on Gen. Early's line, & to report to Gen. Fitz Lee at Clark's Mt.

I am Sir

Yr. obdt. Servt.

A. G. Perkins
A.A.G.

Gen Ramseur[131]

> Oct 9th/63

Dear Bro.

I have time to write you but a line. We are making a flank move to attack [Maj. Gen. George G.] Meade. May Our Heavenly Father grant us another great victory. May He shield our heads in the day of Battle. I must caution you again to feel as little uneasiness as possible. Trust the event to God & pray for us all. Love to my Precious Home Loves. May our Heavenly Father keep, protect, bless & soon unite us all in peace and safety. Accept a Brothers warmest love. I commit my Loved Ones to you. Oh! How hard it has been this cruel separation from my Beloved Nellie. God bless her & all my home Loves.

As Ever Devotedly

Yr Brother

S. D. Ramseur[132]

---

129. Orange (Virginia) Light Artillery.
130. NCOAH.
131. NCOAH.
132. PC.

Woodside, outside Milton, North Carolina, in the nineteenth century

Oct 9th/63

My Own Beloved Nellie,

I have time to write you but a few lines. The long pent up storm cloud is about to burst. We are now mak[ing] a flank move to attack the Enemy. God grant us a glorious success. Oh! My Precious Heart's darling how my love for you warms & brightens in these trying times. My Darling, my heart is overflowing with love & tenderness. God grant us a speedy termination to this cruel war with an honorable & glorious peace. Pray for me My Beloved Darling. May Our God protect us in the hour of danger. May He give us Grace to be prepared for any dispensation of His Providence. May He enable us all to submit cheerfully to His Will, and with thankful hearts say Thy Will be done.

My Beloved One. Goodbye. Oh! May it please Our Father to let me live and speedily to unite us in holy and happy wedlock. Love to all. God bless you all. Accept my Beloved, My Heart's Darling, My all. Love, pure tender & devoted overflowing from my heart. Love to my Home Loves. May God keep them all. Accept a kiss & God bless you. My Darling pray for me continually. Ever Yr Own Dod[133]

133. SHC.

The flanking movement failed to achieve its objective at Bristoe Station, and the Federals withdrew to safety. After the Army of Northern Virginia returned to the south bank of the Rappahannock, Ramseur returned to Nellie's family home at Milton. He finally fulfilled his ardent quest and married Nellie at Woodside on October 28, 1863.

6

Brigade Commander (II), November 1863–May 1864

THE NEWLYWEDS spent the next month in the embrace of their families in Milton and Lincolnton, and in the mountains of western North Carolina. Only reluctantly did Ramseur return to military duties. He found that in his absence his brigade engaged in a skirmish on November 7 at Kelly's Ford, losing a quarter of its men. The Thirtieth North Carolina regiment showed poorly, with almost 300 soldiers surrendering to the Yankees.

> Camp on the Rapidan
> Nov 24th 1863
>
> My Own Darling Wife,
>
> We arrived here safely last night. I am sorry to say that I find my Brigade reduced more than I expected by the fight at Kelly's Ford, which affair, I fear, was rather badly managed by the Offrs. in command. The men fought bravely and well. My loss was 290 captured, and about fifty killed and wounded.[1] Every body seems glad to see me. And as one of my offrs. just remarked, my presence seemed to reanimate the Brigade so that it was again as of old, joyous and gay, daring and brave.
>
> Like a proper soldier, I have been very busy, inquiring into matters concerning the Interior police of my camp, and examining our line of fortifications. I have found it necessary to inaugurate some changes already. I expect to be kept very busy for two or three weeks yet.

1. Colonel Cox served as interim brigade commander. The Federals crossed Kelly's Ford on the Rappahannock River, encountering the Second North Carolina, which slowed the advance by firing from rifle pits. When the Thirtieth North Carolina was sent forward in support, a large number of its soldiers were captured when they refused to leave buildings they occupied for shelter. *OR*, 29(1):612, 632.

Oh! My Darling Wife, *how* I have *missed* you! It is so hard to be thus separated from you altho' it is only for a short time, as we hope. I am going out this evening to search after a boarding house for you. I hope Caleb will be well enough to bring you on next week. You must tell him to drive off the chills & be ready to come on when I write for him. I do hope the poor fellow will recover entirely. I fear I can not wait *patiently* longer than next week. In fact, I know I can not for I am being far from *patiently* waiting now. But you know my notions of duty, so that I bear all things as cheerfully as possible.

Although I feel this separation from you so keenly, yet I have bright hopes of passing the winter in pleasant quarters and with my Darling Wife as my companion. I saw Gen'l. Rodes but a short time this morning. He said, wait a week or two and we will fix up famously for the winter. He will bring Mrs. Rodes here, and I expect we will occupy a vacant house near our Camp. All of us. Would that not be nice? But I will write you more fully of all of our arrangements next time I write.

I so much wish you had been in Richmond with me. All my Friends were ready and waiting to offer you their congratulations. Mrs. Huger & Mrs. [Celestine] Preston especially were anxious to see you. Both send much love to you and say they will surely call on you when you pass thro' if they know when you are in the City.

I went to the Monumental Church ("Piskey") Sunday morn'g. & to Dr. Minnegerode's Sunday Eve'g.[2] and heard two excellent sermons. I did not go to *Our Church*,[3] because all of them were occupied by Brothers, Members of the Great Methodist Conference.

And now Darling Little Wife, let me ask you some questions. How are you Dearest? Have you borne my absence bravely and cheerfully as I wanted you to do? Have you visited your friends & had a pleasant time? Have you been *right well*, even since I left? Have you thought of me often at the evening hour when our most tender love seemed even more sweet, more tender, more removed from all things earthly? Have you, My Heart's Darling, my precious Wife, Have you prayed for me, at the hour when we used to pray together to our Heavenly Father to bless us? Your prayers, My Darling Wife are most precious to me! Oh! May Our Blessed Saviour ever dwell richly in our hearts! May the Holy Spirit enable us to work continu-

2. Monumental Church was erected at Broad and College Streets to honor the dead in the Christmas 1811 fire at the Richmond Theatre. Dr. Charles F. E. Minnigerode was the rector at St. Paul's Episcopal Church at Ninth and Grace Streets, where President Davis and Gen. R. E. Lee often worshipped.

3. Presumably, a Presbyterian church.

ally in the service of our blessed Master. May we both be Christians pure and stead-fast after the Example of our blessed Lord!

I have written in great haste My Darling Wife. Oh! *How* my heart yearns after your sweet society! May a Kind and Merciful Providence soon permit us to meet again in health and comfort.

Give much love to Mama, Sis' Mary, and all. Tell Caleb to write to me. His horse has improved considerably! I shall certainly expect a letter from you tomorrow, and very often. Oh! My Beloved Wife, I do want to be with you *so! so much*!!! Darling, Goodbye. May Our Father & Our God keep us & bless us is my daily prayer. With love and kisses, you know how much, yr devoted Husband[4]

Near Morton's Ford on

The Rapidan

Nov. 26th/63

My Own Darling Wife

I intended writing you a long letter today but the Yankees have had us out all day. We have just returned to Camp, preparing for a big fight in a day or two. My Darling Wife must be cheerful and hopeful and trust-ful. Pray for me My Precious Darling. Pray for our soldiers & our beloved Country! Oh! May our Heavenly Father be with us & bless our arms and in all things enable us to say, "Thy Will be done" cheerfully and resignedly.

The enemy have been crossing all day in heavy force about 12 miles below us. This will necessitate our changing our line to meet them. I am very sorry for this, because we are compelled to give up our intrenchments & meet them in the open field. However, we are hopeful, trusting that He who orders all things aright will be with us and bless us. Oh! My Darling Wife, how my heart yearns towards you. My love for you increases more and more every day. May our blessed Savior bless us both & may the Holy Spirit enable us to love & serve Him.

Love to all. Accept my heart's best love my precious wife. May Our Father & Our God bless, protect & save us! Oh! May we be permitted to meet soon again to love & serve Him.

Write to me very soon & very often. 'Tis so hard to say Good-bye. God bless you My Beloved Wife. Accept love and kisses from your Devoted Husband[5]

4. SHC.
5. SHC.

During the following night, Rodes's division received orders to redeploy from Morton's Ford to Mine Run where, after an initial skirmish, the Confederates entrenched in anticipation of a Federal attack from across the stream. Ramseur's correspondence was interrupted at this point. But after the maneuvering on both sides, the expected clash of forces never materialized.[6] He soon returned to his former campsite to explain what had happened.

> At My Old Camp
> near Morton's Ford
> Dec. 3rd/63
>
> My Own Darling Wife,
>
> For more than one long week, I have been deprived of the pleasure of writing to you. Not the least hardship of our recent short but severe campaign has been my inability to communicate with you & the certainty that you were suffering from great and constant anxiety on my account.
>
> I hope, and have hoped, that true to your promise, you would bear this trial, and all others, as becomes a Soldier's wife, that you would not take upon yourself unnecessary troubles by anticipating bad news. Have I been right?
>
> Well, in a few words, the Yanks came over to whip us. They have ingloriously retreated without carrying out their purpose. One of our Divisions (Maj Gen'l. Johnston's) in marching to his position in line of battle, was attacked by an Entire Corps & one Div'n. of another Corps of the Enemy. These, after a sharp fight of two hours, he repulsed with very great loss. Sunday Monday & Tuesday, we waited in line for the Yanks to attack. Failing to come up the mark, as we expected. Tuesday night Gen'l. Lee made his dispositions to attack the Enemy. But lo! When Wednesday Morning's sun arose, the Yanks were across & crossing the river. They commenced retreating Tuesday night at dark & kept up the retreat until 12 o clock next day, with our army in hot pursuit.[7] This attempt on their part is the most cowardly of the war and for its moral effect must be damaging to Yankeedom. Altho' they have 65 000 troops they were afraid to attack Gen'l. Lee's 30 000 when they came over too for that very purpose. We are quiet for

6. Meade's Army of the Potomac had initiated a campaign to turn Lee's right flank and force him back to Richmond. The division commanded by Maj. Gen. Edward Johnson (not "Johnston") was moving to the left flank of Ewell's Second Corps line when it came under fire. Graham and Skoch, *Mine Run*, 53–57.

7. Rodes described these movements from Sunday, November 29, to Wednesday, December 2, in the after-action report of his division. *OR*, 29(1):876–79.

the present. How long it will remain so I can not say, but a few days will certainly determine. As soon as quiet is restored & our troops are snugly fixed in winter quarters, I want you to come on to the army. Is Caleb well enough to bring you. I hope so.

Oh! My sweet little Wife. You do not know how much I have missed you. How constantly (tho' in line of battle & in range of Yankee small arms) I have thought of you. How earnestly I have longed for even *one* short happy hour with you. How, all thro' these trials and hardships I have endured, your love has cheered me in the performance of all my duties. My Precious Darling Wife I love you more and more every day. Our Father in Heaven has mercifully spared my life thro' many dangers. Oh! May He soon give us strength to overcome our enemies and to establish a strong permanent Government, in which the all controlling principle will be love for Him and obedience to His commandments. Oh! May our God soon grant us Independence & peace & may He give *us* Grace to love Him & to serve him faithfully forever more.

I am very tired my beloved wife, so I must close. Will write soon. Telegraphed yesterday.

Have rec'd. your letter of the 23rd Inst. & *no other*. Do *you write* as you promised you would? You do not know how I enjoy yr letters! How I am disappointed & heart sick when they do not come. Mr. H[arding] was here a short while ago. He is well.

Accept my whole heart full of love & many kisses from your own

Devoted Dod[8]

Camp near Morton's Ford
Dec. 7th 1863

My Own Darling Wife,

Your precious letters of the 28th Ult. and the 2nd Inst. were received just yesterday and the day before. Truly I am sorry that the mails are so uncertain and irregular. I wrote you as soon as I got to my camp. The next day the Yankees caused us to move. Of course when in "line of battle" with the Enemy close in front, I do not have time, which I so much desire to write to you. But tho' I did not write myself, I sent word to Mr Harding to write every day. In addition I sent you three telegrams by the only opportunities I had. Since the Enemy has so ingloriously retreated, I have written you twice. This makes thrice. You are right My Own Beloved, in ascribing all fault to the mails, for believe me, *now*, that I am so cruelly

8. SHC.

separated from my Heart's Darling, the dearest privilege and sweetest pleasure I enjoy, is communion with you. Even though it be by this slow & uncertain medium of letter writing, My Darling Nellie, do you know *how* precious your letters are to me? Before we were married they were my delight, but now that you are my Beloved Wife, they are infinitely, inexpressibly more so. How much I have missed you, My Darling, it is impossible to say. I have thought of you morning, evening and night. I have longed for your sweet company all through the weary days & the long dreary nights. I have never known before how dearly I loved you. The saddest thought I now entertain is that every day I am passing away from you is gone *forever*. But my Precious Wife, I feel and believe that I am doing my duty. And tho' it is hard to be thus separated from you, I believe it is right & I am therefore content. Let us believe so & all will be well!

I am and have been very much troubled at not being able to secure a comfortable and suitable boarding house for you in the vicinity of my camp. But I hope this difficulty will soon be obviated by our removal. It is rumoured that we will move to the vicinity of Orange C.H. in a few days. I hope so as then I will hope to have you with me very soon. However much I dislike to write it, I must say that it will impossible for you to come on to the Army until we move away from here. I know I can rely upon my Darling Wife being brave & patient. The time will soon come my Own Beloved Nellie when we will again be united in love. When my heart grows weak & weary, I think of you My Darling Wife & gain strength.

Tell Caleb for me that he *must not* come on 'til I write for him. When he does come, let him bring a certificate from Uncle Charles[9] extending his furlough. This simply for his easy passage on the trains. Of course I do not need such a certificate.

I was sorry to hear of George's ill success in Richmond. I think he ought to be his own overseer.[10] That will exempt him & some one ought to remain at Woodside. Mr. Harding is well. He slept with me last night & we talked of home & the loved ones there. Do excuse this letter. My pen is miserable and my ink execrable. Write to me very often. Accept my heart overflowing full of love. Oh! How I *do* want to be with you! Love to all. May God bless, keep & comfort you my Beloved Wife is my constant prayer.

Yr Devoted Husband[11]

9. As a physician, Caleb and Ramseur's uncle in Milton could provide the necessary certification to substantiate Caleb's incapacity due to recurring bouts of typhoid fever.

10. With the death of their father, one brother (Dod) dead and the other (Caleb) in the army, eighteen-year-old George was responsible for managing the real assets of the Richmond family.

11. SHC.

Camp near Morton's Ford
Dec 8th 1863

My Dear Brother,

   Since my return to the army I have been so constantly occupied as to
prevent me from writing home as often as I desire. I am astonished at
Meade's last move. He came with orders from Old Abe to find Gen'l. Lee
& fight him. His force was at least 60 000. Some estimate it at 80 000.
He found we waited in line of battle opposite his, Sunday, Monday & Tuesday. Gen'l. Lee became tired waiting for Meade to attack & Tuesday night
made dispositions to attack him Wednesday morning. With the rising sun,
we moved forward. The Yankee fires were burning but the rascals had
cowardly sneaked off during the night. We pursued & captured about 1000
prisoners. Captured men say that they were twice ordered to assault our
positions, but that [Maj. Gen. Gouverneur K.] Warren's Corps refused to
advance. This statement is partially corroborated by the northern papers.[12]
Had Meade attacked I verily believe he would have been cut all to pieces.
The effect of his campaign is obliged to be damaging to his army. No army
can pursue so cowardly a course & escape the result of demoralization &
disgrace.

   Would that I could look as hopefully to the West as to this Army.
Bragg's Army seems to have been disgracefully routed without any thing
approaching a stubborn fight.[13] I fear it will be hard to restore confidence
to his shattered & demoralized masses. Beauregard is the man to do it,
if anybody. But I see the Pres't. is still blindly holding on to Bragg. His
Stubborness may yet prove our greatest disaster.[14] But let me not despair!
Croaking does not [illegible]

   I can not tell you how much I miss my Darling Little Wife. It is very
hard to have the Honey Moon this suddenly & cruelly cut short. The un-

12. Northern newspapers reported that the enemy's extensive entrenchments caused Warren
to halt and await further instructions. The Washington press stated that by slowly moving into position, the northern troops allowed their adversaries to strengthen their defenses. The subsequent
retrograde by the Federals was said to exacerbate their relaxed discipline. *New York Times*, Dec. 4,
1863; *Evening Star* [Washington, D.C.], Dec. 5, 1863.

13. The months-long Chattanooga campaign had concluded ignobly for the Confederates when
Bragg's army withdrew into Georgia in disarray.

14. The disaster at Chattanooga was too much even for Jefferson Davis. As was his custom in
times of criticism, Bragg submitted his resignation to Richmond, but this time, to his surprise, it
was accepted. Davis's blind loyalty to Bragg over the preceding seventeen months had, indeed, cost
the Confederate army in the west thousands of soldiers who could never be replaced. But Ramseur
was not prescient as to Bragg's replacement. At the end of December, Gen. Joseph E. Johnston
was appointed commander of the Army of Tennessee. Interestingly, neither he nor Beauregard,
Ramseur's choice, was popular with Davis.

certainty of our movements and the utter impossibility of procuring any suitable boarding house in the vicinity of my former camp have induced me to wait until we move into Winter Qurs. before I send for Nellie. It is hard to be thus separated, but I submit as cheerfully as possible with the conviction that I am doing my duty.

With reference to yr appt. as comissary to my Brig. I am sorry to tell you that Maj [James W.] Miller has just ret'd. from N.C. where he unsuccessfully applied for a transfer to Post duty. If you have to go into service, come on here & I will find a place for you, tho' I am afraid not a commission. There is no law or order preventing a person exempted from service by any proper means from volunteering as aid. I therefore suggest that you hold onto yr Receiver office, which will exempt you, & volunteer on my Staff. I have four horses. You can use one, & I'll pay yr Mess bill, so you will be at little expense. If you come, bring me a Servant, if one can be hired in yr country, but I do not think it *at all* advisable for you to leave until every thing becomes quiet in Western N.C. I very much fear our peaceful South will have an army quartered on it this Winter.

I don't know what I'll do if John Phifer backs out from our trade.[15] Every thing is so high I can hardly live in the plainest way on my pay. Will you see Jack & learn what he will do for me? For the first time in many months I am right unwell, with severe cold & dysentery. Hope to be well again in a few days. Do write me often & fully. Love to all at Home. [illegible]. Rec'd. Luly's letter last night. May God bless & keep us all & soon reunite us in peace & safety. Yr devoted Brother S.D.R.[16]

Camp near Morton's Ford
Dec. 9th 1863

My Own Darling Wife,

I wrote you the night before last with such a miserable pen and such bad ink that I fear you found great difficulty in deciphering my scribbling. Oh! How grievously I miss you these long (short) days! I did not think it *possible* for me to miss you *so much*! The truth is I love you as I told you more than a year ago, *far more* than your *cousinly* share. I long for your sweet presence all the day long, and throughout the cold, dreary lonesome

---

15. To augment his often erratic pay from the Confederate government, Ramseur had entered into an arrangement to produce yarn at the Laurel Hill Factory in Lincolnton owned by his Uncle John. Ramseur's anxiety was due, no doubt, to the sense of duty he continually felt to supplement his family's income.

16. PC.

night I continuously wish for my own beloved beautiful Wife! But I must bow cheerfully to the decrees of military necessity. Very soon I hope we will move away from this desolate region, and then I will hope to have the cheering, elevating influence of your society to make glad my tour of duty with the Army of No. Va. Today I have been very lonesome. My tent is quite comfortable with blazing fire in my *brick* fire place. Only your sweet presence is wanted to make me satisfied.

I had no idea, when I bade you, Goodbye, that so long a time would elapse before seeing you again. Now I hope to see you next week. If the Division does not move before then will my Precious Wife be willing to come on with Caleb & stay at Col. Crockford's[17] about 20 miles from here, where I will have an opportunity of being with you *only once a week*! It seems to me, very selfish in me, to ask you to come from your sweet home among Strangers when I will have to leave you the greater part of the time. But I leave all this to you. Do not come until I can get your answer to this note, & you can receive my reply. However I hope, as I said before, that the Division will move to some point where we can be together all the time. Maj [Thomas M.] Smith told me yesterday that he certainly intended bringing his wife to the army this winter. May be you can come on together. Tell Caleb that Mr. C. B. Root[18] has succeeded in getting 4 yds of cloth in Raleigh, for each Mr. Harding himself & myself. $10 pr yd. in all $120. Tell him to pay for it if he has the opportunity & have it brought to Milton. If he or Mr. H. can spare it I want to get 2 yds from them so, that after repaying 2 yds to Maj Miller I will have enough to make me an overcoat. Tell Caleb that we are living on bread & beef & to bring us something to make it more palatable, catsup, pickle or something. Your Sorghum Cake was delightful & Capt Gales, Mr. H. & I enjoyed it much.

I sent to Richmond yesterday for your horse. Have you gotten a riding habit? Don't forget it. I told you, My Sweet little Wife, that I intended to make you an allowance of half of my pay. In accordance with that provision I have now "subject to your orders" $100. Oh! My Sweetheart! How I do want to see you! I sometimes feel like it would not take much persuasion to make me *desert*! How I sympathize with some of my poor fellows who have not seen their wife & children for two years!

---

17. John Crockford was a contractor for the Orange and Alexandria Railroad who had worked with the Virginia military authorities in Northern Virginia before the state seceded. *OR*, 51(2):98.

18. Charles B. Root was a prominent Raleigh jeweler. Murray, *Wake, Capital County of North Carolina*, 1:264, 482, 545, Appendix D.

Had a letter from Luly the other day. All well. She complains of not hearing from you. They all insist on your spending the winter at my home provided you do not join me in the army. This would be my wish too, My Precious Darling, if agreeable to your wishes. If you stop long enough in Richmond, send to Mrs. Huger, near the corner of 5th (or 6th) & Cary Streets. They want so much to see you.

Does My Heart's Darling, my beautiful little wife, know how much I love her? How constantly I long for her sweet society? How frequently I make spirit visits to her in her quiet home? Sometimes, when nobody intrudes, I spend an hour or rather hours, in recalling every scene & incident of the past happy year! I think of my visit to Woodside last fall, of my short wounded furlough after Chancelorsville, and of my last and best visit, when I was rendered one of the happiest of men by securing you, my beloved Nellie as My Wife. 'Tis so pleasant to live over again in imagination these green spots in the "dead past." Ah! my Sweetest, best wife, could this cruel war end in our independence & safety, how proudly would I enter upon the race that is before us! How confidently, with your sweet sympathy & the blessing of God, would I encounter & overcome all obstacles & dangers! Truly, that will be a happy day when the Angel of Peace shall once more visit our unfortunate bleeding country! May that day be not far distant!

How is Mama? Sis' Mary? Lucy, George & all? Give each and all much love for me. Would that I could make you a telegraphic visit & deliver it in *propria persona* [personally]. Write me very often. I have rec'd. only three letters from you since my return! I will write to you every other day. Will you do the same?

In the Army of No. Va. there is nothing at all new. The Yanks are reported to have fallen back to Fauquier [County], destroying the Rail Road behind them. This will prevent any active operations (I think) on our part during the winter. So there seems to be nothing now to do but to build winter quarters, drill, discipline & organize our troops for the Spring Campaign. This will be very pleasant duty for me, provided my wife is here to help me. Not otherwise. Tell Caleb that Captain Coughenour has been permanently assigned as Inspector of my Brigade, that his horse has greatly improved but is still *powerful poor*. Do write to me often my own Darling Wife. Do not allow any thing short of sickness prevent you from performing this charitable office. You do not know how precious your letters are to me, away up here in this Wilderness. I wait anxiously for the mail & if no letter comes, I really feel *almost* disposed to complain. Am invited to dinner today at 5o clock at Lt. Col Lea's quarters.[19] *The hour* is fashionable enough to promise something good. Mr. Harding staid with me last night. He is well, but mighty blue! Accept my heart full of love My Own Darling Nellie! my beloved wife. May our Father & our God bless us, protect us, give us strength & Grace to love & serve Him, and may He soon unite us in peace & safety is my constant prayer. Devotedly your

Own Husband[20]

> Thursday morning
> Dec. 10th/63

Our mails have been irregular for the past few days, hence my letter did not go off this morning. I will have an opportunity to send you a few lines in addition this morning. There seems to be an impression among knowing ones that if the weather continues good for a week or two longer, we will make another move forward. I give you this for what it is worth, at the same time expressing the belief that our active operations for the Winter are over. Mr. Harding was over to see me this morning. He mentioned that he had just rec'd. a letter from his wife in which she said, that you were still greatly disappointed in not hearing from me. There is something wrong about the mails. I am sure I have written you nearly every other day for the last week. I hope you will get tons of these letters.

My Precious Darling Wife. Do write to me often. Let us make this cruel separation as bearable as possible by frequent communication. Give my love to all at Woodside. I have suffered severely with cold for several days, but am much better today. I do hope our present suspense will soon be over & that you will come soon to gladden my heart. Accept more love than I can express. May God bless My Heart's Darling, My own beloved Wife. Yr Devoted Husband D. R.[21]

19. John W. Lea of Mississippi was a member of the June 1861 class at West Point who resigned from the Academy in 1860 due to the impending conflict. Commander of Company I (from Caswell County), Fifth North Carolina Infantry, at the outset of the war, Lea was commanding the regiment by December 1863, and just before Appomattox would take command of the brigade from the injured Brig. Gen. Robert D. Johnston. *Register of Graduates and Former Cadets*, 251; James C. MacRae and C. M. Busbee, "Fifth Regiment," in Clark, *Histories*, 1:281, 290–91; Walter A. Montgomery, "Twelfth Regiment," in Clark, *Histories*, 1:651.

20. SHC.

21. SHC.

Camp near Morton's Ford

Dec. 12th 1863

My Own Darling Wife,

Your precious letter, sent by Maj. Hunt,[22] was received yesterday. How gladly I welcomed it! I am very much troubled to know that you have suffered so much anxiety by reason of my letters not reaching you. I cannot account for the mismanagement in our mails. Had you rec'd. my first letter, you would have been prepared for an interval of silence, for I told you in it of the slow operations regularly, if at all, while the Yanks were advancing with the intention of "Whipping us." I do hope you have by this time rec'd. some of my letters. This one is *the 5th*. Have you rec'd. all? Your sweet letters, My Darling Wife, are more precious to me, than any thing else. So highly are they prized that I find myself looking for one every day and feeling much disappointed when it does not come. Ah! you do not know how it gladdens my heart to hear the joyful message, "a letter from your wife!" My tent seems a palace and I am as happy as I possibly can be, so far away from my beautiful little Wife! Then, My Heart's Darling, write often, write fully, all about your Dear Self. I promise to write as often as I can. I love egotistical letters from those I love! You must write about my sweet little Wife. Tell me what you do, what you think, who you see &c &c, and I will promise to be as egotistical as I generally have been.

To begin then I'll tell you of a famous dinner I attended the other day at Lt Col Lea's quarters. He had invited four of his West Point Classmates & myself, making five West Pointers. Only two could attend, Col. Willis[23] & Myself. We had a nice Whisky Toddy before dinner. Roast beef, served with onions (I've forgotten the French), boiled ham and cabbage, sweet potatoes, Irish ditto, baked & fried, & splendid sour pickles. 2nd Course. Sweet potatoe pies, & Blackberry jam ditto. Coffee (pure) & cigars (Havana). What think you of such a dinner in Camp? 'Twas famous! We are all indebted to Lea's Good Wife for sending him these good things. We had a good time talking over old times! How many cigars do you suppose I smoked? Five! With a headache to begin with. You may guess that I suffered severely from this indulgence, but I must tell you that the toddy, the good dinner, the coffee, or the cigars, or all together cured me altogether. Your Presence, only, My Darling Sweet Heart, can effect my perfect cure

22. In June, Leonard H. Hunt had been promoted to major, assistant adjutant and inspector general, on General Pender's staff. Krick, *Staff Officers in Gray*, 167.

23. Edward S. Willis was also a member of the West Point class of June 1861 who had resigned early to join the southern war effort and was now serving with the Twelfth Georgia Infantry. *Register of Graduates and Former Cadets*, 251; Krick, *Lee's Colonels*, 373.

of body and mind. I am becoming so impatient to see you that as soon as I receive a reply to my letter asking your consent to stay at Col. Crockford's, I will telegraph for you and Caleb to come on. Tell Caleb to be sure to telegraph me both from Barkesdale's[24] and from Richmond when you will reach Orange C.H. Tell Caleb also that Hunter did not come on as I expected. That I have hired a small boy (a poor Sot) temporarily. If possible, he should secure a good servant. One can not get on well without such an one this winter. I hope he will bring a good boy with him. I will very willingly pay $25 pr month, clothe & feed him.

I have hunted industriously over this neighbourhood for a boarding house for you. You will have to be contented seeing me occasionally at Col. C's until our Division moves back, which cant possibly be put off more than two weeks longer at furthest. Then I hope we will move to a more hospitable neighbourhood. Col. Grimes wrote for his wife yesterday. She will remain at Orange C.H.

You do not know how gloomy the day has been, dark and rainy and gloomy. But I have spent it very pleasantly in my cozy tent. First by arranging and examining my official business. Then in reading a part of "Cosette."[25] Then in giving orders for the day. And now by writing to my own Darling Wife. This is the dearest privilege, the highest pleasure I now enjoy. How transportingly delightfully happy I will be when you do come! Ah! me! It seems impossible for me to wait another week or two. Would you rather remain at home until after Christmas. Use your pleasure. But expect a telegram to come on very soon. I will go to see Col. C. next week early and will telegraph you from Orange C.H.

You know Darling how pleased I was with my Yarn trade as I called it. Well, what do you think Mr. Schenck writes me about it? Why, that "Mr. Phifer seems to have forgotten all about his promised trade with you." I wonder if he does intend to forget his word. I would be as poor as a Church mouse, all my life, before people should feel it necessary, to make me put down a trade or promise in writing before they could be satisfied. And yet, if this promise is not kept, it will be the 2nd time I have been deceived in that question & I will never trust that man again. But say nothing 'bout this, My Darling. I may be judging too hastily. Let us be patient.

I must close now, My Own Darling, & leave you, for other duties. How reluctantly I give you up! Even for a short time. My Beloved Darling Wife,

24. Barksdale was a hamlet with a railroad station fourteen miles north of Halifax Court House, Virginia, between the Dan and Banister Rivers. Martin, *A New and Comprehensive Gazetteer*, 184.

25. Cosette is a heroine in Victor Hugo's *Les Misérables*, which was first published in French in 1862 in France and New York. An English translation also appeared in 1862. Volume Two was entitled "Cosette."

be assured of my continued increasing love and devotion. May our Father in Heaven bless us & comfort us & soon unite us in health & peace. I always pray specially for you My Precious Wife, & that yr prayers for me may be answered. Love to all. My *Heart full* for yr Dear *Self*.

Yr Devoted Husband[26]

Near Morton's Ford Va.

Dec 15th 1863

My Own Darling Wife,

I intended writing to you yesterday but was prevented by camp duties. I expected before now, my Sweetest Darling, to have written for you to come on to the Army, but really, matters look *so threatening* at present that I do not yet feel it advisable to send for you.

Can not tell you *how sad* I am every day to feel that the time I have to wait before seeing you is thus prolonged. But, My Darling Wife, in the midst of this great uncertainty I feel that it is safest and best for you to remain at home.

It pains me very much thus to postpone the time when I will have the pleasure of again welcoming you. But you know, that it is best for me to do my duty. I know you appreciate my feelings of duty and affection sufficiently well to know that I write this for your own well being. The entire Yankee Army is encamped within striking distance of us. We have rumours of their advance & surely every indication justifies us in preparing & being prepared for it. We hear also of the Yanks advancing down the valley so as to strike the Va. & East Tenn. R.R. thus cutting Longstreets communications. This has necessitated the sending of a force from here under command of Maj Gen'l. Early.[27] When the Yanks here [hear] of our sending troops away from here, I think they will be induced to push forward. I believe, since the Western Yank Army has halted, that their policy will be to put that Army in an entrenched position & send [Lt. Gen. Ulysses S.] Grant & 2000 or 3000 men to reinforce this Army of the Potomac, or to push forward their Tenn Army on the south of the Va & Tenn R.R. toward Richmond. Nous verrons. [We will see.] Whatever they try to do, I hope & trust that our noble leaders and gallant Army will be in time to baulk them.

26. SHC.

27. The report of Early's subsequent operations in the Shenandoah Valley covers the period December 16–23, 1863. *OR*, 29(1):970.

But enough of this cruel war! I prefer to write about your Darling Self. Do you know how much I have been disappointed in not receiving a letter from you this week. My last was yr letter of the 7th Inst sent by Maj Hunt which I recd. on the 12th Inst. Like you, I feel sure that you have written & the fault all lies in the miserable mails. Tonight, I hope to receive a letter tonight. If not, I will be entirely disconsolate all day tomorrow. Now, tell Caleb, that I say, he must not become impatient. He ought to be glad of this opportunity. Tell him I say he *must* be gay & happy, enjoy the privilege to the full extent & when I send for him, to come on well & cheerful. I do not need him as badly now as I did before Capt Coughenour was assigned to duty on my Staff.[28]

I expect My Darling Sweetheart that it will be after Christmas before I write for you. Be content therefore & joyous with the assurance that I'll send for you as soon the situation will possibly allow of it. You must appreciate my Darling Wife, what a self denying sacrifice I make in thus postponing your coming. It is all done out of over watchful anxiety for you, who are dearer to me than all the world beside.

I have not heard from home for some time. When last heard from all were well. Do My Darling write to me oftener. Your letters are the sunshine of this dark life. Were you not all amused at old Abe's proclamation.[29] Really he takes it for granted that we are all whipped. I think the Old Abe has much work ahead of him before he can persuade us to accept his terms. Don't you?

Well My Darling Wife, I must close. Sorry to write you such a hasty note, but I know you will excuse it under the circumstances. Do give my love to all at Woodside. Mr. H is well & sends love. Do write very often to me. 'Tis the best thing you can do for me. May our Father in Heaven bless, keep & protect us & speedily unite us in love is the prayer of

Yr Devoted Husband[30]

28. Coughenour served as assistant adjutant and inspector general on the brigade staff. William R. Cox, "The Anderson-Ramseur-Cox Brigade," in Clark, *Histories*, 4:462.

29. On December 8, 1863, President Lincoln had issued an amnesty proclamation pardoning anyone who participated in the rebellion if he or she would take an oath to the Union and accept all laws and proclamations regarding emancipation. Persons excepted from the provisions of this decree included high-ranking officers in the Confederate military and those who resigned commissions in the U.S. armed forces to join the southern war effort, either of which would have excluded Ramseur. Richardson, *A Compilation of the Messages and Papers of the Presidents*, 8:314–16.

30. SHC.

Camp near Morton's Ford Va.

Dec. 17th 1863

My Dear Darling Wife,

The cold rain is falling fast and all without is dark and dreary. My fire gives to my tent a cheerful aspect, the more striking from contrast. But My Beloved I must tell you I am a *little blue.* Last night I laid on my Soldier pallet and revelled in dreams of my Darling Wife far, far away. I was happy then in the almost certain anticipation of receiving a messenger of Love from my absent Darling by the mail I was then waiting for. Alas. Our fondest, brightest hopes are often doomed to fade. Very soon, I heard my mail carrier say, "A large mail but nothing for Head Quarters!" I could not credit it, & was not satisfied until the entire mail had been closely reexamined. Oh! the horrid, tantalizing mails! I do hope, my best Loved Nellie, that you are not caused the same degree of suffering and anxiety from the same cause; but I know you do not give way to this feeling. I know you do not. You are brave and patient and happy! Is it not so, Darling?

Your health, My Precious Wife, (What an *inestimable* priceless treasure is your health to me, to us!) requires *now*, more than ever, that you should be cheerful, happy, contented and above all things free from apprehensions and alarms! Will you not promise me, My Own beautiful Wife, that you will fully, freely, faithfully trust all things, my life, your life, our happiness, our all, into the hands and safe keeping of Our Father in Heaven? You will, I know you will. And, therefore, *I* rest satisfied and happy. What a precious hope, what a sweet consolation, we have in that certain knowledge that Our Father and Our God cares for us, guides us, protects us in all dangers, delivers us in all temptations and finally will save us throughout all Eternity!

If this rain continues two days longer it will effectually put a stop to all further active operations, at least, for two weeks to come. In that time we may expect more wintry weather, & hence a cessation of hostilities from necessity. If I could get an answer to my letter asking your consent to come on to Col. Crockford's, I think I would telegraph you to come at once. I do hope to hear from you tonight. Really I will not know how to control myself, unless I hear from you very soon. My last letter was the 7th Inst., nearly *two weeks* old! I have heard from home since then, and have rec'd. a letter from David, as far south as Atlanta, dated the 10th.[31]

---

31. On October 12, 1863, David Ramseur was ordered to report for duty to the medical director at Marietta, Georgia. He was subsequently assigned to an Atlanta hospital. David Ramseur, Confederate Generals, Staff Officers, and Non-regimental Enlisted Men, CMSR, RG 109, NARA.

Can it be possible there is something wrong in *your* post office? Luly is
very anxious to have you spend the winter at home. Mr. Schenck gives
me great credit for self denial & a host of other virtues, in concluding to
leave my Wife at home. I wonder who informed him thus wisely? I think it
would be anything else but commendable in me to leave my Wife at home,
when there was any possible chance of having her with me in comfort
and safety. At [the] same time, I feel it necessary above all other considerations to provide *first* for My Darling's comfort and security from danger.
And this is the cause of the long waiting on my part to send for you. Oh!
My Darling's Sweetheart! You do not know *how* I want to see you! Can you
imagine how wildly joyous I will be to welcome you once more! I love to
anticipate the joys, all the little circumstances of our next meeting. Ah!
May it occur soon, very soon!

I have been kept very busy since my return. Very many of my officers
are absent, sick and wounded, and several are prisoners. Some of those
who remain have grown careless & inattentive to the strict performance
of duty. This necessitates constant vigilance on my part. I am convinced
that I will have to proceed against some of my offrs in the most rigorous
manner, unless they very speedily and decidedly mend their ways. I am determined, by every effort of mine, to keep up the high and enviable reputation my Brigade has so gloriously won. I wish you were here to help me!
Ah! if I had your sweet, soothing sympathy, after the duties and trials of
the day are over, I am sure I could do my duty better and in much kinder
spirit than I now do. Let us hope that your gentle influence will soon be
given.

There is nothing at all new in the army. We are drilling twice a day,
conscripts three times. You see us preparing for coming emergencies. I
do hope Congress will pass some sensible laws this session, improving the
currency & increasing the army by enrolling every man who has employed
a substitute. How would you like to see your friend Mr. Bruce[32] trudging
thro' the mud with a musket?

Your horse has safely arrived. He is a capital little animal, very small,
almost a pony. I think you will be pleased with him. How I wish you were
here to ride with me. Day before yesterday the weather was magnificent,
the atmosphere was more transparent than I ever saw it, blue mountains
seemed almost in speaking distance. I took a long ride along the river
& the bordering hills. How earnestly my Heart wished for your sweet

---

32. J. Wilkins Bruce was a well-to-do local resident who was a co-founder of the Milton Farmer's Bank and the Milton and Sutherlin Railroad Company. Powell, *When the Past Refused to Die*,
334, 505.

presence. I felt that my "other heart" was absent, that other heart without which I can not live in peace and happiness. I know you would have enjoyed a ride over such a country on such a day & with such an escort! Would you not, my beautiful Wife? Dearest Nellie, I will close now, waiting and hoping for the coming of the mail. I will continue to write to you every other day. Will you do likewise? Do give my very best love to our Loved ones at Woodside. To Uncle C. & Aunt Prissie.

Accept Darling Wife my Hearts best, richest, dearest Love. May our Father in Heaven keep & bless us! Your devoted Husband[33]

Head Quarters Ramseur's Brig

Dec. 18th 1863

I wrote you yesterday. My Darling Wife, but my letter was not put in the mail this morning. I will therefore add a few lines tonight. Your precious letter of the 15th Inst. came last night. I can not tell you how glad I was to get it. The last date before this one was the 7th, nearly *two weeks* without a letter from my wife. You mention having just rec'd. my letter of the 3rd. Surely it does not require eleven days for a letter to reach you. But so it seems to have done.

Tell George I very much fear his horses have the *glanders*, a terrible disease, the more so as it is contagious.[34] I think he had better put them in the small stable in the corner of the lot & await further developments.

At any rate, he had better keep them away from the mules, nor allow the mules to go into their stables. In fact, it is almost dangerous to keep the mules in proximity to their stables.

My Darling Wife, I love you so devotedly, so tenderly. I need only your presence to make me happy. How I love to dream of the joyous days of peace again, when we will live together in a modest unassuming, but Oh! such a happy little cottage! I find that I could live thus far away from the world's ignoble strife, & be perfectly happy & contented with my Heart's Darling! Ah! Do you not long for the coming of such a day?

I wrote to Lu & Fanny today. Really! I feel that they have some reason to complain of my silence. I excused my self however by telling them that every letter from "my wife" counted *one* from me & I had no doubt you had written frequently. Was I right?

---

33. SHC.

34. Glanders is characterized by inflation or ulceration of the nasal mucous membranes and lymph nodes and module formation in the lungs and spleen, making it fatal to horses and donkeys.

I feel tonight that I would give all I am worth to be with you in your quiet happy home during the Christmas holidays! But I hope to have you here by that time.

I hope you have rec'd. my other letters since you last wrote. I have written several since the 3rd Inst. Do write to me oftener.

My Darling Precious Wife, I wish I could take you in my arms tonight & tell you how dearly I love you.

I have thought of you very often today. Would that this cruelness were over & we were living in peace & happiness, enjoying all the beautiful things in this world of ours. But Patience! Patience!! More toil! More suffering is still in store for us. Let us bear all with fortitude and resignation. Love to all. I am remarkably well except a slight cold. Do write often, my dear Darling Wife. With a heart full of love and a thousand sweet Kisses.

Your own Devoted Dod[35]

The hiatus in the succession of letters from Ramseur to Nellie over the next three months was due to her arrival in Virginia on December 30 to be with her new husband. The sole exception was a quick note penned at his headquarters before an unexpected assignment on February 4.

One of Ramseur's tasks during this period was endorsing the claim of James Magruder, a wealthy farmer in Orange County, Virginia, who owned land valued at $44,000 in the 1860 Census. Magruder alleged damage to his timber, fencing, and crops by Confederate troops during the summer and fall of 1862. In assessing the request, Ramseur joined Generals Trimble, Rodes, Colquitt, and Iverson, along with Colonels Grimes and John T. Mercer, and Capt. Albert H. Campbell, a topographical engineer. They appraised the claim to be in excess of the quantity of fuel and forage consumed by troops camped on Magruder's land. Upon receipt of these endorsements on January 21, 1864, the Quartermaster Department decided to withhold any payment until "a reasonable assessment" was made.[36]

> Camp six miles from Orange C.H.
> Jan. 12th 1864
>
> My Dear Bro.
>
> I have been so busy recently as to neglect my correspondents. Nellie came on the 30th Dec. I staid with her, at Col. Crockford's, 9 miles from

35. SHC.

36. Quarter Master Department, Register of Claims, 1863–64, Chap. 5, Vol. 44, entry 3415, RG 109, NARA.

my Camp, until the 2nd Jan, when I was ordered with my Command to picket our Div'n. front on the Rapid Ann, some 12 miles from my camp. Here I remained on picket, very cold & uncomfortable, until the 9th Inst., when returned to camp. I went to Col C's last Sat & remained until yesterday when I brought Nellie to Mr. Kendall's (a *plain* good country-man)[37] about 2 miles from my Camp. I have just come to camp from there. I remain here, attending to business from 7 a.m. till 4 p.m. when I hasten away to my little wife. Can you imagine *how much* I enjoy her society? Nellie grows sweeter, prettier & smarter every day. Ah, it is a *good thing* to have a wife! And such a wife!!!

My famous box came to me, while I was on picket half starved. I paid $75 freight on it. But I tell you it was worth hundreds. It came safely, with the exception of the sweet potatoes which were spoiled & a jug of Sorghum (I think) which was broken. The brandy came in well & lasted me & staff 2 days. I got 4 drinks. Generous wasn't I? The salad & chow-chow was splendid. Ditto butter & *eggs*.

A Mr. Dillon will leave Statesville between the 4th & 6th of next month with a lot of boxes for the 4th Reg't. He brings them on monthly, I believe. He came to offer to bring anything for me that I could have sent to Statesville (to Mr. Frank Alexander R.R. Ag't.) by the 5th of Feb'y. next. If you can send me another box, thro' him, it will be most acceptable. I wont expect so large a box. Dried fruit, Irish potatoes & onions are the most acceptable vegetables. Butter & eggs of course are acceptable, but these hard times I wont expect them unless they are abundant. Chow chow cant be beat. Tell Luly to send me 4 or 5 dinner plates if she can spare them. Buy me a set of knives & forks at *Sallie's* Country Store. I forget the name. Also a pocket knife or *two*, from Harding's. And if you can possibly make the maise [maize], send me a gallon of whiskey & brandy each. This is almost indispensable to camp life. I don't think I will need the $300 sent me by Mr. Lander. I sold a horse the other day that was falling away, for want of long forage & promised to take his departure, unless better fed, for $650. I might send you $800 or so. I wrote "Uncle Jack" a kind note the other day. Think it will fix the trade he promised me. Tell Father to approach him again on the subject.

Do write me frequently. Yr letters & yr affection is to me most dear. I'll give you an essay on the state of the country soon. Nil desperandum

---

37. Thomas G. Kendall's wealth amounted to $9,000 in real estate and $20,000 in personal property, including nineteen slaves, making him a well-to-do "plain good countryman." U.S. Census Office, *Eighth Census, 1860: Slave Inhabitants.*

[Do not despair] is my motto. If Nellie knew I was writing she would send much love to all. She loves you very dearly. I'll try to write home more frequently this winter, or get my wife to do it for me. Heard from David the other day. He writes soberly, but is anxious to return to Richmond which I am anxious for him *not to do*.

You may tell the girls to hone Aunt Betty for something for my box.

If you can buy me a nice calf skin do so. I'll need a pr of boots a month hence. Let Aleck[38] make them without the huge tops that cost so much. I don't care for them to come higher than my knee.

Give love to all at home. Kiss Sallie & the Little Ones for me. My God bless you my dear Brother. Ever & Truly yrs. Dod[39]

Camp Ramseur's Brig.

Jan 28th 1864

My Dear Brother,

I have been very busily engaged recently. This together with the expectation of a letter from you has prevented my writing sooner. How are you? Not blue, I hope. My spirits are much higher than they have been. Do you know that for nearly a month our men rec'd. 1 ⅛ lbs. of flour & from ⅛ to ¼ lbs. meat pr day. Nothing else. This made me believe—now things are better. The men get between ¼ to ½ lbs. meat pr day, & we are willing to whip Yankeedom when cared for in that way. The Army must be fed even if people at home must go without it. The spirit of our soldiers is all right. Yesterday my Brigade passed the following resolution unanimously. Resolved "That we declare ourselves enlisted in the cause of Southern Rights and Southern Independence as long as one armed foe shall remain on our soil. That we declare ourselves *in for the war* without condition, & this we do most cheerfully as is our bounden duty." What do you think of that? Send Croakers to the army for comfort and courage! [Brig. Gen. Cullen A.] Battle's Brig, Doles' Brig, Johnston's Brig & some of this Div. (Daniels' is on picket & cant be heard from) have passed similar resolutions. So our glorious Division, one which has rec'd. the praise of Gen'l. Lee both at Chancelorsville & Gettysburg, has shown to the world that we intend to *fight the thing out*, that we *wont be whipped* as long as anybody is left to fight. Would you not be proud to occupy a high position in such a Div'n. of such an Army.

38. A black boot-maker in Lincolnton at this time, according to local lore.
39. PC.

Why Don't you write to me? I am positively longing for a letter from you. Nellie is very comfortably situated near my Camp. She rides over with me sometimes & spends the day in Camp. She wrote Sally a long letter last week, which I hope [illegible] will answer soon.

'Tis not necessary to say how much I enjoy soldiering when I have my little wife to help me. Ah! I am being happy now. It is well that it is so, for soon we must separate, and then the tremendous campaign which everybody is anticipating will burst forth. I do pray that I may be able to do my duty through all coming dangers, that our Father & our God will enable us, this year to triumph over our enemies & to conquer a glorious peace. Whatever lot may be reserved for me I pray & trust, that I may be ready & prepared to obey the call of Providence. Oh! that I had my brave men who were killed at Chancelorsville. Would that my Brig was as large as then. Now I have now scarcely one thousand men for duty.

What is the news at home? The weather here is so warm & sunshiny. It makes me think of the spring time gardening of younger days. I suppose you are fixing up yr garden. Do persuade Father to raise all sorts of vegetables in the greatest abundance. Tell Fanny she ought to limit the negroes to ⅛ to ¼ lb. of meat, when they have vegetables. Our whole people should do this & send the surplus to the army. Write me a long letter about home matters. Tell me about Father's farming, how much corn &c he will plant, & where.

What about Jack Phifer's yarn trade? I wrote him a letter of thanks for the apples he sent me & reminded him of his promise. Did he say anything about it? I hope he will come up to his promise. Living up here *is high.* The Confederacy dont increase our pay in proportion to the depreciations of the currency. My pay *now* amts to $13.50 in Gold pr month. But I hope I can squeeze through even this if Jack Phifer will do as he promised.

I am glad to believe that Cong. will not force you into the field.[40] I dont want you to come till you are obliged to because I dont believe you could survive the exposure. If you are obliged to come, come to me & I'll find some place for you. Give my love to every body at home. Do write to me fully about home matters. Would you be surprized to hear that I look for your letters as anxiously as I used to look for letters from my Sweet heart. In fact, my wife says she is convinced that she is not my first & only love, that I fell in love with you years ago & that I prove constant still. To this,

40. David Schenck held an exemption from military service as a receiver for the Confederate government. But as the need for men to serve in the military became dire, Schenck's status and that of other similarly situated men came under closer scrutiny. In their correspondence in the weeks ahead, Ramseur and Schenck would return to this subject more than once.

I plead Guilty, & assure you, that one of the purest and best emotions I enjoy is my unchanging affection for you my dear Brother and best friend. May God bless you & all of yours! May He soon permit us to meet again! to meet in a peaceful independent country, & if this may not be permitted, Oh! may we meet as members of the same unbroken family around His throne in Heaven.

Love & kisses from my Wife & my self to all at home, to Sallie Doddie & little Lucy. Don't let Doddie forget me! With a Brother's love & a Brother's prayers. As ever Yours Dod[41]

Hd Qr's in Camp
Feb. 4th 1864

My Darling Little Wife,

Gen'l. Rodes has gone off with two Brigades & will be absent some days. Gen'l. Doles will come up this morning & I will have to relieve him on Picket.

Show yourself a Soldier's wife now by being cheerful & happy. I send you letters from Luly & one from Lue. Hope they will help you to drive away the blues.

And now, my Darling, don't be sick. I wish I could send you some books, but I cant find any. Accept my heart full of love. May God bless you and keep you and soon reunite us in safety.

With a kiss, Yr Devoted Husband[42]

Orange C.H. February 12 [1864]

My Dear Bro,

Your kind letters and Sallie's of the 8th Inst came to hand in due time. I thank you very much for your kind letters & can only repeat what I wrote before, that yr letters do me more good now than all else, beside the society of my wife.

I send you herewith my will. If it is not in proper form write me one & send it to me for signature. We had a little excitement here last week caused by the Yankees crossing in our front.[43] Oh! for the spirit of Jackson. We ought to have captured & killed the entire batch, & would have done so, had my plans been adopted by Lt Gen'l. Ewell. But enough. I made a

---

41. PC.

42. SHC.

43. On February 6, Union troops crossed the Rapidan at Morton's Ford. The Confederates pinned them down for a while, only to allow them to re-cross the river under cover of darkness. *OR*, 33:141–43; Graham and Skoch, *Mine Run*, 91–94.

narrow escape, riding into the Yanks without warning from our worthless Art'y. But I escaped unhurt, tho' some of their shots whistled uncomfortably close to my ears. Write me soon & very fully. Get Jack Phifer to keep his promise made me. Where are 700 Cav'y. going thro' our quiet town?[44] Did they burn your fences? I am in great haste. Nellie is well & sends love to all. She is a pearl with out price. Love & kisses to all.

God bless you & yours

Yr Devoted Bro.

S. D. Ramseur[45]

Camp near Orange C.H.

Feb 16th 1864

My Dear Brother,

I feel like writing you a long letter this morning, and had set out to do so, hoping that I may not be interrupted before I can fill this mammouth sheet. I have been looking for a letter from you, detailing the *State* of public feeling at home &c and largely devoted to home affairs. May be I exact much of you as a correspondent, take up too much of your time! But I am sure you would be amply repaid for the [illegible] did you know how refreshing & comforting yr letters prove. I told Nellie this morning that if I was not busy today, I intended to write you in order to provoke a reply. Nellie & I both agreed that we would be most happy to spend this day with you and Sallie & yr little ones. Really, I have felt a little home sick lately. I want you all to see my Darling little wife. "What does the Gen'l. think of Married Life?" Decided that it is the greatest Institution since [illegible]. Why, at this rate, My Dear Bro. I am perfectly willing, as far as *I* am concerned, that the War should continue [illegible]

I wish you could spend a day with us. I leave our comfortable boarding House, about 9 every morn'g., come over here and attend to Camp Matters. Genly leave about 3 P.M. & dine at 4 P.M. Then Nellie and I have all the evening to ourselves. You *know* we have a cosy, comfortable *spooney* time. I assure you, I am the happiest man in the world when I mount my horse leaving Camp & Camp business behind me at a gallop & hasten home to my little wife! But you have been along, & are still travelling, a similar road. Oh! for peace and a plantation. I feel no desire for aught else

---

44. Ramseur may have been referring to Confederate soldiers terrorizing citizens while appropriating horses for the cavalry and artillery as well as other property, as reported later from Catawba County, adjacent to Lincoln County. *Raleigh Weekly Standard*, May 18, 1864.

45. PC.

now than a happy home, and a quiet useful life. Do not think that I am growing careless or indifferent in the performance of my duty. Far from it. I am still active & energetic. My Brig. will be in fine condition next Spring. *Small*, 'tis sadly true, but true as steel with an Esprit de Corps of which I am truly proud, as I am to a certain degree the framer of it. I promise you a good account of us. Tho' I declare I am sometimes blue because my command is so small. I have 1200 muskets *for duty*. If the Yanks would send our prisoners back I would get 400 prisoners taken from me at Kelly's Ford, whilst I was at home last fall. The Spirit of this glorious army is *all right*. Would that we had Jackson & 30 000 more men. But I do sincerely trust that an all wise and merciful Providence will yet order all things for our ultimate good in the Coming Campaign!

Has not the influence of so many soldiers from this army, who have been on Furlough recently, operated for good among your weak kneed gentry? I argue from the breaking up of several convention meetings that Holden's [illegible] are on the sure road to destruction.

I am pleased to see the Confederate start under such able leadership and with such favourable prospects![46] I think it will & can do much good.

I have heard it said that Holden will be a candidate for nex[t] Gov. Surely this can not be. If indeed he does run, will not Vance beat him badly. Surely, Surely, North Carolina is not so *low*, so *disloyal*, as to bow to Holden as Gov. If so, then Good bye to the Old State, whose history might be so high, proud & glorious, but whose fair fame has been tarnished by the blackest of all traitors.[47] But I wont allow myself to think of such a possibility.

What is the news at home. How much land is Father cultivating? I think he had better store his yarn away, unless he needs money or sees a good investment. If John Phifer will only sell me the yarn he promised I can get along very comfortably. If he will sell the few bunches pr day, I think it will be well to store them away for awhile, or only sell enough

46. In February President Davis had called for suspension of the writ of habeas corpus and the extension of conscription. He and the Confederate Congress were negotiating the details of a veterans home for disabled officers and soldiers. Davis had also issued an address giving encouragement for the forthcoming spring campaign. Meanwhile, the Congress had enacted a prohibition on the importation of luxuries and instated restrictions on cargo carried by blockade runners leaving southern ports. *OR*, Series IV, 3:67–70, 80–82, 104–5, 107–10, 114–15.

47. Although a member of the North Carolina secession convention who had signed the secession ordnance in 1861, by 1864 Holden had become a leader in the southern peace movement. His willingness to make concessions and end the struggle was contrary to Ramseur's stated intention to fight on until full independence had been achieved. Current, *Encyclopedia of the Confederacy*, 2:781–82.

to pay for more, but I leave all these things to you, satisfied that you will manage it all for the best.

You notice the Mil'y. Bill has passed Congress[48] & if the Pres't signs it, as I think he will, I will be entitled to another Aid with the rank of 1st Lt. I will promote Caleb to Capt. I will keep this place open for you, or for an emergency. I don't think you will be required "to join" by the late Mil'y. bill. So you had better not come. If you are determined to come I will give you the above place, but what's the use of yr exposing yr life, when it is not absolutely necessary! I don't need you, but if you must come, I must have you. If you decide like a sensible man to stay at home, I think I'll offer the place to George Phifer. Do excuse this letter. I have been interrupted a dozen times & cant be properly held responsible for connection &c.

Give love to all. What do you hear from David? I am anxious to hear from him. Love & kisses to all. Write soon. Ever Your devoted Brother

S. D. Ramseur[49]

Camp Ramseur's Brig [illegible]

March 11th/64

Col. R. H. Chilton
Chf of Staff A.N.V.

Col:

I have the honour to apply for five (5) days leave of absence to visit Richmond and Barks dale Station on the R[ichmond] & Danville Rail Road, for the following reasons.

I have at present in the 2nd N.C. Reg't. two Comps., one without a Com'd. Off'r. the other with but two, and both much below the minimum of enlisted men present for duty. I desire to have these two Comps. consolidated. Col [Peter] Mallett Ch'f. of Conscription for N.C. has, I learn, six detached comp. of Inf'y. as a Post guard at Raleigh N.C. I desire to obtain from the Hon Sec'y. of War an order for one of these Comp's. to report to Col Cox Comd'g. 2nd N.C. to fill the vacancy proposed above. Col Cox has now but 180 muskets. He has but seven (7) absent without leave. He is a gallant & efficient Offr. & is anxious for this change. I desire furthermore to accompany Mrs. Ramseur on her way home. This application is made

---

48. As the pool of manpower in the South was being depleted, the Confederate Congress considered a number of bills dealing with conscription, exemption from military service, and the size, nature, and composition of general staffs.

49. PC.

in the belief that active operations will not require my presence here this week & with the hope of more efficiently organizing one of my best Reg'ts. I am Col very Resp'y.

S. D. Ramseur
Brig. Gen'l.[50]

Camp near Orange C.H.
March 13th/64

Dear Brother,

Your letter was rec'd. as soon as the mails came to us after Kilpatrick's raid[51] and right glad was I to get so cheerful an account of home matters, y'r. own views & feelings &c. After some stir up here from some Yankee moves, we are again quiet, and some of us are enjoying the society of our wives. Ah! I tell you these "Winter Quarters" are delightful, a charming respite to the hardships of active service.

Well, we are enjoying a long rest before entering upon a hard and long campaign. I promise you we will do good work this summer. Our prospects are brightening every where; on all sides, our little affairs have been successes. The enemy's affairs have been failures. Our armies will soon be increased by the arrival of 25 000 veterans from Northern prisons whose hearts are full of bitterness towards their cowardly oppressors. You may have heard too that we expect to have a larger and well mounted (I wish we could say, well disciplined) cav'y. force this spring. Most of Stewart's Cav'y. has been sent far to the rear this winter to rest & to eat up the [illegible] forage. They will come back in good condition. Well now tho' I do not approve of stating numbers in general, I send you the following promises on condition that you keep them to yourself. If we get back our prisoners, which seems more certain, Gen'l. Lee will have in the two corps now with him, about 45 000 Inf'y 2500 Art'y (200 guns) and about 10 000 well mounted Cav'y. Should Longstreet (leaving Maj Gen'l. [John C.] Breckenridge with his (B's) div'n. of Inf'y. and Ransom's Cav'y. in S.W. Va.) bring his gallant corps back to this army, we will number additionally 20 000 Inf'y. & 1200 Art'y.[52]

50. Letters Received by Confederate Adjutant General and the Confederate Quarter Master General, 1861–65, entry 480 R 1864, RG 109, NARA.

51. Brig. Gen. Judson Kilpatrick had led a cavalry force of 3,500 troopers on an unsuccessful raid intended to free Union prisoners held in Richmond.

52. On April 7, Longstreet was ordered with that part of his command originally with the Army of Northern Virginia back to the Rapidan to rejoin R. E. Lee. OR, 32(3):756.

With this Army, we will crush Meade, *before* crossing the Potomac.
I believe we can do it, and with Heaven's blessing I believe we *will do* it.
Should we cripple Meade so as to destroy, or considerably demoralize
his army, we could possess Maryland and Southern Penn'a., subsist there
while the Yanks draw troops from the West (they dare not draw them from
elsewhere), then retire to the South of the Potomac with all the cattle &c,
we could transport & there await the onset of this new army. In the meantime, Joe Johnston must change his usual tactics & advance & Kentucky
will be redeemed. In the mean time the Yankee debt will go piling up.
Gold will mount higher. Yanks will consider "the job" bigger than they expected, in which all concerned are apt to be hurt. Old Abe will be defeated
for Pres't., & the people will be ready & anxious to sustain the peace policy
of the new Pres't.

In this hasty sketch I have left out of consideration the effect of French
recognition, of which our today's papers have such *cheering reports*.[53] I do
not allow myself to be cheered too extravagantly by promised intervention. Surely, truth and justice long ago required our recognition. Nations
are governed by selfish motives. Is it necessary to the prosperity of France
that we should accomplish our Independence? If so, will this necessity justify the danger of intervention? There are so many considerations of policy
to enter the question, that I have little hope from it.[54] I fear Louis Nap'n.
will not care to entangle himself in our affairs.[55] However this may be, I
confidently expect that we will be enabled to whip the Yanks but single-
handed, by the assistance of the Lord of Hosts!

I have time to add but a few lines. I have written this hastily in our
court room, so you will have to excuse scattering. The Court is about to

53. The *Daily Richmond Examiner* of March 2 and 9, 1864, interpreted Emperor Napoleon III's
call for a congress of European powers as a sign of his increasing influence, which could result in
recognition of the Confederate States. France was portrayed as the one European power favorable
to the southern cause and a potential ally in Mexico. The *Richmond Dispatch* of March 13 reprinted
the views of French officers published in the *Boston Courier*, that men of the Union army lacked
discipline and the force on the Potomac was "an armed multitude, but not an army." The day after
Ramseur's letter, the *Examiner* cited northern sources as circulating a rumor that France had decided to recognize the Confederate States. Another tack, cited in the same edition of the *Examiner*,
was advanced by the *London Post* correspondent in Paris, who hypothesized that a neutral power
like France could act as an intermediary to bring the war to conclusion.

54. The French-Confederate dialogue during the spring of 1864 seemed focused on release of
the CSS *Rappahannock*, a British dispatch boat being refitted as a commerce raider for the Confederacy in the port of Calais, raising fundamental questions about the rights of belligerents and the
obligations of neutrals. Case and Spencer, *The United States and France*, 500–509.

55. In midsummer, Emperor Napoleon III of France did, in fact, order his foreign minister to
release the *Rappahannock*, although without effect. Case and Spencer, *The United States and France*,
507.

adjourn, and I must go home & see my Wife. Ah My Dear Brother. This [illegible] Wife of mine is the joy & sunshine of the world to me. I am going to hold on to her here as long as possible. Then she will go home & to Lincolnton for the summer. I know you will take the best care possible of her. I only wish I could make [illegible] of your party *occasionally* during the Summer, but that can only be by being wounded, which I wont be anxious for. Love to all. Kisses too. Write often. The Army is for Vance.[56] *We Secessionists cant beat him.* God bless you. With much love

Yr affcte. Bro. S. D. R.[57]

Wednesday [March] 16th [1864][58]

Dear Bro.

I am sitting by my little Wife & Caleb has come over to dine with us. I was reading Caleb yr views on Vance, when Caleb pulled this letter out of his pocket & said he forgot to send it the other day. I am glad to get such good accounts from you. You will have to go for Vance. The Army is for him.

Make the investment for me that you spoke of. I would rather that J. Phifer would keep his promise & sell me the yarn.

By the way, here is some home news. I want you to know, so that you'll know how to act. Aunt Pris writes Mr. Harding that J. B. Barrett[59] called on her in Milton & had a long talk. He said that Mr. Richmond got scared & caused his failure. He didn't blame himself for any of his troubles. The matter was different in L'n. *He had introduced* Elisha *there*! Mr. Ramseur was a good sort of man, & he intended to send his lawyer Mr. Reid to L'n

56. The soldier vote was 13,209 for Vance and 1,824 for Holden. Lefler and Newsome, *North Carolina, The History of a Southern State*, 447.

57. PC.

58. Over the preceding two weeks, Ramseur had served as president of a board of examiners, consisting of Col. Samuel B. Pickens, Twelfth Alabama Regiment, and Colonel Cox, Second North Carolina Regiment, convened to determine the fitness for duty of certain members of Rodes's division. The most ambiguous case involved Capt. William M. Hammond, assistant adjutant general in Daniel's Brigade, who contended that the weather in northern Virginia was deleterious to his health. After hearing witnesses, considering the evidence, and deliberating in private, the board recommended that Hammond be transferred to Florida or a port with a temperate and consistent climate. He was consequently assigned to inspection duty in the Southeast. Hammond, Confederate Generals, Staff Officers, and Non-regimental Enlisted Men, CMSR, RG 109, NARA; Letters Received by Confederate Adjutant General and the Confederate Quarter Master General, 1861–65, entry 247 J 1864, RG 109, NARA.

59. John B. Barrett, born in New York circa 1822, was listed as a Milton merchant in the 1850 Census. U.S. Census Office, *Seventh Census, 1850*.

to satisfy all parties &c. Nellie rec'd. Lue's letter. Will send an answer soon. If you send my boots by express, have them *fully valued*.

Love to all. Let me hear from you frequently. God bless you.

S. D. R.[60]

Hd. Qrs. 2nd Army Corps

March 19th 1864

General S. Cooper
A & I General
C.S.A.

General.

The undersigned General Officers of this corps respectfully request, in our own behalf and that of the other officers in our commands, that Paragraphs III & IV General Orders No. 28, A & I Gen'l. Office, current series, be amended, so as to allow officers on duty in the field to *purchase rations* from the Commissary Department in addition to *the one* which the order allows them to draw.

The necessity for some action of the sort is obvious from the fact that, it is absolutely necessary that officers should keep servants, the regulations very properly forbid the employment of enlisted men in menial capacities and we are obliged to employ servants for cooks, grooms, &c. To provide food for these with the order as it now stands is utterly impossible. For in the first place all articles of provision are held at such prices in the country, that no officer's pay, on which the majority are dependent, would enable him to buy them. And, in the second place, were prices more reasonable, there are no means of purchasing in the vicinity of the army, for the country in which we operate is almost entirely denuded of supplies, the citizens having barely enough for their own support and no surplus for sale.

Very Respectfully
Yr Obt. Servants

R. S. Ewell
Lieut. Gen'l. Comdg Corps

Extra supplies of candles, salt &c ought to be sold on campaigns or transportation would be increased.

J A Early
Maj. Gen'l. Comdg Division

60. PC.

To be limited to one ration for a servant on certification that servant is actually employed on duty in the field. J A Early

Harry T. Hays
Brig. Genl. Comdg Brig.

J. B. Gordon
Brig. Genl. Comdg Brig.

R. E. Rodes
Maj. Gen'l. Comdg Division

C. A. Battle
Brig. Gen'l. Com'g Brigade

Junius Daniel
Brig Gen'l. Comdg Brigade

S. D. Ramseur
Brig. Gen'l. Comd'g. Brig[61]

Hd Qrs Out Post
April 15th 64

My Darling Wife,

Caleb came today bringing your notes. Oh! How much I miss you! How dearly I love you! How earnestly I wish for your sweet presence even now!

Have I been blue. Not blue but somewhat sad. I can not drive away the contemplation of the long months that must slowly drag away before I can again press my Darling to my heart. But My Dearest Darling Wife, I am not often this sad. I am so happy in remembering the past winter with every little incident, every precious association, every joyous emotion! Ah! how much happiness our good God gave us! Nor does He now leave us without hope. What sweet recollection, what precious anticipations cheer our absence!

I feel so hopeful about the coming campaign. I have never felt so encouraged before. Surely Our Father will bless His faithful people. The prayers of the Righteous availeth much. May our people forsake their sins and turn humbly to Our God, and in perfected faith call upon Him to deliver us from our sins and the power of our Enemies! My Little Darling will not forget to pray for me, I know. Pray also, my Beloved, for our suffering Country and our cause. The Lord will hear and answer the prayers of His People!

61. Letters Received by Confederate Adjutant General and the Confederate Quarter Master General, 1861–65, entry 146 E 1864, RG 109, NARA.

Oh! How I miss your sweet companionship in my daily devotion! but tho' separated so far from each other, is it not a precious privilege to meet daily at the "Mercy Seat"?[62]

I am sorry Caleb did not go on home with you. I am afraid you had some trouble at the river & besides they all wanted to see him so much. I hope you had a safe & pleasant journey home. Write me all about it. My greatest pleasure now will be to read your letters. After the promises you have made me, I know I will have that pleasure often. I am anxious for the time to arrive when the welcome visitors will begin to come regularly. The fact is My Darling Little Wife, I have to say, as Maj. Smith does, I am growing more lover like every day. I do so love to think of you, of our past happiness, of every precious incident of our Courtship and marriage, and to anticipate the coming of that good time when, by God's blessing we will be permitted to live together in peace and happiness and usefulness! But really I must not write you too much love for fear that you may think me too sad, too much overcome by your absence.

I am endeavoring to be cheerful and happy. The best way to be so, I know by past experience, is to perform faithfully all our duties. Coming on picket immediately was a relief. Here I have some thing to keep me actively engaged all the time. So far the Yanks have been more quiet than I ever saw them before, so much so that at one time I thought they had vamoosed, but I found very soon I was mistaken. When we go back to camp I am going to try to get my Brigade in tip top trim. I expect some of the lazy fellows will be sorry you left me so soon.

I am going to take mighty good care of myself for your sweet sake. My tooth has been extremely painful. At one time it was so bad I sent for Dr. [John E.] Logan to extract it, but he was so long in procuring the proper instrument that the tooth got easy before he came. For the past day or two it has been free from pain but very sore. At the first opportunity I will either have it filled or extracted. Strange to say I have not much missed the luxurious fare Mrs. [Elizabeth] Kendall gave us. We have nothing but bread and meat & not much of that, but somehow I have not *longed* for anything else. Don't know how long I can remain so easily pleased. You know we expect Congress to relieve us from the operation of the present unfair bill. When that is done we will get along finely, especially if we go to Pennsylvania this Summer, as many of us hope to do.

I will leave this unclosed 'till tomorrow when it will go to the Office. I don't want to stop, but twilight is coming on. May Our God bless My

---

62. The mercy seat was the gold covering on the ark of the covenant, regarded as the resting place of the throne of God. Exodus 25:17–22.

Darling this sweet Sabbath Evening. May we both unite our heads in praising Him. Dearest Darling, Best Loved, Good Night.

Monday Morning [April 18, 1864]. The birds are singing merrily, the trees are blossoming beautifully and the sun is shining warmly. Every thing on this side of the river is emblematical of peace and happiness. On the other side the mountains are covered with Snowy Caps and the sound of Yankee drums rolls over at us reminding of Winter and cold. [illegible] must take this as a happy omen that soon here we may have Peace and happiness. Whilst there all will be confusion and Anarchy! So mote it be!

I imagine you this morning walking through the yard admiring and gathering flowers, *wishing for me* and thinking how you will write *all* you wish to tell me. Perhaps at this very moment you are writing loving tender words to me. Pleasant thought! Ah! Is it not a precious privilege thus to commune so lovingly with those far away who are so dear to our hearts? My Darling Little Pet, My precious little Wife. I do love you more tenderly more devotedly every day. Oh! this cruel separation! terrible war! May God in mercy speedily deliver us from the hands of our Enemies. Then when Beautiful Peace shall once more visit our land how thankful and peaceful will be our hearts united on earth to be separated no more, except in the short passage to our Eternal Heavenly Home, where no parting is known. Dearest Wife let us be hopeful and thankful and prayerful. Let us pray for Grace, to bow submissively to God's Holy Will! Pray for me Darling Wife. Let us feel that we meet *together* at the foot of the Cross! If God be for us, who can prevail against us?[63]

I have no news to write you, but I shall expect a letter full of news from you. I hope you found all well at home. Give my love to Mama, Sis Mary, Lue and all. Tell them to take the best possible care of my Darling.

By the first opportunity I will send you some money. Should you want any before this, if George can spare it, borrow from him and when you go to Lincolnton Mr. Schenck will refund. If G. can not spare it, write to Mr. S. and he will furnish it to you.

You must write often to my Loves at home. Your letters are very precious to them. Caleb rec'd. a letter from George on his return. Says G. must certainly send him a pr. of boots. Entre nous [Between us] I think G. is dangerously smitten with Miss Jane. You will have to take care of him, or Cupid will seize him before the Conscript Offr. gets a chance.

It is so hard to leave you My Precious Little Wife but I must do so. Write me all about your most precious self. Are you well? perfectly well?

63. Paraphrase of Romans 8:31.

Do not they all think you look well? I shall await your letter with impatient anxiety.

May Our Heavenly Father bless us and comfort us and save us in His heavenly Home is my constant prayer. Caleb joins me in love to all. Says he feels much better since his trip to Richmond. Good by My Darling Wife.

Your devoted husband. S. D. R.

I send you a letter from Sis' Mary which came yesterday. You will perceive that it was written in Feb. Two mo's. ago!

Longstreet is said to be at Gen'l. Lee's H'd. Qrs., his troops at Charlottesville.[64] The impression seems to be that we will whip Grant before he can concentrate.

When you write to Luly tell her not to let Fanny go out until she has perfect recovery. The great danger from measles is in exposure too soon. I'll write home as soon as I find time. You must certainly go to L'n. this Summer. When do you think of going? Accept My Dearest Darling immeasurable love and many Kisses from Your Devoted Husband[65]

> Camp near Orange C.H.
> April 24th 64

My Precious Wife

I was again delighted last night by reception of another love messenger from you. Do you know how much good it did me? I feel really ashamed that I have allowed a whole week to lapse since writing to you but I promise you that I'll do better in future. We have been greatly excited and delighted at the good news that is coming to us from N.C.[66] Truly Gen'l. Hoke has done gallantly. He deserves credit for his good judgement and skill. I hope to hear still more news of the same good sort. Having obtained command of the water, there is nothing to prevent the capture of Washington & Newberne. I'll write to congratulate Gen'l. H. soon.

I have not visited Mr. Kendall's since you left. Indeed, my duties con-

---

64. Longstreet's two divisions assembled at Charlottesville on April 21. Piston, *Lee's Tarnished Lieutenant*, 87.

65. SHC.

66. Hoke's attack on the Federal garrison at Plymouth, North Carolina, on April 20 resulted in the surrender of 2,400 men and the capture of needed food, equipment, and ordnance; the capitulation provided the Confederacy with its first victory along the Atlantic coast in a long time. Hoke reported capturing one brigadier, 1,600 men, stores, and twenty-five artillery pieces. Barefoot, *General Robert F. Hoke*, 148, 150; OR, 51:870.

fine me so closely that I get away from my camp very little. I have not yet been to Orange, tho' I expected to go up to Church today. We are getting ready for an arduous Summer Campaign. Our heart's are full of hope. I pray most earnestly that Our Heavenly Father will so order all things that our Enemy will be driven back in confusion, that his heart may be changed so that he will be persuaded to let us depart in peace. Oh! I do pray that we may be established as an independent people, a people known and recognized as God's Peculiar People! Our men are full of hope and courage. Our Army is in fine condition and I believe we all feel that with the blessing of Providence we will this Summer conquer a glorious peace. Let us pray for the happy consummation!

I am so glad My Darling Wife to know that you are so well and safe and happy at your sweet home. 'Tis such a relief to me to know that those who are dear to me are safe in their own homes! May the foot of the invader never again pollute our soil! I was much amused at your description of Mrs. Evans. I agree with you. She ought to be careful, she might make revelations improper for the uninitiated.[67] You did not tell me in your last any thing about your health. I am delighted at Aunt Pris' estimate of you. I am sure you know how anxious I am that you should be cheerful and happy and hopeful. I will be anxious to know that you have never been heard to complain or despond.

My Little Darling let us keep our hearts full of hope and trust and love. You know how happy I am to know that you write to me regularly. How I welcome the good mail days that bring your letters! My tooth after troubling me a week has learned good manners & is now very quiet. Caleb has been a little ailing the past week. I have offered him a furlough but he says he isn't sick enough for that. If he gets really sick I'll insist on his going home. So tell Mama to have no fear concerning him. We have no local news. We are all wraped up in the glorious news from Hoke. We are full of hope for the future! May God bless us and deliver us from the power of our Enemies.

This is a very unsatisfactory letter. I promise to write you a much longer one very soon. Deo Volente [God willing]. Write me long letters about your darling self. Have you heard from home recently. Give my love to Mama Sis' Mary & all. Tell George I say he must try to raise some bread & meat for the army. Has Grandma come home. I forgot to enclose yr letter

---

67. Her husband, Charles Napoleon Bonaparte Evans, was owner and editor of the *Milton Chronicle*, and she was therefore privy to information not intended to be shared with the general public. Powell, *When the Past Refused to Die*, 402.

from Sis' M in my last. Caleb sends love. Says don't let George forget his boots. Says tell G. to let the girls alone and "pitch in" to work.

I hope to get another letter tomorrow. How cheering thus to hear from you so often.

May God bless and preserve you My Darling Wife is the prayer of yr

Devoted Husband[68]

Adjutant and Inspector General's Office

Richmond, April 25th 1864

[Extract]

SPECIAL ORDERS

No. 96

xx Leaves of Absence, for the times here in specified are granted the following named officers:

Brig. Gen'l. S. D. Ramseur, P.A.C.S.

Five (5) days

By command of the Secretary of War.

Jno. Withers

Assistant Adjutant General[69]

Camp near Orange C.H.

April 28th 1864

My Own Darling Wife,

Your sweet letter of the 22nd Inst. came day before yesterday. It is impossible for me to tell you how precious, how cheering and how comforting are these sweet messengers of love and sympathy which now come so often! I intended to write you a long letter yesterday but I thought I could improve one of my Regts. (the 30th) by drilling it myself yesterday mor'g. for two hours that together with the eve'g. Brig. drill, for two hours and a half, made me so tired as to remove the inclination and desire to write you the intended *long letter*.

Last night I heard a most excellent sermon from Rev. Mr. Powers, Chaplain of the 14th Reg't., delivered to the Offrs. of the Brigade! It was one of the best sermons I ever listened to. His text "No man liveth to him-

---

68. SHC.

69. Letters Received by Confederate Adjutant General and the Confederate Quarter Master General, 1861–1865, entry 630 R 1864, RG 109, NARA.

self alone, and no man dieth to himself alone."[70] He showed our dependence upon one another, showed the influence of the Offrs. over their men and each other, and then very earnestly pressed upon them the duty and necessity of making this influence operate for good, temporal and eternal.

I have been hard at work for some time drilling my command. I tell you I have the finest and most gallant Brigade in this Army. With God's help we will give a good account of ourselves in the coming Campaign. I have been sorry to see that the Richmond papers have been spreading alarm and anxiety throughout the country by publishing the reports of demoralized cavalrymen and "reliable" gentlemen to the effect that our armies were in line of battle, a general engagement imminent &c &c.[71] Do not allow such things, My Darling Little Wife, [to] annoy or alarm you! In all these things be hopeful and trustful. Do not alarm yourself in anticipation. Do not believe a battle has been fought until you are positively informed that such has been the fact. Do not credit *any* rumoured movements. And finally do not believe the *rumoured* results of an engagement when you know one has taken place. By following my advice in these matters, My Precious little Darling, you will save yourself much unnecessary anxiety and anguish of mind.

I was very much surprised last night on receiving from the Sec'y. of War a furlough for five days. It was granted (by mistake I suppose) on the application I sent up when you were about leaving for home. I felt greatly inclined to go off on this permission to see you for a day. How delightful that would have been, but when I remembered it was granted thro' misapprehension, that the reason for which it was asked no longer obtained, I felt that I would have been taking undue advantage of the authorities by making use of the leave. Inclination would have led me to you my Heart's Darling, but duty requires me to remain at my post. I know Gen'l. Lee will approve of my course. Don't you Dearest?

I have been greatly excited and delighted at Gen'l. Hoke's success at Plymouth. I am glad the Pres't. has promoted him for it.[72] In this war we must judge men by their actions. Success is certainly, whether justly or not (I will not determine) the test of merit.

I have been looking most anxiously for further favourable news from the Old North State. I certainly expect to hear of the capture or evacuation

70. Romans 14:7–8.
71. *Richmond Enquirer*, Apr. 26, 1864; *Richmond Sentinel*, Apr. 27, 1864.
72. Hoke was promoted to major general, effective April 20, 1864.

of New Berne. With the command of the water, I don't see what can prevent this result.[73]

Last night I rec'd. a long letter from Mr. S. and one from Luly. Luly seems to intend her letters for *us*, so I will enclose it to you.

I am so glad, My Darling Wife, to know that you have a safe and early means of going to my home. I sincerely trust the visit will do you great good. I am sorry I have not yet been able to draw and forward to you money of the new currency.[74] If you can borrow enough to take you to Lincolnton, Mr. Schenck will refund and furnish you with all you want. He holds some of my funds. Draw on him whenever you need money.

David has been assigned to duty with the 14th Reg't. of my Brigade.[75] I am expecting him to come up every day. Hope he'll do better here. When you go to my home, Darling Wife, you must not allow *anything* to interfere with your regular letter days. Oh! you don't know how precious your letters are to me. They are my chiefest delight, my joy, my comfort! Would, My Precious Darling, that I could tell you all the warm constant devoted love which always fills my heart for you. I do *so* want to see you! May Our Heavenly Father in mercy grant that this cruel separation may soon terminate, that this cruel war may speedily be brought to an honourable and peaceful end; and that our Confederacy may be established among the Nations of the Earth as Our God's own peculiar people!

I must now reluctantly say goodbye. A most disagreeable duty awaits me. I have to march my Brigade out to witness the execution of three miserable deserters.[76] Oh! why will these poor miserable men commit this crime and folly.

The mail carrier is waiting and the drums are beating for the reg't. to

73. Here Ramseur was in error. Looking ahead to a spring offensive engineered by Grant (the newly appointed general-in-chief of the Federal army), Lee insisted that the task force sent to lay siege to New Bern be returned to the Army of Northern Virginia. *OR*, 33:1278–79. Hoke's victory provided a rationale for declaring the New Bern campaign a success and reinforcing Lee's beleaguered command.

74. By act of the Confederate Congress on February 17, 1864, outstanding currency was to be exchanged at a discount for new notes. The new bills had red lace overprinted on the same faces with crude backs substituted for the old. The measure was so ineffective in retiring excess money, which was intended to strengthen the Confederacy's monetary rating, that the deadline and penalty date were extended in December. Ball, *Financial Failure and Confederate Defeat*, 188–89.

75. On April 23, David Ramseur was ordered by the Medical Director's Office, Army of Tennessee, to report to the Fourteenth North Carolina Regiment. That army's register for May 31, 1864, listed him as being absent without leave since April 16. He was absent again in February 1865 and placed under arrest. David Ramseur, Confederate Generals, Staff Officers, and Non-regimental Enlisted Men, CMSR, RG 109, NARA.

76. A year earlier, Governor Vance had pleaded for leniency for North Carolina deserters after issuing a proclamation appealing to their patriotism to return to the colors. *OR*, 18:928.

form. How joyfully I now look for the coming of the mails. This eve'g. I have two chances of getting a letter. Yrs of Monday by mail. Yrs of yesterday by Caesar.[77] Two letters from My Beloved Little Wife! Is not that joy enough for one day! Caleb is much better. He is complaining about not hearing from home, says he is entirely ignored & that he does not intend to write another letter until *somebody* writes to him. Give Lue a scolding for me for not writing to C. Mr. H. is on Picket with his Regt this week. I'll go down again next week. Love to all. Accept my precious Darling Little Wife, my heart overflowing full of love. May God bless, keep & save you & me. With a thousand kisses. Yr devoted Husband S. D. R.[78]

Near Orange C.H.
Ap'l. 30th Saturday/64

My Own Darling Wife

Your recent letter written last Sabbath came on Wednesday. I am so sorry to hear of your very bad cold. How did you catch it? Wearing thin shoes? You tell me not to be anxious. I am not anxious about any result, but my Heart's Darling, I can't help feeling anxious to hear from you again & to be assured that you are again perfectly well.[79] I do so long to be with you these bright beautiful days. Seems to me I miss you more and more every day. May our Heavenly Father give us strength to bear cheerfully this cruel but necessary Separation. May He strengthen our hearts and nerve our arms for the coming conflict and enable us to gain decisive victories which will bring the war to an end, and to us, independence and peace! I have been very busy since you left. I have not yet had an opportunity to visit anywhere. When I do get the chance I will certainly take great pleasure in visiting our friends the Crockfords. I would go to Orange tomorrow but Mr. Powers will have communion in his Chapel, and I will attend there. Think of me, my Precious Darling, and pray that these blessed opportunities may be refreshing and redoun[d] to the eternal salvation of my soul.

Caleb is very much disappointed that Caesar did not arrive Wednesday. He is afraid that Caesar was arrested & detained in Richmond. If Caesar started Wednesday I suppose I will have to wait until the midday of next

---

77. Caesar was a faithful retainer of the Richmond family in Milton. His wartime service in the field with General Ramseur apparently made a lasting impression upon him, as the 1870 Census for Lincoln County, North Carolina, lists "Cesar Ramsour" as a black, sixty-six-year-old farm laborer.

78. SHC.

79. By this time, Ramseur must have learned that Nellie was carrying their child, and his letters throughout the spring and summer would lovingly reflect his concern for her health.

week before getting another letter from My Best Beloved. Speaking of going to Lincolnton, Do you know an order from the War Department forbids travelling on the Cars? Will it not be well to write to Hillsboro to know certainly whether or not you will be permitted to get on the cars there? I hope nothing will prevent your visit. I believe it will do you much good, and I am sure it will greatly gratify the loved ones at Home. Can you not take Sis' Mary with you? Tell her I say if possible she must go. The mountain air will benefit both Richmond & herself. Hope she will go.

There is no news here. The Yanks thus far have been unusually quiet. In fact we have had but one rumour tho' I see the Richmond papers represent us in Line of battle and an engagement imminent.[80]

Caleb has almost entirely recovered & is improving daily. He is very anxious to hear from home & I almost confess I agree with him in thinking he is somewhat badly treated. I wish you could witness my Brigade drills. I believe, I know you would be edified. I am closing before I desire. Have kept the mail carrier waiting for some time. 'Tis better to send a short letter than postpone it till tomorrow. Thank you, My Beloved Wife, for all your sweet letters. You are so good and so sweet. Wish I could kiss you a thousand times this morn'g. Love to all.

Hope to hear you are entirely well in your next. Write me long letters. Dont you want to come back to the Army? May God bless, protect and speedily reunite us in peace and happiness is my constant prayer. With love and kisses,

Yr Devoted Husband[81]

Camp near Orange C.H.

Apl 30th/64

My Dear Brother

I have time to write you but a few lines. You remember a silver watch I left with [illegible]. I forgot to bring it with me & it belongs to one of my men & he needs it. Will you send it to me by the 1st safe opportunity. Also an overcoat I sent to Phillips in Charlotte some two months ago. I'll need it this summer.

David has not yet reported for duty, nor have I heard a word from him since he left. Has he been at home? I advised him exactly in accordance with yr views.

---

80. *Richmond Sentinel*, Apr. 28, 30, 1864; *Daily Richmond Examiner*, Apr. 30, 1864.
81. SHC.

Is it possible for you to get a good free Negro to wait on me? Can you not scare one into it by the conscription? As a teamster or on fortifications they will have hard fare & hard work & $4 pr month. As my Svr't. they will live as I do, have little to do, & get clothing food & $15 or $20 pr month. If you can get me a good reliable servant send me a box of some thing to eat by him for three weeks. Since Nellie left I have lived only on fat, strong bacon & coarse corn meal without a sifter. I assure you it's using me badly. I would cheerfully give $50 for one of our old time dinners.

If you can send me a few hams & some vegetables, dried fruit, pickles, anything, do it. You can appropriate some of my money to it. I'll send you $500 in new currency as soon as the opportunity offers. Supply Nellie's wants.

I'll write you a long letter soon. Every thing is perfectly quiet.

Write me the news. Love to all. God bless & protect you & yours.

Good bye

Yr Affte. Brother

S. D. R.[82]

> Camp Ramseur's Brig
> near Orange May 2nd/64

My Darling Wife,

I do not like to write you hurriedly, but it seemed that my last few letters have all been short & hasty. I am now just about to start on picket. I sent my Brigade down this morning at day light. I have been on the B'd. examining Mr. J. Forney Johnston[83] for a L't. in the regular Army. We were very easy on him & let him pass. Tho' his examination was not remarkably brilliant.

Oh! my Precious Darling, You don't know how much your letters rec'd. by Caesar, have delighted me! Mr. Harding and Caleb & I were sitting in my tent, talking over home affairs, when Caesar came in & gave us our letters from those we love best in this world! My Sweetest darling, you don't know how my heart was gladdened by your sweet letters! 'Tis strange you don't receive my letters. I have written you frequently & regularly. Some

---

82. PC.

83. A native of Lincoln County, Joseph Forney Johnston had enlisted in the Confederate army while attending military school in Alabama, eventually rising to the rank of captain. He later served as governor (1896–1900) and U.S. senator (1907–13) from Alabama. Powell, *North Carolina Biography*, 3:305.

of my letters must have miscarried. Hope you will receive them all after
while.

I feel very hopeful of the final result. If I had time I would give you a
long lecture about not feeling uneasy, anxious &c.

Tell Sis Mary that we all enjoyed her cake *hugely*. I had been confined
so closely that I could not get to Mr. Kendall's until last Sat'y. when Col.
G[rimes] and I called on the good people. They were very glad to see us,
gave us a splendid dinner, asked many questions about you &c &c. I fear
the active campaign will soon prevent us from enjoying their hospitality
again. I did so wish for you. The flowers were all in bloom. A great many
wild violets, iris &c. I walked about the yard, looked at our dear old room
and felt Oh! to have my little Darling with me! But I wont give you an account of my gloomy thoughts. When next I go over there, I'll endeavor
to enjoy the good dinner, remember the happy past, and not allow my
thoughts to grow despondent.

I hope you will excuse this disconnected scrawl. I've been writing in
Maj Miller's tent, with Col Grimes, Col Cox, & several others have been
chatting to each other & frequently to me. Now I must stop & leave for the
Outposts. I know you will excuse this note. I send it because I know you
would rather have this than nothing. Love to all. If nothing prevents I'll
write you a long letter tomorrow from picket. May God bless & keep you
My Precious Darling. With a heart full of love.

Yr devoted Husband[84]

H'd Qrs on Out Post
May 3rd/64

My Precious Darling Wife,

I wrote you very hastily last Monday [May 2]. Hope you'll excuse that
and all of my hurried letters. Today I have carefully examined our front,
watched the Yankees dashing about on the other side to discover if possible their future movements. We have heard rumours of their intended
advance for several days, but I could discover but little change in the appearance of their camps. When they do come, I pray that we may be prepared to meet them and to push them back with terrible loss.

I have just discovered that I have commenced this letter on the last
instead of the first page.

84. SHC.

Today I was much surprised by a visit from my old friend & West Point chum Gibbes. He is now on duty with the Artillery of this Army & his Camp is not far from me.[85]

Of course all thoughts and speculations now turn to the coming battle. We hope and believe that we will be enabled to come off victorious. God grant it may be so! Our army is in splendid condition and I learn Gen'l. Lee says, he has never before been so nearly the equal of the Yanks in numbers. All things look bright and cheering! May be Sun of Peace soon return to gladden & beautify our land.

I wish you could just ride with me along the banks of this beautiful river. The Valley of the Rapidan is beautiful beyond expression. How I did wish you could enjoy a ride with me this morning. I think I never saw so many wild violets and iris before. One hill was really blue with them! Dont you wish you could see them with me! Ah! My Darling Wife, how poor and unsatisfactory are the beauties and delights of this world when not shared with you! May the time soon come when we can enjoy all these delights together! I am now looking for a sweet long letter from you tomorrow. I hope it will come! How I will welcome it! Does my little Darling know how I want to see & be with her. Seems to me I can not wait much longer until I see you. I feel I would give any thing to be with you tonight, but patience! Oh! that I may learn patience and contentment and resignation!! Unless I learn by your next, that you have not gone to L'n., I'll direct my letters there. I do hope you will have a pleasant and beneficial visit. I know it will do Father & my dear Sister so much good to have you with them. I think it will be well for you to remain *All* Summer if you think you can do so. At any rate stay as long as possible.

You must write me all the gossip of the Burg. Will it not be pleasant for you to attend the Gen'l. Assembly[86] with Miss Ellen Smith? I think so. There is no news with us. We have expected to hear of the capture of Newberne[87] before now but probably we were too sanguine. Every body has

---

85. Maj. Wade Hampton Gibbes was assigned to Cabell's Artillery Battalion in the First Corps Artillery. Gibbes would be reassigned to command the Thirteenth Virginia Light Artillery Battalion on June 10, 1864. He reportedly began the war in notable fashion by firing some of the first rounds at Fort Sumter. Sibley, *The Confederate Order of Battle*, 1:68, 75; *OR*, 36(1):1051; Aimone, "Much to Sadden—and Little to Cheer," 24.

86. The General Assembly was the highest governing body in the Presbyterian Church of the Confederate States of America, as it remains in the Presbyterian Church of the United States of America today.

87. After Hoke's stirring triumph at Plymouth, the Confederates launched one final expedition against New Bern in early May before Lee recalled Pickett's Division to help defend against the massive multipronged Federal offensive approaching Richmond.

retired & as I must rise early I must say Good night. I am very reluctant to leave you & send you an Iris. I fear all its sweetness will be lost before it reaches you. Give my love to the Dear Ones at *Woodside*. I'll write to you soon to L'n. May our Father & our God bless my beloved Darling Wife is my constant prayer. With a heart full of love & a good night kiss from Yr Husband[88]

MAY 5 [1864]—5 a.m.

MAJOR DANIEL:[89]

I had crossed Mountain Run when (3 a.m.) I received orders from General Ewell, dated 1 a.m., to keep my pickets on the river until I was satisfied there was no enemy in Culpeper to attack our rear, or until I was ordered to rejoin the corps. I have just gotten back under that order. As yet can discover nothing on account of the fog. As far as can be seen all is quiet. The troops are tired from the forced march to get back by daylight. If I discover no considerable force I'll start to join you again.

S. D. RAMSEUR
Brigadier-General[90]

Ramseur's correspondence with his wife was interrupted by fighting that broke out in the Wilderness and moved on to Spotsylvania Court House. Grant crossed the Rapidan on May 4. Ramseur's initial mission caused him to miss the opening clash the following day. On May 6, he was called from reserve to fill the gap between Rodes's division and the rest of the army two miles away to the south along the Orange Plank Road. His troops strengthened the line, thereby preventing Burnside's IX Corps from splitting the Confederate defense.

Ramseur's men joined the rest of Ewell's Second Corps in marching toward Spotsylvania Court House on May 8. The troop movement was again aimed at precluding the Federals from gaining direct access to the Confederate capital. En route, Ramseur received a message desperately requesting help at the county seat, which the Confederate First Corps and Stuart's cavalry had reached just before the Union troops arrived. Ramseur quickened the pace and succeeded in driving the enemy back and removing the threat to his compatriots' flank.

88. SHC.
89. Maj. John W. Daniel, Early's assistant adjutant general.
90. *OR*, 51(2):890.

It was only two days later when Ramseur's brigade was again in the thick of the fighting. From their defensive position on the lower part of a salient known as the Mule Shoe, the North Carolinians joined the Confederate counterattack to restore the line after northern regiments pierced their defenses. A hard rain on May 11 prevented the battle from resuming, allowing Ramseur time to write home.

May 11th/64

My Darling Wife

We are still on line of Battle, the Enemy threatening. We have a strong position & if they attack us we will slaughter them terribly. Their loss up to this time has been immense. Our victory I hope & trust will be complete, decisive & glorious. God has been very good and merciful to us. Let us bless and magnify his great name. My loss thus far has been slight. This is the greatest battle the world ever witnessed. The Yankees loss I think is 35 000 (thirty five thousand) killed and wounded, and about 5 000 (five thousand prisoners), ours about 5 000 (five thousand) killed, wounded & prisoners.[91] May our Heavenly Father continue to bestow his merciful kindness upon us. Oh! May He who is the righteous Judge of all, grant us a complete victory and a glorious peace.

Caleb was struck in the wrist, but is not hurt. The skin was not broken. Jimmy Stinson was wounded slightly thro' the leg.[92] My life has been wonderfully and most mercifully preserved. Let us unitedly thank our God for His merciful Kindness toward us. Have telegraphed you on every occasion. Will continue to do so. Pray for me my Beloved Wife. Love to all of my Home Loves. Tell Mr. S. that I have captured a little flag for Doddie.

In great haste, and with a heart full of love. Write soon & often. May Our Father & our God keep, bless & protect us & speedily reunite us in peace & happiness. Good bye Darling Wife.

Yr Own devoted Husband

S. D. R.

Written on Yankee papers.
Wish I could send you some.[93]

91. As was often the case in the Civil War, Ramseur's estimate of enemy casualties was exaggerated: he cites twice the actual number who fell during the entire two weeks of operations, while the extent of Confederate losses remains uncertain. Matter, *If It Takes All Summer*, 348.

92. Stinson was acting as a courier when wounded. William R. Cox, "The Anderson-Ramseur-Cox Brigade," in Clark, *Histories*, 4:463–64.

93. SHC.

Monday 16th May/64

My Precious Darling,

I have an opportunity of writing you a line. My life has been mercifully preserved. Oh! let us praise and bless God for all His goodness & merciful kindness so continually shown toward us. Caleb is safe. Capt. Hines a prisoner.[94] Maj Smith safe. Poor Gen'l. Daniel is killed.[95]

By the bad conduct of *one* Brig[96] last Thursday our loss was heavy, and matters looked scarey for awhile. My Brig has behaved splendidly.

I have telegraphed you frequently. You see I am working with my left hand. I have a slight wound in my right arm. My Darling I must stop now. Your prayers have been answered. Continue to pray. Love to all. May God bless, keep, protect & soon reunite us in peace & happiness.

Devotedly Your Own Husband[97]

Battle field near Spotsylvania C.H.

May 19th/64

My Own Precious Darling

By the mercy of an All Kind Providence I am still spared to write you a hasty note. On the 12th my Brigade did some of the best fighting of the war. My loss has been heavy especially in men, the officers getting off quite well comparatively. I was slightly wounded thro' the arm (right) just below the elbow. My Yankee horse was shot severely. He still lives. I also rec'd. four holes in my overcoat. Some of our troops behaved shamefully. Caleb is well. So is Maj Smith & Capt Evans.[98] The Yankees have been quiet for two days, with the exception of a feeble assault on our lines yesterday which was easily repulsed. I think they are anticipating to strike the R.R. in our rear. Their loss has been immense. 50 000 is about the correct

94. Hines had been promoted to captain and commander of Company I, Forty-fifth North Carolina Infantry, on June 25, 1863. He was captured at Spotsylvania Court House on May 10, 1864. Manarin, *North Carolina Troops*, 11:107.

95. Junius Daniel was mortally wounded in the abdomen on May 12 while trying to recapture the Confederate works at the tip of the Bloody Angle at Spotsylvania. Rhea, *The Battles for Spotsylvania Court House*, 268.

96. Ramseur may well be referring to Brig. Gen. George H. Steuart's brigade, which broke at the Bloody Angle.

97. SHC.

98. Trained as a lawyer, Capt. Thomas C. Evans was the son of the editor of the *Milton Chronicle*, C. N. B. Evans, and commander of Company C ("The Milton Blues"), Thirteenth North Carolina Regiment. Manarin, *North Carolina Troops*, 5:309; Powell, *When the Past Refused to Die*, 183, 188, 190.

estimate. Ours about 15 000 in killed, wounded & prisoners. 5000 being prisoners.

May a merciful Providence continue to bless our arms and give us a complete decisive & glorious victory, a victory which will ensure peace and independence to our struggling Confederacy.

The Rail Roads are cut & hence I suppose I will not hear from you for some time. This is a great hardship. I have not rec'd. one of your sweet letters for more than two weeks.

I do hope My Hearts Darling that you are well hopeful and cheerful. Put your trust in God. Pray for me, for our noble army, for all God's people and for the success of our cause. Give my best love to all at Home. Accept my heart full of love. Oh! how I so want to see you! Continue to write to me. I'll get your letters after while. The papers have not done me justice yet, but it will be all right yet. Let us My Precious Darling continue to hope & pray. Let us put our trust & confidence in Him who is willing & able to help us in every extremity.

I have telegraphed you at every opportunity. Am so anxious to hear from you. *It is important* that you should be free from anxiety & alarm at this time. Try to be hopeful & cheerful.

Love to all my home Loves. May our God bless, comfort, sustain & preserve you. With my heart full of love & with many kisses.

Yr own S. D. R.[99]

If Ramseur's men had helped plug the gap in the Mule Shoe on May 10, two days later they may well have preserved Lee's entire army.[100] Called once again to the most extended point of the southern entrenchments known from then on as the Bloody Angle, his brigade fought the enemy musket-to-musket, at one point employing bayonets to drive the Federals from their toehold in the Confederate earthworks. Ramseur was wounded early in the contest but struggled to keep up with his men. The battle raged for twenty hours until well after midnight before the defenders pulled back into a new line only recently prepared by their engineers.[101]

Three days of rain prevented more fighting until the Federals again pushed into the southern front, only to be repulsed by the North Carolin-

99. SHC.

100. One of his subordinate regimental commanders at the time who temporarily took charge of the brigade when Ramseur was wounded, quoted Lee as saying, "We had saved his army." Grimes, *Extract of Letters of Major-Gen'l. Bryan Grimes*, 54.

101. *OR*, 36(1):1072–73.

ians and other defenders. On May 19, word that Grant's forces were sliding off to the southeast, continuing their march on Richmond, caused Lee to order Ewell to advance against the Union right to determine the enemy's whereabouts. Once more, Ramseur's brigade made contact and drove forward, only to be halted by pressure on its flanks resulting in a standup fight with no cover.

May 20th 1864

My Precious Darling,

Again by the mercy of God I have an opportunity to tell you of my safety & that of Caleb. We had a terrible fight yesterday eve'ng. & last night. My Brig. behaved splendidly & lost severely. I hope & pray that God will grant us a decisive & ultimate victory. Love to all. In haste. Oh, How I want to see you! My little wound is doing well. Continue to pray for me. God bless you Darling. I want to hear from you *so much*. Be hopeful cheerful trustful & prayerful. With a heart full of love with prayers for yr happiness. Your own S. D. R.[102]

May 23rd/64

My Darling Wife,

My troops are now marching to our right to take position. I have an opportunity of sending you a *line*.

I am very well. My wound is doing remarkably well. Caleb is well. David is with me. Our Army is all right. If Grant comes on he'll find us prepared. Oh! How I want to see you. Communication is reopened. Write often. God bless & preserve you My Darling. Love to all at home.

With heart full of love. Your Devoted Husband[103]

On the night of May 20, Grant resumed his drive past the Confederate right. Lee redeployed his forces again, this time behind the North Anna River at Hanover Junction, where Ramseur's brigade skirmished with the Federals, May 23–26. At his first opportunity in an official report ten weeks later, Ramseur summarized the brigade's operations under his leadership during May. While self-serving, his account sums up his final days as a brigade commander.

102. SHC.
103. SHC.

Camp near Winchester
August 10, 1864

GENERAL: Your note of 16th ultimo was received a few days ago. I take the first opportunity to reply. The copy of my report of the fight of the 12th of May has been misplaced. I therefore sent you a copy of my report of the operations of my brigade from 4th of May until 27th of May. This report is very brief, and hastily written. It does not do justice to the brave officers and men under my command, but in the midst of a most active campaign it was the best I could do. Being separated from my brigade I have not been able to procure a list of killed and wounded. This list will be forwarded at my first opportunity. I have left to yourself and General Rodes to represent me fairly in all these fights. After my disaster of the 20th ultimo (which I have asked Major New[104] to explain to you in person), I need all the encouragement you can give me.

With the assurances of my very high esteem, I am, general, your obedient servant,

S. D. RAMSEUR
Major-General

Lieut. Gen. R. S. Ewell[105]

Headquarters Early's Division
August 3, 1864

In accordance with the request of Major-General Rodes, I have the honor to submit the following brief account of the operations of my brigade from May 4 until May 27, when I was assigned to the command of this division.

I was on outpost duty with my brigade at Raccoon Ford when the enemy crossed at Germanna and Ely's Fords on May 3 and 4. I was left with my own brigade, three regiments of [Brig. Gen. John] Pegram's brigade, and three regiments from [Maj. Gen. Edward] Johnson's division, to resist any crossing the enemy might attempt on my front, which extended from Rapidan Station to Mitchell's Ford. On the morning of the 6th, I discovered, by a reconnaissance as far as Culpeper Court-House, that the main body of the enemy had crossed to the south side of the river. I

104. John P. H. New was an assistant adjutant general on Ramseur's staff. Krick, *Staff Officers in Gray*, 230.
105. *OR*, 36(1):1080–81.

therefore moved rapidly and rejoined the corps that night, taking position in echelon on the extreme left to protect Major-General Johnson's left flank.

On the morning of the 7th I was moved in rear of our center as a reserve either to Major-Generals Johnson or Rodes. Burnside's corps moved to envelop General Rodes' right and cut off the Second Corps from the army. The distance from General Rodes to Lieut. Gen. A. P. Hill's left being about a mile, General Rodes ordered me to form on Brigadier-General Daniel's right and to push back Burnsides's advance. Moving at a double-quick, I arrived just in time to check a large flanking party of the enemy, and by strengthening and extending my skirmish line half a mile to the right of my line I turned the enemy's line, and by a dashing charge with my skirmishers, under the gallant Major [Edwin A.] Osborne, of the Fourth North Carolina Regiment, drove not only the enemy's skirmishers, but his line of battle, back fully half a mile, capturing some prisoners and the knapsacks and shelter-tents of an entire regiment. This advance on our right enabled our right to connect with Lieutenant-General Hill's left. On the night of the 7th marched to the right, and on the 8th by a wonderfully rapid march arrived just in time to prevent, by a vigorous charge, the Fifth Corps from turning General Humphrys'[106] right flank. In this charge we drove the enemy back half a mile into his intrenchments. My brigade was then withdrawn and constructed intrenchments on the right of [Maj. Gen. Joseph B.] Kershaw's division.

On the 9th, 10th, and 11th constant and sometimes heavy skirmishing with the enemy.

In anticipation of an attack on my front on the morning of May 12, I had my brigade under arms at early dawn. Very soon, I heard a terrible assault on my right. From the direction of the fire I soon discovered the enemy on my right. I therefore moved the Second North Carolina Regiment, which I had in reserve, to a position on the right perpendicular to my line of battle. The enemy had broken entirely through Major-General Johnson's line and was massing his troops for a farther advance. Major-General Rodes directed me to check the enemy's advance and to drive him back. To do this, I formed my brigade in a line parallel to the two lines of works (which the enemy had taken and were holding) in the following order: On the right, Thirtieth North Carolina, Colonel Parker; on the left, Fourteenth North Carolina, Colonel Bennett; right center, Second

106. Brig. Gen. Benjamin G. Humphreys.

North Carolina, Colonel Cox; left center, Fourth North Carolina, Colonel Grimes. This formation was made under a severe fire.

Before ordering the charge I cautioned the men to keep the alignment, not to fire, to move slowly until the command "Charge," and then to move forward on the run, shouting "charge," and not to pause until both lines of works were ours.

How gallantly and successfully my orders were executed. Major-General Rodes and Lieutenant-General Ewell can testify, for they both witnessed it. Two lines of Yankees were driven pell-mell out and over both lines of our original works with great loss. This was done without any assistance on my immediate right. The enemy still held the breast-works on my right, enfilading my line with a destructive fire, at the same time heavily assaulting my right front. In this extremity Colonel Bennett, Fourteenth North Carolina, offered to take his regiment from left to right under a severe fire, and drive back the growing masses of the enemy on my right. This bold and hazardous offer was accepted as a forlorn hope. It was successfully executed; the enemy was driven from my immediate right, and the works were held, notwithstanding the enemy still enfiladed my line from part of our works in front of Harris' brigade, on my right, which he held until the last. For this all honor is due to Colonel Bennett and the gallant officers and men of his regiment. The enemy was driven out at 7:30 a.m. on the 12th. We held the works under a direct and enfilade fire until 3 a.m. on the 13th, when, in obedience to orders, I withdrew to a new line.

In this action I cannot too highly commend the conduct of both officers and men. Having had my horse shot under me, and shortly after receiving a ball through my arm, I was prevented from giving the command to charge. Colonel Grimes, Fourth North Carolina, seeing this, his regiment being battalion of direction, gave the command "Charge" exactly at the right time. To Colonels Parker, Grimes, Bennett, and Cox, to the gallant officers and patriotic men of my little brigade, this country owes much for the successful charge, which I verily believe turned the fortune of the day at that point in our favor. Our loss here was severe. From the 13th to 19th lay in line on the left of our corps.

About 3 p.m. [on May 19] the corps was moved across the Ny River to attack the enemy in flank and rear. My brigade was in front. Some half hour after the enemy discovered our movement, and when further delay, as I thought, would cause disaster, I offered to attack with my brigade. I advanced and drove the enemy rapidly and with severe loss until my flanks were both partially enveloped. I then retired about 200 yards and reformed my line, with Grimes' brigade on my left and Battle's on my right. At this moment the troops of Johnson's division, now under General Gordon,[107] on Grimes' left, were flanked and retreated in disorder. This compelled our line to fall back to our first position. Here a heavy force attacked us. Fortunately Pegram's gallant brigade came in on my left in elegant style just as the enemy were about to turn me there. Several attacks of the enemy were repulsed, and we were able to hold our position until night, when we quietly and safely withdrew to our original lines.

The conduct of my brigade on this occasion Major-General Rodes witnessed and can testify to. I may be pardoned for feeling that the steady bravery of my troops largely contributed to the repulse of the enemy's heavy force and the salvation of our corps. Marched to Hanover Junction on May 22. On the 23d, 24th, 25th, and 26th skirmished with the enemy. On the 27th moved toward the Chickahominy. Relieved from the command of my brigade and assigned to Early's division on this day.

"While we envy not others their merited glory," we feel it to be our bounden duty to North Carolina, to our gallant soldiers, and to our dead heroes, that we should be fairly represented in history's story. We therefore call upon our major-general and lieutenant-general, both of whom witnessed our conduct on May 12 and 13, to tell our fellow-citizens how we did our duty.

Respectfully submitted.

S. D. RAMSEUR
Major-General

Major Peyton,
Assistant Adjutant-General[108]

---

107. Maj. Gen. John B. Gordon.
108. *OR*, 36(1):1081–83.

7

Division Commander,
May–October 1864

AS FIGHTING PROGRESSED during May, Ewell's precarious health declined. It was said that he could no longer continue to campaign without respite. Early assumed temporary control of Lee's Second Corps, and Ramseur was selected to succeed him as division commander. Ramseur's first trial under fire as a senior commander ensued quickly on May 30, the eve of his last birthday. He was promoted to the rank of major general at the age of twenty-seven years and one day, the youngest West Pointer to achieve this rank in the Confederate army.

Grant's flanking movements advanced toward the Chickahominy River and to the east of Lee's army. The southern defense shifted to remain positioned between the Federals and Richmond. Early's corps headed toward the crossroads at Bethesda Church, with its commander and Ramseur in the van. Encountering what seemed initially to be a single Union cannon impeding their advance from the left flank ahead, Ramseur dispatched Brig. Gen. John Pegram's brigade to silence it. When Pegram's men entered the field in front of the artillery piece, they were decimated by massed ordnance on their right. Critics blamed Ramseur for the carnage that followed his attack because he did not first ascertain the strength of his opponent or the perils posed by the terrain ahead.

Ramseur's command was still deployed along a line between Bethesda Church and Mechanicsville on June 3, when Grant launched an all-out offensive now known as Cold Harbor. Ramseur was with his sharpshooters as fighting erupted, and again narrowly avoided death when his mount fell, throwing him to the ground. Horse and rider arose and escaped through a hail of fire. While another close call was subsequently recounted to his wife, Ramseur's first letters home as a division commander focus on successes achieved in his last month as a brigadier.

Line of Battle Hanover Junction

May 30th/64

My Darling Little Wife

Your sweet letter of the 11th Inst came to hand today. How rejoiced I was to hear from you, to know that you are cheerful and happy, that you are hopeful and well. You see my wound is getting so well that I can again use my right hand. I only suffer now from a little soreness. I am very well and have been enabled to keep up wonderfully well throughout all the exposure and fatigue of the past few weeks. My Brigade has fought splendidly and suffered severely. In the great battle of the 12th Inst. I retook that part of the work near to Gen'l. Rodes position, from which Johnston's [Johnson's] Division had been driven by the Enemy. This charge of my Brigade is universally spoken of in the highest terms by Offrs. of distinction. Gen'l. Ewell called me the hero of the day &c. Gen'l. Lee sent for me to thank me. Again on the 19th Inst when our Corps was almost entirely enveloped & every thing looked squally I rec'd. an order to retreat which I protested against declaring that I could & would hold the enemy in check. The order was revoked, the Yankee advance repulsed & our Corps saved from heavy loss.

I have been sorry on your account that the newspapers have not done me justice but you know correspondents write what is told them. They see nothing being too far to the rear and I am sure I will not trumpet my own praises. I send you a letter from the correspondent of the London Herald. The part taken by my sharpshooters is literally true but is not all the truth. I led my skirmishers in that charge.

Every thing has been very quiet today. I don't believe we will fight here. We are strongly entrenched & I believe Grant has entrenched also. I think therefore that Grant will attempt another flank movement. If so, I think Gen'l. Lee will attack him before he can entrench although our noble chief would rather that Grant w'd. attack him. Continue my Darling to be hopeful, trustful & prayerful. Be constant in prayer. Be cheerful and hopeful. Trust in prayer and God's Providence. My life has been mercifully spared by an able Kind Providence. I firmly believe this to be in answer to your prayers.

Do give my love to all at home. I do wish my Precious Darling that I could spend a few days or even hours with you. You don't *know*! how I want to see you. Enjoy all the pleasures of your sweet home. Would that I could join you a little while this evening. All is quiet here now. Continue to write to me regularly. Write long letters. I think I'll get most if not all of them. Our events can be referred to in such a way that nobody will be the wiser even if yr letters should be intercepted which is not at all probable.

Are you perfectly well? I'll write to you whenever I can. Caleb is well & sends love. Love to all at home. May Our Father & Our God bless, protect, comfort & mercifully save My Darling Wife & may the same Kind Providence soon reunite us in peace & happiness & love. Good bye Darling. Devotedly Yr own Husband[1]

HEADQUARTERS EARLY'S DIVISION
May 31, 1864

Lieut. Col. A. S. PENDLETON
Assistant Adjutant-General

COLONEL: The cavalry picket has been driven in on the Cold Harbor road obliquely in front of our right. Two prisoners from the Fourth Maryland state that the Fifth Corps is over in that direction intrenching. I think this report of the prisoners, taken in connection with the driving in of our cavalry pickets, is worthy of being reported to General Early.

I am, very respectfully,

S. D. RAMSEUR,
Brigadier-General, Commanding Division.[2]

Lines opposite Grant
May 31st 1864

My Precious Darling Wife,

I have just read two sweet letters from you of the 23rd & 25th Inst. I have thought of you so often & so tenderly during this arduous & bloody campaign. Oh! how I have sometimes longed to lay my head in your lap & rest. I am so glad you are well, hopeful & cheerful. May God preserve you so until the end. I do rejoice that you are so happy with my home Loves. Truly My Own Darling we have abundant cause for thankfulness & gratitude to Almighty God for His wonderful goodness & mercy so constantly shown toward us! My life has been spared I verily believe in answer to

1. SHC.
2. *OR*, 51(2):975.

your special prayers! In the terrible battles of the 12th 19th & 30th my life was mercifully spared. I have been placed in command of Early's Division. Yesterday we had a hard fight[3] in which my friend Col Willis was killed[4] and Maj Smith very seriously if not mortally, wounded.[5] I feel sorry for his poor wife. I cant tell you what Grant is going to do. He seems to have given up his plans of attack. Our glorious army is in splendid spirits. I hope & believe & pray that we will be able to overthrow Grant. If so the war will be brought to an end. Let us pray for such a consummation. Our strength is in the Lord. He is our strength & hope.

My wound is nearly well. It was very slight through the arm just below the elbow. Will be perfectly well in a few days I hope. David is with me, is well & doing well. Give my love to all at home. May God bless & preserve you. Let us put all our trust & confidence in him. May He very soon cause this cruel war to end & reunite us in peace & safety, happiness and independence.

Love to all. My heart full I send you, My Heart's Darling. Good bye. May God bless & preserve you is my constant prayer. With kisses & love

Yr Devoted Husband

This is my Birthday. I send you a birthday Kiss & hope before another year rolls around to be permitted to live with you in peace & quiet. With love

Yr own Husband[6]

Confederate States of America
WAR DEPARTMENT
Richmond, June 1, 1864

Sir:

You are hereby informed that the President, by and with the advice and consent of the Senate, has appointed you to temporary rank of Major General, under Act approved May 31st 1864. In the Provisional Army in the service of the Confederate States: to rank as such from the first day of June one thousand eight hundred and sixty four.

3. At Bethesda Church.
4. Willis was serving as commander of the Twelfth Georgia Regiment when he was mortally wounded. *Register of Graduates and Former Cadets*, 251.
5. Smith died as a result of wounds suffered while commanding the Forty-fifth North Carolina Regiment. Cyrus B. Watson, "Forty-Fifth Regiment," in Clark, *Histories*, 3:38.
6. SHC.

Immediately on receipt hereof, please to communicate to this Department through the Adjutant and Inspector General's Office, your acceptance or non-acceptance of said appointment; and with your letter of acceptance, return to the Adjutant and Inspector General the OATH, herewith enclosed, properly filled up, SUBSCRIBED and ATTESTED, reporting at the same time your AGE, RESIDENCE when appointed and the STATE in which you were BORN.

Should you accept, you will report for duty to General R. E. Lee for assignment to the Command of Early's Division A.N.Va

James A. Seddon
Secretary of War

Major Gen S. D. Ramseur
Commanding &c
P.A.C.S.[7]

Head Quarters

DEPARTMENT NORTHERN VIRGINIA

4th June 1864

[Extract]

SPECIAL ORDER

The following named officers having been appointed to the temporary rank of the positions indicated, are assigned to duty as set forth apposite their respective names.

Major General S. D. Ramseur to the temporary command of Early's Division Ewell's Corps.

By command of Gen. R. E. Lee

W H Taylor[8]
A.A. General

Major Gen'l. Ramseur
Thru:
Gen'l. Early[9]

---

7. NCOAH.
8. Lt. Col. Walter H. Taylor.
9. NCOAH.

Near Richmond
June 4th/64

My Darling Wife,

I am sitting in [the] rear of our breast works on the ground. Our skirmishers and the Yankees are keeping up a continual popping at each other
out in front from their respective pits. This is light skirmishing. Occasionally the Yanks fire a Shell at us. Far off on our right (some two miles) there
seems to be heavy Skirmishing, sometimes approaching a battle, musketry
& Artillery booming continually. Yesterday Grant attacked several times
at different points of our line and was repulsed at every point.[10] If he will
continue these (a bullet came so close to me just then as to make me jump
& spoil the k in the last word above our "Yanks"; you must feel no uneasiness, the bullets go over our breast works) attacks I verily believe by the
blessing of Providence his Army will be utterly destroyed.

I rec'd, a letter from Mr S. yesterday, which I was so glad to get. Thank
him for it. He says he has been somewhat astonished to see so little of my
name in the papers.

You know I don't keep a news paper correspondent with me nor do I
seek out the Special correspondent of any of our city papers. It is not in a
spirit of boasting that I caution the following facts. On the 7th I drove off
a *Division* of Burnsides Corp that was attempting to turn Gen'l. Daniel's
flank.[11] In the great fight of the 12th My Brig. more than any other saved
the day. We made the most daring and effective charge I ever saw, retak-
ing two lines of our works from the Yanks & holding them under a terrific direct, enfilade and reverse fire from 7.30 a.m. Thursday until 3.30
a.m. Friday. For the work of my Brigade that 12th day, I was thanked on
the field by Maj Gen'l. Rodes & Lt Gen'l. Ewell. And Gen'l. Lee sent for
me and thanked me & thru me my Gallant Brig. for our good service &
gallant conduct. Lt Gen'l. Ewell told me I was the "Hero of the day." Isn't
this better than partial, predjudiced (and often incorrect) newspaper accounts. On the 19th my Brig again made *two* gallant charges, driving the
Enemy with severe loss, and when the Yanks concentrated an overwhelming force against our little Corps (we had been reduced from 17 000 to
7000 but this is a secret. Most of the loss of the Army has fallen upon our
Corps) and threatened our utter annihilation when many Confederate
troops were running to the rear, I checked the enemy's advance & assisted

---

10. Ramseur understates the army-wide attack along the line at Cold Harbor on June 3.

11. Ewell reported that skirmishers under command of Ramseur surprised a division of Burnside's Ninth Corps that was entrenching and put them to flight with a sudden attack, taking possession of hundreds of knapsacks. *OR,* 36(1):1071.

by Daniels Brig & Pegram's Va Brig saved the day of that glorious Corps. [illegible] that my services are appreciated by my military superiors. When Gen'l. Early took command of the Corps (Gen'l. Ewell is sick) I was taken out of another division & assigned to the command of Early's Division which I now command.

There is a rumour that I have been made Maj Gen'l. If so, I will endeavour to do my whole duty. I will be the more rejoiced on your account. 1st because you will be pleased at honours conferred upon me & 2nd because I'll not be so much exposed. If I am a Division Commander now and stay further off from the line, I'll tell you of my escapes. I have had three horses shot under me & disabled, one of these was struck three times. In addition to these, the pony was also slightly wounded in the leg but not disabled. My saddle was shot through the pommel. I got four holes through my overcoat beside the ball which passed through my arm.

I tell you these things, my Darling Wife in order that you may be still more grateful to our Heavenly Father for His most wonderful and merciful preservation of my life. Truly we should render unto Him prayers of thanksgiving & praise continually for all His Mercies so recently & so continually shewn towards us. Your prayers my precious wife have thus far been answered. Oh may God grant an answer to them all. May we be His devoted children here. May He bring this war to a speedy close giving us independence and His special blessing.

It is raining on my paper so I must close. Do write often. Every day is not too often. Don't feel uneasy. I think we will confine our operation to the defensive. Love to all. Oh how I want to see you. Accept my devoted love and a thousand Kisses. Your devoted Husband[12]

Army near Chickahominy
June 7th/64

My Darling Wife,

I have rec'd. four letters from you in the last three days, the latest dated May 30th. How rejoiced I am to know that you all are well, hopeful & trustful. Continue to write to me My Dearest. Your letters are my chiefest delight and comfort.

Mr. Harding has just left me. He returned last night, having left Woodside yesterday morning. You know he took Maj. Smith's body to his friend's. All were well at Woodside & house was so beautiful, so peaceful. Ah! how I wish we could all meet there together in peace & happiness!

12. SHC.

I have been unwell several days. Bread & meat & (frequently) muddy water has given me a slight Diarrhea. I rec'd. some vegetables & pickles. Can't you send me a box by some body?

Every thing is quiet today. More so than it has been for a month past. Grant's losses have been tremendous. Ours have been heavy, especially in Offrs.

Don't be alarmed about Grant getting to Richmond. He may & probably will make many more desperate efforts to move us out of his way, but by the blessing of Almighty God we will defeat his plans.

Caleb is very well and sends you much love & many thanks for your recent note.

My Darling, let us unite in prayer, night and morning to thank God for his loving Kindness to us and to beseach His blessing upon our Cause. Give love to all of my Dear Ones. Excuse brevity. I have been up a great deal & lost much sleep, and will leave you now to take advantage of this lull in the storm & nap a little. Give love to all my friends. Oh! how I long to be with you all. Write frequently. Yr letters come very promptly. Accept my heart full of love My Darling little Wife. May God continue His love and mercy to us. May we be prepared for His Providence and have Grace given us equal to the day!

Good bye, Darling. My heart overflows with love and desire to be with you. Heaven bless my sweet little Wife. Yr devoted Husband.

P.S. I am appointed Major Gen'l. to date from June 1st/64.
Mr. H. brought me two bottles of pickled cherries. So good![13]

Army near Richmond
June 9th/64

My Precious Darling,

I know you would rather get a few lines than none at all & therefore I send you hastily this short note. We have been very quiet all day, no artillery & very little musketry along our lines. I have been asleep for nearly 20 hours. I have just made Caesar *bathe* me thoroughly and after a change of clothing I have taken a mint julep a friend sent me and am now waiting to eat some bacon & bread & as a variety some onions & pickle cherries which Mr. Harding brought me. Now if the mail carrier will bring me a letter from my Wife I will be as comfortable and happy as possible under the circumstances.

13. SHC.

Grant seems to have grown tame recently. I believe he will now attempt a Siege. I don't think he will attack our lines again unless he gets a very heavy reinforcement. He will probably cross to the South Side and attempt to cut our communication.

We must be brave and patient. Perseverance must be our motto. We must never relax our efforts! Liberty is worth great & immense Sacrafices! You must be patient too My Darling. Continue to hope, be constant in prayer, be cheerful, trustful, and happy. Let us hope and pray that the time may soon come when War will cease and we may remain in happiness and peace to enjoy all the delights of being together.

I have just rec'd. a letter and bundle from Jimmy Stinson who is wounded in Richmond. The bundle contains a small bottle of "Spirits"! and some thing to eat. There! now, a third interruption sounds in the way of orders. So I must close hurriedly. God bless you my Darling. Love to all. Write often. Caleb is well. Tell the children to write to me.

With a heart full of love, Your devoted Husband

S. D. R.[14]

Head Quarters Early's Div'n.
June 11th 1864

My Darling Wife

Today I rec'd. a short letter from Bro' Dave & am glad to hear such good accounts from you all at home. I have been disappointed in not getting a letter from you today, but I know it is not your fault. The mails I know are very irregular.

We have been very quiet for a few days. Grant is resting for another grand effort. May the Lord continue His merciful assistance to us & enable us to baffle all the designs of our cruel enemy. I expect Grant is endeavouring to throw a force to the South bank of the James. Gen'l. Lee is watching him. We have cause for thankfulness & gratitude in that we have been enabled to check the immense hosts of our enemy thus far.

Let us be hopeful and patient. We have many trials, dangers & hardships yet to bear, but persevering courage and a firm reliance upon an all wise Providence will enable us to come off victoriously.

Mr. H. tells me that Mama is very anxious for you to return to Woodside. I leave this entirely to you. I have some new money I am anxious to send you but am afraid to trust it to the mails. If I can not find an opportunity to send it soon I will send it by express to Mr. Schenck.

14. SHC.

Caleb is very well, and I have nearly entirely recovered. Col Grimes has been appointed Brigadier & assigned to Daniels' Brig. I believe I wrote you that I had Early's Div'n.

The Twilight is deepening to dark, so I must close. I send you these few lines frequently, knowing they will be full of comfort to you. Continue to pray for me, My Beloved. Oh! I wish I could spend tomorrow with you. I rec'd. the sweet influences of your gentle spirit after the storms of the past month. May our God speedily grant us peace! Oh! May the time soon come when Wars shall cease and all God's people rejoice in peace & happiness.

Do give my love to all my Dear Ones at home. Tell Mr. S. to write to me frequently. What regt is Charlie in.[15] Who is his Com'dg. Offr.

Write to me very often my best beloved.

Your letters are my priceless treasures these trying times. God bless & protect you My Darling Wife.

With a heart full of love

Yr Devoted Husband

S. D. R.[16]

The sixteen-day hiatus in Ramseur's correspondence began early on the morning of June 13, when Early led his corps westward into the Shenandoah Valley where Maj. Gen. David Hunter was threatening the key Confederate transportation and logistics center at Lynchburg. Ramseur's troops were aboard the lead train heading across the Orange and Alexandria rail line. Arriving in Lynchburg, they formed a defense west of town. Ramseur held in place until the southern resistance was fully formed. Hunter's indecisiveness in taking Lynchburg, even with a force far larger than Early's, saved the day for the Confederates. Instead, Hunter withdrew down the valley with Ramseur leading a pursuit that lasted until the Federals disappeared over the ridgeline to the west. Early was now free to continue northward, which he did with Ramseur once again in the van. Ramseur's troops passed through Lexington, where they somberly viewed the grave of "Stonewall" Jackson and the ruins of the Virginia Military Institute burned by Hunter's intruders. By the time Ramseur next wrote to Nellie, he and his men had covered well over 200 miles on foot, but the hardest marching and fighting on this incursion were yet to come.

15. Ramseur refers to his brother, who would have been seventeen years old in 1864.
16. SHC.

Staunton Va

June 27th/64

Precious Wife,

I have time to write you a line & tell you that I am well. We have had the hardest march of the war. Couldn't catch Hunter but we hope yet to strike the Yanks a heavy blow. Caleb is well as is Mr. Hn. Dont be anxious if you fail to hear from us. We are going still farther, & all our communication will be cut. We hope to relieve Richmond & make Yankeedom smart, in a sore place, so is not proper to write more of mil'y. matters. I may be pardoned for saying that I am making a reputation as Maj Gen'l. The greatest hardship I have to endure is my separation from you. May the time soon come, my Darling, when we will know no more separation in this world. Oh! how I want to see you. Accept my heart full of love. Love to all at home. May God bless you & soon reunite us. Yr Devoted Husband S. D. R.

Caleb says he'll write next August.[17]

New Market Va

June 30th 1864

My Darling Wife,

I write you a few lines this morning, hoping by some good fortune, they may arrive safely. I don't know when we will send another mail to the rear. We intend to cut loose from our communication & *take Washington* (?) or try.

We have marched tremendously. Hunter only escaped us, from the fact that *our* Cavalry was demoralized, and he had stolen enough horses to mount his entire Command.

Caleb & Mr. H. & Myself are well.

My Darling! I want to see you. Oh! so much! I dreamed about you last eve'g. & it was so sweet to meet you even in dream land.

I have not time to write more now. I send this to Milton, thinking probably you have returned there.

Caleb sends love to you & all at home. Says he wants you to feel no uneasiness on his account.

Do not feel anxious if you fail to hear from us. Necessarily we will be cut off from further communication for some time. Do give my warmest

17. SHC.

love to all my precious Home Loves! With a heart overflowing with love
for you My Precious Wife, and with the hope that this war may be brought
to a close this year so that we may soon live together in safety happiness &
peace. And with my earnest prayers for your health & happiness.

Your Devoted Lover & Husband

S. D. R.

Continue to write to me. Direct to Maj Gen'l. S. D. R. comd'g. Early's Div'n.
2nd Corps A.N.Va. Richmond Va & in the left hand corner Post Master
please forward. Accept love & Kisses from your Husband.

Write to Mr. S. & tell him the news from me. Tell him the Confederacy
owes me pay from the 1st of March.[18]

Sharpsburg Md.[19]

July 7th/64

My Darling Wife

Cut loose from the Confederacy I have an opportunity to send you by
hand a letter of few lines. I have been very well. Caleb also. Saw David yesterday. He is well. We are all doing well. Rec'd. two precious letters from
you yesterday, of the 10th & 16th of June. Oh! I am so rejoiced to hear
from you. You must not allow yourself to feel uneasy about me now that
we have no means of communication. Rest assured I will write by every
opportunity. Give my love to all at Home. I think it will be well for you to
return to Woodside. I wish I had an opportunity to send you some money.
The Gov't. owes me from the 1st of March.

Continue to write to me. Some of your letters will reach me.

Love to all of my Dear [illegible] Home Loves. Pray for me My Darling
Wife unceasingly. May God bless protect & keep us both, and may He
grant us the victory over our enemies & very soon establish us in independence, peace & happiness.

Accept my heart full of love. May God bless & protect you, & soon reunite us is the constant prayer of yr devoted Husband. S. D. R.[20]

18. SHC.

19. Kyd Douglas wrote that on the way to Sharpsburg he took Early, Gordon, Breckinridge, and
Ramseur to his father's house on the Maryland bank of the Potomac. Douglas, *I Rode with Stonewall*,
293.

20. SHC.

Sharpsburg Md
July 7th/64

My Own Darling Wife,

I have just finished a hasty note to you directed to Lincolnton; in order that I may have another chance, I enclose this in Mama's Letter.

You must not feel uneasy if you fail to hear from us. I cannot tell how long we will be absent from the Confederacy. Ah! Me! I do hope we will soon be able to retire to our sweet home and our Dear Ones, very soon. I rec'd. two letters from you yesterday, of the 10th & 16th of June. The greatest deprivation I experience.

We are doing very well but have plenty of hard work to do.

I must close my Darling Wife. I can not tell you how my heart yearns to see you and be with you. Ah My Darling Wife, when this terrible war is over, may we not enjoy living together in a quiet happy refined home? Oh! May our Heavenly Father in mercy hear our prayers and grant us peace.

Excuse haste, My Precious Darling.

May God bless you and keep you, comfort and sustain you, and speedily reunite us in happiness and peace.

Accept my heart full of Love

Good bye My Beloved, Yr Husband[21]

Near Leesburg Va. July 15th/64

My Darling Wife,

I seize the first opportunity since returning to Va. to write you very hastily. I have just learned that a courier leaves in the morning for Richmond & I hope my letter will reach you by this means.

We have been hard at work since I last wrote you. Took Harpers Ferry on the 4th Inst. Marched to Frederick Md. Whipped the Yankees there.[22] Marched to the District of Columbia and halted within five miles of Washington City.

Natural obstacles alone prevented our taking Washington. The heat & dust was so great that our men could not possibly march further. Time was thus given the Enemy to get a sufficient force into his works to prevent

---

21. SHC.

22. While Ramseur may have considered the battle of the Monocacy on July 9, 1864, to be a Confederate victory, from a strategic perspective the delay caused by Federal defenders bought time for Union forces to coalesce in the ramparts guarding Washington, D.C., thereby denying Early's invaders an easier opportunity to enter the capital city.

our capturing them.[23] We have however accomplished a good deal, and I hope will still do good work for our cause.

The great hardship of the campaign has been the absence of your dear letters. You do not know how intensely I long to hear from you. I feel that a budget of letters from home would so refresh & invigorate me, as to enable me to make all our long marches over again. David was left behind in charge of the wounded of Rodes' Div'n. near Washington.[24] I hope the Yankees will treat him kindly. Tell homeloves not to be uneasy concerning him.

Caleb is very well. So is Mr. Harding. Mr. H. has just left me. He will try to get a furlough as soon as everything grows more quiet.

I suppose you have returned to Woodside & therefore I direct there. I have been unusually well throughout this campaign. As the months pass by, I think of Winter Quarters & the hope of seeing you. How delightful 'twould be to know certainly that I will be with you again in a few months.

Our rumours from Richmond are very pleasing![25] May our Heavenly Father turn back our enemies with a terrible defeat. Oh! My Precious Darling, let us continue to pray for peace and independence!

Do give my best love to all the Dear ones at Woodside. I would write more, but my Courier is waiting to go to Hd. Qrs. with our mail & reports. Continue to write to me. I hope to get within reach of mail communication some day & then what a treat I'll have reading *all* your letters!

Accept my Sweetest Darling my heart's best, richest, warmest love. May God keep you, protect you, comfort & sustain you in these days of trial. And May He in much mercy soon reunite us in safety & happiness with a country free & independent. With Love inexpressible, Yr. Devoted Husband.

Caleb sends love. Mr. H. left before this opportunity to write was known or he w'd. doubtless have written.[26]

23. Ramseur refers to Fort Stevens on the capital's northern outskirts, where President Lincoln observed the skirmishes on July 11 and 12.

24. David Ramseur was serving as surgeon with the Fourteenth North Carolina when he was captured near Washington, D.C., on July 13, 1864, and sent to Old Capitol Prison. Manarin, *North Carolina Troops*, 5:395.

25. The absence of a major engagement near the Confederate capital while the attention of the Union high command was temporarily diverted by Early's threat to Washington may have given Ramseur cause for optimism.

26. SHC.

Berryville Va July 19th/64

My Darling Wife,

Last night I rec'd. your most welcome letter of the 25th Ult. by Lt. [J. Forney] Johnston. I assure you it was most gladly welcomed! You don't know how precious a letter from my Hearts Best Love is to me. It is like an Angel's visit to an exile from home & country. We are now resting after our grand march. Yesterday the Yankees attacked Gen'l. Rodes Div'n. but were repulsed with great loss. I regret to say the Col Wood of my old Brig was killed & Col Owens of Daniels Brig severely if not mortally wounded.[27] The Yanks withdrew last night & to all appearances we will have a quiet day. Caleb & Mr. H. are very well. David was left in charge of our wounded at Washington. I hope the Yanks will treat him well.

I am anxious to send you some money, but as yet have found no opportunity. I will send you $1000 by the 1st opportunity. In the mean time you must borrow. I hope my Darling Wife that you will continue hopeful, prayerful & full of health. Oh! that I could be with you even tho' it be for a short time. I think of you so frequently and with so much tenderness and love. May God bless you my Precious Wife. Oh! may He soon bring this terrible war to a close and permit us again to live together in happiness and peace! I have written these few lines in haste, hoping they may reach you safely. We are all very well. Don't feel anxious about us! Do give my best love to dear Mama & all at home. *Write to me often.* Most of them I receive. May our Heavenly Father bless protect you & very soon reunite us in happiness & peace.

Yr Devoted Husband

Don't tell any body about the bad conduct of my troops. S. D. R.[28]

Hd Qrs Early's Div'n.

July 23rd/64

My own Darling Wife,

Again I have escaped the ordeal of battle. I am greatly mortified at the result. My men behaved shamefully. They ran from the Enemy, and for the first time in my life I am deeply mortified at the conduct of troops under my command. Had these men behaved like my old Brigade would have

27. James H. Wood was killed and William A. Owens was mortally wounded in skirmishing at Snicker's Gap, July 18–19. Krick, *Lee's Colonels*, 272, 378.

28. SHC.

done under similar circumstances, a disgraceful retreat would have been a brilliant victory. Caleb & I are both safe, wonderful to say. God grant that we may be greatful and feel to Whom our thanks are due. Mr. H. is well.

Excuse haste. Accept my heart full of love. Oh how I long to see you, to rest with you and to receive your sweet sympathy. May God grant us a safe & speedy issue out of all our terrible trials and great dangers.

Do please continue to write to me. I'll get most of your letters. Those I don't get, will be of no use to anybody. Love to all. Accept my heart full of love. God bless & keep you & me & soon reunite us in happiness & peace.

Your devoted Husband S. D. R.[29]

Near Strasburg Va.
July 23th 1864

My Darling Precious Wife

I wrote you a short letter this morning. Now I have more leisure and will write again. Our trip into M'd. was a success. I see the Richmond papers are "pitching into" Gen'l. Early for not taking Washington.[30] If he had attempted it he would have been repulsed with great loss, and then these same Wise Acres would have condemned him for recklessness. The fight of the 20th at Winchester where my Div'n. was engaged, ought to have been a victory. Our men for some unaccountable reason became panic striken & after a fight of five minutes ran off of the field in wild disorder. I did all in my power to stop them, but 'twas impossible. Officers who are acquainted with all the facts not only do acquit me of all blame but unhesitatingly declare that had the troops behaved with their usual steadiness we would have gained a glorious victory.

I am sure I did all that mortal man could do. Yet newspaper editors & stay at home Croakers will sit back in safe places and condemn me. I do hope My Darling Wife, that you will be as little affected by these things as I am. I must request that you will endeavour to pass all such things by without notice.

---

29. SHC.

30. The *Richmond Sentinel*'s special correspondent reported that when Early's army drew up within cannon range of the northern capital, "The enthusiasm of the army was unbounded and the belief was pretty general that we could and would take the place," yet no attempt was made. The *Daily Richmond Examiner* quoted the *Washington Chronicle*: "The rebels might have dashed into Washington and effected its capture, if not its occupation." The invaders were said in the *Richmond Dispatch* to have gone where they wanted and done what they pleased without opposition, except at Monocacy bridge. *Richmond Sentinel*, July 26, 1864; *Daily Richmond Examiner*, July 18, 19, 1864; *Richmond Dispatch*, July 18, 1864.

I am sorry I was unable to procure you any goods in M'd. A pair of
kid gloves with the compliments of Col [Alexander S.] Pendleton, Gen'l.
Early's Ad't. Gen'l. is about all I have to send you. We are now preparing
for another advance. Hope we may be as successful in our military movements and even more so in procuring stores.

I bought a beautiful little mare in M'd. for you, but as usual with me in
the fight at Winchester, she was shot in the foot and I fear permanently
disabled. I rec'd. your precious letter by Lt Johnston several days ago. If
I could only have [a] daily letter from you assuring me that you are well
happy & hopeful I could be far more content myself at this terrible Separation! Do continue to write to me regularly. You can write so that even if
your letters are lost no one will be the wiser thereby.

I am anxious to send you some money, and at the very first opportunity
will do so. In the mean time you must borrow from some friend.

The papers mention a rumour to the effect that Grant has been killed
by a shell.[31] If so, I think we have cause for rejoicing! The news from
northern G'a. looks bad. I hope now however that Gen'l. Hood will be able
to drive Sherman back. From the Mississippi, we have glorious news.[32] All
of La except New Orleans, all of Arkansas & all of Texas in our possession.
Price, at the head of a large & growing Army, moving into Missouri. Oh!
If we can be successful at Richmond & in G'a., I believe we can see the
beginning of the end of this horrible war. I believe I wrote you that David
was left in charge of our wounded near Washington. He did not object to
staying. I hope the Yanks will not treat him well.[33] Caleb will write home
today. You must scold him for not writing oftener.

I must bid you goodbye My Darling Nellie. How I want to be with you!
How I want to see you! I love you My Darling more & better every day. I
miss your sweet companionship. Oh! so grievously. God grant that very
soon this cruel war may end, and that we may very soon be reunited to
live in a happy home. Accept my heart's overflowing affection.

God bless, keep, protect & save you and me to be soon united in happiness and love. Devotedly Husband[34]

31. The *Daily Richmond Examiner* cited Yankee prisoners and a deserter as sources, one saying
Grant's left arm had been shattered by a shell. The *Richmond Sentinel* published rumors of his
death, as well, as did the *Raleigh Confederate*. *Daily Richmond Examiner*, July 18, 20, 21; *Richmond
Sentinel*, July 18, 20; *The Confederate*, July 26, 1864.

32. Ramseur could only be referring to fighting at Harrisburg, Mississippi on July 14, that resulted in losses to the Federals sufficient for them to withdraw to Memphis, leaving the area open
for Lt. Gen. Nathan Bedford Forrest to operate freely.

33. Was Ramseur afraid that otherwise David would defect, or is this simply misstated?

34. SHC.

Camp near Martinsburg
July 28th/64

My Darling Wife,

I have time only to write you a line. I tried to get something nice in M. today but everything is gone. I could find nothing in any of the stores until I came to a bonnet shop. I reckon you'll laugh at my selection but I bought out the concern & I'm sure that's all that could have been expected of me.

No news. The Yanks whipped me t'other day. Twas mighty hard to bear at first, but I am getting used to it. However, we paid 'em back on the 24th.[35] We have driven 'em across the river & expect to follow in a few days. Accept my heart full of love. Write often. How I want to see you.

I sent the box of hats &c to Mr. Toles in Raleigh.[36] You must write to Miss Witty to take care of it for you until you can send for it.

Good bye my Precious Darling.

May God bless you

Your Devoted Husband

Do not feel anxious about me. Caleb is well & joins me in love to all.

Hope this weary war will terminate next year. What good news from G'a.[37] Oh! May the Lord deliver us from the hands of our enemies. Love to all. With my heart full of love My Darling Wife. Good night. With a Kiss from your devoted Husband[38]

Camp near Martinsburg
Aug 1st/64

My Darling Wife

I stopped a gentleman going to the rear just now to write you a few lines. Your precious letter of the 23rd ult. was rec'd. on 30th. How glad I was to hear that you were safely & happily at home. You must continue to write to me. Give me an account of your trip from L'n. I send you a band-box of hats from here. These were the only articles I could get. You must

---

35. Ramseur refers to the engagement at Kernstown, Virginia, in which Bvt. Maj. Gen. George Crook's dismounted cavalry was routed. *OR*, 37(1):286, 37(2):601.

36. This is quite possibly William H. Toles, a free mulatto from Person County (adjacent to Caswell County) who worked as a laborer and may well have been known to Nellie's family.

37. Ramseur must have been referring to exaggerated reports of a Confederate victory, as often appeared initially, after the clash in Atlanta on July 22 that took the life of U.S. Maj. Gen. James B. McPherson. See, for example, the *Daily Richmond Examiner*, July 25, 26, 1864.

38. SHC.

not quarrel with me for failure. Our orders were positive on the matter of taking property for private use & you know I always obey orders.[39]

I suppose Mr. Harding has reached home & has the pleasure of greeting his daughter.

I rec'd. yr. letter by Lt Johnston.

Caleb & myself are well.

Oh! how I do want to be with you. May our Heavenly Father in mercy stop this terrible war, cleanse us from all sin, and speedily reunite us in happiness and peace.

Accept my heart full of love My beloved wife. God bless, keep, protect & sustain you. Love to all.

With love & kisses

Yr. devoted Husband

S. D. R.

P.S. I sent you $400 by Mr. H. As soon as I have an opportunity I'll send you more. With love inexpressible

Yours forever

Most devotedly

S. D. R.

The bandbox was directed to Mr. C. H. Richmond care of Mr. Toles at Raleigh. Send to Mr. Toles for it as soon as you can.[40]

Camp near Martinsburg Va.
Aug't. 1st 64

My Dear Brother

I have been too hard at work for some time past to write you.

I consider our Campaign to M'd. a success. People say we could have taken Wash'n. That might have been done the 1st day we got there had our troops been fresh, but they were nearly exhausted. I marched from Frederick City to Wash'n. (42) forty-two miles with but two (2) hours rest. The heat & dust were terrible, water scarce & everything combined to make the march a terrible one. The next morning the Yanks had more men behind the strongest field works I ever saw than we had in front of them.

David was left in charge of the wounded from Rodes' Div'n. I did not know of this or I would have prevented it.

39. *OR*, 37(2):592.
40. SHC.

You have no doubt seen an article in the Richmond Sentinel giving an account of the whipping the Yanks gave this Div'n. on the 20th Inst.[41] That acct. is false. You will no doubt see & hear other false accts. For yr own satisfaction I write you a hasty history of the affair.

I had 1800 infantry at Winchester, & Vaughan's Com'd. I ordered Vaughan [Brig. Gen. John C. Vaughn] to drive some Yankee Cav'y. back to Bunker Hill. This was at 5 0 c'k a.m. I had marched all night (17 miles) to W. & my Inf'y. was too tired to go farther & camp (as I was ordered to do) at Newtown 9 miles in the opposite direction that night.

Vaughan was out, driving sometimes & falling back sometimes before the Yankees whom he represented to be in *small force*. Finally I heard musketing about 2 miles off & moved the Div'n. to attack the Yanks. I rode ahead & met Cav'y. coming back. Saw Gen'l. Vaughan & asked him what force was in his front. He said "a small force, one reg't. Inf'y. & one Reg't. Cav'y. & a 4 gun batt'y." This agreed with several other reports he had sent back during the day. Now here was an old Cav'y. Brigadier, who had been out skirmishing with the En'y. all day. (it was now 4 P.m.) Of course I was justified in believing & acting on his report.

I therefore moved [Brig. Gen. W. Gaston] Lewis' (Hoke's old Brigade) & Johnston's into line & advanced, with Pegram's Brig in reserve. The country was wooded right here so that the En'y. could not be seen. Before going far some of Vaughan's Cav'y. rushed thro' Lewis Brig. The Yanks advanced rapidly. Johnston's Brig broke & dispersed those in his front, & I was just on the point of ordering Lewis to charge when the troops on the left broke & ran away in the most perfect rout I ever saw. This was taken up from left to right. It was a perfect & unaccountable panic. I tried in vain to stop them & often expected to lose my life in so doing.

To sum up. 1st I was deceived by the Cav'y. & have got the witnesses to prove it. 2nd I had whipped part of the Yankee line & if the troops had stood & fought as they usually do, instead of a defeat, I would have gained a brilliant victory.

I am very well. Write to me a long letter. Direct to Maj Gen'l. S. D. R. Comd'g. Early's Div, Army of the Valley of Va.

I'm looking over my letter & see I have omitted to mention the Yankee

41. In a column-long report, the *Sentinel*'s special correspondent ("Soldat") cited "[the Confederate] loss in the unfortunate affair [as] about 800 killed, wounded and captured, besides Kirkpatrick's battery of artillery of four pieces." He identified the reasons for the defeat as not sending skirmishers sufficiently forward, marching up too near the rapidly advancing enemy line, and "bad management in sending [the battery] even in front of the infantry and within two hundred yards of the enemy before unlimbering." Ramseur was not mentioned by name. *Richmond Sentinel*, July 26, 1864.

forces. Instead of the regts. as reported, I was attacked by [Brig. Gen. William W.] Averell's Division, 3700 strong.

I censured my command severely for running. I called it unnecessary & cowardly. For this reason I've no doubt there will be a good deal of correspondence about it. I think I've got every body in a fighting humour & they'll do better next time.

Love to all. God bless & keep you & grant us a speedy & happy union in independent peace. Yr Affte. Brother[42]

Woodside August 3rd 1864

Now that you are far away my dear husband, and almost entirely cut off from us, it seems almost useless to write regularly, as I have done previously, but as the regular days come around for writing to you, my darling, I cant bear to let them escape unheeded. It is such a relief to surrender my heart to you, and such a pleasure to tell you all my thoughts & feelings & the deep, lasting affection I feel for you.

I hope you may get these letters sooner than I think. At any rate, you will find on your return from Maryland a budget of them awaiting you.

We get nothing reliable whatever from the Army of the Valley. *Northern* Papers report firing in the direction of Washington. This is another time of trial we have to pass through, but I am very hopeful, trusting that our Kind Father who has watched over you so mercifully through so many dangers, will continue his loving kindness & tender mercies unto us. If we could only hear from you, this separation could be better borne, but I suppose that, at present is almost impossible. It does seem that our trials and sufferings of the present time ought to teach us submission, resignation, & our dependence on a Higher Power, but we are still wicked & rebellious, we are not yet sufficiently punished, our pride is not humbled, our hearts are hard & cold & proud still.[43]

I do hope, my dear husband that you have by this time received some of my letters written before you left the Valley. I have written very often. I have only heard from you once since Mr. Harding came home. I think I must have letters on the way somewhere. I will get them sooner or later I suppose. I had such a pleasant comforting letter from Mr. Schenck last night. He had just heard of the disaster to your command, had only seen

42. PC.

43. Here Nellie repeats an often-heard explanation when a people, who believe God to be on their side, suffer a defeat and rationalize that it was brought about by their own pride and wickedness.

the accounts in the Examiner[44] which were very much exaggerated. He seemed to feel no uneasiness about the result of the affair, knew that you were not to blame and all would *come out right* in the end.

None of your friends nor indeed *anyone* in this part of the country seem inclined to censure you in the least, but simply express regret that the affair should have happened. I do not expect you, my dear husband, to pass through this war & rise to fame, without passing through some shadows for a moment. No man ever did yet; our Christian fortitude is called into action now too. Let us not succumb to this first trial of faith, but act with that firm confidance which your name, talents & character well justify.

I have written a short letter this evening, but will atone for it by sending you a long one next time. All join me in love to you & Caleb, all are well & doing well. Take good care of your self my Dearest, for my sake.

May God bless you, devotedly your wife Nellie.

I hope you will bring me some Yankee paper. This is miserable.[45]

Camp near Winchester Va.
Aug 10th/64

My Darling Wife, today I rec'd. yours of the 3rd only 7 days after it was written. How glad I am that you continue to write regularly to me! I cant imagine why my letters do not reach you as punctually as come to me. I have written to you frequently, tho' not regularly, since Mr. Harding left, and you certainly ought to have rec'd. more than one letter from me.

Well, we have again been into M'd. In fact, we (*part* of this army) have crossed the river twice since Mr. H. left us. We have made very short visits each time. Now we are back at Winchester and the Yanks are at Charlestown & Berryville under *Hooker* at least three times our numbers. Why

---

44. On July 25, the *Daily Richmond Examiner* announced that Ramseur's "command [was] cut to pieces or captured, and he himself had lost an arm," based on "reports." Citing an official dispatch the following day, the paper stated that on July 20, "General Ramseur with a brigade was sent north from Winchester on a reconnaissance, and found the enemy in much heavier force than he expected, and was beaten back with a loss of two hundred and fifty men killed, wounded, and missing." The account of "Ramseur's defeat" on July 27 called it "a nasty affair," saying, "Ramseur led his division up the turnpike with empty guns, at the route step and in route order—that is, in that extreme degree of irregularity and confusion in which only Confederate troops know how to march." The enemy fired into their ranks, routing them "with scarcely a show of resistance." Finally, on July 28, the *Examiner* editorialized about "the deplorable affair in which Ramseur's division was humiliated in the dust. A scandalous affair!" The commentary went on to describe the encounter as "a disaster such as never before fell on any portion of the army of Northern Virginia, and such, we trust, as will never again be known on the soil of the State."

45. SHC.

they do not advance, I do not know, but we expect stirring times before long. I do hope, for more reasons than I have time to give, that we may be enabled to whip them soundly, & that my command may redeem itself.

You say in one of yr late letters that you think the statements made in the papers should be corrected at once.[46] I must confess I was made very angry by some of the editorials I have seen & I felt disposed to write a true acc't. of the affair over my own signature, but on reflection I saw this would be unwise & improper. So I've borne it all in silence resting satisfied that official reports will properly explain the whole affair when the history of this war is compiled. I have great satisfaction in telling you, that none of my Mil. Superiors blame me. I have had the kindest assurances of sympathy & confidence from Gen'ls. Early, Rodes & Gordon! In fact, I have heard no one reflect against me except men who ran away from the fight, & offrs. whose commands behaved badly & who know that I have unhesitatingly said so. But enough of this, it don't trouble me much. So don't think it. I am so sorry to hear such bad news from the corn crops &c. I do hope that refreshing showers may yet restore the corn &c.

Oh! My Sweetest Darling. How I do want to see & be with you. I do feel this terrible separation so keenly. Ah! So much of our young lives are passed in anxiety far from sympathy & mutual encouragement. What would I not give to be with you this eve'g. Tomorrow I think we will be on the move, probably towards Culpeper. We have certainly expected an advance on this side of the M'ts, but the Yanks have gone on the other side & we will probably go there to stop them.

In our last raid I succeeded in getting 5 yds. of wte. Flannel, 5 yds. linen, 5 yds. [illegible] cambric, a pr. of gloves & a dress pattern. These things were all I could get as I had a limited am't. of *Yankee* money & Confed. money would not pass. The art[icles] were all selected by a young man on my staff. I hope they will suit. I'll send them by 1st opportunity. Also a pr. of blk kid gloves sent to you with the compliments of Col. Pendleton A.A.G. of our Army of the Valley.

Tell Mr. Harding I envy him in the enjoyment of home. Ah me! If I could see & be with my Darling little wife, I would not complain. I'd be willing to fight a battle every day, if I could be with my sweet little wife every eve'g. But, my Darling, be patient, be hopeful, be trustful!

Let us pray for each other [illegible] separated here. Let us meet at a

46. Nellie may have been thinking of accounts published in the *Raleigh Confederate*. On July 30, it reprinted an article from the *Richmond Enquirer* "demand[ing] investigation. All reports agree that General Ramseur was completely surprised." The *Enquirer* went on to report rumors that Ramseur was under arrest. On August 2, the *Confederate*'s own source ("Sigma") retold the story from a soldier's point of view, characterizing it as "a sad affair."

throne of Grace. Give my love to all the dear ones at home. Have you got the box of hats? I'll send the bundle I now have by 1st chance. Caleb is well. I hope you will scold him constantly for not writing to his mother. My Sweetest Darling write to me often. I'll get most of y'r. letters & those that are lost will not benefit any one else. Do give my love to all. Accept my heart full of love & pray for me my Precious Wife. May God bless us & soon reunite us in happiness & peace. With love & kisses Yr. Own Husband[47]

Camp near Strausburg Va.

Aug't. 15th/64

My Darling Precious Wife

It has been almost a week since I rec'd. yr last precious letter. I suppose the regular mail trains have been interfered with by the movement of Anderson's troops from Richmond up this way.[48] I hope soon to receive a whole batch of precious documents.

Oh! My Sweetest Darling. How I long to be with you at *this* time. I really think that every hour I am engaged with military matters, my thoughts fly to you. *Do* you know how I want to be with you? Ah! My Heart's Most Precious Darling! You are the light and delight of my life. I live for you. And Oh! your love makes life so delightful for me.

Today and yesterday, we have been waiting for the Yankees to attack. They are too strong for us to attack & I am pretty sure they are afraid to attack us in our present position. Hence I expect we will at least rest from our marches for a few days. If so, you may expect an epistle from me every day.

You must not feel any longer anxious about my health &c. Every body tells me that I am looking remarkably well. I am however growing bald quite fast, so you may imagine that it will not be long before I am quite *slick on top.*

But seriously, My Darling, had it not been for the outrageous conduct of my troops at Winchester, I would be in as fine spirits as 'tis possible for me to be away from my sweet little wife. I am sorry you allow newspaper scribblers to trouble you so much. Their accounts are received principally from runaways or the friends of troops not especially distinguished for good conduct. I do assure you My Darling for your own satisfaction (and I care more for your opinion than for anyone else's) that if this Div'n. had

---

47. SHC.

48. Lt. Gen. Richard H. Anderson was dispatched to join Early in a coordinated attack on Sheridan. *OR*, 43(1):997.

fought as my old Brigade was & is in the habit of fighting I would have whipped Gen'l. Averell most thoroughly. But you must say nothing about the above. It will do no good. I am glad to assure you that my Mil'y. Superiors attach no blame whatever to me. And if you could have heard all the kind sayings expressing perfect confidence in me, urging me not to feel badly &c, you would know that your husband is well appreciated by the chiefs of this army.

I was interrupted to go to dinner. I give you bill of fare. 1st course, nice light bread, butter, new onions, irish potatoes, roast beef. 2nd course, light bread, butter, scrambled eggs. 3rd course, bread, butter & molasses. What think you of that fare? Are we not living *high*? We certainly are, for soldiers!

My Precious, I have just again been interrupted to go to the lines. Do Write me all about yourself. You don't & cant know my anxiety. Do tell me all. I sent you a small bundle the other day, to be left with Mr. Callum in Danville.[49] Did you get it? If not send for it by first opportunity. Caleb is well & sends love. He is looking better than I ever saw him before. Really I think the girls would all fall in love with him now.

Write me a long letter of news, but let it all be news about yourself. Oh! My Darling, beautiful wife, how I do want to see you and be with you. Let us be brave and courageous, patient and hopeful, and all will yet be well.

I am greatly encouraged by signs in the north. If we hold out against Sherman (there is the vital point) hold Richmond & keep the trans-Mississippi as 'tis, I believe we may expect a speedy peace.

Write home for me frequently, & tell them I'm too much engaged to write often. What has become of Charley? Is he at Goldsboro? I'm much concerned about him. Do give my best love to all my Dear Relatives in Milton. Where is Grandma? I hope she has ret'd. as I think that portion of Va. liable to Raids.

I have been writing at a galloping rate. So you must excuse. Don't fail to write to me regularly. Y'r. letters are my ch'f. delight. What is my little niece to be named?[50]

Write to me soon!

Accept My Sweetest Darling, my heart's best love. May our God keep us & bless us & soon reunite us in peace & happiness. Good bye with a kiss.

Yr devoted Husband[51]

49. James R. Callum was a druggist from North Carolina. U.S. Census Office, *Eighth Census,* 1860.

50. Ramseur refers to the newborn daughter of Mary and E. H. Harding, named Anne.

51. SHC.

Camp near Winchester
Aug't. 20, 1864

My Dear Brother,

Your kind & most welcome letter of the 11th rec'd. yesterday. I have been so constantly employed I am compelled to write hurriedly.

You know how I dislike news paper controversy & hence my reasons (& besides that such publications are unmilitary) for not correcting some of the outrageous falsehoods that have been published about the affair of the 20th Ult.

You say Gen'l. Lewis says that reconnaissance was not sufficient &c. I'll write you a hasty history of the affair. At 6 p.m. on the 19th I rec'd. orders to march from Camp four miles beyond Berryville to Winchester. 17 miles to reach Winchester before or by day light & to drive back a force reported to be advancing from Martinsburg and to camp that night (the 20th) at Newtown 7 miles south of Winchester (after having had all our stores & sick & wounded removed from Winchester).

I marched to a position 2 miles north of Winchester by daylight (19 mls., 2 ½ pr. hour). The men were very tired & I directed Brig. Gen'l. Vaughn to take his own & Col [George] Jackson's Brigades of Cav'y. & go out and meet the En'y. & if possible to drive him back. This was at daylight. During the day I rec'd. several reports from Gen'l. Vaughan all agreeing that the En'y. was in small force.

At 12 o clock Gen'l. V. sent me word that he needed a battery! At the same time asking me *how far* I wished him to drive the En'y. I sent him a batt'y. of 4 guns & told him to drive them to Bunker Hill 12 miles north of Winchester. At 2 p.m. he sent a Staff Offr. to me to request that I would put my Div'n. in ambush for the En'y. & that he would draw them into it, that there were only *four* regts. of Cav'y. out in his front. I declined this proposition for the following reasons which were expressed to him, i.e. 1st The stores were now nearly all removed & that I was about to march to Newtown 9 miles off where I had to encamp. 2nd that the men were very tired from the rapid march of the night before & that there was no place where I could find woods enough for an ambuscade within four miles of Winchester. Going so far w'd. necessitate a march of 2 miles to the front, 4 mls. back to Winchester & 7 to Newtown. 13 mls. I heard nothing more from Vaughan until 4 p.m. when I heard musketry near me. I immediately got my command under arms & moved to the front. I met Gen'l. V. & his Cav'y. coming back. I asked him why he was falling back. He replied "in order that the En'y. might be more certainly repulsed." I then asked what force the En'y. had. He replied "One Reg't. Cav'y., one Reg't. Inf'y. & four guns." Now here was the statement of an old Brigadier who had recently commanded a Div'n. of Infantry[52] who had been skirmishing from sunrise till 4 p.m. with the En'y. over four miles of country. Of course I was justified in believing his report correct. I acted upon it & was mistaken & defeated.

Notwithstanding Vaughan's incorrect reports, had the men fought, had they staid with me, had they *followed where I repeatedly led*, I would have been victorious. The following were my dispositions. I immediately put Lewis' Brig. in line in a good position with his skirmishers but 50 yds in front (this was to induce the reported small force to come to close quarters). Soon after Lewis line was formed I discovered three large Regts. advancing rapidly on his Right. I sent Johnston to meet them.

About five minutes after the firing commenced the Yanks in front of Johnston & the right of Lewis were broken to pieces. I had discovered just as the firing commenced that the Yankee line overlapped Lewis left about 200 yds. I immediately ordered Gen'l. Lilly[53] who was in line behind Lewis to form on Lewis' left. Lilly was slow about moving & before he got in position the 57th & 54th [North Carolina Infantry Regiments] broke & ran like Sheep. I was on the right with Johnston's Brigade at this time. I immediately gallopped to the left & by every means endeavoured to check the flying panic stricken men.

All the regts. took up the panic from left to right. The woods were of such a nature that the men on the Right could not see the cause of the running on the left. They only knew that every thing on the left was routed & they imagined there was sufficient cause for it & joined in. Certain am I that there was no occasion for any running. The Yankees out numbered us about six hundred men, but if the left regts. of Lewis Brig. had stood 5 minutes longer, I would have charged & turned their left flank with Johnston's Brigade which had already broken the line in his front, and Lilly would soon have been upon Lewis' left. There was no necessity or excuse for those regts. to run.

52. Ramseur is overreaching here. Vaughn had seen service in the Mexican War, witnessed the bombardment of Fort Sumter, fought at Bull Run and in the Vicksburg campaign, and ridden with Early on the Washington raid. There is no indication in his military service record, however, of his ever having commanded a division. Vaughn, Confederate Generals, Staff Officers, and Non-regimental Enlisted Men, CMSR, RG 109, NARA; Warner, *Generals in Gray*, 316–17.

53. Brig. Gen. Robert D. Lilley had commanded Early's old brigade earlier in the 1864 campaign and been wounded three times, resulting in his arm being amputated at Winchester. Ramseur consistently misspells Lilley's surname without the "e."

There may have been some necessity for the left reg't. to throw back its left wing or even to retire in good [order] some hundred yds. Instead of this it was an unnecessary rout. Look at the losses, *nearly all* of which occurred after the running commenced, 24 killed, 16 wounded in the Enemy's hands, 52 brought off & 142 prisoners, total 234. Remember nearly all of this loss was after the rout began. I did every thing that mortal man could to stop the runaways. By appealing to the "Brave Men (if any were there)" to follow me I succeeded finally in stopping a few. The Yankees did not pursue vigorously. 15 minutes after my men ran Averell withdrew most of his Inf'y. leaving only dismounted Cav'y. in our front. His Inf'y. withdrew four miles. His loss was 30 buried on the field (their graves are marked & we have counted them) & they admit a loss of 192 wounded. All this was done on my right in front of which I have told you the Yankees broke. Had the left done as well what praises would have been sounded for me!

I don't want you to publish anything about this matter. My Mil'y. Superiors are perfectly satisfied with my conduct.

In the subsequent fight the men behaved well. They are doing well now. They are much shamed of their former conduct & I think I'm getting up a good spirit among them.

I am appointed Maj. Gen'l. temporarily, that is while I have command of Early's Div'n. which I suppose will be as long as he is Lt. Gen'l. (which *he* is temporarily) or if his app't. is made permanent, I think mine will be. Tho' I understand that the friends of a certain Virginian are making use of the Winchester disaster to cry me down in Richmond.[54]

I retain Early's old staff except an additional aid, & I will give that to Lt. [Randolph] Ridgely, who dared all things & was shot down near me trying to assist me in rallying the men.

I cant write more at present. You may read this to my *true* friends. I dont care a snap for the opinion of others because my own conscience is free of all blame.

Love to all. Write soon. Your letters giving home news are most welcome.

Give kisses to the children. Did Jimmy Stinson ever send Doddie his flag? I hope so. We are now at Charlestown. Expect a big fight soon. God

54. Ramseur's biographer hypothesizes that the unnamed Virginian being touted for Ramseur's command was John Pegram. This hypothesis is strengthened by Pegram's being selected for Ramseur's command after Rodes was killed on September 19 and Ramseur was appointed to lead his division. Gallagher, *Stephen Dodson Ramseur*, 199 (n. 62).

bless you & yours. Do, my Dear Brother, pray for me that I may have Grace sufficient unto the day that I may feel the assurance that I am one of God's children. God bless you all. Yr devoted Brother, S. D. R.[55]

The heavy engagement at Stephenson's Depot (or Rutherford's Farm) on July 20, 1864, evinces Ramseur's aggressiveness and impetuosity as a combat commander, traits evident earlier at Bethesda Church. The clash also provides insight into how he coped with stress bred by the adversity that followed. He was heavily criticized in the press in Virginia and North Carolina for recklessness in not ascertaining the size and disposition of the enemy before advancing and contravening Early's orders to remain on the defensive. He likely heard that some southerners were calling the battle "Ramseur's Defeat," or even "Ramseur's Butt."[56]

The intensity of the furor is clear in Rodes's observation that "the men and main officers concerned have succeeded in winning public opinion to their side and have very nearly ruined Ramseur. . . . His reputation is ruined, and he is deprived of his permanent promotion."[57] Ramseur chose not to argue his case in the press but sought instead to convince the two confidants who mattered most, Nellie and Schenck. Pride seemed to prevent Ramseur from admitting that his own misjudgment had contributed to the rout.[58]

While acknowledging that the Yankees had "whipped" him, he declared that his superiors did not blame him for the debacle. In Ramseur's telling, the cavalry commander provided inaccurate intelligence, Lewis's brigade had broken and run, igniting panic all along his line, and the whole division refused to fight. Ramseur cited 1,800 infantrymen under his command plus cavalry (1,300 strong, although unspecified), versus Averell's 3,700 combatants. Periodic strength reports indicate the North Carolinians' actual strength at over 2,000 foot soldiers, confronting 1,350 Federal riflemen and 1,000 mounted troopers.[59] Nor was Ramseur attacked by Averell's Division; his column marched into the Federal battle line.

Rodes tempered his public criticism, stating only that, "Of course if Ramseur had put Pegram's brigade in the front line the disaster might have

55. PC.

56. Patchan, *Shenandoah Summer*, 151.

57. *OR*, 37(1):353.

58. After the war, David Ramseur sought to repair the damage to his brother's reputation, as shown in his reference to this matter in a letter to R. E. Lee, February 22, 1866, Lee Headquarters Papers, MSS3 L 515, 592–94, Virginia Historical Society, Richmond.

59. Patchan, *Shenandoah Summer*, 347–48 (n. 5).

been averted, but who knows!"[60] After the war, Early went further: "General Ramseur did not take the proper precautions in advancing, and his division while moving by the flank, was suddenly met by a larger force under Averell, advancing in line of battle, and the result was Ramseur was thrown into confusion, and compelled to retire with the loss of four pieces of artillery and a number in killed and wounded."[61]

Camp near Bunker Hill
Aug 28th/64

Last night, my Beloved Wife, I rec'd. two letters from you, one of the 18th, the other of the 21st Inst. *Do you know how* much good those letters did me? After a long march and a sharp skirmish I had gone to bed & was thinking of my absent Darling, when your letters were handed to me. I am so glad to know that you continue cheerful and hopeful all through these terrible days. I do *so long* to be with you more than ever. When you long for me so much, courage my Little Wife! May be I will be permitted to come and see you before long.

Do you know that I am beginning to believe with Uncle Charles, that we will very soon have peace. Every body seems to think that the peace party will carry the election in the north. Oh! May these expectations be realized. Oh! that very soon this terrible war may cease and we may be permitted to live together in happiness and peace.

I am so glad my Beloved to know that your health continues good at this time. I do pray that you may be sustained in your approaching trial. Let us be confident, hopeful and cheerful as thus one will be the better prepared for every trial. It is such a pleasure, My Darling, to be permitted to write to you often. I wish I had time to write oftener and more fully. My letters would all be filled with love for you and longings to be with you. Is there anything you want that I can send you? I have a bottle of fine old French brandy I'll send you by the very 1st safe opportunity. I also have some money I am anxious to send you; hope an opportunity may offer very soon.

---

60. *OR*, 37(1):353.

61. Harding, "Sketch of Major General S. D. Ramseur," 39. Averell reported capturing seventeen officers, 250 enlisted men, and a four-gun battery. Another couple hundred Confederates may well have been killed and wounded. The Federal losses were twenty-seven killed and 184 wounded in the infantry. *OR*, 37(1):327. One of Ramseur's subordinate commanders that day stated twenty-seven years later that Brig. Gen. W. G. Lewis had criticized Vaughn for making imprecise statements and excused Ramseur from being "altogether responsible for the mistake that occurred." Cox, *Life and Character*, 36.

Would the Pony be of any service at Woodside? He is too small for the carriage. It is very difficult to get a good horse up here. All captured horses are at once handed over to the Quarter Master for Gov't. use. Caleb has swapped Tarheel & has made a good trade, tho' his horse is too light for harness. If I have an opportunity I will purchase a horse for the carriage & send him home by Caesar. There is no news with us. We followed the Yankees to their strong hold at Harper's Ferry. Offered them battle there several days and are now in striking distance of them at this place.[62] If they choose to come out & fight us, I think Gen'l. Early will accomodate them. We have had good news from Richmond.[63] May God grant us a great victory there and at Atlanta, which is the point of great interest to me.

Have you rec'd. a package I sent you by a Soldier going home on furlough? It was directed to the care Mr. James Callum, Danville. I am sorry I did not get more *plunder* when we were in Maryland the first time, but you know I was full of business & had not time to look out for goods.

I suppose you have heard that David has returned safely from Yankee prison.[64] He has furlough for 20 days. I hope he will return via Milton.

You would be astonished to see me now. I weigh about one hundred and fifty and *look as handsome* as you ever saw me *with my hat on.* You must be prepared to see me nearly if not quite bald. I dont know what would so much restore my hair as to lay my head in your lap & have you to comb it for me every morning and evening! Would you not wish to apply the remedy? I am sure I would submit to it most willingly.

I have not heard from home for a long time. You must scold the children and Mr. Schenck for treating me so badly. I suppose they are all well or I would have heard it. Has George determined to go to the Army. Advise him for me to join the Artillery. He will find that easiest &c.[65]

Tell Mr. Harding I say he had better remain at home until his cutaneous gets entirely well. In fact, say to him that I think he ought to get a church near Milton and remain at home altogether.

I hope my Darling Little Wife that you receive all of my letters. I have written you very frequently of late. You know the R R President & the P[ost] M[aster] Gen'l. have had a fuss which interferes materially with our

---

62. Early demonstrated around Harpers Ferry, August 22–25, without provoking a major engagement. Long, *The Civil War Day by Day*, 559–60.

63. Ramseur may be referring to early reports of the battle at Reams' Station on August 25.

64. David Ramseur was transferred from Old Capitol Prison to Fort Delaware and then to City Point, Virginia, where he was exchanged on August 12, 1864. Manarin, *North Carolina Troops*, 5:395.

65. There is no record of George Richmond's serving in the Confederate army.

mails.[66] Whenever we are quiet I will write to you very often. If you fail to receive my letters do not become uneasy for we are so situated frequently that even when we have the opportunity to write we have no way to send our letters to the rear.

Ah! My Beautiful Beloved How I do wish I could spend this day with you at Woodside, but I hope to be with you before long & this hope cheers me up. May we soon realize it. Good bye My Precious Wife & may our God keep us bless us & soon reunite us is the constant prayer of yr devoted Husband.[67]

Camp near Bunker Hill Va.

Aug 29/64

My Own Darling Wife

This morning, much to my surprise, we are quiet. How long we will remain so is very doubtful. In fact, I have everything now ready to move. Thus you see our life is one of constant action. Marching & Counter Marching. Maneuvering & sometimes a little fighting. So far we have been very successful. God grant that we may continue to strike telling blows for our bleeding country.

I am growing more hopeful about the ending of the war. Every man whose opinion I have asked and who has had an opportunity of learning the feeling of the Yankee people & soldiers, assures me that the North is tired of war and will elect an out & out unconditional Peace Man at the Presidential Election next November.

I sincerely trust that these opinions may be very speedily verified. For myself, I think *now* as I did a few months ago that everything depends upon the result of operations at Richmond and Atlanta. If we are enabled to baffle all of Grant's movements and to drive back Sherman, it does seem to me that the Yankee Nation will be forced to conclude that the task of subjugating the South is more than they can accomplish! At all events we have reason for great gratitude to the Giver of all Good for his wonderful mercy so continuously shown towards us during this tremendous campaign. Let us be humble thankful and prayerful, putting all of our trust in the Lord of Hosts, who is our Father & our God. What a precious thought! If the Lord is for us, who can prevail against us?[68]

66. The president of the Virginia Central Railroad, along with the other railway executives, were engaged in a long-term quarrel with the Confederate Post Office Department over the rates of pay and contractual requirements involved in carrying the mail. Black, *Railroads of the Confederacy*, 226–27.

67. SHC.

68. Again, Ramseur paraphrases Romans 8:31.

My beautiful Darling, how earnestly I long to be with you *now*. Every morning and evening my thoughts hasten home to you My Beloved. Could we be permitted to see each other even for a short while, how much would we be encouraged and strengthened. But stern duty separates us. Let us bear it bravely, and the time will soon come when we will receive our reward! Rich Reward! reunion in peace, independence and happiness!!!

There is nothing new. Caleb & I are looking & feeling well. You must scold Caleb for not writing oftener. He has more time than I have.

I have written hurriedly. You must put up with short letters with the assurance that I feel like writing volumes of love and sympathy to you. I will write as often as I can & you must feel no anxiety if you fail to get letters regularly from me. Any movement & irregular mail facilities may prevent my letters from reaching you regularly. Have you heard from Lincolnton recently? They seem to have forgotten me. Give my best love to Mama & Grandma and to all.

Never neglect an opportunity to write to me. Accept my Heart's overflowing love. God bless you, comfort & sustain you in every trial.

With love inexpressible and many kisses.

Yr devoted Husband[69]

> Camp near Bunker Hill
> Aug 30th/64

My Own Darling Wife

Since I last wrote you I have had quite a sharp skirmish with the Enemy's Cavalry in which I drove them two or three miles.[70] I have not rec'd. a letter from you for several days and am becoming very anxious to hear again that you are well cheerful and happy.

Just as I finished the above sentence, my mail man came in with a "No letter for your General." I know my letters are on the road and that the senseless quarrels between the R.R. Pres't. & the P.M. Gen'l. by which all our letters are detained, prevents me from hearing regularly and quickly from My Heart's Darling. Isn't this too bad.

I had a long conversation today with an escaped prisoner. He escaped from the cars in the state of N.Y. three weeks ago & has travelled through the country on foot to this point. He represents the peace party at the

---

69. SHC.

70. Bvt. Maj. Gen. Alfred T. A. Torbert, chief of cavalry of the Middle Military Division in the Shenandoah Valley, reported that on August 29, in the face of the enemy in force, his third brigade executed an orderly retrograde to Charleston, where it made a stand, forcing the enemy to retire. *OR*, 43(1):95; Warner, *Generals in Blue*, 508–9.

North to be very strong & daily increasing, says that a peace man will be elected President by an overwhelming majority and that we will have peace in three months. Dont you hope that his predictions may prove correct?

Nearly every body talks about the prospect for peace. Gen'l. Rodes says we will have an armistice & peace this year. Every thing looks bright for our cause. We have just heard of Gen'l. Hills brilliant victory on the Weldon Rail Road.[71] *Three North Carolina Brigades!* Hurrah for the Old North State! I hope Richmond papers will do our gallant troops full credit for their glorious achievement.

What is the news in old Milton? What, especially at Woodside? How is my Darling Wife this beautiful evening? How do you look and feel and think? I love to recall your darling features, to remember your precious love, to recall your sweet sympathy in times gone by, and to look forward to a happy reunion with you when we will rejoice together in peace and happiness in a sweet little home of our own. May the day be not far distant when we will realize the full fruition of our long and dearly cherished hopes! But we must be patient, patient & brave.

Gen'l. Grimes was over to see me the other day. He asked very particularly about you. Sent kindest regards for himself and wife.

What has become of Capt. Evans[72] & his buxom wife. As Caleb says I expect she is *buxomer* than ever! I hope David will return by Woodside. I want to hear exactly how you look. Would that I could satisfy myself by a personal inspection. But I know you are prettier and sweeter and better than ever if that were possible.

Ah! My Beautiful Darling Wife, how I do long to see you, to be with you, to live with you. How much we would enjoy together our beautiful month of September. Do you remember our love making this time two years ago. What precious hours were those. The memory of them is sweet to me now! Would that we could talk over those dear old days together. I am in a writing, loving mood this evening, but when am I not so, when I let my thoughts roam away to my Beautiful little Wife. Will you write me oftener & long letters. You must not expect long letters from me. I'll try to

71. In the battle of Reams' Station south of Petersburg, Maj. Gen. A. P. Hill defeated Maj. Gen. Winfield Hancock's Second Corps in a surprise attack, causing it to withdraw temporarily. Horn, *The Destruction of the Weldon Railroad*, 167–75; Charles M. Stedman, "Reams Station. 25 August, 1864," in Clark, *Histories*, 5:211–12.

72. Evans was wounded in the neck and mouth at Spotsylvania Court House and hospitalized in Richmond, May 23, 1864. He may well have returned to Milton to convalesce before rejoining Ramseur's command on September 13. Manarin, *North Carolina Troops*, 5:309.

write frequently. Do give my love to all at Woodside & in Milton. Ask Mr. Harding to send me a description of his daughter.

I leave you very reluctantly. I'll wrap up in my blanket & dream of you. Accept my Heart's best love. I commend you to the care of Him who causes all things to work together for good to those who love Him. Good bye Dearest.

Yr Husband[73]

Camp near Bunker Hill Va.

Aug 31st/64

My Own Darling Wife

Next to the pleasure of being with you is the privilege of writing to you frequently and regularly. I certainly expected a long letter from you before now. I suppose it will surely come this evening. At any rate it is better to hope on, believing that you are well and that all things are working together for the best.

We have been at camp at this place for several days, enjoying a longer rest than at any one time or place since we left Richmond. The Yankees have felt our position twice since we came here but each time they were made to pay for their temerity. Today every thing promises to be quiet, tho' I have heard some firing at our Out Posts. Whenever quiet reigns about me and I have leisure to give free scope to my thoughts I hasten home, in spiritus [in spirit], to where my Heart's darling is. Where my thoughts love to dwell and where I would be!

My Sweetest Darling, My Heart's Queen, my Best beloved, My beautiful little Wife, how earnestly, increasingly I long to be with you, to share your joys & help bear your trials and to sympathise with your every thought word and deed!

Let us hope and trust and pray that a better brighter happier time is coming for our afflicted country. Surely this awful carnage will not longer, much longer be permitted. The war clouds seem now to be passing away, and the sweet voice of peace is beginning to be heard even where war advocates were most numerous and violent. May we not hope that moderate Counsels will prevail at Chicago! That wise and good men will unite to stop the great carnival of blood which Lincoln has inaugurated! Peace is sighed for by us all. Peace is in the air. Every paper we get from the North, whether Republican or Copperhead, talks of, and longs for peace. True the Abolition papers say we must have the *restored* Union and after that peace.

73. SHC.

At the same time we note with hopeful pleasure that many, and the number is increasing, leading journals at the north now boldly advocate Peace, with union if possible, but Peace at any cost, on any condition! Whilst we have reason to hope for an end of this terrible war let us not forget that much yet remains to be done, that the brightest hopes are sometimes dashed to the ground. Then with a firm confidence in the justice of our Cause and the favour of heaven let us "learn to labour and to wait."[74]

I do want to meet some one who has seen you and talked with you. I want to know *how* you look, how you talk &c. Wont you give me a long, full and accurate scribbling of Your Dear Self? My Sweetest Little Wife, you must write me more about yourself for you are *infinitely* dearer to me than *all* the world besides. I wish I could give expression in this letter to the intensity, the deep devotion, of my love for you. But Dearest little wife, this is impossible. You must know my love for you by that you feel for me. Let us hope that very soon we will meet in our happy home. And *then* Dearest *how* inexpressibly happy we will be in each other's love.

There is now nothing new with us. We are rejoicing over Gen'l. A. P. Hill's victory on the Weldon R.R. We hope to hear further good news from that Quarter. If the pony will be any service at Woodside I will send him home, or if you wish it I will endeavor to purchase, or trade for a horse for George. I am anxious for you to have the use of the carriage.

Have you heard from Lincolnton lately? Really they treat me very shabbily but I suppose it is because I have not had time to write to them.

Do give my love to Mama, Grandma & all. Caleb & myself are both very well. You cannot write too often or too much to me. God bless you my Darling Precious Wife. Pray for me! Your prayers will and have availed much. It is so sweet and comforting to know that I have a pious wife who prays for my safety and salvation.

Remember me kindly to your & my friends. Has Miss Anne W. a beau. Poor Hines. I fear his imprisonment will tell against him.[75] Tell Mr. H. to write to me. Love to all. And my beloved Wife accept the warm overflowing love of

Your Devoted Husband[76]

74. The last line of Longfellow's "Psalm of Life."
75. Hines was first confined at Fort Delaware. By the date of Ramseur's letter, he had been taken to Morris Island, South Carolina, where he was one of "The Immortal 600" held in a pen under the shelling of Confederate artillery fire. After forty-five days, the southern officer-prisoners were transferred to imprisonment at Fort Pulaski, Georgia. John L. Cantwell, "N.C. Officers Prisoners Under Fire at Morris Island" in Clark, *Histories*, 4:721; Joslyn, *The Biographical Roster of the Immortal 600*, 139.
76. SHC.

No. 1
Camp near Winchester Va.
Sept. 6th/64

My Own Darling Wife

Last week I wrote you several letters whilst we were resting at Bunker Hill. Since my last we have been marching and maneuvering (fighting very little) to draw the Yankees out of their entrenchments to fight us, but they wont come. They have a larger force of Inf'y. and Art'y. than we, and a much larger force of Cav'y. We think we can whip their Inf'y. & have several times offered them battle which they invariably decline. Their mounted forces annoy us a great deal, keeping us constantly on the watch to prevent a surprise or the capture of our supply trains.

Today is cold, rainy & disagreeable generally. How I do long to spend it with you! Ah! My Darling how increasingly, intimately, all absorbingly my heart is wrapped up in you! God, in mercy, grant that this cruel war may speedily be brought to a close and we be permitted to rejoin our loved ones at our happy homes! My Darling, this is certainly a time to try our souls. We see in Yankee papers that Sherman has defeated Hood and captured Atlanta![77] We do not wish to believe this, but still we are compelled to be apprehensive and anxious. Our bright hopes for peace depend upon the success of our armies in the field.

Even tho' Sherman takes Atlanta, provided he does not destroy or disorganize Hood's army, it will still be all right as long as Gen'l. Lee (God bless our old Hero!) and his glorious army continue to baffle the tremendous efforts made to capture Richmond and overrun Virginia. So let us be hopeful. Our own accounts may put a different face upon Western news. You will have learned before this reaches you that McClellan and Pendleton are the nominees of the Chicago Convention.[78] Their platform is ingeniously contrived to mean War or Peace, so as to catch all of the opponents of the Lincoln Administration and to be governed by events between now & the election. If our armies then hold their own, suffer no crushing disasters before the next election, we may reasonably confidently expect a termination of this war. Let us therefore devote all our energies to the defense of our country. Let us continue to persevere in prayer and suplication to the Ruler of all the Nations that He will have mercy upon us, wash us from our sins, and grant us Peace!

77. The Confederates evacuated Atlanta on September 1, and Sherman pronounced the city "fairly won" when he occupied it the following day. Long, *The Civil War Day by Day*, 564–65.

78. McClellan and George H. Pendleton of Ohio won nominations for president and vice president, respectively, at the Democratic convention in Chicago on August 31, 1864.

Yr letter of the 28th Ult. has been rec'd. Yr letters generally come now 5 or 6 days after they are written. How gratifying to hear so regularly from you, to know that you continue well, hopeful & cheerful. I do hope you receive my hasty letters as promptly as yr last has come to me. In order that you may know certainly whether my letters fail to reach you, I will number them from this one.

What is the news at Woodside. I send you a receipt for making apple butter. You have heard us all speak of it. Tell Sis' Mary her husband can recommend it & as it requires no store things, except a few spices. You will perceive 'tis the cheapest preserves we can now have. You must be sure to have some made this fall. The apples must be ripe or nearly so. I predict you will be pleased with this recipe. I rec'd. a long letter from dear Luly yesterday. All are well and longing for us to be with them! David was still there & expected to reach the army this week. Hope he will bring me a long letter from you. If our army moves forward again, I will get you a Circular Cloak. (I've forgotten the technical name)[79] They are all the rage now, and though quite expensive are valuable for the large quantity of cloth they contain &c. I am anxious to send you a bottle of fine old brandy I have for you. My Precious Wife, I do hope that we will have a respite from our labours before long. If we go back up the Valley as far as Strausburg soon (as I think we will do so before long) and every thing promises quiet, I intend to ask for a furlough to come & see you. I dont know whether my application will be granted, but I'm right hopeful about it.

My Sweetest little Wife, I must now leave you. The sun is coming out & I predict orders for a move before long. Caleb is well & sends love. He rec'd. George's letter & is curious to know why he closed so abruptly. Do give my best love to all at Woodside. Tell Grandma that we cant use Confederate money in M'd. & we have to give six dollars Confed for one greenback. I gave for the hats & bonnet $22 greenbacks or $132 Confedte. for the other package $18 greenback or $108 Confedte. That was quite cheap I think, don't you. Tell Grandma I'm very economical. I know she'll be pleased with the apple butter. Do write often. Accept my heart's overflowing love. God bless you, My Darling Wife

Yr Devoted Husband[80]

---

79. Talma Mantle, a circular cloak of velvet or satin, usually hooded, sometimes with a collar or cape, fashionable in the mid- and late-nineteenth century.

80. SHC.

No. 2

Camp near Winchester

Sept. 7th/64

My Own Darling Wife,

Bright and joyous Sunshine succeeds the cold, dreary rain of yesterday. Let us hope that Sweet Peace will very soon succeed the terrible carnage of this cruel war.

We hear through Yankee papers of a disaster to our Arms at Atlanta, but after the false accounts published in their papers of the fight at Reams Station we receive their accounts with much hesitation.[81]

Still we can not but feel anxious to hear our own accounts, and to know the truth of the matter. It is our duty to bear disaster bravely. We must do it and bend all of our energies of mind & body to the great work of doing well our part in the defence of our country and the maintainence of our rights.

Should Atlanta fall, unless Hoods Army is *greatly* injured, the blow will only have a temporary moral effect, which successful resistance there & elsewhere will soon counteract. I must confess I am imbibing strongly the general feeling that we will soon have Peace. I think the platform of the Chicago convention contrived so as to mean Peace or War according to the temper of the People and the issues of this Campaign. If we continue merely to "hold our own" (to use a vulgarism) and the peace party (already large & growing) will continue to gain accessions as rapidly in the two months before the elections as it has in the two months just passed, then I believe the Peace Construction will be put upon the Chicago Convention platform. Let us pray for peace. That the *minds* & hearts of our Enemies may be turned from War & that our Heavenly Father will establish us in peace & independence. That we may be a Nation whose God is the Lord! An Example of National Christianity to the Nations of the Earth!

I have rec'd. no letter from you My Beloved Wife for some time. Of course a few days over the regular mail day seems a very long time to me. I fear the irregularity caused by the R.R. squabble will often interfere with our regular correspondence, but this must not prevent our letters from being regularly *started*. They will reach their destination sooner or later & will be received with a hearty welcome whether early or late. How I do wish I could stroll with you through the woods this sweet September day! How sweet 'twould be to review the happy days of September/62.

81. On Aug. 28, 1864, the *New York Herald* reported "the enemy withdrawing from the field, leaving their dead and wounded on the ground," the mark of defeat during the Civil War.

Ah me. I love to live over the days of our early love, courtship, & marriage. Sometimes when my work is done I give memory a loose rein and Oh! it is so sweet to live over again the happy days Lang Syne [long since]. The contrast between *then* and now is some times painful but anticipation of "a good time coming" is more delightful on account of present hardships. How proud I will be to tell *our children* that I fought and helped to win some of the great battles of this Second War of Independence![82] Wont you My Darling.

The Yankee Cav'y. has just come upon my picket posts. They are reconnoitering our positions. Trying to find out our whereabouts. Our cav'y. is greatly inferior in number & equipments & efficiency to the Yankee Cavalry. The consequence is, that our Inf'y. is constantly called upon to do work that the Cav'y. should perform. This service, tho' annoying, is not dangerous.

I sent you a receipt yesterday, you must be sure to try. Ripe Sweet Apples make fried apple fritter. Ripe sour apples give to it a pleasant acidity. I know Grandma will be pleased with the apple butter because it is nice and *so cheap.* When you write to Luly thank her for her nice letter & tell her you answer it for me.

I am very well, indeed. In fact, I have been perfectly well with the exception of a few days/everyday since we left R[ichmond]. Write to Father. He loves you so much 'twould please him. Love to All. Excuse haste & rambling. I live for you My Darling. Your love is my richest treasure. How I long to be with you. Accept kisses innumerable. God bless you & me & soon unite us in peace & happiness.

Your Devoted Husband

You will have to excuse short and hasty letter. I will try to write often, and it is better to hear often even though our letters are short. You must write me long letters. You cant write too much if you will write about your precious self.[83]

No. 3
Camp near Bunker Hill
Sept. 10th/64

My Own Darling Wife

I intended to write you yesterday, but postponed it to hear from you. Last night rec'd. yours of the 3rd Inst. All day today have been in the sad-

---

82. A name commonly applied by Americans to the War of 1812, the term was adopted by some southerners for the war of secession, 1861–65.

83. SHC.

dle in a cold rain. Tonight tho' quite tired, I cannot sleep until I write you a short note to let you know that I am well & that my heart's first & most earnest desire is to be with you at this time. I can not tell you how much, how constantly, how sympathisingly I think of you. My heart yearns to be with you very beautiful Beloved. God grant that this cruel war may be shortly ended & that we may meet in happiness and peace in a dear little house of our own.

Today David came just from home. He looks remarkably well. I am much disappointed that he did not stop at Woodside. He says all are well & full of hopes of peace. He thinks little Lucy[84] is *very* delicate & will require careful nurturing to raise her.

The girls, he says, talk about us all the time &c. We ran the Yankee Cav'y. several miles today[85] & I expect we'll have to take the back track tomorrow ourselves as we are much exposed to flanking moves here. I am afraid I can not get the cloth for yr cloak. If we go forward, I will try to get it.

News from Hood is not so bad as at first reported. His army is intact & that is the great point.

Let us continue to be hopeful & cheerful. Let us pray without ceasing for the success of our army & for peace! Excuse my great haste. Love to all. God bless you my Beloved Wife. Oh! may we very soon be happily & duly reunited. Good bye Devotedly Husband[86]

No. 4
Camp near Bunker Hill
Sept 12th/64

My Own Darling Wife

Last night I wrote you very briefly, thinking that we would continue our move this morning & prevent my writing today. The heavy rain yesterday and last night keeps us in camp today and thus affords me an opportunity to write you more at length this morning. Do you know that I have rec'd. no letters from you for a long time, but I see the R'l. R'd. difficulty has been settled, and I hope our letters will now come to us more promptly & regularly. Y'r. letter by Mr. Hines,[87] written on the 17th

---

84. Sallie and David Schenck's second child.

85. Averell reported that on the morning of September 10, three brigades of Confederate cavalry and an infantry brigade of Rodes's Division attacked his First U.S. Cavalry Brigade, compelling it to withdraw. *OR*, 43(2):66.

86. SHC.

87. Benjamin Hines, the father of Capt. Samuel H. Hines, was a stage contractor in Milton who may well have journeyed northward to obtain information on his son's whereabouts as a prisoner of war. U.S. Census Office, *Eighth Census, 1860*.

Ult. was handed me yesterday. Tho' greatly behind the times, it was very welcome.

Oh My Beloved Wife, how I do long to be with you at Woodside today! It does seem to me, that our separation grows harder to bear every day. What would I not give to lay my head in your lap and listen to the love notes of Auld Lang Syne. I sometimes think what mutual comfort, happiness and encouragement we would both derive from even a short meeting but my Dearest this can not be now. So let us prove ourselves brave and worthy the blood of our ancestors. Let us endeavor to do our whole duty with cheerfulness and devotion. Let us be cheerful and hopeful, humble and submissive under the dispensation of a kind Providence, and let us put all our Faith & Trust in Him who is ready and willing to save even to the uttermost all who truly repent and come to Him for succour! My Beloved Little Wife, you do not know how much I miss your sympathy and example as a member of Christ's flock. Would that we could read and digest together today God's Holy word, and together bow before His Mercy Seat and implore pardon and blessing from a loving Merciful Father! What a sweet privilege we enjoy in our separation. Tho' far away from each other we can yet meet around one common Mercy Seat. Let us, My Darling Wife, meet often at the Throne of Grace. Your prayers, I am satisfied, have heretofore availed much in the preservation of my life. Pray for the salvation of my soul, for my growth in spiritual Graces, that I may be in deed and in truth a devoted follower of the meek and lowly Jesus.

I would like so much to hear Mr. Harding preach today. We have been so actively campaigning that religious services have been very seldom held in camp. Tell Mr. H. I think he ought to get a church near Milton and remain at home for the balance of the war.

David gives me a very cheerful account of home [illegible] He says the young people are very gay. Parties are all the rage: Mrs. Hoke is the *largest* woman in the Confederacy. She classes Bob[88] with Beauregard. Ben Guion[89] is to marry Miss Katie Caldwell.[90] I believe there is no other gossip worth mentioning. An order has just come for me to move my Division back to its old camp near Winchester. So I will have to close rather abruptly. I did want to write you a long letter, but in this I have been dis-

88. Her son, Maj. Gen. Robert Hoke.

89. Benjamin Guion, a thirty-seven-year-old engineer, was living with David Schenck's father in Lincolnton at the time of the 1860 Census. Dr. Schenck died on December 20, 1861. U.S. Census Office, *Eighth Census, 1860.*

90. Catherine C. Caldwell, eighteen-year-old daughter of Dr. Pinckney C. Caldwell of Charlotte. Sherrill, *Annals of Lincoln County,* 261.

appointed but I will hope to write you a long letter very soon. Do continue to write to me very often. I cant tell you how precious your letters are to me. I am so glad to continue to hear that you are well, hopeful and cheerful Be brave My Beloved Wife. Patience, Patience! and all, let us hope, will yet be well.

Do give my love to all the loved ones at Woodside. Accept for yourself my heart overflowing full of love. Write very soon.

May God bless us & keep us and very speedily reunite us in health happiness and peace.

Devotedly yr

Husband[91]

No. 5
Camp near Winchester
Sept 14th/64

My Own Darling Wife

I was again disappointed yesterday evening in not receiving a letter from you. I know you have written regularly and I expect I will get a large package when your precious letters do come. We are again quiet today and my thoughts have been on a visit to my heart's best Beloved! How sweet it is, My Darling Wife, thus to forget the hardships of war and visit in thought our Sweet Ones at our Sweet home! Would that we could occasionally come in propria persona [in person] to visit you for even a few short hours! It's as David says, If we could be two people, the war would not be so hard to bear. Our campaign though a very active and arduous one, I think has been far more free from vexations and trials upon our patience and endurance than the campaign about Richmond would have been. We have enjoyed a great variety of scenes & travelled over, and sojourned in the most beautiful part of the Valley of Virginia. I have had pure water, a few vegetables and plenty of fresh meat. Altogether we consider ourselves very fortunate thus far. If we have an active Winter Campaign, we will not fare so well, tho' I believe I would rather campaign here during the Winter than remain in the trenches at Richmond & Petersburg. One great advantage I would have there would be the fact of being so much nearer to you.

I wish you could see this magnificent valley at this beautiful season of the year. Although plantations are ruined and the blackened ruins of once

91. SHC.

splendid mansions are to be seen on all sides, yet nature is still trium-
phant. The hand of the destroyer has not despoiled though in some places
it has greatly marred the natural beauty of this lovely valley. You know the
Valley lies between the Blue Ridge Mts. on the East and the Alleghenies on
the West. It varies in width from three miles at Strausburg to twenty-five
at the Potomac. Magnificent meadows, beautiful forests and broad undu-
lating fields rich in grass and clover are every where to be seen. Truly it
does seem sacraligeous to despoil such an Eden-like spot by the cruel ravages of war! Sometimes as I ride through this desolated country, my heart
overflows with gratitude to the Giver of Every Good, that our sweet homes
have thus far been spared the ravages of war. That My Loved Ones have
never known the terrour and anxiety caused by the presence of our mean
cowardly foes. Foes who respect neither helpless age nor tender woman.
Surely a just God will visit upon such a nation and such an army the just
indignation of His terrible wrath!

Last week I wrote you several letters in which I spoke hopefully of
coming peace, provided no great military disaster visited our arms. I still
hope and believe as I then wrote you. The Yankees, 'tis true, have Atlanta
and Yankee-like are making a tremendous glorification over it. But Hood's
Army is intact. Sherman is far away from his base of supplies and it does
seem to me, *if* our Cav'y. is *at all energetic* his position is obliged to prove
very dangerous to him. I still hope for good news from Georgia. At Richmond all efforts of Grant's Grand Army have heretofore been baffled by
our noble General and his gallant troops. We should feel so thankful and
grateful to the Ruler of Nations that He has so successfully delivered us
from the hands of our powerful enemies!

In the "Valley District" we have forced old Abe to send a heavy force to
check our peregrinations. We have at least 45 000 or 50 000 men opposed
to us. We have offered them battle several times on a fair field. Every offer
has been declined, the Yankees running behind their breastworks whenever we advance. We are thus accomplishing much good by neutralizing
(holding in check) this large force. We are gathering all the wheat in this
wonderfully productive valley, enough to supply ourselves and send large
surplus to Gen'l. Lee's Army. We have also sent Gen'l. Lee several hundred
beef cattle &c. At this time the Yankees hold less of the territory of this old
Commonwealth than at any time since 1862.

We learn from gentlemen recently from the North that the Peace Party
is growing rapidly, that McClellan will be elected and that his election will
bring peace provided always that we continue to hold our own against the
Yankee armies.

Yesterday I rec'd. a letter from Charley and was much pleased to see the improvement he has made since his last letter. He really wrote a very creditable letter, is pleased with the Army life but is very anxious to get into a regular army as he calls Gen'l. Lee's Army. Poor boy, he may have that to do before long.[92] David looks remarkably well. Says he will never let the Yankees get hold of him again &c.[93] Fair Miss Bonney who is an out & out Union woman, says the Rebels will soon be put down &c. Strange that sensible people can be so blind, even mad.

But I have written gossip enough, have I not My Darling? I would much rather write love letters to you than any other kind. It seems so natural to tell you I love you above every body and every thing this world contains. I wish I could be with you, take you [on] my lap, call you my own Darling Little Wife and express (in a small degree at least) by a thousand attentions how precious you are to me! This wish is ever in my heart and frequently on my tongue. We must continue hopeful, brave and cheerful. We must do well our part in this great struggle for our Independence. And then when this cruel war is over how satisfactorily we can look back and review our trials and our labours during this dark and bloody time. I do hope My Beloved little Wife that you continue well and cheerful. I am growing so *anxious* to hear from you. You have written often. Haven't you Dearest? You must write to Luly for me. I am really so much occupied by a thousand little things & big things too, that I have not interrupted duty to write home as often as I wish. Give my love to Grandma, Mama & all at Woodside. Tell Mr. H. I have been looking for his promised letters. Write often. Accept My Beloved Darling, my most beautiful Wife, my heart's best truest warmest love. May our God bless us, keep us, & soon reunite us in health, happiness & peace. Devotedly Yr Husband[94]

No. 6
Camp near Winchester Va.
Sept. 14th 1864

My Own Darling Wife

I am sitting in a leaky tent with Caleb [and] Majors [Henry Kyd] Douglas and New (Adjutants General), chatting and joking on the comfort! of

---

92. Dodson's younger brother is listed in December 1864 as sergeant-major of the Second Regiment of junior reserves, later the Seventy-first North Carolina Regiment. David E. McKinne, "Seventy-First Regiment," in Clark, *Histories*, 4:28.

93. Ironically, Dr. Ramseur practiced medicine in New York City after the war. Davidson College, *Semi-Centennial Catalogue of Davidson College*, 105.

94. SHC.

our position. Just now one remarks "how I would enjoy a warm carpet & parlour full of pretty girls and plenty of music?" Give me a comfortable library with a blazing wood fire, an arm chair, hot whiskey, punch and a box of "Cigars" says another. "If the General will let me go to Winchester and spend the day with my little Sweetest heart, I would not envy either of you the consummation of your wishes" &c &c. The first speaker, you guess, was Caleb, the second Major New, the 3rd Maj. Douglas, who is engaged to a beautiful and highly accomplished little Lady in Winchester. I did not express my wish. Can you guess what it would have been? Ah! My Beautiful Darling I would not envy others the possession of worlds could I only be with you in health, happiness & peace! Sometimes I grow very impatient and feel that I can not possibly wait much longer for a move up the Valley and a furlough, but this is only when Selfishness gets the better of Patriotism. I long to be with you all the time, but I believe I have learned to subject my wishes to my duty.

I wish you could take a peek at my Hd. Qrs. You would observe two small tents, rather the [illegible] two wagons with their shivering mules, but the interesting and attractive feature would be a flock of ducks and chickens taking shelter under these wagons. We are really growing fat up here. With Yankee money, we can buy almost any thing for the table except sugar and coffee. Bill of fare for breakfast: Mutton chops, *Ducks*, raw tomatoes, fried apples (a Valley dish, very nice) and fresh butter. You see we are living well in a beautiful country and if it were not for the constant watchfulness and almost daily moves we would be as well content as 'tis possible to be away from home.

Day before yesterday, I rode into town and took tea at Mr. Conrad's a Gentleman of the old school with a lovely and accomplished Wife and two beautiful daughters, one of whom the "Belle of the Valley" is Major D's sweetheart.[95] With music and genial conversation the hours slipped away rapidly. You may judge how I enjoyed the visit from the fact that I remained until 11 o'clock. Of course, Mrs. C. & her daughters asked about you and you know nothing does me more good than to talk with pretty sweet women about my belle/beau[96] ideal [model of excellence] of their

---

95. Elizabeth and Robert Y. Conrad had two daughters, Catherine and Sarah, ages twenty-two and nineteen at the time of the 1860 Census. The younger, Sarah or "Sallie," was supposedly betrothed to Douglas. Douglas, *I Rode with Stonewall*, 381 (n. 5). U.S. Census Office, *Eighth Census, 1860.*

96. Perhaps the ardent Francophile could not recall the gender of the word "ideal" (masculine) and so included both forms of the adjective ("beautiful" and "handsome"). The correct adjective, however, is "bel," for reasons of pronunciation.

sex. Mrs. C. insists that if "our army" goes into winter quarters below Winchester, that is between Winchester and the Potomac, that I must bring you to spend the Winter with [illegible]. What do you say, Darling Wife, to spending another Winter with the Army. You would rather and so would I that we would spend it together at home, but there is time enough to talk about these things. I have no idea that we will remain for the Winter so far down the Valley as Winchester. In fact, I have been expecting daily that Gen'l. Early would move back towards Staunton.

We have had no news from Richmond or the West for several days. I do hope we may be enabled to continue to baffle Grant and to drive back Sherman. I think every thing depends upon this Fall campaign. If we whip the Yankees every where or even, if we can manage to prevent them from gaining any Important Successes, I surely believe that the Peace Party will have grown sufficiently strong to compel a cessation of hostilities. Whatever course the North pursues *our duty is very plain*. We must fight this fight out. There must be no turning back now. Too much precious blood has been shed for the maintainance of our rights, too great a gulph has been opened up between us & our foes to allow even the idea of reunion to be entertained. No! No! We can & we must bear & suffer all things rather than give up to Yankees & mercenaries our glorious Birthrights.

[illegible] Oh Me! how I long to be with you! Even for a day, for an hour! I have not had a letter from you since yrs of the 31st Ult. It would be a most welcome sight to see another dear letter from you. How are you now my Sweet little Darling? I am so anxious to hear from you. My tenderest sympathies and most devoted love abide with you. When I think how much you need me now to caress and comfort you, it is so hard to stay away. Were you perfectly well and [illegible] this cruel separation. But Darling Wife we must both be humble, cheerful and obedient to the Will of Our Heavenly Father. I do fervently pray that you may be [illegible] brought through your trial, and that it may result to us both in the greatest blessing and delight and happiness of our lives. Do write to me Darling as often as [illegible] Without your letters this life is far more dreary. With them, and the assurance that you are well and happy, I can bear almost anything.

Caleb is well. He wrote to George yesterday & I presume gave him all the news. I am sorry to tell you that "Frank" has never entirely recovered from the distemper he had last winter. He is very delicate & is not doing well. Are you willing that I should swap him for a larger horse. You can consider yr horse as Mr. S.'s present. You asked some time ago, if I had gotten any cloths for Myself in M'd. I am sorry to say no. I will need a few socks like those you made me last winter. I think I can make out on every thing else at least until I come home. Give my best love to Mama & all. Accept My Precious Darling my whole heart overflowing full for your Sweet Self.

May our God bless & preserve us & reunite us speedily in happiness and peace. Devotedly Husband[97]

No. 7
Camp near Winchester
Sept 16th/64

My Own Darling Wife

Your long precious letter of the 7th Inst. was rec'd. yesterday. After waiting most anxiously for it more than a week, you must imagine how eagerly it was read and reread! If I could get such a letter every day I could bear this separation much more contentedly. I feel sure that you do not get all my letters. There has at no time elapsed as long as a week that I have failed to write to you. A short note at least. Last week and this I have written nearly every day. I hope you will get all of my letters some of these days.

It does me so much good to know that you are "as well and strong as you ever were." Every letter I get from you gives me hope that all will be well with you. And when there is the least doubt about my being with you, this is a source of great comfort to me. But I do not yet give up the hope of being with you.

I will not apply for a furlough as long as we are facing the foe, but if Gen'l. Early moves back to Strausburg & the Yankees do not follow us up closely, I think I may be spared to visit you if it be even for a few days.

There is nothing new here. We are constantly kept on the alert by Yankee Cav'y. who out number ours so much as to do with them pretty much as they please.

We are still *living* very well. I gave you a bill of fare of our breakfast t'other day. Let me tell you our dinner today.

1st Old fashioned, homemade vegetable soup. 1st rate.

2nd Roast Beef, roast turkey apple sauce &c.

3rd bread butter & molasses.

Is not that doing well for camp life? How the poor fellows in the trenches at Petersburg would rejoice at such a meal!

---

97. SHC.

What does Uncle Charles think of McClellan's letter of acceptance? Is it not a little more warlike than he anticipated?[98] I suppose he thinks as I do that everything depends upon our armies. If we can successfully resist the Yankee thousands now being hurled against us, all will be well. But if we allow the Yankees to gain any great victories over us, then we must expect to see the war spirit rise with their renewed hopes of success.

I must confess I was greatly surprised to hear that Grandma had ridden on horseback to see you before breakfast. I declare she is indeed a wonderful woman, physically as well so mentally. I wonder if her Granddaughter will so preserve her health as to accomplish such a feat half a century hence!

I wish I could be with you this evening my beloved wife in your sweet home. The atmosphere is so pure, transparent and beautiful. All nature seems to be smiling. Wherever I turn, some beautiful scene reminds me of days that are gone and of *the one* beautiful, beloved being who is far away!

With what a longing heart do I look to the return of the pissing days of Peace! Would that our wishes could be granted! How soon would the distance which separates us be annihilated. And we would know separation no more in this world. But My Own Beloved Wife, we must be brave and patient, with a firm faith and hope, bearing all things, ever unto the end, until our independence has been achieved.

Caleb is very well & looking remarkably well. You will have to scold him for his shortcomings as a correspondent. I have spoken to him frequently about it. He says he "don't like to write letters nohow." I am very glad to hear that I have some cloth at home for a coat. I had entirely forgotten it. My wedding coat is getting right worn so I'll be glad to have another made when I come home. I need a few prs cotton socks, and a pr of warm gloves for winter. I know it will give you pleasure to knit them for me. I dont think we will soon again advance up this part of the Valley, so I will not be able to get you the cloak you want. Can you not get one in Richmond?

Have you rec'd. none of the letters I wrote you last & this week? I certainly have written a dozen *or more* in the last two weeks.

Give my love to Mama and all at Woodside & in Milton. Do write often & at length.

98. McClellan wrote that "the Union is the one condition of peace," and continued to say that he could not face his gallant comrades in the army and navy and tell them he had abandoned the Union for which they risked their lives. *New York Times*, September 9, 1864. As Ramseur was determined to achieve complete independence for the southern states, this appeared war-like to him.

Accept my heart overflowing full of love. May God bless us, keep us, and very soon reunite us in health, happiness and peace, is the earnest prayer of your devoted husband.

Give my love to your friends Misses Anne & Jane. Tell them, I say, the best thing they can do for themselves and *our Country* is to marry some brave gallant soldiers. Goodbye My Love. Oh! How I want to be with you. S. D. R.[99]

No. 8

Camp near Winchester Va.

Sep'r. 17th 1864

My Own Darling Wife

I wrote you a hurried note yesterday and will have to do the same today. Lt [Plato] Durham goes home tomorrow and I will send you a bottle of brandy by him to the care of Mr. Callum at Danville. Is it safe to send money to you in the same way? I dont know what means you have of getting the money from Danville. I think I will risk some that way & if you tell me it is safe I will send more as opportunity offers. Well, then, I send you in this letter $300 (three hundred dollars).

There is nothing new in our front. This morning the Yankee Cav'y. drove in our Cav'y. before my Inf'y., but were soon driven back.[100] I do not know how long we will remain here quietly! I have been expecting a move for some days. Since McClellan's letter of acceptance has reached us we are not so hopeful of a speedy peace. However neither platforms nor letters will avail any thing. *Every thing* depends upon the issue of this fall campaign! If we are enabled to hold our own, or more certainly, if we are enabled to defeat the Yankees decisively at Richmond or in Georgia or anywhere else, then you may expect to hear a loud and strong demand for Peace coming from all quarters of the North. If on the other hand we suffer defeat and disaster at any important point, the war cry will be renewed and the Rebellion on its last legs will be trumpeted through Yankee land. Every thing depends upon the blessing of God upon our arms. Let us pray increasingly for His aid and interference in our behalf. Let us put our whole trust in Him, feeling sure that He will do all things for the best.

The lovely days and beautiful nights of Sep'r. are now upon us. Last night I did so long to be with you. Every thing was so beautiful and peaceful. How much I do regret to lose all this precious time of our young life.

---

99. SHC.

100. Ramseur may well have been referring to the affair at Limestone Ridge. *OR*, 43(1):531.

And to be separated from you is to lose it all. But I am sure there is wisdom and goodness hidden from us under all the dark clouds now overhanging us.

Caleb is very well. Sends love to all. Do write to me very often. Excuse this hasty note. Give my love to all our loved ones. Accept my heart's best, truest tenderest love for your dear self. Goodbye Dearest. Hus[band][101]

Camp Near Winchester
Sept 17th/64[102]

My Dear Brother

Yr letter by David was rec'd. some time ago. I w'd. have answered sooner but we have been so continually on the line [illegible] that I have scarcely had the opportunity. As to my present status, it remains unchanged. I am at a loss to know [illegible] meddlesome individual [illegible] start and circulate the [illegible] rumours in the rear, concerning me. I assure you I have lost nothing in the Army—the whole fault of the disaster at this place is put where it belongs, on the Cav'y. & part of Lewis' men who ran most shamefully without fighting five minutes.

There is no news here. We are neutralizing (holding in check) here about 30 000 Inf'y. and 6000 or 8000 Cav'y., so you see our little army is kept constantly on the go. We are all somewhat disappointed at McClellan's [illegible] of acceptance. It [illegible] makes little difference [illegible] who is elected. Our [illegible] is & must be [illegible] armies. We must [illegible] support them, and all will be well. Not other [illegible] be. I do hope we can yet bring troops enough to resist Sherman. I consider his position a very critical one, if we can only concentrate enough troops from south & transMississippi to enable Hood to take the offensive.

I rec'd. a letter from Charley the other day, and am very pleased to see the improvement he has made. I wrote him that I would endeavour to find him a place with me next spring. I have app'd. Lt Ridgely, who acted very gallantly & was severely wounded at Winchester one of my aids de camp.

David is very well and doing well. Write me a long letter giving me a full account of home affairs. Is Jack P[hifer] still allowing Father to get yarn or has he closed his shutters on him?

We are having delightful weather [illegible] in the Valley. If the Yankees Cav'y. [illegible] superior in numbers [illegible] so busy, we would have comparatively a pleasant time.

101. SHC.
102. The writing in this letter is heavily overlaid with ink blots, smudges, and fingerprints.

You may imagine I am anxious to be at Woodside *at this time* but I will have to sacrafice my heart's earnest wishes to patriotism. Do write me a long letter. Give my love to Father [illegible] to Sallie & yr little Ones.

May God bless you all. In haste [illegible]

[illegible] can give you an account of our run away at Winchester.

S. D. R.[103]

Daily maneuvering and fighting had begun as Maj. Gen. Philip H. Sheridan executed Grant's orders to clear the Shenandoah Valley of Confederate forces, denying them access to the livestock and provisions available there.[104] Early had attempted to take the initiative against his larger adversary by moving down the Valley toward Martinsburg with Rodes's and Gordon's divisions, leaving Ramseur's understrength command, numbering 1,700 soldiers, facing a Federal force of 40,000 men. On September 19, while marching along the Berryville Pike toward Winchester, Sheridan's army crashed into Johnston's brigade. Ramseur quickly positioned his other brigades and succeeded in holding off the Federals until Early could bring up his other commands and form a line of battle. In delaying the Union advance, Ramseur saved his army from a complete rout in a clash remembered as the third battle of Winchester. The Confederates then withdrew up the Valley. Sheridan pushed steadily after them, skirmishing at every opportunity, destroying rails, buildings, and fields as he went.

At Fisher's Hill, just south of Strasburg, Early formed a defense. On the afternoon of September 22, one of Sheridan's three corps moved around Early's flank and overwhelmed the dismounted cavalry protecting the Confederates' far left. The southern resistance crumbled, butternut defenders streaming to the rear. After nightfall, Ramseur and the other senior officers succeeded in reorganizing their units. Early's little army then resumed its retreat toward Staunton. It was September 25 before Ramseur could send a brief message home. Despite the defeats suffered over the preceding week and his opponent's overwhelming numbers, Ramseur tried to project a note of optimism so as not to alarm his wife, due to go into labor any day.

103. PC.
104. *OR*, 43(1):698.

Camp near Port Republic
Sept 25th/64

My Own Darling Wife

I am too tired to write you a long letter this eve'g. The Yankees in over-whelming numbers have driven us back to this point. On the 19th our men fought splendidly at Winchester. On the 22nd the whole army stampeded without much of a fight. We lost a good many prisoners & guns. Now I think we will hold the Yanks here.

Caleb & I are well. C. has been slightly scratched on the forehead & on the leg, but was not badly enough hurt to quit. He is now perfectly well. Our loss has been very heavy, especially in offrs. This is a sad blow, coming as it does on the heels of the affair at Atlanta. But let us not be discouraged & all will be well.

I will write you more fully soon. Give our love to all. May God bless & keep you my precious Darling is my constant prayer. I do want to see you Oh! so much!

Give my love to all. Excuse haste &c. Write often. Accept my heart full of love. Devotedly, Husband[105]

Richmond
29 Sept. 1864

Dear Mrs Ramseur,

I send you a telegram I received yesterday from the General, and would have sent you a dispatch immediately, but he had sent me a message by a gentleman telling me he had sent a dispatch, & asked him to call & see me. But I saw him before the telegram arrived and I sent one off to you immediately.

We are in a little excitement as the enemy are now near the city, and quite a sharp engagement is going on. They took one of our lines of in-trenchments this morning, but I hope we will drive them off during the day.

Yrs very truly

Thomas Pinckney[106]

---

105. SHC.

106. Lieutenant Pinckney was former vice aide-de-camp to General Huger and was now sta-tioned in Richmond in the Conscription Bureau. Krick, *Staff Officers in Gray*, 244. SHC.

THE SOUTHERN EXPRESS COMPANY

Dispatched by Telegraph from Richmond 23 via Raleigh 25

To Mrs. S. D. Ramseur Lincolnton N C

> Your brother and myself are well.
>
> S. D. Ramseur [107]

THE SOUTHERN TELEGRAPH COMPANIES

Received at Richmond Sept 1864

By telegraph from Charlottesville 27 *To* Thos. Pinckney

Cons[cription] Bu[reau]

> Telegh Mrs. Richmond that Caleb & myself
> are perfectly safe
> S. D. Ramseur [108]

Camp near Waynesboro Va

Sept 30th/64

My Darling Wife

I have time for a line to you. Caleb & I are well. We checked the Yankees at Port Republic. We are recruiting here & I hope in a few days will be able to drive the Yanks out of the Valley. Rec'd. your previous letters of the 17th & 18th Insts. Continue to write. Keep brave & cheerful & hopeful.

I sent you $300 in a letter, care of Mr. Callum. Have you rec'd. it? Excuse great haste. Accept my heart full of love my Darling Wife from

Yr Devoted Husband [109]

Camp near Wadesboro Va.

Sept 30th 1864

My Own Darling Wife

I have been too busy and too much mortified to write to you for several days. At Winchester after hard fighting we had prevailed against the largely superior forces in our front & on our right. When the Enemy's Cav'y. in heavy force broke our Cav'y. on the left & created a terrible disorder throughout our line. You know we lost my friend Gen'l. Rodes. [110] We then fell back to Strausburg (or Fisher's Hill). Here the Enemy concentrated heavily on our weak point (guarded by our Cav'y.) drove everything before them there and then poured in our left and rear. I am sorry to say

---

107. SHC.

108. SHC.

109. SHC.

110. Rodes was knocked from his horse by a bullet in the head on September 19, 1864. *OR*, 43(1):555; Krick, "Robert Emmett Rodes."

that our men were very much stampeded & did not keep cool or fight as well as they have heretofore done.

We then retreated to Port Republic & from there to this point 12 miles from Staunton. I am daily expecting Gen'l. Early to advance. I believe if we could get enough Cav'y., even to hold the Yankee Cav'y. in check, that our infantry can drive back Sheridan forces.

I cant tell you my beloved wife how much I have thought of you the past week. I do hope you have not given up your bright hopeful spirit. Anybody can be hopeful when everything is prosperous. *Adversity calls forth the nobler qualities of our natures.* Continue my Beloved to be brave hopeful and trustful. Cease not to pray for us and our cause. Remember how grateful we should be for so many mercies. Nothing but God's mercy has spared our lives.

I still feel confident of the final triumph of our cause. It may be a long and weary time before our independence is established. We must steel ourselves for great trials. Let us learn to labour and to wait. Above all things let us never dispair of the Republic. Let us work and pray with a brave heart for any fate. Clouds may obscure, but the Sun of liberty will soon shine in all its brightness.

I can not begin to tell you my own beloved Wife how intensely I long to be with you. As *the day* approaches I grow more and more anxious to be with you. But these recent battles & defeats will render it almost impossible for me to leave this Army. So My Beloved Darling Wife, be brave & cheerful. Be assured that all the devoted sympathy of your doting Husband is with you. God grant you strength and courage, faith & hope. And may you come through your great trial with health & strength & great happiness. Oh! to be with you I would give any thing I possess.

Give love to all for Caleb & me. We want to see you all. May God keep us & bless us & very speedily reunite us in health, happiness & peace is my constant prayer. God bless my Darling Wife.

Devotedly Husband[111]

Camp near Staunton Va.
Oct. 2nd/64

My Own Precious Nellie,

This has been a very quiet lovely Sabbath day. My thoughts have so often sought you in your quiet home. I can not tell you *how much* I have thought of you in the last few days. I do hope, My Darling Wife, that you

111. SHC.

have not allowed the bad news from the Army of the Valley District to discourage you. We must bear up bravely in the midst of disaster. Nor can we always hope to be successful. We must be prepared for any event, with brave hearts for any fate. I hope in a few days we will be enabled to go after the Yankees and drive them down the Valley. At Present we are all anxiety to hear from Richmond. We have all sorts of rumours. I do hope and pray that Gen'l. Lee may be enabled to overcome and drive Grant away from before Richmond.

I have not heard from you my Beloved Wife since the 18th of last month. I know you have written to me and R.R. irregularities have prevented me from getting your letters. Maybe I'll hear from you today.

David got a letter from Luly yesterday. All well and having quite a pleasant time. One of the girls is speaking of going to make you a visit this fall. I hope they will get to Woodside in time to be of service to you.

I am so anxious about my little frail wife. Oh! that this cruel war were over and I could be with you continuously. But we must do our duty bravely, hoping for a happy ending of all our troubles.

I sent you some time ago, by Lt Durham, to the care of Mr. Callum $300. Have you rec'd. it. The Gov't. owes me now from the 1st of June, and I could send you several hundred dollars if I had a safe way.

Our disaster in the Valley, with Hood's at Atlanta makes me think the war party will triumph at the North. But tho' peace may be a long way off, I feel sure that Justice & Right will finally triumph. Then let us never despair, but move ourselves to greater exertions and prepare to endure greater privations and hardships. Surely all true Southrons would prefer *anything* to *submission*.

Caleb and I are well, very well. We both look *well*. You know *how well*, My Darling Little Wife. You don't know how *intensely* I love you. Every day I live, I learn more and more how my heart is devoted to you. When I come home to you, how sweet it will be to talk over all these things together. Ah! Me! how I long for you to be well and happy.

May we learn wisdom from our trials. You must write and telegraph me if any thing happens. Telegraph to Maj. Gen. R—. Care of Gen'l. Early, Army of the Valley. My anxiety is actually painful. Do give my love to all. I'll try to write to you frequently, tho' our movements may prevent. Accept my heart full of love & believe me yr devoted Lover.

May God bless & keep you My Darling Lover[112]

112. SHC.

Camp near Staunton Va
Oct 5th/64

My Own Darling Wife,

I have been without a letter from you since the 18th Ult, the date of y'r. last. I cant tell you how full of anxiety I am to hear from you. I think of you at all times, when mil'y. duties do not imperatively require my attention. I have dreamed of you very frequently, and always with reference to the great event of our lives. Last night, I visited you in dreams and we were *so* happy together. Ah! Me! How I do long to be with you My Beloved Wife, in your sweet home. But these are times calling for great sacrafices. We must bear separation, hardship and danger for the sake of our Country. We must dare and do in the cause of liberty. We must never yield an inch or relax any effort in the defence of our homes or the establishment of our nationality. Then let us be brave, hopeful, cheerful, doing well our duty and leaving the result to God.

After the death of Gen'l. Rodes I was assigned to the Command of his Division. This is very pleasing to me. Direct yr letters hereafter to Maj Gen'l. R, Army of the Valley, and they will reach me sooner than by the old address. We have been very quiet for several days, but I expect active service before the month is out. We are very anxious about Richmond. The Yankees are said to be sending a force towards Orange C.H. They seem to stick to McClellan's plan of approaching Richmond from three directions.[113] Everything calls for all the bravery we possess, *every effort* in our power, to meet and hurl back our cruel foes.

Whilst we fight battles our beloved Wives and Sisters and Mothers must be constant and earnest in prayer. Oh! May our Heavenly Father give us courage and strength and wisdom to overcome and drive back our powerful and cruel enemies. My Darling Little Wife pray for me as you have ever done. And May Our God hear and answer yr prayers for the sake of His dear Son!

I have no news to tell you, absolutely none. We have had no mail from Richmond for 3 days. I do hope to hear from you today. Telegraph me to Staunton. I would like to get a telegram from you daily until the crisis is past. Wont you send them to me? I hope Luly or Fanny will be with you. Oh! that I could be there too!

---

113. While difficult to understand from a historical perspective, Ramseur's calculus of McClellan's plan must have added the threat of McDowell's corps to Richmond from the north, with its later design to advance on Petersburg, to the main body's intent to march on the capital up the Peninsula.

I know that you are in the best hands. I know Mama & Grandma will do every thing for you, but yet I do so long to add my loving sympathy to all that they can do. God grant that this cruel separation may not be of much longer continuance.

When active operations cease up here, I will endeavour to get home. The weather will soon make any extensive operations impracticable, and just as soon as I can conscientiously leave my post of duty, I will hasten home to my beloved wife.

I hope that a happy meeting will very soon be speedily granted to us. I have just read your sweet letter of the 28th Inst. brought by Mr. H. Oh! how rejoiced I am to hear from you again my own beloved wife. I fear you have allowed yourself to suffer too much from anxiety for *us*. Do not My Sweetest Wife let these things trouble you so much. I fear greatly you will seriously injure your health by so much anxiety! But I hope otherwise. Mr. H. has not yet gotten up from the depot. I expect him tomorrow and then I will enjoy cross questioning him to my heart's content. I have not written near all I wish, but I must leave you which I do very reluctantly. I hope I may dream about you again tonight. Do give my love to all of our dear relatives & friends. Write very often. Accept my beautiful beloved *Nellie* my heart's best, warmest, truest love. May God bless, keep & speedily reunite us in happiness & peace is the earnest prayer of your devoted Husband.[114]

H'd Qrs Rodes' Division
New Market Va Oct 10th/64

My Dear Brother

Your letter of the 22nd Ult was rec'd. last evening. I was truly glad to learn that all of my loved ones were well. I am sorry to learn my Dear Brother, that you are sometimes so low-spirited and despondent—that "life at times becomes almost hateful to you" that "were it not for your wife and children you could quit this weary world &c." You ought not, must not indulge such thoughts. This is a time of great trial. We are all called on to show that we are made of the true metal. Let us then be brave cheerful and trustful. Remembering that Might is not Right. But that God is just and will order all things for the good of His People and the honour of His Kingdom. He moves in a mysterious way His wonders to perform.[115] Let us do well our part and pray God to give us *Faith* and *Strength*.

You speak of entering the Army? It will be the height of folly for you to

114. SHC.
115. William Cowper in "Light Shining Out of Darkness," Olney Collection, 1779.

enter the ranks. You could not stand the Service a week. If you are determined to join the Army, come to me and I will have a place for you. I propose the following plan. Retain your place as Receiver. This will exempt
you and enable me to appoint you Volunteer Aid de Camp. The law does
not allow a person liable to conscription to be app'd. Aid de Camp. Hence
you must hold on to your app't. as Receiver. Beside you will not be under
Military Control, other than mine, and I can let you go home whenever
you wish &c. What do you think of my proposal. I'll furnish you a horse &
provide for you at my mess.

Since Gen'l. Rodes death I have been assigned to command his Division. Pegram to command Early's old Div'n. I am the ranking Officer in
this old Div'n. and my app't. ought to be made permanent. But you know
I have from the first made it a principle not to ask for promotion. I have
no friends *at Court*. I am advised that others are moving for the permanent
app't.

I should not object to a move being made for me. Some influential
North Carolinians should write to Gen'l. Bragg,[116] stating that there are
2 N.C. Brigades in this Div'n., that I am the ranking Offr. and entitled to
the Div'n. on that ground, and 3rd on acct of my past services for an acct
of which reference may be made to Gen'ls. Lee, Ewell & Early. This much
I can say, that I *made* Early's old Div'n. do splendid fighting at Winchester
& held my position *unaided* from early dawn until 9 o'clock, when the
Yankees in overwhelming force broke my Div'n. and they did some tall
running, I tried by exhortation & example to stop them. It wouldn't do. So
I took a musket and rode to the foremost and knocked him down. I then
knocked every man on the head who refused to halt and by this means
and the exertions of my staff and some gallant offrs. of the Brigs. I got the
div'n. again in line, charged the Yanks & drove them some 400 yds. where
they overpowered me again, and I ordered the Div'n. back to a strong position which I held against several attacks. At this time, 10 o'clock the other
troops of the Army were coming up to my assistance. Gen'l. Rodes came
first, then Gordon then [Brig. Gen. Gabriel C.] Wharton. We had whipped
their Inf'y. when their Cav'y. 7000 or 8000 strong broke our Cav'y. on our
left [and] got in behind us, followed by a strong column of Inf'y. There
arose a panic from the left. 1st Wharton's & Gordon's commands broke all
to pieces. Rodes' Div'n. came off in tolerable order. And I brought up the
rear, my Div'n. organization unbroken. I was rear Guard and repulsed several attacks and saved our wagons and artillery. I have no army correspon-

116. Since being relieved of command of the Army of Tennessee the previous December, Bragg
had been serving in Richmond as a supernumerary senior military adviser to President Davis.

dent or you would have seen the above in print. At Fisher's Hill, our Cav'y. gave way and the Yankees poured in our flank & rear necessitating a hasty withdrawal.

I shall say nothing now as to the disposition of forces that brought this about, but when the proper time comes I shall state my opinion very plainly.

Yesterday Gen'l. Early sent our Cav'y. without any supports at least 20 miles to the front, with all their Art'y. & wagons. The Yanks pounced on them with Inf'y. & Division Cav'y. force & took some wagons & several pieces of Art'y. from them.[117] I declare I am sick at heart from these repeated disasters, but I hope this is the last. My great anxiety is for the safety of Richmond. Unless Gen'l. Lee is soon reinforced the City must fall. But I fear I am adding to your Blues. Don't Give Up. We are bound to succeed. The God of Justice will order all things [for] our Good.

Give love to all. I will give my will to David to keep. David is having a right hard time, but it is doing him good. He is behaving very well indeed. Caleb & David join me in love to you all. Do write as soon as you read this, a long home letter. How much corn, wheat & sorghum did you & Father make. Love to Sallie & yr little ones. May God bless & keep you all.

Yr. devoted Brother[118]

Camp near New Market Va.
Oct. 10th 1864

My Own Darling Wife

Yesterday my Courier handed me a letter from Mr. S, one from Charley and *three* from your dear Self. Yours were dated respectively 23rd 26th Sept. and 30th ditto.

Do you know how much better I feel after getting these letters from you. I have been questioning Mr. Harding too, and he tells me you are perfectly well and "sweet accordin." Oh me! how I want to be with you. Every day I think more and more about you. I cant help feeling the most intense anxiety and solicitude on your behalf. Since our disasters over here in the Valley, my prospects for a furlough are greatly diminished. I think my duty is plain. I ought not to leave *now* even if I could do so.

So my Beloved Darling you must be brave and cheerful without me for a while, a short while I hope. I do earnestly pray that your life may not be endangered. That you may be soon restored to health. And that both

117. The cavalry duel took place at Tom's Brook. *OR*, 43(2):327, 329, 339.
118. PC.

of our hearts may be gladdened and our natures improved by the issue of your confinement. Oh! My beautiful Darling Wife! I can not begin to write what I feel now that you need so much my presence and sympathy. I do so long to be with you! 'Tis the greatest trial of my life to be separated from you *now*! But these trials do us good, even as gold is refined by the fire. When in God's good Providence we are permitted again to meet and live together in Peace, we can look back to these dark days as the time when we were tried and not found wanting. I hope and pray that we may be benefited spiritually as well as mentally by the trials to which we are now subjected.

Mr. S. writes me that all are well at home, that Father tho' much discouraged by the late disasters to our army, is still hopeful as to the final result. I agree with you in your remarks about the Croakers. I must confess, I would be willing to take a musket and fight to the bitter end, rather than submit to these miserable Yankees. I think they have placed themselves outside of the pale of civilization by the course they have pursued in this Campaign. This beautiful and fertile Valley has been totally destroyed. Sheridan has had *some* houses, *all* the mills & barns, every straw & wheat stack burned. This Valley is one great desert. I do not see how these poor people are to live. We have to haul our supplies from away up the Valley. It is rumoured that the Yankees are rebuilding the Manassa Gap Rail Road. If this is so, Sheridan will not give up his hold upon the Valley and we will probably remain here for the Winter, unless Gen'l. Lee becomes so hard pressed that we will have to go to him. It is (or rather was, before our disasters) more pleasant campaigning in the Valley than in those terrible trenches before Richmond.

My hope now is from Hood. I do hope he may be enabled to overwhelm Sherman and send reinforcements to our great Gen'l. Lee. When Providence smiled on us here, one always had bad news from the West. May we not hope now for cheer and support from that Quarter?

The last private advices I had from Georgia were very encouraging. Time is an important element. I believe Hood will whip Sherman. I hope he'll do it quickly.

I rec'd. a long, kind letter from Col. Frank Huger[119] a few days ago. He is full of hope and sprightliness. Says his sister Mrs. Preston has the finest boy (so she says) in the Confederacy. May be we will have something to say about that some of these days. Nous verrons! [We will see!]

---

119. At this time, Ramseur's West Point chum was serving in the rank of lieutenant colonel as an artillery battalion commander in the First Corps Artillery of the Army of Northern Virginia. Sibley, *The Confederate Order of Battle*, 1:138.

I have not been writing to you so often recently My Darling Wife, because I have been either so constantly occupied or (I must acknowledge it) so much mortified at the recent disasters to our Army of the Valley that I could not write with any pleasure. There is something now to write about. Dr. David has just come in & sends love to you. He is very well and is doing well. Caleb sends love & will write soon. Mr. H was with me sometime today. He is very homesick, talks about his babies all the time. Do give my love to all! Write as often as you can. Telegraph anything that happens to you. If you need me I'll try to get home. Telegraph to Maj Gen'l. R. army of the Valley. Near Harrisonburg. Give my very best love to dear Mama. I know she will take the very best care of you. Accept my heart full of love my Beloved Wife. God bless you and keep you and may He in Mercy speedily grant us peace. Yr devoted Husband[120]

> Camp near Strausburg
> Oct 15th/64

Today your letter of the 7th Inst. was rec'd. Yesterday yrs of the 3rd & 5th Insts. were rec'd. I am so rejoiced to know my Beloved wife, that you continue so well in body & mind. I am very anxious now to hear from you by each mail. I can not tell you how I long to be with you now. You must be sure to telegraph me as soon as possible.

We have been offering the Yankees battle for a day or two but they decline it. I think we will have some stirring work before long. I do hope we will be enabled to punish them well. We ought to do so. Tell Mrs. Jeffries that her son, Lt. Jeffries, is unhurt and a prisoner.[121] This is reported by one of our men who was captured with him & who afterwards made his escape.

Late letters from home inform me that all is well & in fine spirits. The girls speak confidently of assisting you this winter. I hope they can do so.

There is no news in our Army. We are all expecting good news from G'a. The Richmond papers hint at something very cheering from that quarter of our Confederacy.[122] I do hope Hood can yet strike a telling blow,

120. SHC.

121. A native of Caswell County, Second Lt. J. Glenn Jeffries of Company I, Forty-fifth North Carolina Regiment, had been captured at Fisher's Hill on September 22 and sent for confinement to Fort Delaware. Forty-fifth North Carolina Regiment, CMSR, RG 109, NARA.

122. A long silence in hearing from the northern conqueror fueled published rumors that the Confederates had reoccupied Atlanta, captured five of Sherman's corps, boxed him up in the city, and taken Rome and 3,000 blacks. At the same time, Hood was said to be poised to cut Sherman's supply lines. *Daily Richmond Examiner*, Oct. 11, 12, 1864; *Richmond Dispatch*, Oct. 15, 1864.

then reinforce Gen'l. Lee. If he can do this we may expect Peace next year. Rec'd. a long letter from my old friend Frank Huger t'other day. Says he has a Nephew. The finest boy in the Confederacy. What do you say to that?

Mr. Harding is still afflicted with cutaneous & homesickness. I have advised him to get a church and resign. I think he ought to be at home to assist Mama if George enters the service, which I suppose he will do.

I wish you could see the mountains surrounding my camp, rich in all the varied hues of autumn. I know you would appreciate and enjoy all their beauties.

When the war is over I think we will have to find a Mountain Home of our own. Would it not be pleasant to cut loose from *nearly* all the world and enjoy life together in peace and quiet. I am writing on my knees without a candle, so you must excuse this hurried note.

Give love to Mama & Grandma & all.

Caleb and Mr. H. are well & send love.

Continue to write to me as often as you are well enough. Accept my heart overflowing full of love.

May God bless & keep you My Heart's Darling, and may He soon permit us to meet in happiness & Peace.

Yr Devoted Husband[123]

Camp near Strausburg Va
Oct 17th/64

My Own Darling Wife,

I rec'd. late last night the following dispatch through the signal corps. "The crisis is over and all is well." Tho' this leaves much to conjecture, yet it has relieved me of the greatest anxiety of my life. I am so anxious to hear from you further. I do hope that "all is well." I hope my darling Precious Wife is well and that our little Darling too is well. Oh! I can not express my feelings when I think of all you have endured and suffered for love of me. My heart is full of love and sympathy for you my beloved Wife. I thought it scarcely possible for me to love you more. But *now* it seems that I love you more devotedly, more tenderly than ever before. Oh! how I long to be with you. I don't know how I can bear to be separated from you much longer. I feel like I *must see you* and *be with you* and *our little Darling*.

Of course I am full of anxiety to hear all the particulars of your illness. I want to know whether we have a son or daughter. I do feel so thankful,

123. SHC.

so grateful to an All-wise and Merciful Father that He has brought you safely through all your trials and that "All is well." Let us endeavour my Darling Precious Wife to live worthy of the Infinitive Love that is showered upon us. Yes, My Darling, My beautiful Wife, after so much mercy shewn to *both of us*, we should be humble, grateful, prayerful Christians.

I am writing in great haste, which I know you will excuse. I will write to you again in the morning. Give love to Mama Sis Mary & all. Tell Sis' Mary, for pity's sake, if not for loves sake, write me a long letter about my little Wife and baby. Oh Me! I want to see you *so bad*. God bless my Darling & may He soon reunite us in happiness & peace a joyful family. Goodbye my sweetest Darling.

With love inexpressible

Your Devoted Husband[124]

There was scant reason for optimism in the Confederate war effort. Reverses in the west and the Federal investiture of Richmond led Ramseur to conclude that President Lincoln and the war hawks would be reelected in the November election, prolonging the struggle. In Ramseur's judgment, Early's inept generalship had led to the series of defeats in the Valley campaign. Among the irreplaceable losses were seasoned division, brigade, and regimental commanders, including gifted leaders like Robert Rodes whom Ramseur had held in high esteem. Although he denied any culpability, Ramseur's own battlefield performance had been spotty at Bethesda Church and Stephenson's Depot, and remained a subject of discussion in the press and among Confederate leaders. Lee had transferred the last units he could spare from Richmond's defense to the Valley. But Early's corps would have little time to replace their lost officers and regroup while Sheridan pressed the shrinking band of Confederates. Early's Valley Army, and Dodson Ramseur himself, were approaching their denouement.

124. SHC.

Death and Aftermath

SHERIDAN'S MISSION was to destroy the military value of the Shenandoah Valley to Lee's army. Early's orders were to threaten Maryland and Pennsylvania in order to engage the largest possible Federal force—troops who otherwise would be available for Grant's disposition outside Richmond. So when Sheridan turned north in early October and began moving down the Valley, burning it as he went, Early followed closely behind, alert to any opportunity to strike a blow at the invaders. On October 14, the Federals halted at Middletown, encamping south of town on Cedar Creek while Sheridan rode back to Washington, D.C., for a strategy conference. Early's topographical engineer soon identified a path over the rugged slope of the Massanutten on the Federals' unprotected left flank. Two division commanders, Ramseur and Gordon, reconnoitered the trail on October 18. That night, Ramseur led his men through two fords on the serpentine North Fork of the Shenandoah River and into position for an early morning strike. Ramseur entered battle with a white flower in his lapel to honor the birth of his new baby, news of the event having just reached him. Years later, Henry Kyd Douglas maintained that Ramseur declared at the outset of the clash, "Douglas I want to win this battle, for I must see my wife and baby."[1]

As often happened in Civil War combat, the battle of Cedar Creek evolved in two distinct phases. The Confederates surprised the enemy before daybreak, driving them from their bivouac areas and earthworks. The attackers' discipline then broke down as the famished southern troops stopped to scavenge food in abandoned Union camps. Early did little to reassemble the units and exploit his advantage. Galvanized by Sheridan's return that

1. Douglas, *I Rode with Stonewall*, 317.

afternoon, the reorganized Federals counterattacked, overwhelming the Confederate left and igniting a rout that swept along the defensive line.[2] Attempting to rally a small band and stop the retreat from the field, Ramseur had two horses shot out from under him. As he was mounting a third, a bullet struck him in the right side, passing through his lungs and lodging below his left arm.

Ramseur's assistant adjutant-general, Robert R. Hutchinson, and his aid-de-camp, Caleb Richmond, tried to lead him to safety. Stalled in the melee of fleeing soldiers, Ramseur's ambulance was taken into custody by Union cavalry and redirected to nearby Belle Grove Plantation, headquarters of both Sheridan and Brig. Gen. George Crook, a corps commander in the Army of the Shenandoah.

Ramseur's final hours were described in a letter from Hutchinson to Nellie, written on the day of Ramseur's death and while seated beside his body. Because of his Confederate sympathies, Hutchinson omitted the names of the Union officers who came to the bedside, robbing the account of its greatest poignancy. Demonstrating the endurance of their friendship, four cadets from Ramseur's West Point days came to honor their fallen friend. Two were classmates, Gen. Wesley Merritt and Col. Alexander C. M. Pennington, and the other two, Brig. Gen. George A. Custer and Capt. Henry A. Du Pont, graduated the following year. Du Pont would later be awarded the Medal of Honor for his bravery at Cedar Creek. Sheridan extended every kindness to the southerners.

Near Strasburg, Va
Oct 20th 1864

Mrs. S. D. Ramseur
Milton, N.C.

Dear Madam,

I do not know how to write to you, how to express my deep sympathy with your gruesome affliction, but the Christian soldier who has gone before us to the other world asked me to do it, and I must not shrink from the performance of this duty however painful. I am writing by the side of him whose last thought was of you and of his God, his country and his

---

2. Provost marshals for two Federal cavalry units cited capturing 161 prisoners, three battle flags, twenty-three artillery pieces, fourteen caissons, seventeen army wagons, six spring wagons and ambulances, ninety-eight horses, sixty-nine mules, and miscellaneous sets of harness. *National Tribune*, March 28, 1908, 7.

Sketch of the mortal wounding of General Ramseur at Cedar Creek
(The Western Reserve Historical Society, Cleveland, Ohio)

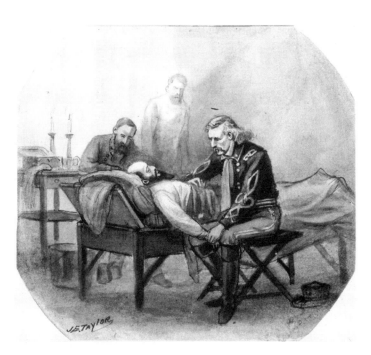

Sketch of Gen. George A. Custer at the bedside of the dying Ramseur
(The Western Reserve Historical Society, Cleveland, Ohio)

duty. He died this day, at 27 minutes past ten a.m., and had at least the consolation of having by his side some who wore the same uniform, and served in the same holy cause as himself. His last moments were peaceful. His wound was painful, but his hope in Christ led him to endure *all* patiently. He received his mortal wound yesterday afternoon, between 5 & 6 p.m., at the post of honor and of danger where he always was. Our troops had fallen back a short distance, but had re-formed and were stubbornly contesting a position on a hill which the enemy attacked from three sides. He exposed himself to every shot cheering & encouraging all. I was not far from him when I saw his horse shot, he procured another, which was shot also and immediately after he received his fatal wound (the second) all in a space of a very few moments. I ran over to him, got some men, & bore him to the rear, your brother joining us on the way. I then went off after an ambulance, found it but saw on returning with it that he had been left, as I thought in the enemy's lines. This fear was soon after dissipated however by seeing him on Capt. Randolph's horse, the Capt running alongside & supporting him, and we got him then to the ambulance I had brought up. I thought he was safe then, not knowing how dangerous was his wound and remained with the rearguard where I was subsequently captured by the enemy's cavalry. I was carried to Gen'l. Sheridans Hd Qrs. and learning that Gen'l. Ramseur had been captured asked & obtained permission to remain with him. The road had been blocked up by wagons, causing a delay that gave the enemy time to get up and take him prisoner just south of Strasburg. Many of his former friends, West Pointers, called to see him yesterday & to day and offered every assistance in their power, Gen'l. Sheridan himself being among the number. He was taken to Gen'l. Sheridan's Hd Qrs, and made as comfortable as circumstances would permit, Dr. Jas Gillespie of Cutshaw's Battln. of Artillery a Confederate Surgeon assisted by the enemy's surgeon attending to him, and doing all that could be done under the circumstances. He suffered a good deal from his wound, the ball having entered his right side, penetrating the right & left lung and lodging near the left side but the end was peaceful and quiet. He spoke continually of you, and sent very many messages to his family but above all to his wife. He told the ambulance driver to tell Genl Hoke that he had died a Christian and done his duty. He told me to give his love and send some of his hair to his darling wife, and often wished that he could once see his wife and little child before he died. He told me to tell you that he had a firm hope in Christ and trusted to meet you hereafter. He died as became a Confederate soldier and a firm believer. I enclose the lock of hair he desired sent to you.

I have turned over to Dr. Gillespie such articles, money &c as he had about him retaining myself as a memento a small pocket comb. I do not know what became of his watch; it was not found in his pocket. I suppose he must have left it somewhere, as I cannot conceive how it could have been stolen. Dr [blank] can give you all particulars omitted here, and will do so. May God comfort you in your affliction, and console you in his own good time is the heartfelt prayer of

R R Hutchinson
Major & A.A.G.
P.A.C.S.[3]

Ramseur's body was embalmed at Belle Grove, attired in the same full uniform with the boutonniere that he had worn on the battlefield, and was placed in a mahogany casket for return to the Confederate lines via the Virginia Peninsula. Under flag of truce, Robert Hoke received the casket outside the Richmond defenses and escorted the body into the city where it lay in state at the national capital. It was November 6 before the train bearing Ramseur's remains arrived in Lincolnton. The coffin was opened for viewing in the Presbyterian church. After the funeral, Ramseur was laid to rest, first in the Hoke family vault and then permanently in the town's Episcopal cemetery.

So soon after the birth of their daughter, Nellie could not travel to Lincolnton for the service and interment. Instead, she sent a bouquet of flowers to be placed on the coffin. Following the funeral, Luly wrote Nellie a mournful account. Condolences arrived from sympathizers near and far, including the mother of Dodson's dear friend since West Point days, Frank Huger. The deceased had executed a new will the day before his death, dividing his estate between Nellie and his sisters. He never learned the name of his child, Mary Dodson, or even her gender.

I, S. D. Ramseur, do make and publish this my last will and testament.

I will that all my debts be first paid out of my monies on hand, and if not enough, to raise a sufficiency by sale of my personal estate.

I will all my personal estate to my wife Ellen Richmond Ramseur and also one half of my real estate.

The other half of my real estate I will to my sisters Lucy, Fannie and Addie Ramseur, during their single life with remainder to the survivors

3. NCOAH.

and at their death or marriage, when their estate ceases, to go to my wife Ellen Richmond Ramseur.

Signed sealed and published this eighteenth (18th) day of October 1864 in presence of

Test'd.

H. A. Whiting

W. S. Mitchell[4]

S. D. Ramseur[5]

Ramseur's lifelong companion, David Schenck, reflected thoughtfully in his diary on the death and his feelings on losing his beloved friend.

Gen'l. Ramseur captured

Oct. 22ed 1864

Today sad, doleful news reaches our family "Gen" Ramseur was seriously wounded and "fell into the hands of the enemy." This is the report from the battle at "Cedar creek" and the valley fought on the 19—. Our family are "full of sorrow" and bowed down in grief. "Dod" has been the idol of the family, to whose safety and honor day by day we have looked, with the most tender and affectionate anxiety. Oh! it is a hard stroke and words nor pen can describe our grief. May God pity him and be merciful to him, shall be our earnest prayer.

"Maj Gen'l. S. D. Ramseur's death"

The telegram from General Sheridan of the Yankee army soon announce to us the death of poor "*Dod*," a man whom I loved with the tenderest affection, with whom my heart was together, who was earliest, warmest, dearest absent friend, in whom I confided any most secret thoughts, and received in return a friendship as warm and sincere. I wept more bitterly than ever tears flowed from me and my spirit was broken within me. My dear, noble friend, those who knew thee prediction in thy youth; thy qualities and goodness but none could bear to foresee thy untimely death, while Fame and Fortune were crowning thee with honor and glory; but God-himself desires thee and once his call found thee ready to obey his call—duty to parents, to country, to

---

4. William S. Mitchell, a surgeon assigned to Rodes's Division. Confederate Generals, Staff Officers, and Non-regimental Enlisted Men, CMSR, RG 109, NARA.

5. SHC.

family, to God had been performed and you were ready for higher duties and pleasures.

General Ramseur died at General Sheridan's Headquarters, on the 20—October 1864, at 27 minutes past 10 o c'k a.m. He received his fatal wound on the 19—at sundown, a minie ball striking him under the right arm and passing through both lungs lodged near the surface on the other side from whence it was extracted. Maj R R Hutchinson of his Staff, who was captured with him was with him in his last moments. "His end" said he, "was peaceful." He told the major "he died a Christian and to tell his wife to meet him hereafter." Also "Tell Gen'l. Hoke I die a Christian I have done my duty." His body was embalmed at Winchester, placed in a mahogany coffin dressed in full uniform and sent by flag of truce to Richmond were [where] it was received by Gen'l. Hoke, and conveyed to Richmond. It there lay one night in state in the Capitol, and was then brought by Major Adams[6] of Gen'l. Hokes staff to Charlotte, there it was received with great honor by the military and civil authorities, and from thence escorted by the military on special trains to Lincolnton. Here it lay in state one day and was then taken to the church, where in presence of the family the coffin was opened. The body was in a perfectly natural state, no signs of decomposition. The features were rigid and face somewhat sunken but easily recognizable. This was on the 6— of October [November]. It was then open to the inspection of the public until Monday 7 Oct [Nov] 2 o ck and was visited by great numbers of people from the country and on Monday the funeral ceremonies performed by Rev R N Davis,[7] in the Presbyterian Church and then conveyed to a vault where they remain for further disposition by the family.

Thus has passed, from early manhood to eternity a pure Christian, a noble patriot, a man "The bravest of the brave," a friend of warmest affections and kindred in all His every virtue which made him lovely here and welcome in heaven.

My dearest friend no page is sacred enough to be inscribed with the love I bore thee; it rests in the depths of my sorrowful heart, which alone can know how I loved thee! May God give me grace to so live that I may one day meet thee in Heaven.[8]

6. James M. Adams was assistant adjutant general to Hoke. Krick, *Staff Officers in Gray*, 58.
7. Ramseur's pastor in Lincolnton.
8. David Schenck, Diary, October 22, 1864,SHC.

Nov. 2d 1864

Mrs. S. D. Ramseur

Dear Madam,

I had hoped to deliver you the letter accompanying this, and the effects of the General in person, but I find it impossible, & therefore send them. You will find every thing safe that he had, also a sadder relic in his pocket book, the ball which was fatal to him.

I am now a prisoner of war,[9] but hope at some future time to be able to give you such particulars of the Generals death as you might wish to hear. Until then, Madam, I bid you adieu, with the deepest sympathy in your affliction.

Very Sincerely Yours,

R. R. Hutchinson[10]

Thomas[ville] Tuesday, Oct. [Nov.] 8th [1864]

I can not let another day pass, dear sister, without writing you a few lines. Oh, my darling, how my heart yearns to have you with me that you might have had the sad, sweet privilege which we have had of kissing his dear face once more. It is a sweet comfort to have him once more although so pale & cold in death. I kissed him for you, dear Nellie, & passed my hands over his dear brow & through his hair & whiskers & longed to have you by my side. He looked so sweet, so peaceful, so natural, just as if he had fallen into a calm sweet slumber. I hope you may yet see him, dear Nellie. Our good God has sent so many mercy to our poor bleeding hearts. We have a full record of his last moments & it is so sweet to know that although he suffered bodily pains, the dear Savior's presence enabled him to bear it all, without a murmur. He sent messages of love to you & all of us so precious to our hearts. All this you will learn from Maj Hutchinson's letter & all the sad, sad relics Cousin Caleb will give you. Also the cross I kiss Sophy Alexander made with the request that it might be sent to you, after he was placed in the vault. Come to us, dear Sister, just as soon as you can. We all want you so much, to have you with us always. The Physicians think, his dear body can be preserved several months. How thankful I am to the kind friends who showed such tender & deep respect for him.

---

9. Hutchinson was taken to Capitol Prison in Washington, D.C., where he was reported to be the following March. *OR*, Series II, 8:372.
10. NCOAH.

I enclose you some flowers which were lying on his breast, when his body came. All the sweet sympathy & respectful attention shown him & *us*, you will see. I could write the sad particulars. I placed your flowers, dear Nellie, by his face. He was *covered* with wreathes of flowers. The whole country mourns his death, & every earthly honor is paid him. You feel how very painful to me must have been my journey home. I can't write to you, as fully as I wished. My heart bleeds for you, dear Sister & prays for you always. God love & bless you & bind up your broken, bleeding heart—give you *patience* under this heart-crushing sorrow, & resignation to His will, who "doeth all things well." He consoled our precious one in the hour of death, so may He comfort us in life & give us *patience* to "run the race set before us"[11] & grace so to live that we may meet him hereafter, an unbroken family in Heaven. Mr. Johnson will go to Milton soon & if you can't come soon, I want Father to go to see you. God sustained him with His strong arms. He prays so tenderly & particularly for you every night. Dear Sister, our hearts are with you always. You are so inexpressibly dear to us all, now, because you were dearest to his heart. God bless you, & your dear baby. We will be so sorry to give up Cousin Caleb tomorrow. We all love him so dearly, & are so sorry he must go. You all are dearer now than ever, to us. Mrs. Monroe's sweet [illegible] & wreath I will send you, if Cousin Caleb can carry it. I want to have it framed & a glass put over it. Dear Nellie, I can't write any more today. The Lord send you a comforter, that shall abide with you forever. Kiss the dear child for us all, & our heart's love & prayers are with you always. God love & bless you, dear Sister. Luly

Warmest love to dear Aunt & Cousin Mary & the other dear ones. I hope Cousin George can stay at home, but I know God will order all things right for us. We will be so anxious to hear from you.

Father is anxious to have your pony. Says he will be so glad to keep it for you this winter. I send little book Miss Valentine gave Brother when he was wounded at Malvern Hill. I marked some passages for you. Tell Cousin Mary to write to us until you are able to write. My every thought is a prayer for you.[12]

For those who had known or loved Dodson Ramseur, discussion of his unique qualities and accomplishments and the events leading up to his death did not cease with his burial. Nellie did not remarry, dying in 1900 and being laid beside her husband in the Lincolnton cemetery.[13] Their

11. Hebrews 12:1.
12. SHC.
13. Stedman, *Life and Character of Major General Stephen D. Ramseur.*

daughter never married and led the effort to keep his memory alive. She unveiled the Ramseur monument on the Cedar Creek battlefield in a 1920 ceremony at which U.S. Representative Charles M. Stedman delivered the eulogy.[14] Mary Dodson Ramseur died in 1935.

Address of Col. H. A. du Pont,[15] September 16, 1920, at the unveiling of the Monument erected to the memory of Major General Stephen D. Ramseur, on the Cedar Creek battlefield, near Middletown, Virginia.

Ladies and Gentlemen and Representatives of the several societies and Historical Commission of North Carolina.

Your invitation to be present at the unveiling of the monument to General Ramseur and to speak of my personal relations with that distinguished son of North Carolina was gladly accepted. As a close friend of my youthful days, I held him in most affectionate remembrance, and as I happened to have been personally concerned in much, if not all, that occurred from the time he fell mortally wounded on the Cedar Creek battlefield, October 19, 1964, until the end came during the early hours of the following day, I was exceedingly desirous that the information in my possession should be imparted to his immediate relatives and friends.

My relations with General Ramseur began when I entered the United States Military Academy at West Point, and, as we all know, youthful associations and friendships are not only the strongest but the most enduring. The course of military instruction and discipline at that admirable institution was then five years, and although he entered the Academy twelve months before I did, we were fellow-cadets there for a period of four years previous to his graduation in 1860. During the last ten months of his sojourn at West Point, our associations were especially close, as he was at that time captain of Company B of the corps of cadets and was quartered on the second floor of the third division of the barracks, in the room next to the second division and facing south. As I then belonged to the cadet non-commissioned staff, I was not tied down to the quarters of any special company, and roomed with my classmate and close

14. Stedman was elected to represent North Carolina in ten successive Congresses, 1911–30. During the Civil War, he served as a private in the Fayetteville Light Infantry Company and as a major in the Forty-ninth North Carolina Infantry. Edward J. Hale, "The 'Bethel' Regiment: The First North Carolina Volunteers," in Clark, *Histories*, 1:123; Charles M. Stedman, "Forty-Fourth Regiment," in Clark, *Histories*, 3:24.

15. The printed version of these remarks uses a small "d" for the speaker's name, contrary to other spelling.

friend, the lamented Hoxton of Virginia,[16] who at that time was a cadet sergeant of B company. As our room likewise faced to the south and was separated only by a narrow corridor from that of Ramseur and his classmate, John M. Kerr, also of North Carolina, we four were thrown very much together and the relations between the two North Carolinians, the Virginian and the Delawarean were exceedingly cordial. At that time Ramseur was very mature for one of his years; somewhat reserved to those who did not know him intimately, but always quiet, courteous and dignified—a young man of strong character and great good sense, as well as a most excellent soldier.

Some twelve months later when Hoxton and I graduated, the Civil War had already begun; and, during the campaign of 1864 in the Valley of Virginia, my old friend Ramseur was a division commander of the Confederate forces under Early, while I was chief of artillery and commander of the artillery brigade of Crook's corps which belonged to General Sheridan's opposing army.

Ramseur fell at the battle of Cedar Creek, October 19, 1864, and it was my sad privilege to meet him once more during his last hours at the Belle Grove house, in full view of this very spot, which was then the headquarters of both Sheridan and Crook. Before relating what occurred, let me first tell you how he happened to be brought to that house, as I believe that I am the only person now living who has any knowledge of the circumstances. To explain them clearly and satisfactorily, it will be necessary to speak of the battle, but I shall try to be as brief as possible.

As a matter of fact, the battle of Cedar Creek consisted of two distinct general engagements, fought on the same day. In the first, which began at 5:25 A.M., and continued until about noon, the Confederate army surprised and completely defeated the Union troops and drove them from the field with heavy loss. Crook's corps, to which I belonged, was a special sufferer, as it was on the left of the Union line and the first objective of the Confederate attack. Our camps were captured and many prisoners taken, among them the senior medical officer of my artillery brigade, Dr. Isaac D. Knight, of Philadelphia, surgeon of volunteers with the rank of major, then a man on the wrong side of sixty and not endowed with a very robust physique, who at his age had no busi-

16. Llewellyn G. Hoxton graduated sixth in the class of 1861 and then resigned his commission to enter the Confederate army, where he rose to the rank of lieutenant colonel in the artillery before being wounded at Trevilian Station, Virginia, in 1864. *Register of Graduates and Former Cadets,* 4–43.

ness in active service with troops in the field. In spite of this, however, he was not only a highly efficient medical officer but also one of the most calm, affable, warm-hearted and sensible men I have ever known. When captured, Surgeon Knight was not sent to the rear with the other Union prisoners, but was set to work in the field hospitals to assist the Confederate medical officers in caring for the wounded, presumably of both armies.

In the second engagement, which began between half-past three and four P.M., the Union army, which meantime had been reformed and re-aligned, attacked the Confederates, who in their turn were disastrously defeated and driven from the field. Early's left was the first to give way and by five o'clock the whole Confederate force was retreating in the utmost disorder down the Valley turnpike and across Cedar Creek, Surgeon Knight of course accompanying it as a prisoner. Ramseur, styled by General Early, "a most gallant and energetic officer whom no disaster appalled," was shot through the lungs while making a supreme effort to hold the Confederate line, and was carried to the rear accompanied by his adjutant-general, Major Hutchinson, his medical officer and two soldiers, one the driver of the ambulance. My batteries were the first to reach the heights on the north bank of Cedar Creek, and I immediately opened fire upon the retreating army which was in full view, little thinking at the time that the guns were trained upon my chief medical officer as well as upon the wounded friend of my youthful days!

As soon as the Union cavalry in pursuit had advanced far enough to come within range of my pieces, I gave the order to cease firing; and at this juncture the following incident occurred, as reported to me next day by Surgeon Knight: When the horsemen were close at hand and so near that the capture of the ambulance was inevitable, Major Hutchinson hailed Surgeon Knight who, as the fates willed it, happened to be trudging along very near the ambulance in which the wounded general lay. Realizing that their respective roles were about to be reversed, he accosted the quondam prisoner as follows: "We surrender to you, sir!" Surgeon Knight, who took in the situation, upon receiving the surrender of the general with his two staff officers and two Confederate soldiers, ordered the ambulance to be halted and turned to the rear. When the cavalry came up, Knight claimed the five prisoners, took them back directly to the Belle Grove house, which was Sheridan's headquarters, and turned them over the chief medical officer of the Union army, Surgeon [James T.] Ghiselin of Maryland.

Ramseur was at once installed in one of the most commodious bed-
rooms in the house and all possible steps taken, in cooperation with
his own medical officer, to mitigate his sufferings. The best evidence
of the very special consideration extended to the wounded division
commander lies in the fact that his adjutant-general as well as his two
soldiers were permitted to stay with him. In recent years I have often
thought of the striking contrast between the treatment then and there
accorded to General Ramseur and the gross brutality displayed by our
German foes during the great conflict which has so recently ended.

The battle was over and night had fallen: after seeing that my remaining men and horses had all the attention possible under the circumstances, it suddenly dawned upon me that I was almost completely
exhausted, mentally and physically; that I had not tasted food for more
than twenty-four hours; that I had been almost continuously in the
saddle since half-part five in the morning; and, worst of all, that I had
no abiding place, as my personal effects had been taken by the enemy
when our camp was captured in the morning. The only recourse was to
seek food and shelter at the headquarters of my corps, which, as before
stated, were with the army headquarters at the Belle Grove house. One
of the first persons I met there was General Torbert, of Delaware, the
commander of the Union cavalry corps, who lost no time in telling me
that Ramseur was lying mortally wounded in the house, which information so acutely shocked and distressed me that I forgot for the time my
own necessities and hastened upstairs to see him.[17]

The room was absolutely still—Ramseur, clad in his major general's
uniform, lay on his back in the bed, his eyes closed. At the other end of
the room were the four Confederates, the surgeon examining medicine
bottles on the windowsill: on his right as he faced the window sat Major
Hutchinson, and on his left in the corner of the room stood the two Confederate soldiers, seemingly men of middle age. Approaching the bed I
said: "Ramseur, do you know me?" mentioning my name; he opened
his eyes, in which I saw recognition and apparently a gleam of pleasure.
So great was my physical exhaustion that I seated myself as quietly as
possible on the side-rail of the bedstead, but the almost imperceptible
jar thus occasioned gave the sufferer a thrill of pain, to my extreme distress. Speaking with the greatest effort he said to me: "Du Pont, you

17. Ramseur was placed in a bedroom on the first residential floor of the plantation house, accessible by climbing a full flight of steps outside the house from the ground below.

don't know how I suffer," and then relapsed into silence and closed his eyes—not, however, before extending his hand and firmly grasping and holding mine. I was deeply moved. Strange as it may seem—illogical, if you please—in that supreme moment he turned with content and satisfaction to the one person present who though officially a foe, was still, as he instinctively felt, the steadfast personal friend of former days!

As his condition was hopeless and his time short, the Confederate surgeon very wisely sought only to relieve the excruciating pain. The treatment was simple—from a large bottle of laudanum or other opiate on the windowsill he filled a wineglass, and approaching the bed, said: "Drink this, General:" as soon as the sufferer had swallowed the medicine, the medical officer went directly back to the window, carefully refilled the wineglass, returned to the bedside and again said: "Drink this, General." This went on for a considerable time when at length the effect of the opiate became apparent: Ramseur's hand slowly and gradually relaxed in mine and finally became limp—he was unconscious and remained so until his death several hours later!

Had he been in possession of his faculties, I would have stayed to the end, but as nothing more could be done and my need of food and rest was no longer to be ignored, I withdrew and after getting something to eat fell into a profound slumber. Upon awakening next morning I went directly to Surgeon Ghiselin and arranged with him to have General Ramseur's remains sent through the lines to his family.

Such, my friends, is the brief statement of my personal relations with that gallant soldier and splendid son of the old North State.[18]

Accounts of Ramseur's death invoke the principles of *ars moriendi* (the art of dying), ideals arising in the Middle Ages. The elements of a "good death," as richly described by historian Drew Faust, were well known and sought after by nineteenth-century Americans.[19] This ideal death is reflected in the condolences and eulogies offered for Ramseur. A fine example is Maj. Hutchinson's letter to Nellie from her husband's deathbed. The writer characterizes the departed as a Christian soldier who did his patriotic duty, details the general's wounding and death, and reports Ramseur's proclamation that he dies a firm believer in God. Nellie was, through

18. Du Pont, *Address of Col. H. A. du Pont, September 16, 1920.*

19. Faust, "The Civil War Soldier and the Art of Dying"; Faust, *This Republic of Suffering*, 10–11, 13–16.

letters from her sister-in-law and others, made a witness to her husband's demise and to the honor paid him in Richmond and at his funeral.

Of great consolation to the widow was the assurance that the deceased's final thoughts and words were of his dearly loved wife and child. Hutchinson also sent personal effects to Milton, including the bullet that killed Ramseur, again part of an effort to link the dead to the family left behind. Ramseur's friends from West Point gathered at his bedside. They took the place of the wife, children, and other close relatives, the preferred company in which to depart life. The important thing was that Ramseur died among friends, companions from his alma mater and comrades in gray. Hutchinson recorded that the general had asked him to assure Nellie that the couple would be reunited in heaven, the ultimate hope a dying man could offer his wife. This surely influenced her decision to wear the black of mourning for the thirty-six years until her death.

Ramseur's conduct had long been consistent with the principles of an artful death. As early as June 5, 1862, he indicated a readiness to die for his beliefs. Ramseur wrote, "Should I fall, I do it willingly, gladly and with the hope that I may be rec'd. into the Company of the Saints On High. Therefore, my wish is that my friends should not mourn for me, but rather think of the time when we shall all meet to part no more." This spiritual preparation, as well as a strong Christian conviction, was part of the *ars moriendi* ethos and was a theme of the condolence letters sent to Nellie. His admirers also evinced an understanding of the custom by recognizing Ramseur's religious devotion, patriotism, and courageous performance of duty, all qualities essential to attaining a heavenly reward.

Abbreviated Family Tree of
Stephen Dodson Ramseur

FAMILY SURNAMES FOUND IN THE TREE *and*
NICKNAMES USED IN CORRESPONDENCE

PART ONE   *Dodson, Richmond, Harding*

Nellie	Ellen Elizabeth Richmond
Lue	Lucy Ann Richmond
Cousin Dod	Stephen D. Richmond

PART TWO   *Ramseur, Ramsour, Schenck, Barrett, Hoyle*

Luly, Lou, Lue	Lucy Ramseur
Ada	Addie E. Ramseur
Charley, Charlie	Charles R. Ramseur
Fannie	Fannie Dodson Ramseur
Doddie	Dodson Ramseur Schenck
Sallie	Sarah Wilfong Ramseur Schenck

PART THREE   *Dodson, Phifer, Motz*

Uncle Charles	Charles Russell Dodson
Aunt Fanny	Frances Ann Dodson
Aunt Pris/Prissie	Priscilla Shaw Harding Dodson
Georgy	George Motz
Aunt Bettie	Elizabeth Ramseur Phifer
Uncle John/Jack	John F. Phifer

Note: The Stephen Dodson Ramseur appearing in
Part 1 and Part 2 is the same individual.

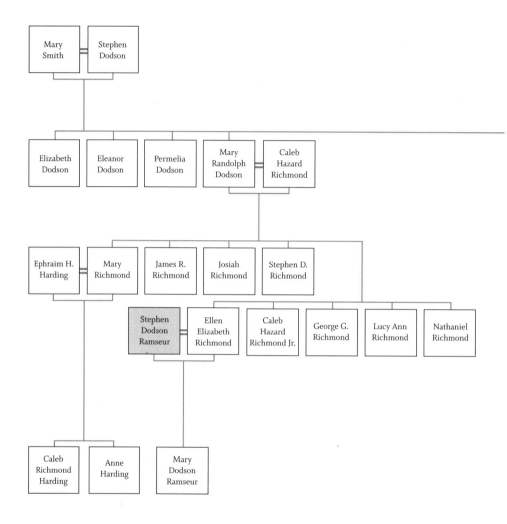

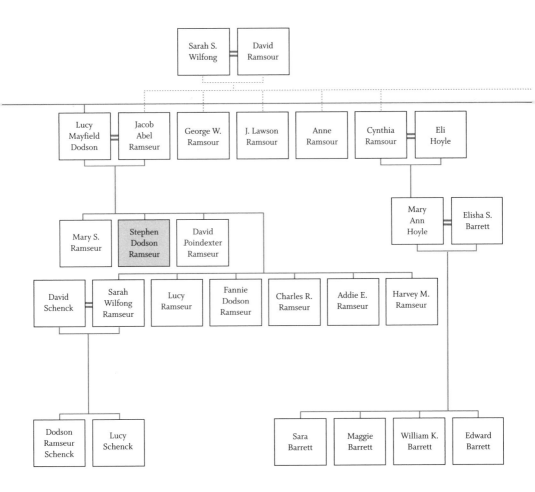

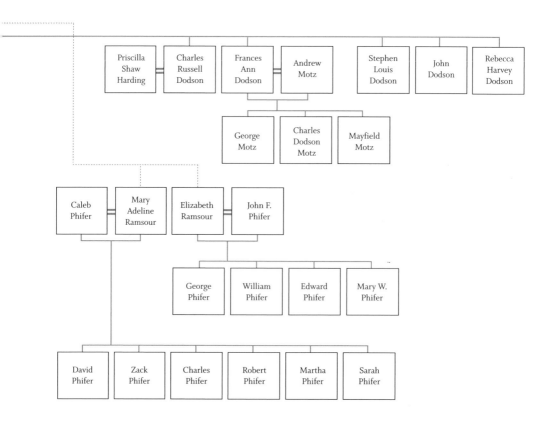

Bibliography

MANUSCRIPTS

Chapel Hill, N.C.
    North Carolina Collection, Wilson Library, University of North Carolina
        David Schenck, comp., *Sketches of Maj.-Gen. Stephen Dodson Ramseur*
    Southern Historical Collection, Wilson Library, University of North Carolina
        Stephen Dodson Ramseur Papers
        David Schenck Diary
        David Schenck Papers (twelve-volume typed transcript was used in the
            preparation of this collection)
Philadelphia, Pa.
    Historical Society of Pennsylvania
        Simon Gratz Collection
Raleigh, N.C.
    Office of Archives and History, North Carolina Department of Cultural Resources
        Lincoln County Civil Action Papers, 1857–59
        Stephen Dodson Ramseur Papers
Richmond, Va.
    Library of Virginia
        D. H. Hill Papers, Accession 32032, Box 2
    Virginia Historical Society
        Lee Headquarters Papers, MSS3 L 515, 592–94
Washington, D.C.
    National Archives and Records Administration
        Record Group 94, Records of the Adjutant General's Office, 1780s–1917
        Record Group 109, War Department Collection of Confederate Records
    U.S. Census Office
        Sixth Census of the United States, 1840
        Seventh Census of the United States, 1850
        Eighth Census of the United States, 1860
        Ninth Census of the United States, 1870

West Point, N.Y.
    U.S. Military Academy
        Official Registers, 1855–1860 (printed)
        Post Orders, 1856–1860
        Register of Delinquency, 1856–1860

PRINTED SOURCES

Books

Avary, Myrta L. *A Virginia Girl in the Civil War 1861–1865.* New York: Appleton, 1903.
Clark, Walter, ed. *Histories of the Several Regiments and Battalions from North Carolina in the Great War 1861–65.* 5 vols. Raleigh: E. M. Uzzell, 1901.
Cox, William R. *Address on the Life and Character of Maj. Gen. Stephen D. Ramseur Before the Ladies' Memorial Association of Raleigh, N.C., May 10th, 1891.* Raleigh: E. M. Uzzell, 1891.
Davidson College. *Catalogue of the Trustees, Faculty, Students and Alumni of Davidson College for the Collegiate Year Closing August, 1854.* Davidson, N.C.
———. *The Semi-Centennial Catalogue of Davidson College, Davidson, N.C., 1837–1887.* Raleigh: E. M. Uzzell, 1891.
Douglas, Henry Kyd. *I Rode with Stonewall.* Chapel Hill: University of North Carolina Press, 1940.
Du Pont, Henry A. *Address of Col. H. A. du Pont, September 16, 1920, at the unveiling of the Monument erected to the memory of Major General Stephen D. Ramseur, on the Cedar Creek battlefield, near Middletown, Virginia.* Winterthur, Del.: H. A. Du Pont, 1920.
Early, Jubal A. *War Memoirs: Autobiographical Sketch and Narrative of the War Between the States.* Bloomington: Indiana University Press, 1960.
Grimes, Bryan. *Extract of Letters of Major-Gen'l. Bryan Grimes, to his Wife, Written While in Active Service in the Army of Northern Virginia.* Compiled by Pulaski Cowper. Raleigh, N.C.: Edwards, Broughton & Co., 1883.
Martin, Joseph. *A New and Comprehensive Gazetteer of Virginia and the District of Columbia.* Charlottesville, Va.: Moseley & Tompkins, 1835.
McClure, Alexander K. *Recollections of Half a Century.* Salem, Mass.: Salem Press, 1902.
The Register of Graduates and Former Cadets of the United States Military Academy West Point, New York. West Point: Association of Graduates, 2005.
Richardson, James D., ed. *A Compilation of the Messages and Papers of the Presidents, Prepared Under the Direction of the Joint Committee on Printing of the House and Senate, Pursuant to an Act of the Fifty-Second Congress of the United States.* Vol. 8. New York: Bureau of National Literature, 1914.
Schaff, Morris. *The Spirit of Old West Point, 1858–1862.* New York: Houghton, Mifflin, 1907.
Scott, Winfield. *Memoirs of Lieut.-General Scott, LL.D. Written by Himself.* Vol. 1. New York: Sheldon, 1864.

Taylor, James E. *The James E. Taylor Sketchbook: With Sheridan Up the Shenandoah Valley in 1864: Leaves from a Special Artist's Sketchbook and Diary*. Dayton, Ohio: Morningside House, 1989.

U.S. Senate. "Report of the Commission Appointed . . . to examine into the organization, system of discipline, and course of instruction of the United States Military Academy at West Point" 36th Cong., 2nd sess., 1860. Doc. 3.

U.S. War Department. *War of the Rebellion: A Compilation of the Official Records of the Union and Confederate Armies in the War of the Rebellion*. 128 vols. Washington, D.C.: U.S. Government Printing Office, 1901.

Wilson, James Harrison. *Under the Flag*. Vol. 1. New York: Appleton, 1912.

Articles and Parts of Books

"The Cloven Foot." *United States Democratic Review* 37 (February 1856): 151–57.

Harding, E. H. "Sketch of Major General S. D. Ramseur." In *Sketches of Maj.-Gen. Stephen Dodson Ramseur*, compiled by David Schenck, 31–42. N.p.: [ca. 1892].

———. "Sketch of Major General S. D. Ramseur," *Land We Love* 5 (May 1868): 1–10.

Terry, William. "'The Stonewall Brigade' at Chancellorsville." *Southern Historical Society Papers* 14 (1896): 364–70.

Wright, Horatio Governour. "West Point and Cadet Life." *Putnam's Monthly Magazine of American Literature, Science, and Art* 4 (July–December 1854): 192–204.

Wright, John Montgomery. "West Point Before the War." *Southern Bivouac* 4 (June 1885): 13–21.

Newspapers

National Tribune, 1908
New York Times, 1863
North Carolina Standard (Raleigh), 1862–64
Raleigh Confederate, 1864
Richmond Dispatch, 1863–64
Richmond Enquirer, 1862
Richmond Examiner, 1864
Richmond Sentinel, 1864
Washington Evening Star, 1863

SECONDARY WORKS

Books

Ambrose, Stephen E. *Duty Honor, Country: A History of West Point*. Baltimore: Johns Hopkins University Press, 1966.

Ball, Douglas B. *Financial Failure and Confederate Defeat*. Urbana: University of Illinois Press, 1991.

Ballard, Michael B. *Vicksburg: The Campaign That Opened the Mississippi*. Chapel Hill: University of North Carolina Press, 2004.

Barefoot, Daniel W. *General Robert F. Hoke: Lee's Modest Warrior*. Winston-Salem, N.C.: John F. Blair, 1996.

Bartlett, Irving H. *John C. Calhoun: A Biography*. New York: Norton, 1993.

Black, Robert C., III. *Railroads of the Confederacy*. Chapel Hill: University of North Carolina Press, 1952.

Boatner, Mark M., III. *The Civil War Dictionary*. New York: David McKay, 1959.

Bridges, Hal. *Lee's Maverick General: Daniel Harvey Hill*. New York: McGraw-Hill, 1961.

Brown, Marvin A. *Our Enduring Past: A Survey of 235 Years of Life and Architecture in Lincoln County, North Carolina*. Lincolnton, N.C.: Lincoln County Historic Properties Commission, 1986.

Case, Lynn M., and Warren F. Spencer. *The United States and France: Civil War Diplomacy*. Philadelphia: University of Pennsylvania Press, 1970.

Congressional Quarterly's Guide to U.S. Elections. 4th ed. 2 vols. Washington, D.C.: CQ Press, 2001.

Cullum, George W. *Biographical Register of the Officers and Graduates of the U.S. Military Academy at West Point, New York, from Its Establishment in 1802, to 1890*. 3 vols. 3rd ed. rev. Cambridge, Mass.: Riverside Press, 1891.

Current, Richard N., ed. *Encyclopedia of the Confederacy*. Vol. 2. New York: Simon & Schuster, 1993.

Davis, William C., ed. *The Confederate General*. Harrisburg, Pa.: National Historical Society, 1991.

Faust, Drew Gilpin. *This Republic of Suffering: Death and the American Civil War*. New York: Knopf, 2008.

Freeman, Douglass Southall. *Lee's Lieutenants: A Study in Command*. New York: Scribner's, 1946.

Furgurson, Ernest B. *Chancellorsville 1863: The Souls of the Brave*. New York: Knopf, 1992.

Gallagher, Gary W. *Stephen Dodson Ramseur: Lee's Gallant General*. Chapel Hill: University of North Carolina Press, 1985.

Gragg, Rod. *Covered with Glory: The 26th North Carolina Infantry at the Battle of Gettysburg*. New York: Harper Collins, 2000.

Graham, Martin F., and George F. Skoch. *Mine Run: A Campaign of Lost Opportunities, October 21, 1863–May 1, 1864*. Lynchburg, Va.: H. E. Howard, 1987.

Heitman, Francis B. *Historical Register and Dictionary of the United States Army from Its Organization*. Vol. 1. Washington, D.C.: Government Printing Office, 1907.

Horn, John. *The Destruction of the Weldon Railroad: Deep Bottom, Globe Tavern, and Reams Station August 14–25, 1864*. Lynchburg, Va.: H. E. Howard, 1991.

Hughes, Nathaniel Cheairs, Jr. *General William J. Hardee: Old Reliable*. Baton Rouge: Louisiana State University Press, 1965.

Joslyn, Mauriel. *The Biographical Roster of the Immortal 600*. Shippensburg, Pa.: White Mane Publishing Company, 1992.

Krick, Robert E. L. *Staff Officers in Gray: Biographical Register of the Staff Officers in the Army of Northern Virginia*. Chapel Hill: University of North Carolina Press, 2003.

Krick, Robert K. *Lee's Colonels: A Biographical Register of the Field Officers of the Army of Northern Virginia*. Dayton, Ohio: Morningside Bookshop, 1979.

Lefler, Hugh Talmage, and Albert Ray Newsome. *North Carolina, The History of a Southern State*. rev. ed. Chapel Hill: University of North Carolina Press, 1963.

Linderman, Gerald F. *Embattled Courage: The Experience of Combat in the American Civil War*. New York: Free Press, 1987.

Long, E. B. *The Civil War Day by Day: An Almanac, 1861–1865*. New York: De Capo, 1971.

Lonn, Ella. *Salt as a Factor in the Confederacy*. New York: Walter Neale, 1933.

Manarin, Louis H., comp. *North Carolina Troops 1861–1865, A Roster*. 15 vols. Raleigh: State Department of Archives and History, 1966.

Matter, William D. *If It Takes All Summer: The Battle of Spotsylvania*. Chapel Hill: University of North Carolina Press, 1988.

McWhiney, Grady. *Southerners and Other Americans*. New York: Basic Books, 1973.

Meynard, Virginia C. *The Venturers: The Hampton, Harrison, and Earle Families of Virginia, South Carolina, and Texas*. Easley, S.C.: Southern History Press, 1981.

Morrison, James L., Jr. *"The Best School": West Point, 1833–1866*. Kent, Ohio: Kent State University Press, 1998.

Murray, Elizabeth Reid. *Wake, Capital County of North Carolina*. Raleigh: Capital County , 1983.

The National Cyclopedia of American Biography. Vols. 7 and 10. New York.: James T. White, 1897, 1909.

North Carolina Department of the Secretary of State. *North Carolina Government, 1585–1979: A Narrative and Statistical History*. Raleigh: 1981.

Nye, Wilbur Sturtevant. *Here Come the Rebels!* Baton Rouge: Louisiana State University Press, 1965.

Patchan, Scott C. *Shenandoah Summer: The 1864 Valley Campaign*. Lincoln: University of Nebraska Press, 2007.

Piston, William Garrett. *Lee's Tarnished Lieutenant: James Longstreet and His Place in Southern History*. Athens: University of Georgia Press, 1987.

Powell, William S., ed. *Dictionary of North Carolina Biography*. 6 vols. Chapel Hill: University of North Carolina Press, 1979–1996.

———. *When the Past Refused to Die: A History of Caswell County, North Carolina, 1777–1977*. Durham, N.C.: Moore Publishing, 1977.

Reed, Rowena. *Combined Operations in the Civil War*. Annapolis, Md.: Naval Institute Press, 1978.

The Register of Graduates and Former Cadets of the United States Military Academy West Point, New York. West Point: Association of Graduates, 2005.

Rhea, Gordon C. *The Battles for Spotsylvania Court House and the Road to Yellow Tavern, May 7–12, 1864*. Baton Rouge: Louisiana State University Press, 1997.

Robertson, James I., Jr. *The Stonewall Brigade*. Baton Rouge: Louisiana State University Press, 1963.

Sherrill, William L. *Annals of Lincoln County, North Carolina, containing interesting and authentic facts of Lincoln county history through the years 1749 to 1937*. Charlotte: Observer printing house, 1937.

Sibley, F. Ray, Jr. *The Confederate Order of Battle*. Shippensburg, Pa.: White Mane Publishing Company, 1996.

Stedman, Charles M. *Life and Character of Major General Stephen D. Ramseur, address of Hon. Charles M. Stedman, of North Carolina, delivered near Winchester, Va., September 15, 1920.* Washington, D.C.: Government Printing Office, 1921.

Warner, Ezra. J. *Generals in Blue: Lives of the Union Commanders.* Baton Rouge: Louisiana State University Press, 1964.

———. *Generals in Gray: Lives of the Confederate Commanders.* Baton Rouge: Louisiana State University Press, 1959.

Wyatt-Brown, Bertram. *Honor and Violence in the Old South.* New York: Oxford University Press, 1986.

Articles

Aimone, Alan and Barbara, "Much to Sadden—and Little to Cheer: The Civil War Years at West Point," *Blue & Gray Magazine* 9 (December 1991): 12–28, 48–64.

Clark, Walter. "Major General Stephen Dodson Ramseur." *North Carolina Booklet* 16 (October 1916): 68–75.

Faust, Drew Gilpin. "The Civil War Soldier and the Art of Dying." *Journal of Southern History* 67 (February 2001): 3–38.

Gallagher, Gary W. "A North Carolinian at West Point: Stephen Dodson Ramseur, 1855–1860." *North Carolina Historical Review* 62 (January 1985): 1–28.

Krick, Robert K. "Robert Emmett Rodes." In *The Confederate General*, edited by William C. Davis. Harrisburg, Pa.: National Historical Society, 1991.

———. "Three Confederate Disasters on Oak Ridge: Failures of Brigade Leadership on the First Day at Gettysburg." In *Three Days at Gettysburg: Essays on Confederate and Union Leadership*, edited by Gary W. Gallagher. Kent, Ohio: Kent State University Press, 1999.

Mushkat, Jerome. "Ben Wood's Fort Lafayette: A Source of Studying the Peace Democrats." *Civil War History* 21 (June 1975): 160–71.

Stedman, Charles H. "Gen. Stephen Dodson Ramseur." *Confederate Veteran* 28 (December 1920): 453–57.

Steiner, Paul E. "Medical-Military Studies on the Civil War. Major General Stephen D. Ramseur, C.S.A." *Military Medicine* 130 (October 1965): 1016–22.

Wert, Jeffry D. "Robert Daniel Johnston." In *The Confederate General*, edited by William C. Davis. Harrisburg, Pa.: National Historical Society, 1991.

Acknowledgments

CLAIMING TO KNOW EVERYTHING about the American Civil War is like being the fastest gun in the West. There's always someone faster. Gary W. Gallagher and Robert K. Krick, scholars and authors with national reputations, are far quicker draws than I, and were both extremely generous with their extensive knowledge and materials related to Stephen Dodson Ramseur.

For day-to-day help, I relied upon the director of the Special Collections at the Alexandria Library, George Combs. His interest in this project preceded mine. George identified resource materials, acquired documents, evaluated my assessments of events, made contact with disparate sources, and provided encouragement, all with his customary tolerance, good humor, and overall appreciation of the Civil War and its chronicles, published and unpublished. A researcher could not expect a compatriot as helpful and loyal as I found in George Combs.

From farther away, two other published authorities on the war once again provided their assistance. At the Museum of the Confederacy in Richmond, John Coski offered help in understanding references that eluded my comprehension. In New Bern, North Carolina, Horace Mewborn uncovered information more readily than I could have done.

Transcribing, understanding, and annotating the correspondence of Stephen Dodson Ramseur required the facility to work in multiple disciplines. Ramseur's West Point years are part of an important prelude to the Civil War that included many well known leaders. It would have been impossible for me to appreciate Ramseur's experiences at West Point without instruction from the humanities librarian at the academy's library, Alan Aimone. Marjorie McNinch, librarian at the Hagley Museum and Library, Wilmington, Delaware, also provided support.

The totality of Ramseur's extant correspondence relates almost as much to his state's history as it does to the war. To appreciate that dimension of the letters I was fortunate to benefit from the services of the staff at the University of North Carolina's Wilson Library. Specifically, I was helped time and again by Matthew Turi and Clark Tew in the Manuscripts Department and Jill Wagy, Harry McKown, and Jason Tomberlin in the North Carolina Collection. Bryan McKown at the South Carolina Department of Archives and History and Jan Blodgett, Davidson College Archivist, were also valuable contributors to my research.

So much of Ramseur's writing concerns his "Home Loves" and their lives in and around Lincolnton, North Carolina; help from knowledgeable residents of this area was compulsory. Ann Dellinger, Lincoln County Historical Society, and Darrell Harkey, Lincoln County Historical Coordinator, repeatedly consulted voluminous files and willingly shared their personal knowledge of local history and genealogy to provide information otherwise unavailable to me. Linda Hoyle at the Charles R. Jonas Library and Brian Brown, Gaston County Public Library, also researched obscure references.

Ramseur's solid grounding in religion, literature, and Latin required consultation with professionals in these fields to discern the meaning and identify the sources of his many quotations and expressions. For that assistance, I thank the Venerable Kenneth Letts, Rev. Mary Kieser, Suzanne Kalil at Alexandria's Kate Waller Barrett Library, and Latin educator Stacey Kenkeremath.

Collaborators in other undertakings came to my assistance once again. Craig Kellermann, John Komoroske, Harry Day, Jon Barlow and Dave Demoney graciously provided special expertise without which I would have been lost. And, finally, the staff of the Special Collections in the library system of Alexandria, Virginia, past and present—Leslie Anderson, Rita Holtz, Barbara Winters, Julie Ballin Patton, Michele Lee, Joyce McMullin, and Ada Valaitis—exhibited their signature competence, patience, and amity. Rita warrants special mention for computerizing a graphic of Ramseur's convoluted extended family, an illustration central to fully understanding his correspondence. To all of the above, and to any others I may have neglected, my heartfelt thanks.

The individual who paid the highest price for this work, however, is my wife, Joy. Without her love, acceptance, and forbearance, I would never have known the Dodsons, Ramseurs, and Richmonds of nineteenth-century North Carolina and the character of their fallen hero, Stephen Dodson Ramseur.

Index